Yuji Kaku

I stuffed this book
full of all the things
I'm most familiar
with. I hope you
enjoy it.

Yuji Kaku debuted as a mangaka in 2009 with the one-shot
"Omoide Zeikan" (Memory Customs), which won an honorable mention in
the 14th *Jump SQ* Comic Grand Prix. He went on to write several other
one-shots before beginning his first series, *Fantasma*, which
ran in *Jump SQ* from 2013 to 2014. His second series, *Hell's Paradise:
Jigokuraku*, ran from 2018 to 2021 on Jump+ and received an anime
adaptation. *Ayashimon* is his third title and started its
serialization in *Weekly Shonen Jump* in November 2021.

AYASHIMON

Volume 1
SHONEN JUMP Edition

Story and Art by
Yuji Kaku

TRANSLATION Adrienne Beck
LETTERING Brandon Bovia
DESIGN Shawn Carrico
WEEKLY SHONEN JUMP EDITOR Rae First
GRAPHIC NOVEL EDITOR Andrew Kuhre Bartosh

Printed in the U.S.A.

Published by VIZ Media, LLC
P.O. Box 77010
San Francisco, CA 94107

10 9 8 7 6 5 4 3 2 1
First Printing, March 2023

VIZ MEDIA
viz.com

SHONEN JUMP

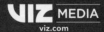

AYASHIMON

I'll Play
with You, Punk

AYASHIMON

1

I'll Play with You, Punk

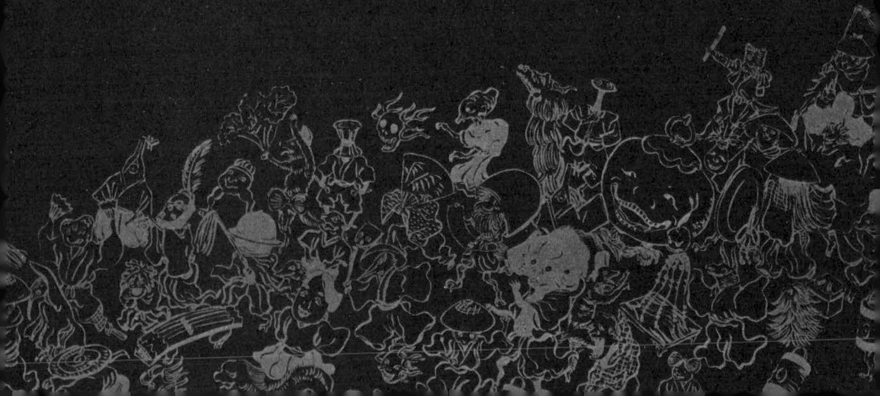

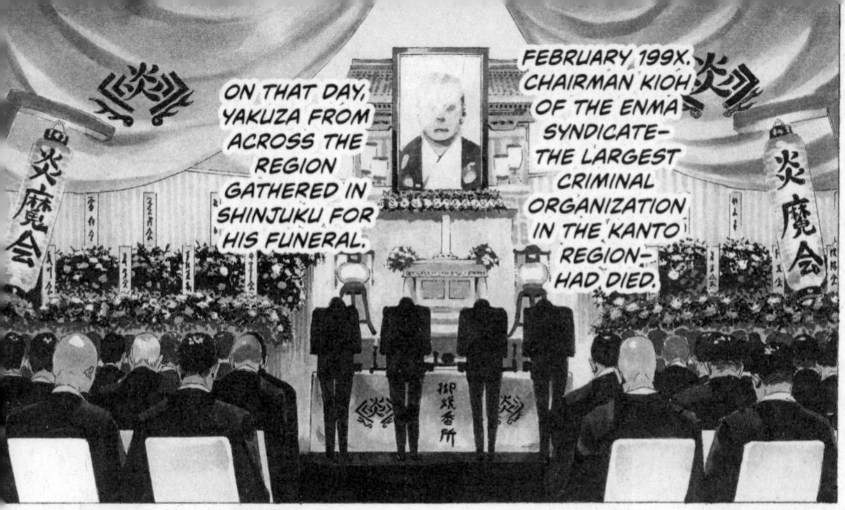
FEBRUARY 199X. CHAIRMAN KIOH OF THE ENMA SYNDICATE— THE LARGEST CRIMINAL ORGANIZATION IN THE KANTO REGION— HAD DIED.
ON THAT DAY, YAKUZA FROM ACROSS THE REGION GATHERED IN SHINJUKU FOR HIS FUNERAL.
炎魔会
炎魔会

*LANTERNS: ENMA SYNDICATE

Chapter 1

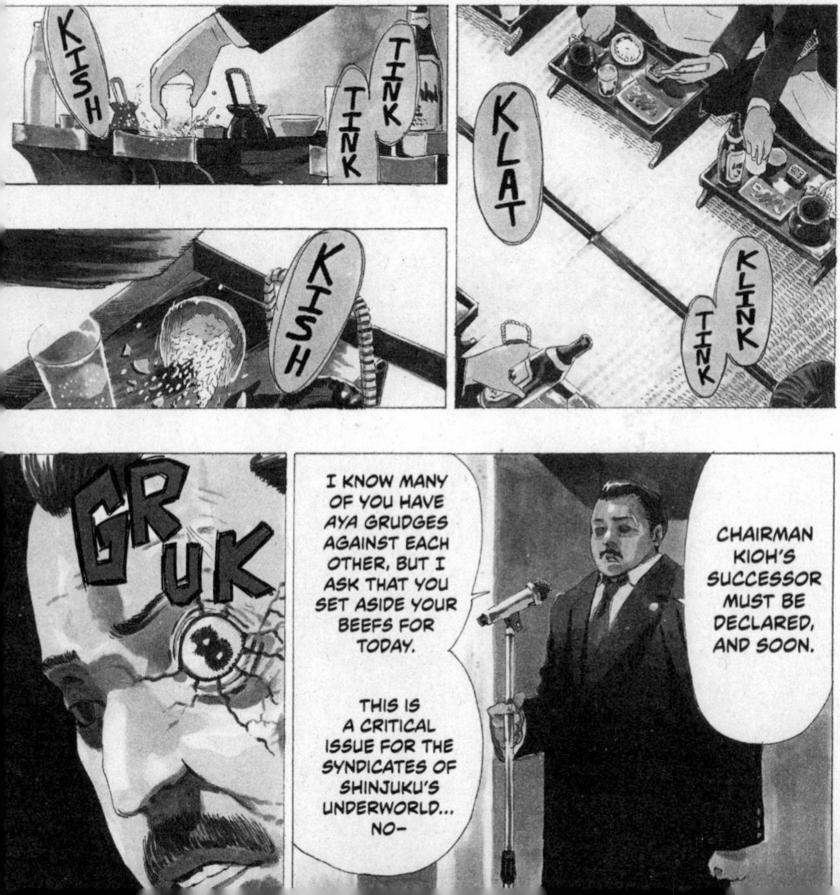
KLAT
KLINK
TINK
KISH
TINK
TINK
KISH
CHAIRMAN KIOH'S SUCCESSOR MUST BE DECLARED, AND SOON.
I KNOW MANY OF YOU HAVE AYA GRUDGES AGAINST EACH OTHER, BUT I ASK THAT YOU SET ASIDE YOUR BEEFS FOR TODAY.
THIS IS A CRITICAL ISSUE FOR THE SYNDICATES OF SHINJUKU'S UNDERWORLD... NO—
GR
UK

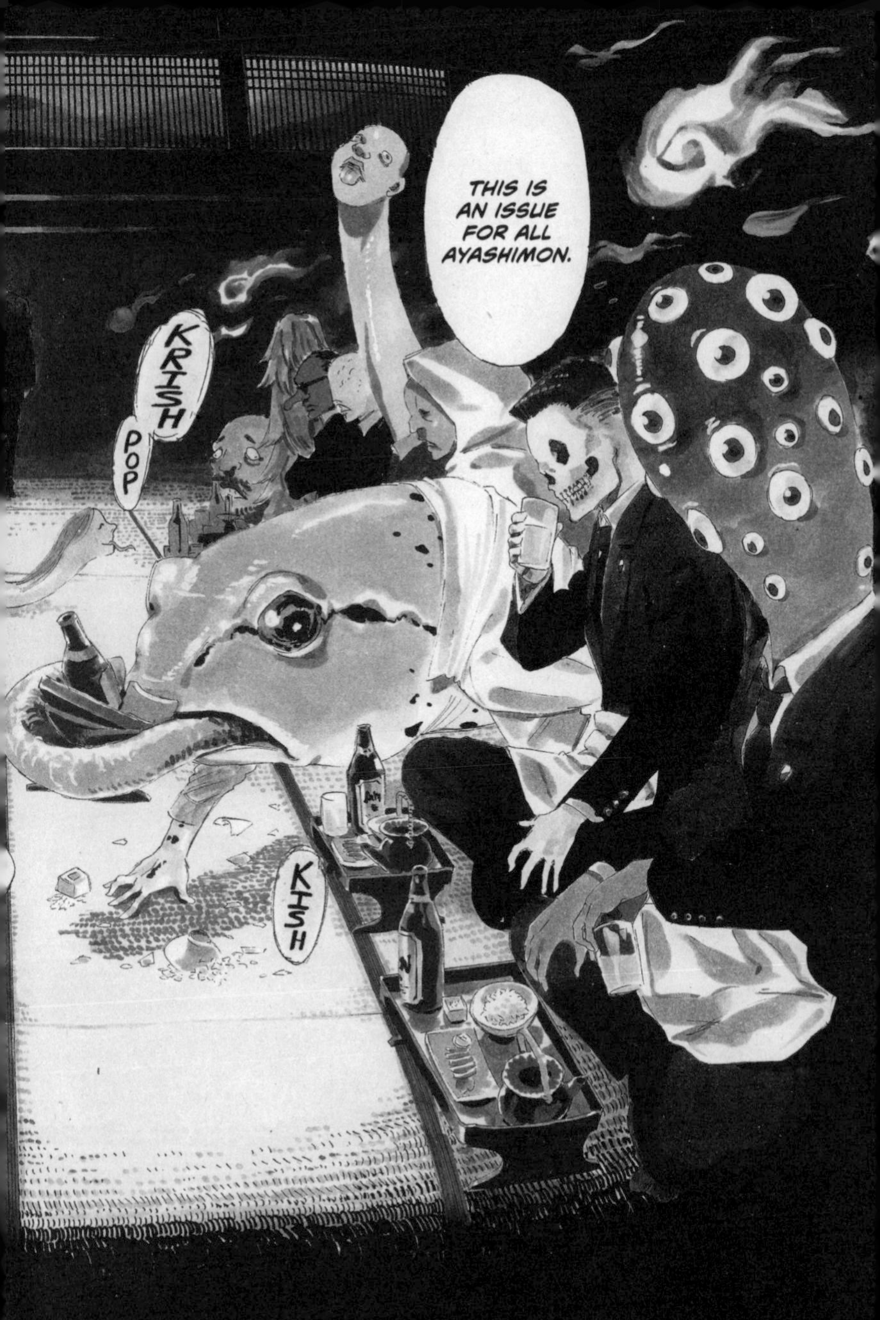
THIS IS AN ISSUE FOR ALL AYASHIMON.
KRISH
POP
KISH

Chapter 1: I'll Play with You, Punk

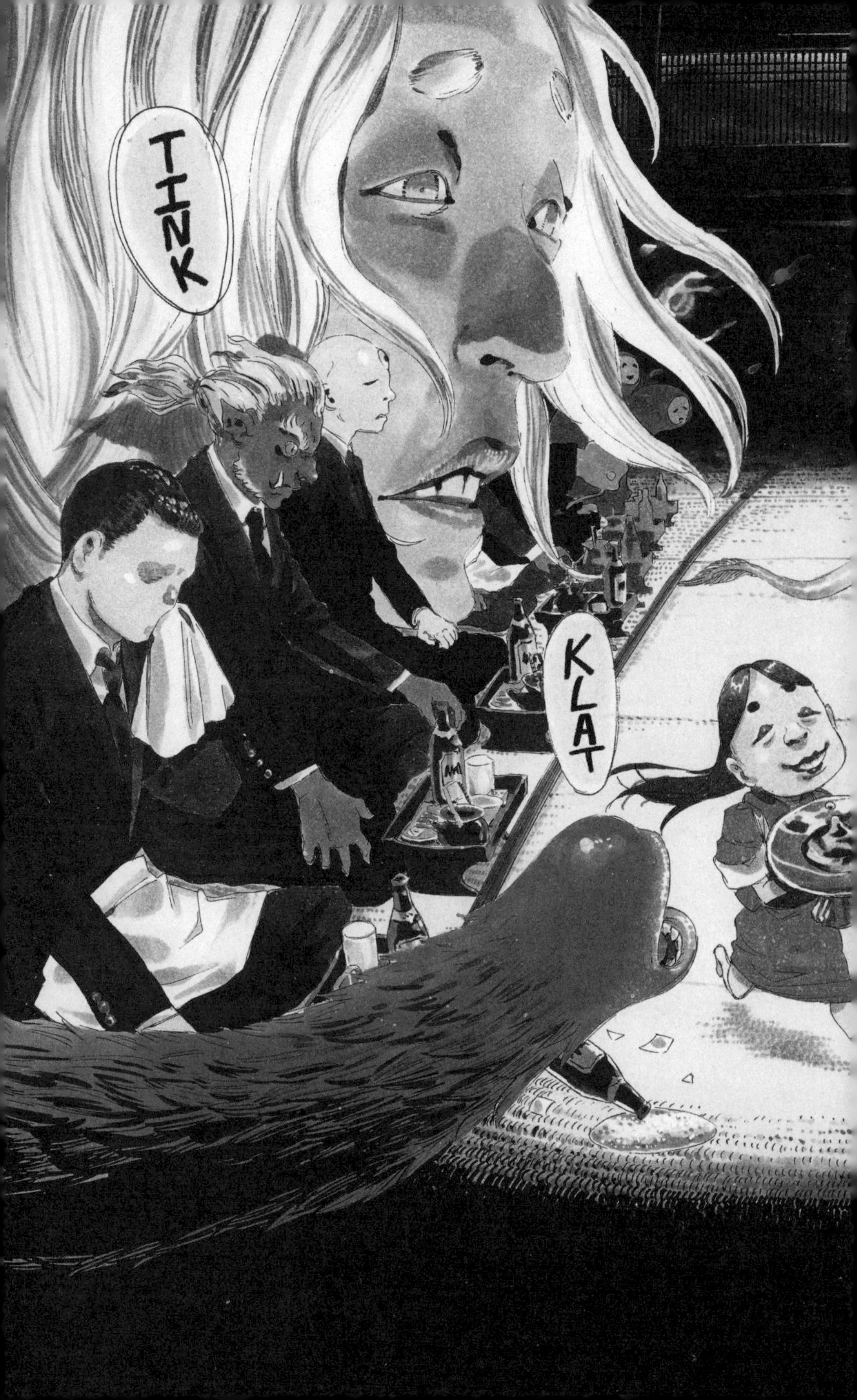
TINK
KLAT

AYASHIMON

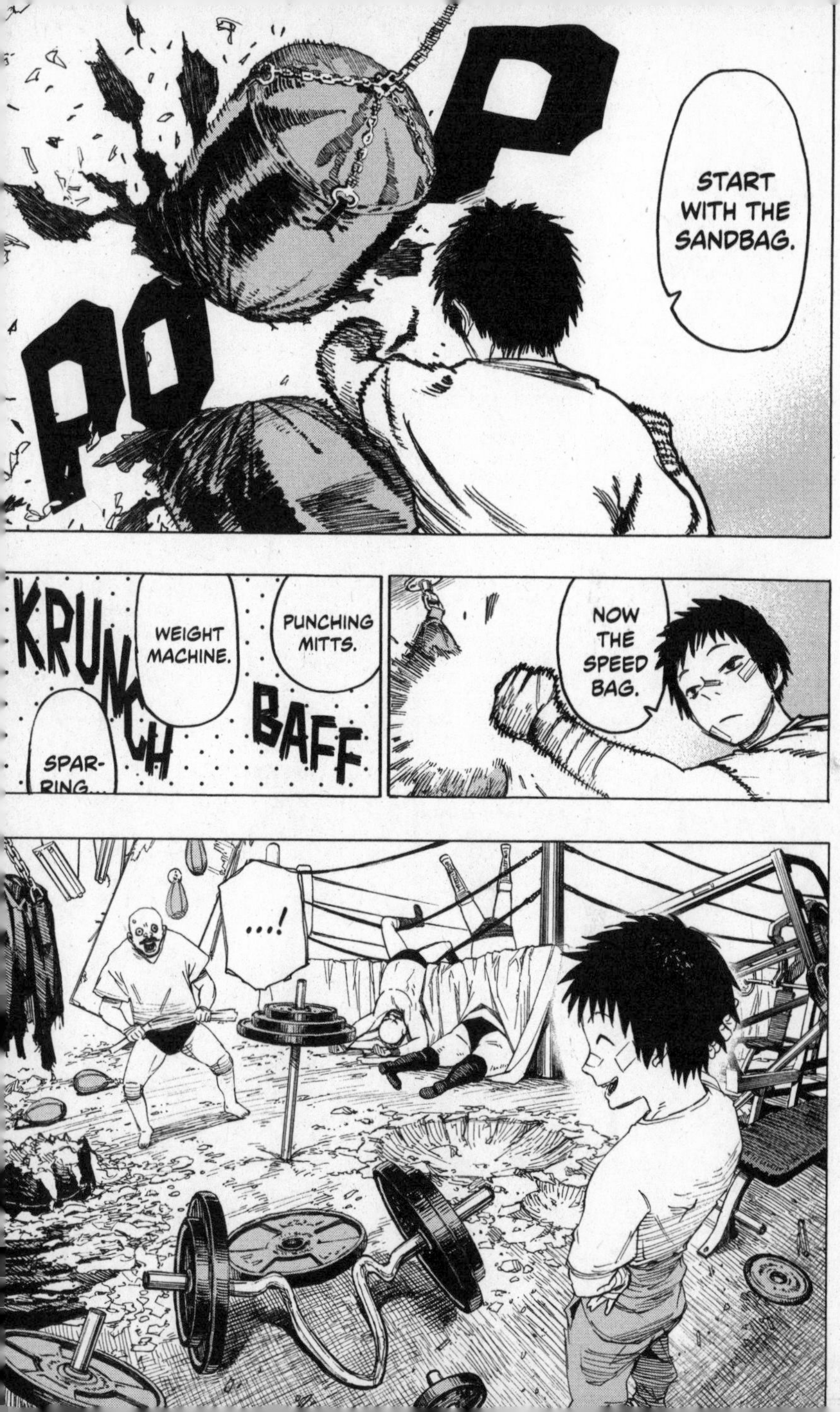
START WITH THE SANDBAG.
NOW THE SPEED BAG.
PUNCHING MITTS.
BAFF
WEIGHT MACHINE.
KRUNCH
SPAR-RING...
...!

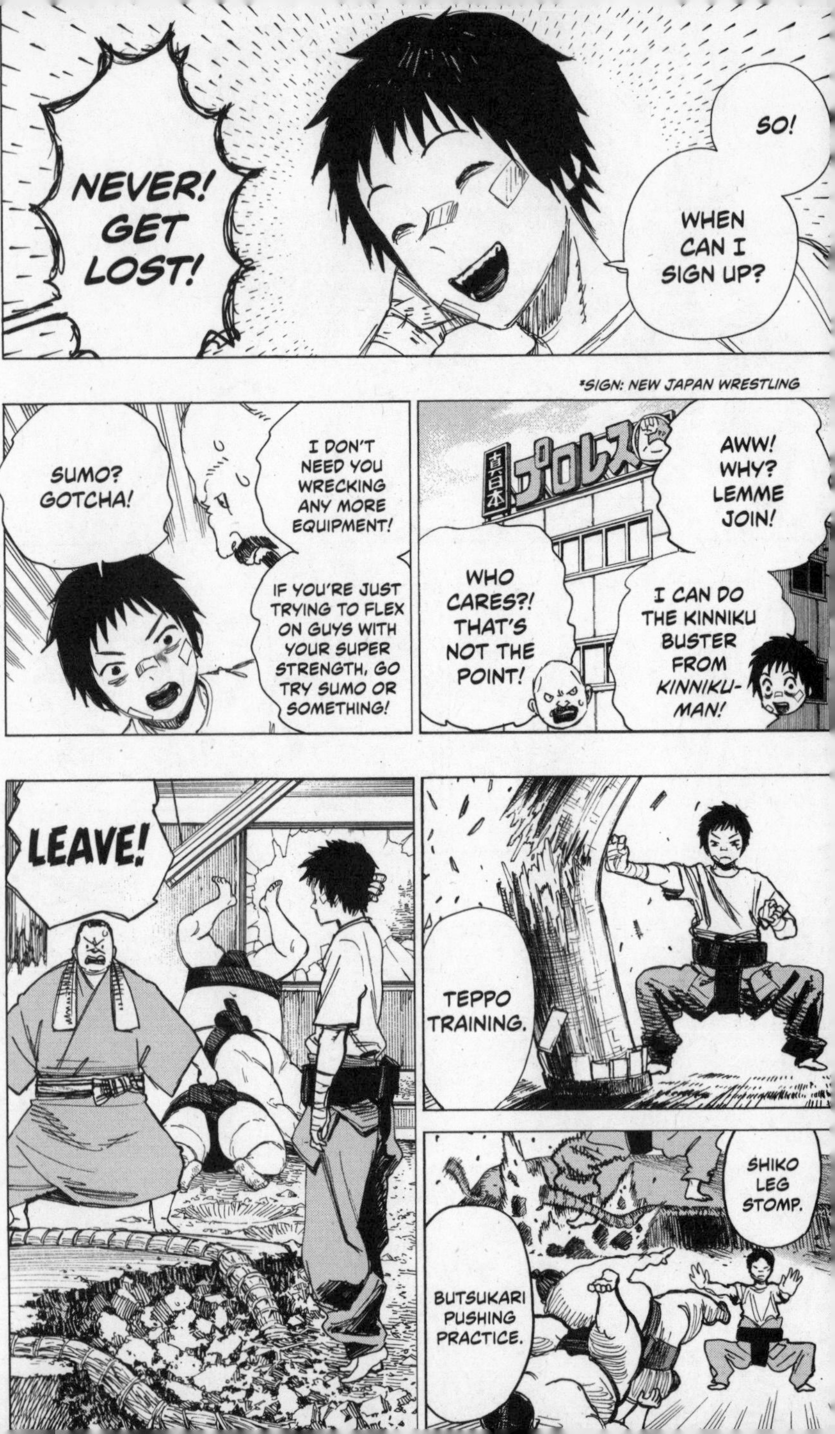
SO!
WHEN CAN I SIGN UP?
NEVER! GET LOST!
*SIGN: NEW JAPAN WRESTLING
AWW! WHY? LEMME JOIN!
I CAN DO THE KINNIKU BUSTER FROM KINNIKU-MAN!
WHO CARES?! THAT'S NOT THE POINT!
I DON'T NEED YOU WRECKING ANY MORE EQUIPMENT!
IF YOU'RE JUST TRYING TO FLEX ON GUYS WITH YOUR SUPER STRENGTH, GO TRY SUMO OR SOMETHING!
SUMO? GOTCHA!
TEPPO TRAINING.
SHIKO LEG STOMP.
BUTSUKARI PUSHING PRACTICE.
LEAVE!

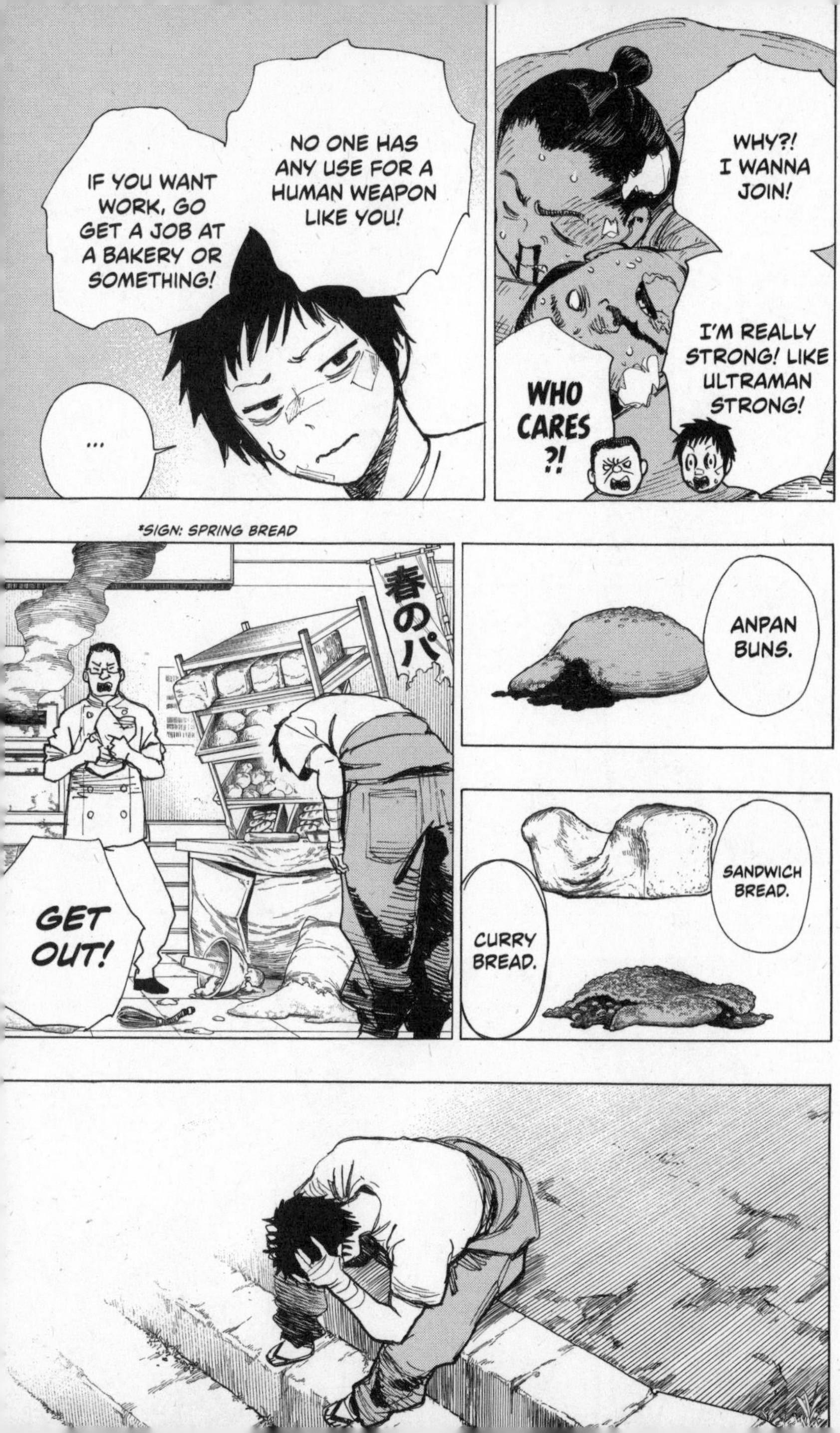
WHY?! I WANNA JOIN!
I'M REALLY STRONG! LIKE ULTRAMAN STRONG!
WHO CARES?!
NO ONE HAS ANY USE FOR A HUMAN WEAPON LIKE YOU!
IF YOU WANT WORK, GO GET A JOB AT A BAKERY OR SOMETHING!
...
ANPAN BUNS.
SANDWICH BREAD.
CURRY BREAD.
*SIGN: SPRING BREAD
春のパ
GET OUT!

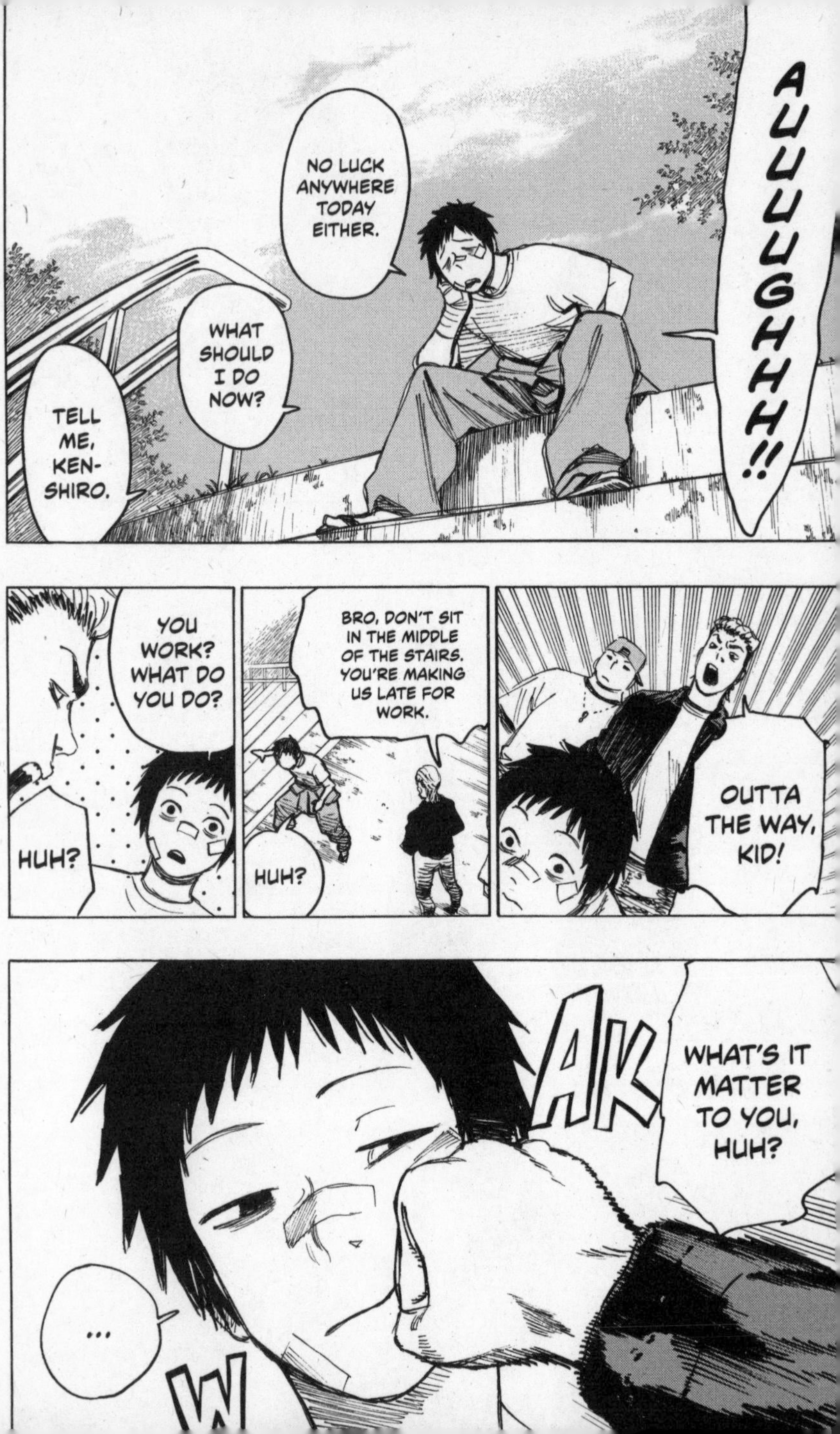
AUUUUGHHHH!!
NO LUCK ANYWHERE TODAY EITHER.
WHAT SHOULD I DO NOW?
TELL ME, KEN-SHIRO.
OUTTA THE WAY, KID!
BRO, DON'T SIT IN THE MIDDLE OF THE STAIRS. YOU'RE MAKING US LATE FOR WORK.
HUH?
YOU WORK? WHAT DO YOU DO?
HUH?
WHAT'S IT MATTER TO YOU, HUH?
AK
...
W

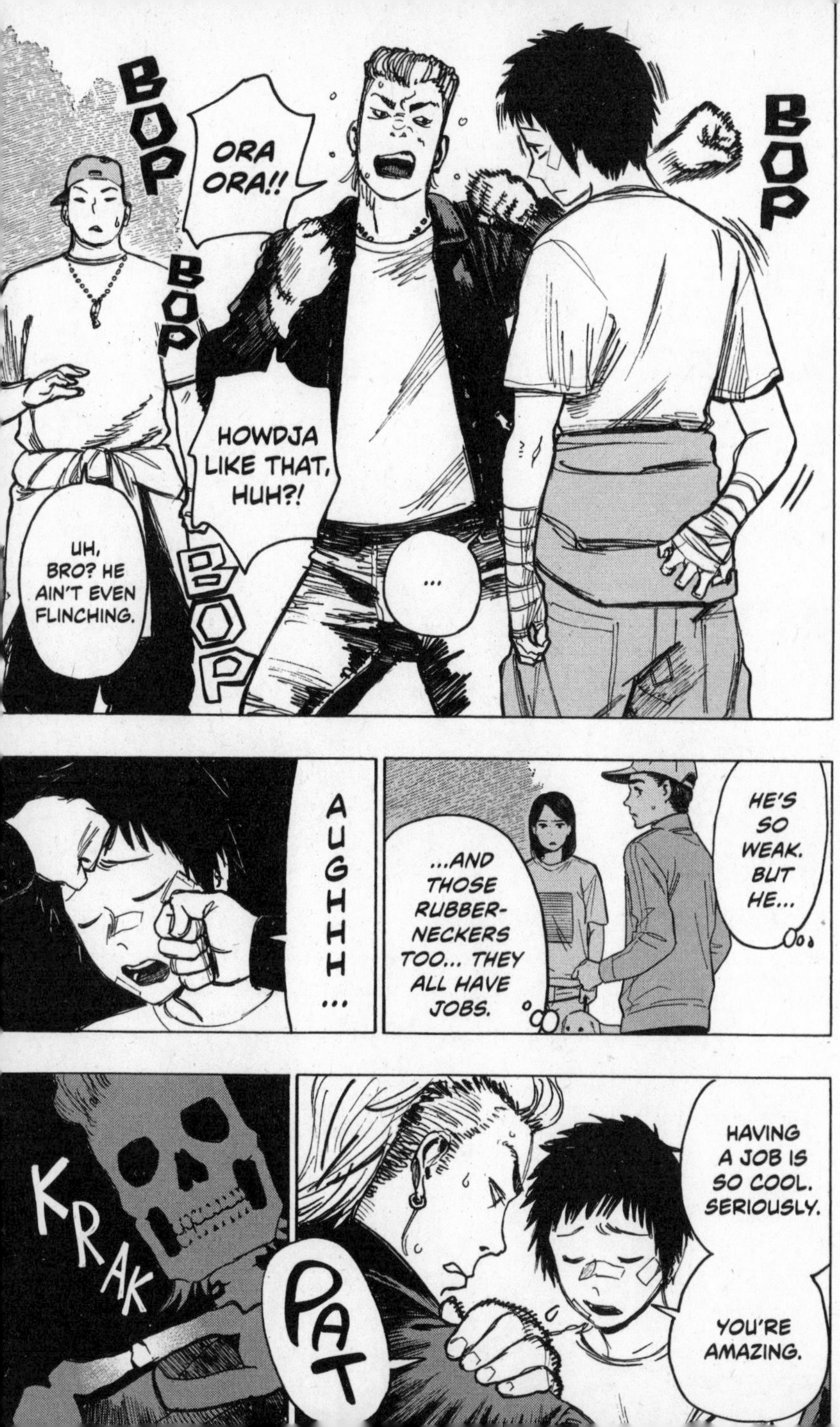
BOP BOP
ORA ORA!!
BOP BOP
BOP BOP
HOWDJA LIKE THAT, HUH?!
...
BOP BOP
UH, BRO? HE AIN'T EVEN FLINCHING.
HE'S SO WEAK. BUT HE...
...AND THOSE RUBBER-NECKERS TOO... THEY ALL HAVE JOBS.
AUGHHH...
HAVING A JOB IS SO COOL. SERIOUSLY.
YOU'RE AMAZING.
PAT
KRAK

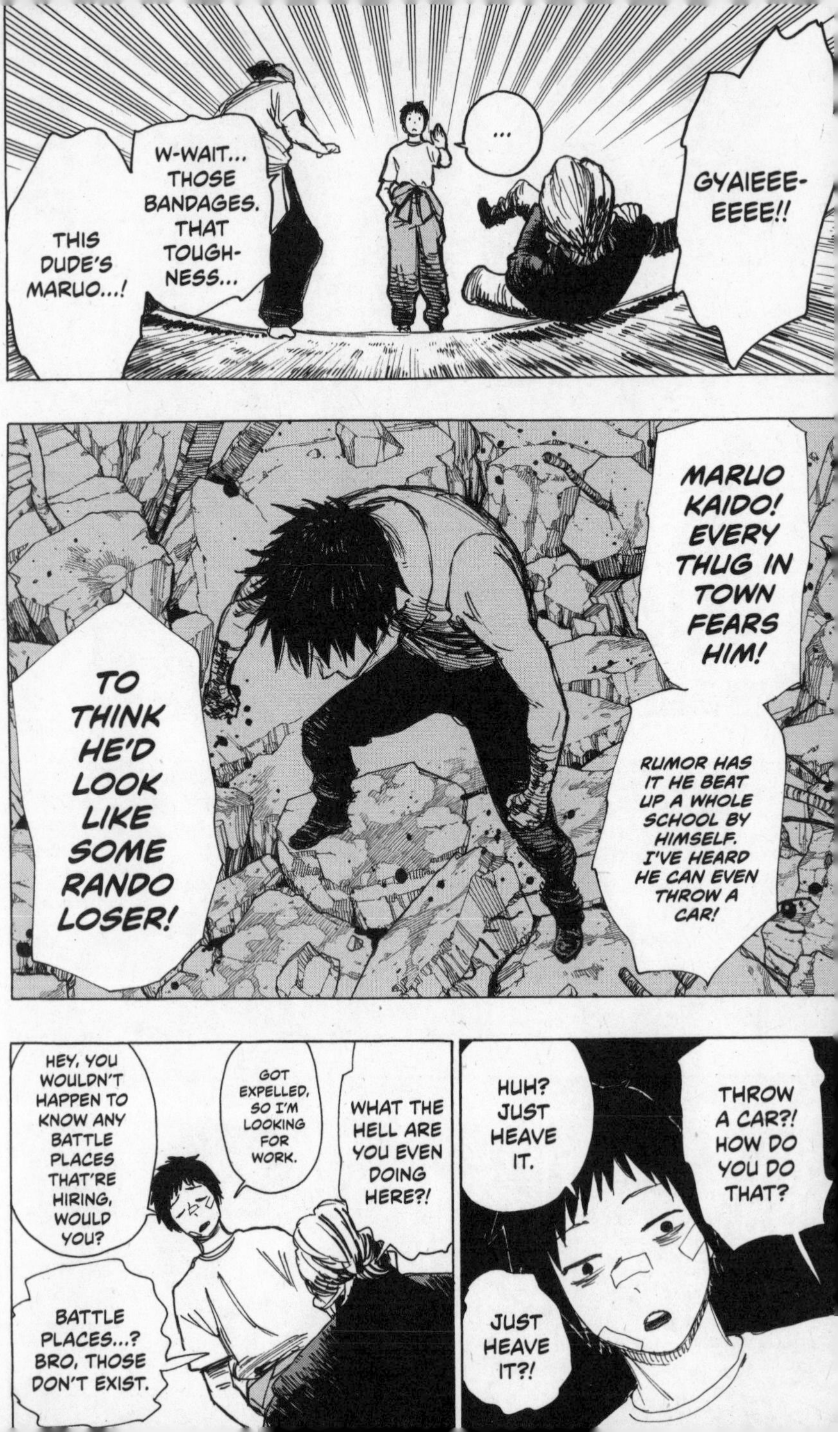
GYAIEEE-EEEE!!
...
W-WAIT... THOSE BANDAGES. THAT TOUGHNESS...
THIS DUDE'S MARUO...!
MARUO KAIDO! EVERY THUG IN TOWN FEARS HIM!
RUMOR HAS IT HE BEAT UP A WHOLE SCHOOL BY HIMSELF. I'VE HEARD HE CAN EVEN THROW A CAR!
TO THINK HE'D LOOK LIKE SOME RANDO LOSER!
THROW A CAR?! HOW DO YOU DO THAT?
HUH? JUST HEAVE IT.
JUST HEAVE IT?!
WHAT THE HELL ARE YOU EVEN DOING HERE?!
GOT EXPELLED, SO I'M LOOKING FOR WORK.
HEY, YOU WOULDN'T HAPPEN TO KNOW ANY BATTLE PLACES THAT'RE HIRING, WOULD YOU?
BATTLE PLACES...? BRO, THOSE DON'T EXIST.

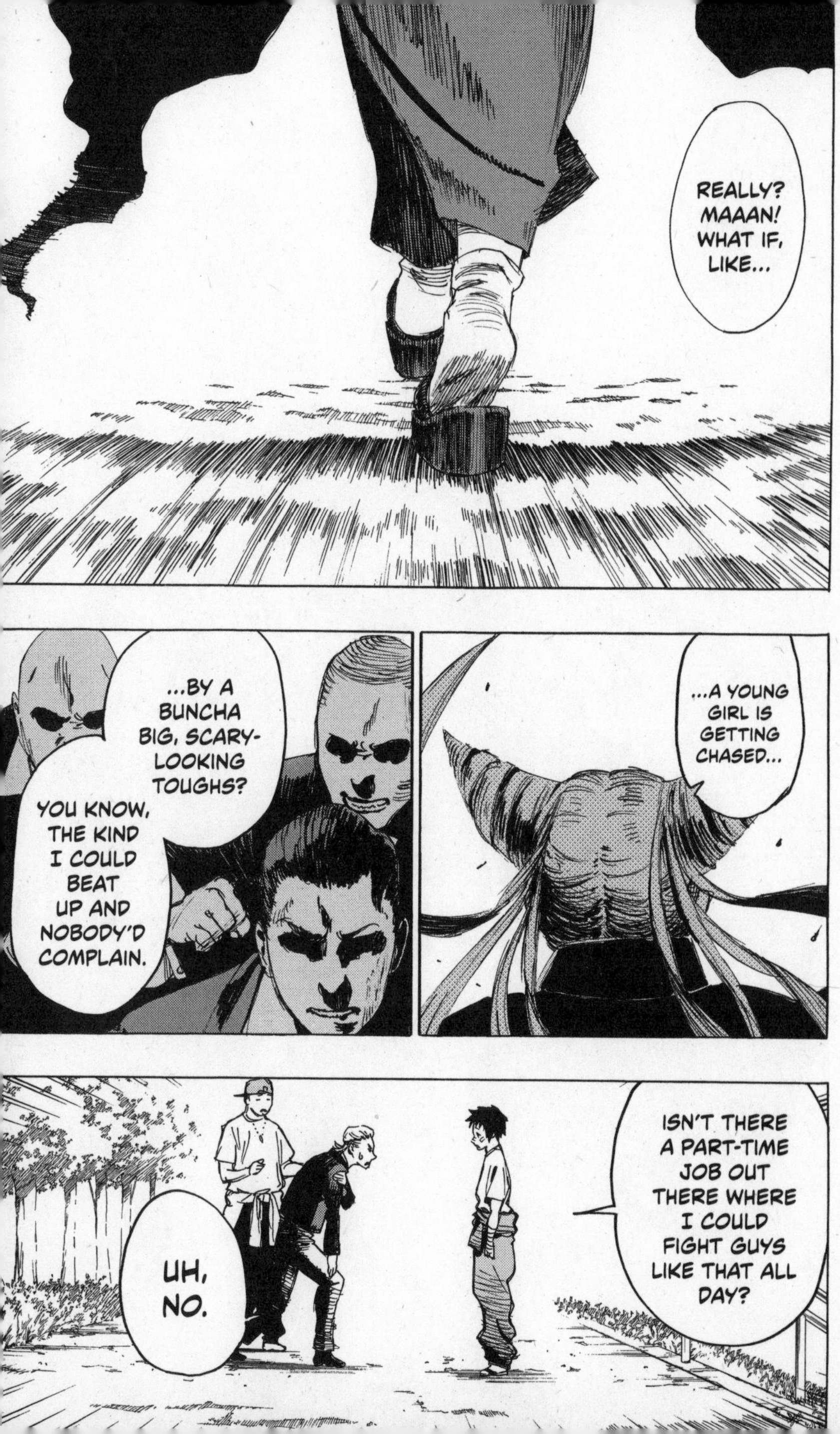
REALLY? MAAAN! WHAT IF, LIKE...
...A YOUNG GIRL IS GETTING CHASED...
...BY A BUNCHA BIG, SCARY-LOOKING TOUGHS?
YOU KNOW, THE KIND I COULD BEAT UP AND NOBODY'D COMPLAIN.
ISN'T THERE A PART-TIME JOB OUT THERE WHERE I COULD FIGHT GUYS LIKE THAT ALL DAY?
UH, NO.

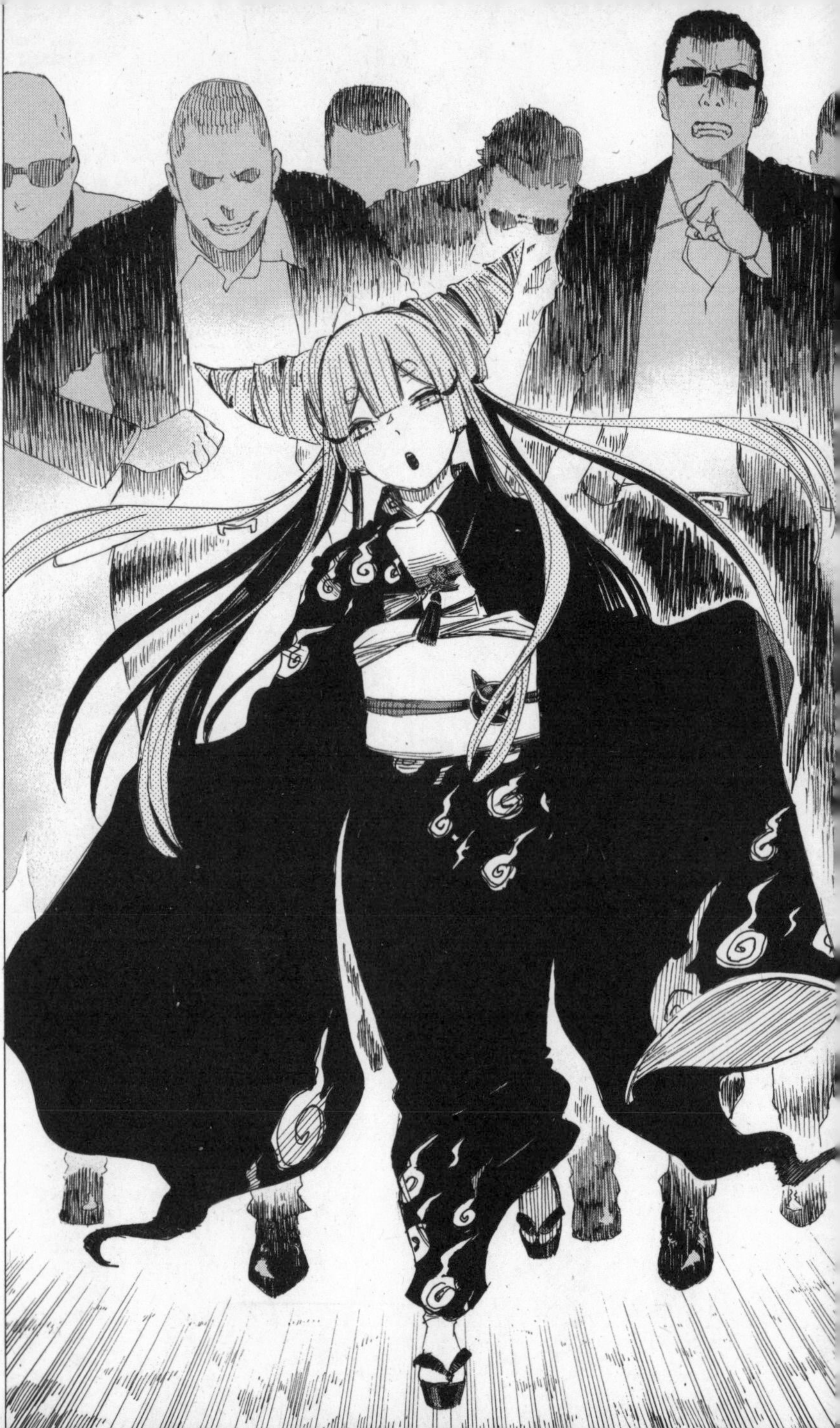

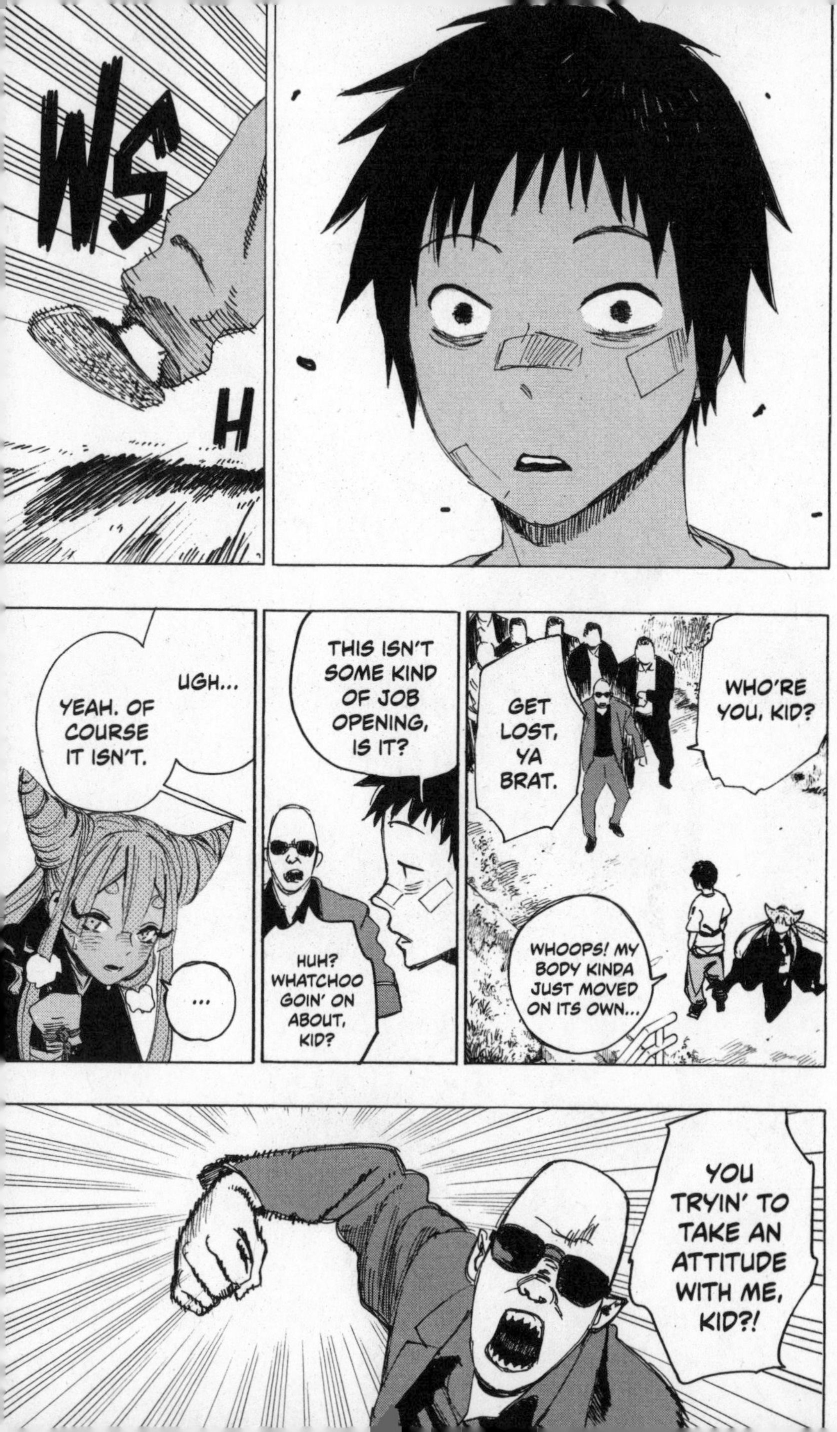
WSH
WHO'RE YOU, KID?
GET LOST, YA BRAT.
WHOOPS! MY BODY KINDA JUST MOVED ON ITS OWN...
THIS ISN'T SOME KIND OF JOB OPENING, IS IT?
HUH? WHATCHOO GOIN' ON ABOUT, KID?
UGH... YEAH. OF COURSE IT ISN'T.
...
YOU TRYIN' TO TAKE AN ATTITUDE WITH ME, KID?!

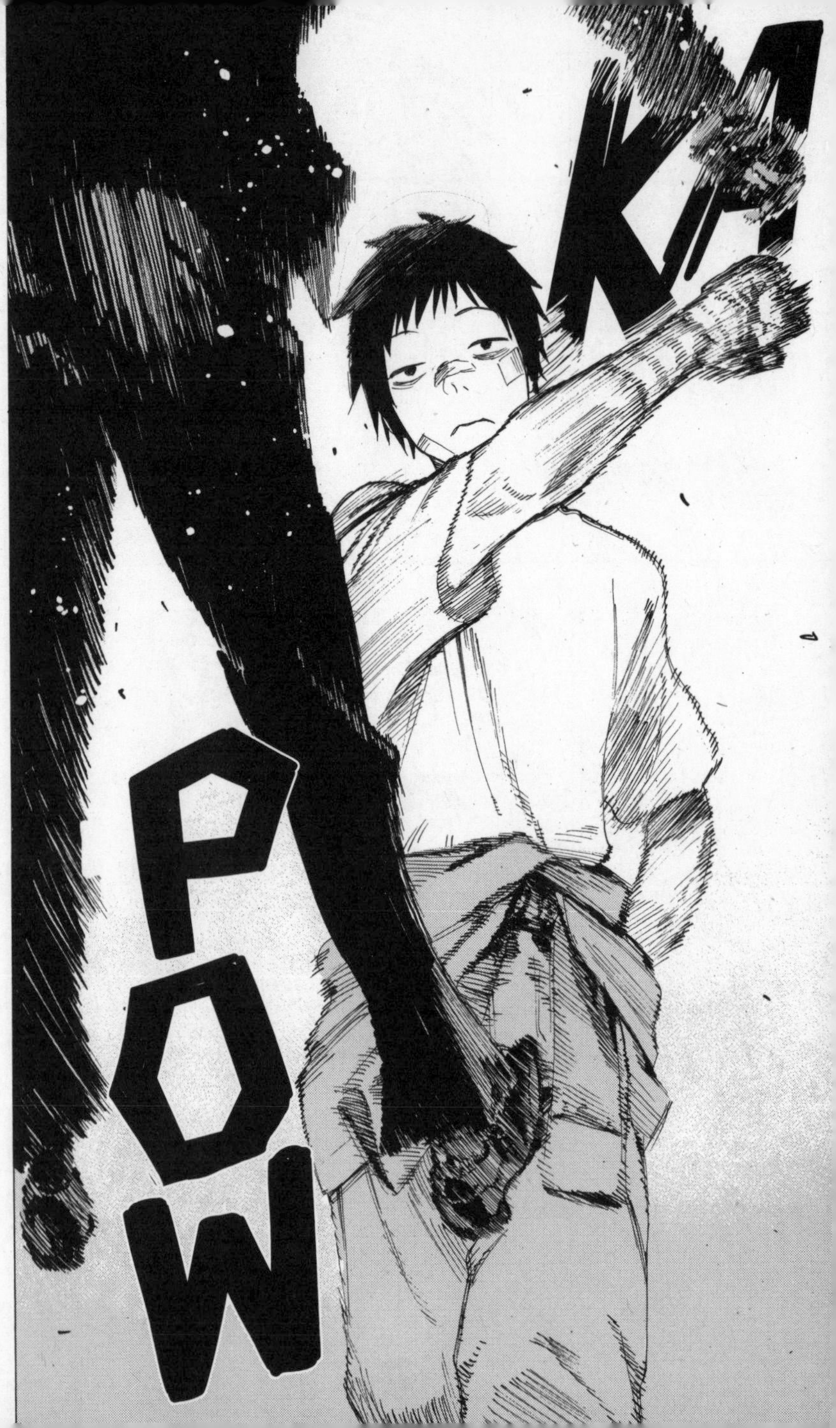
KA
POW

FWMP

NOW YOU'VE DONE IT, KID!

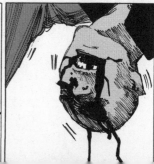

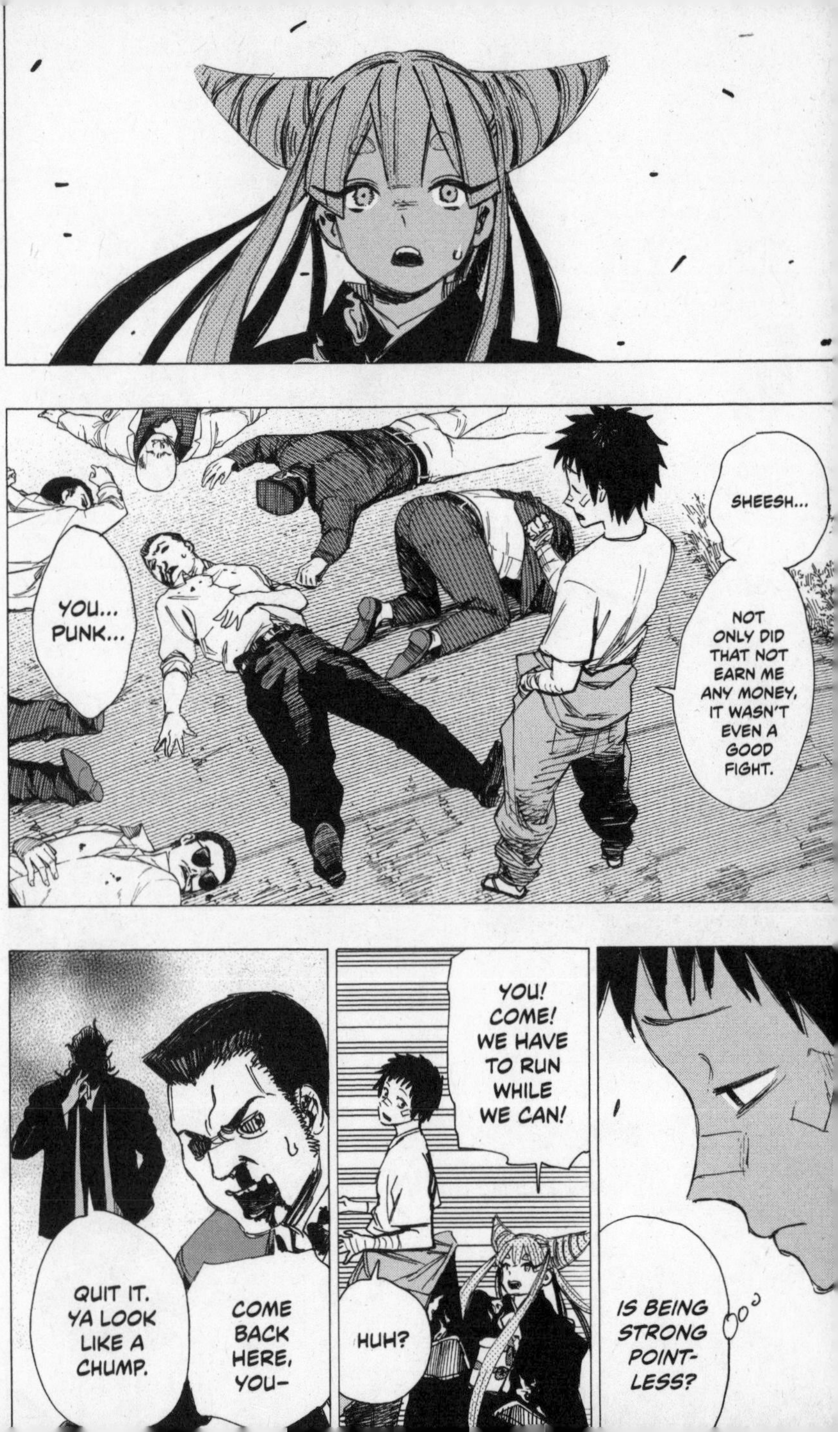
SHEESH...
NOT ONLY DID THAT NOT EARN ME ANY MONEY, IT WASN'T EVEN A GOOD FIGHT.
YOU... PUNK...
IS BEING STRONG POINT-LESS?
YOU! COME! WE HAVE TO RUN WHILE WE CAN!
HUH?
COME BACK HERE, YOU-
QUIT IT. YA LOOK LIKE A CHUMP.

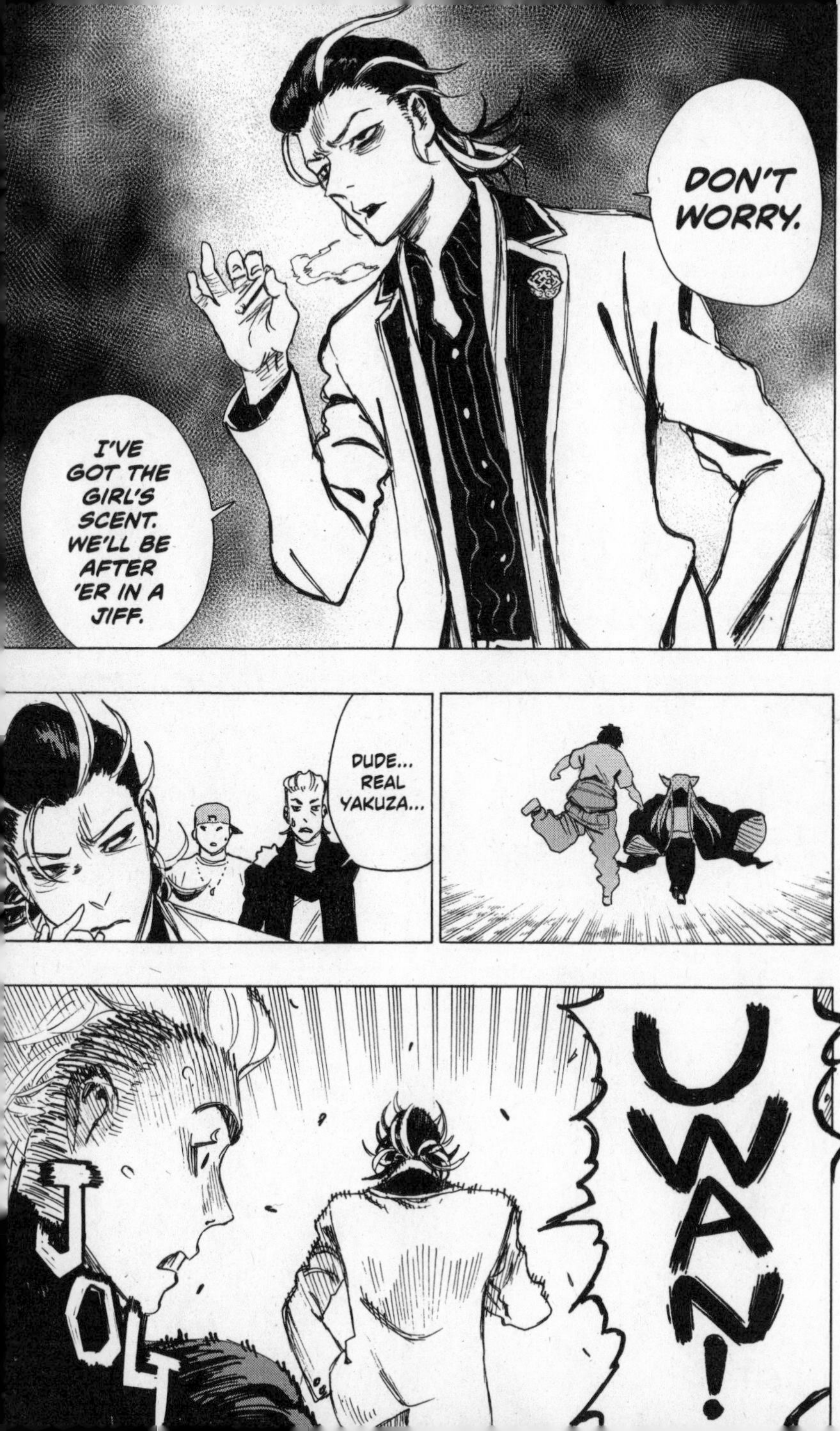
DON'T WORRY.
I'VE GOT THE GIRL'S SCENT. WE'LL BE AFTER 'ER IN A JIFF.
DUDE... REAL YAKUZA...
UWAN!
JOLT

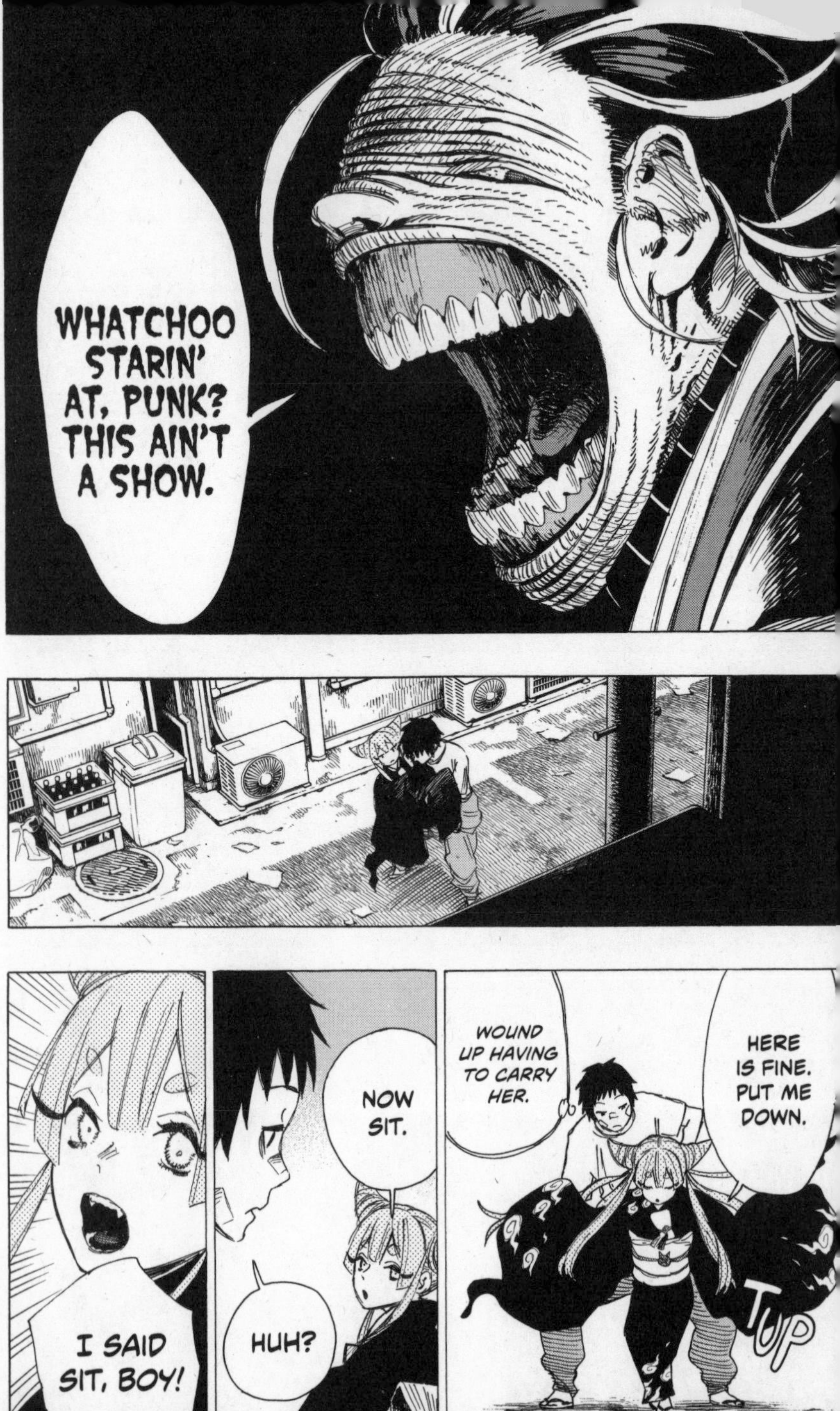
WHATCHOO STARIN' AT, PUNK? THIS AIN'T A SHOW.
HERE IS FINE. PUT ME DOWN.
WOUND UP HAVING TO CARRY HER.
TUP
NOW SIT.
HUH?
I SAID SIT, BOY!

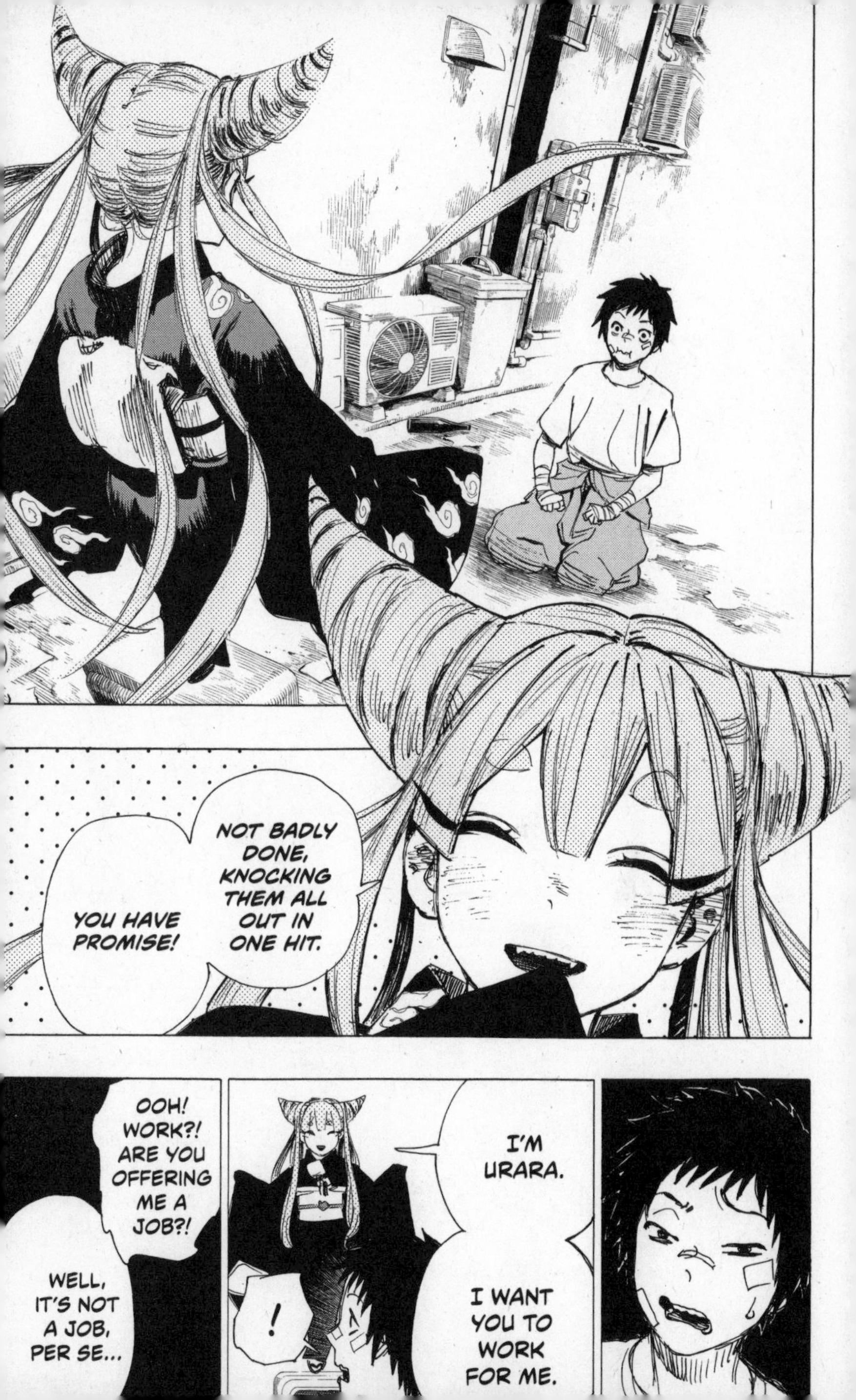
NOT BADLY DONE, KNOCKING THEM ALL OUT IN ONE HIT.
YOU HAVE PROMISE!
I'M URARA.
I WANT YOU TO WORK FOR ME.
!
OOH! WORK?! ARE YOU OFFERING ME A JOB?!
WELL, IT'S NOT A JOB, PER SE...

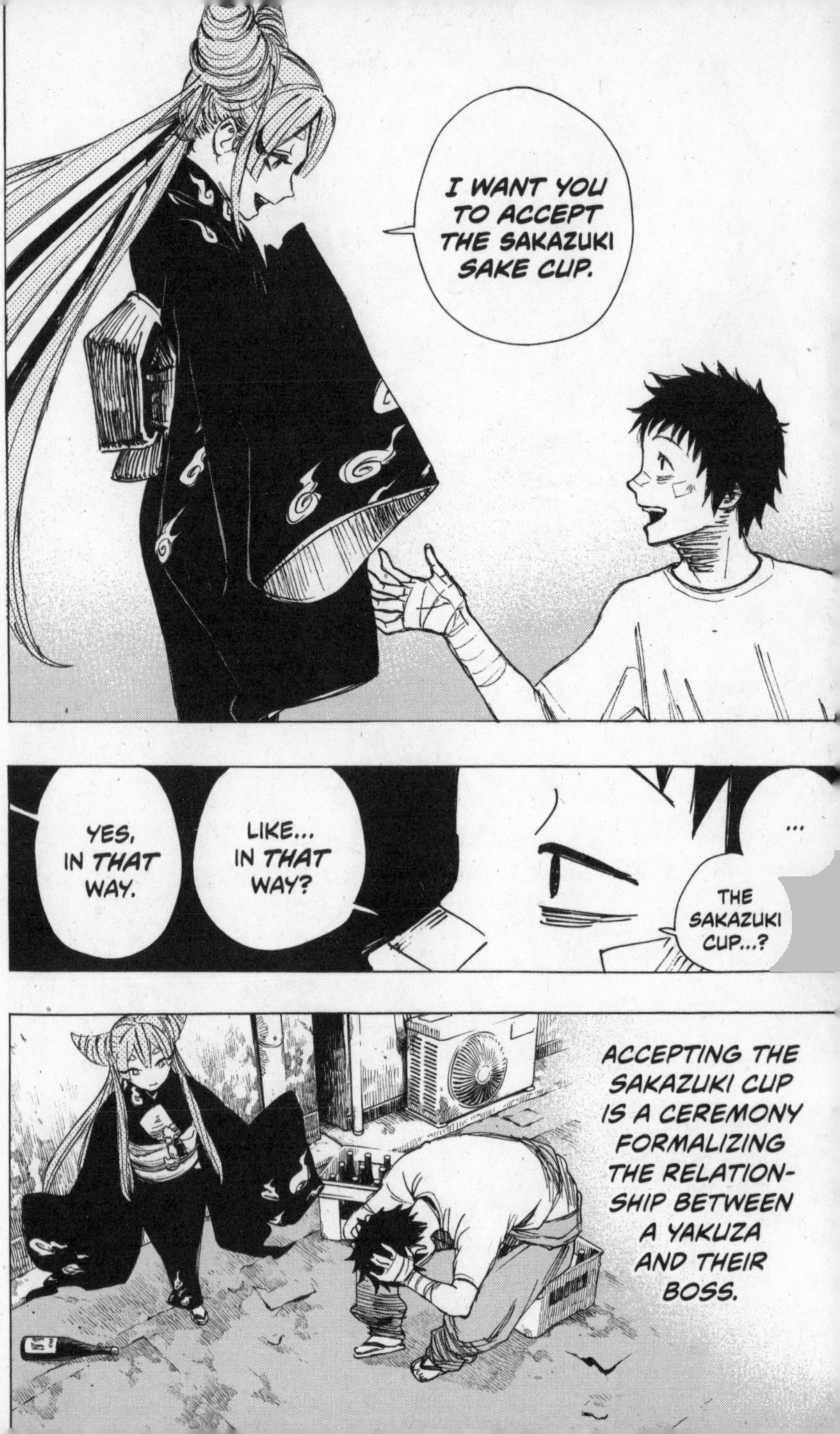
I WANT YOU TO ACCEPT THE SAKAZUKI SAKE CUP.
...
THE SAKAZUKI CUP...?
LIKE... IN *THAT* WAY?
YES, IN *THAT* WAY.
ACCEPTING THE SAKAZUKI CUP IS A CEREMONY FORMALIZING THE RELATIONSHIP BETWEEN A YAKUZA AND THEIR BOSS.

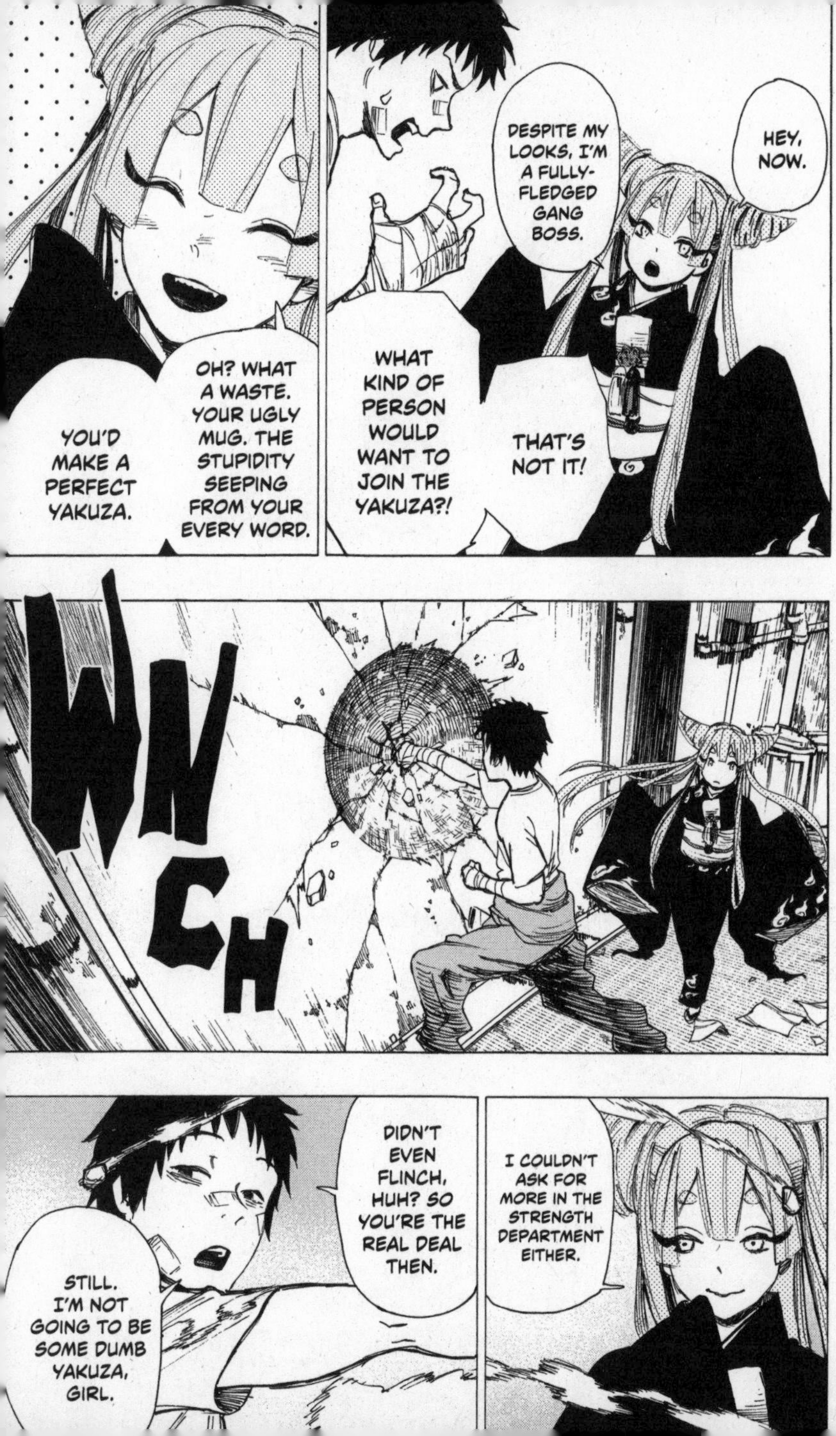
HEY, NOW.
DESPITE MY LOOKS, I'M A FULLY-FLEDGED GANG BOSS.
THAT'S NOT IT!
WHAT KIND OF PERSON WOULD WANT TO JOIN THE YAKUZA?!
OH? WHAT A WASTE. YOUR UGLY MUG. THE STUPIDITY SEEPING FROM YOUR EVERY WORD.
YOU'D MAKE A PERFECT YAKUZA.
WNCH
I COULDN'T ASK FOR MORE IN THE STRENGTH DEPARTMENT EITHER.
DIDN'T EVEN FLINCH, HUH? SO YOU'RE THE REAL DEAL THEN.
STILL. I'M NOT GOING TO BE SOME DUMB YAKUZA, GIRL.

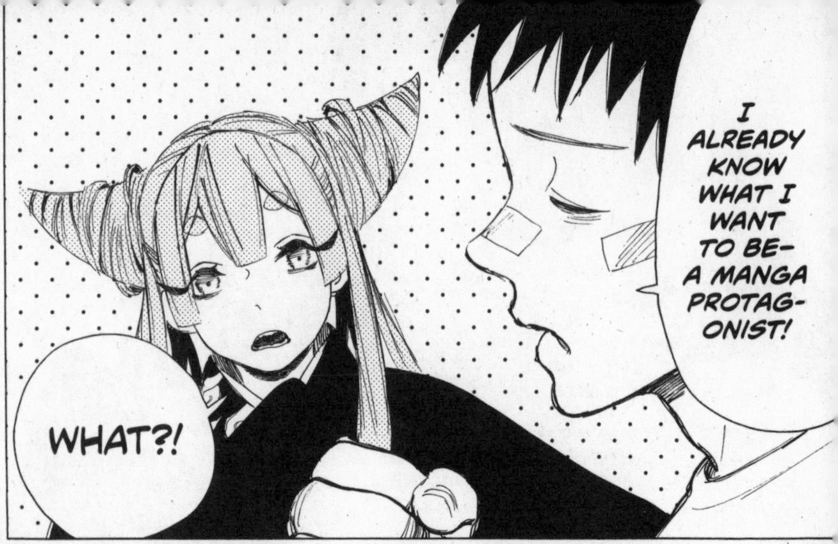
I ALREADY KNOW WHAT I WANT TO BE– A MANGA PROTAG-ONIST!
WHAT?!

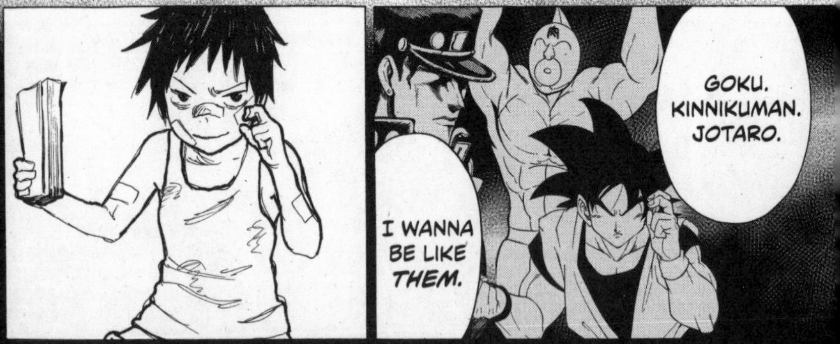
GOKU. KINNIKUMAN. JOTARO.
I WANNA BE LIKE THEM.

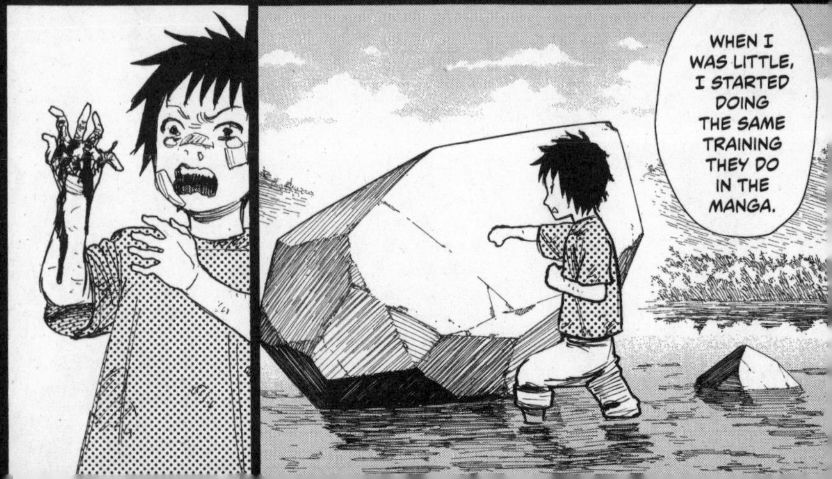
WHEN I WAS LITTLE, I STARTED DOING THE SAME TRAINING THEY DO IN THE MANGA.

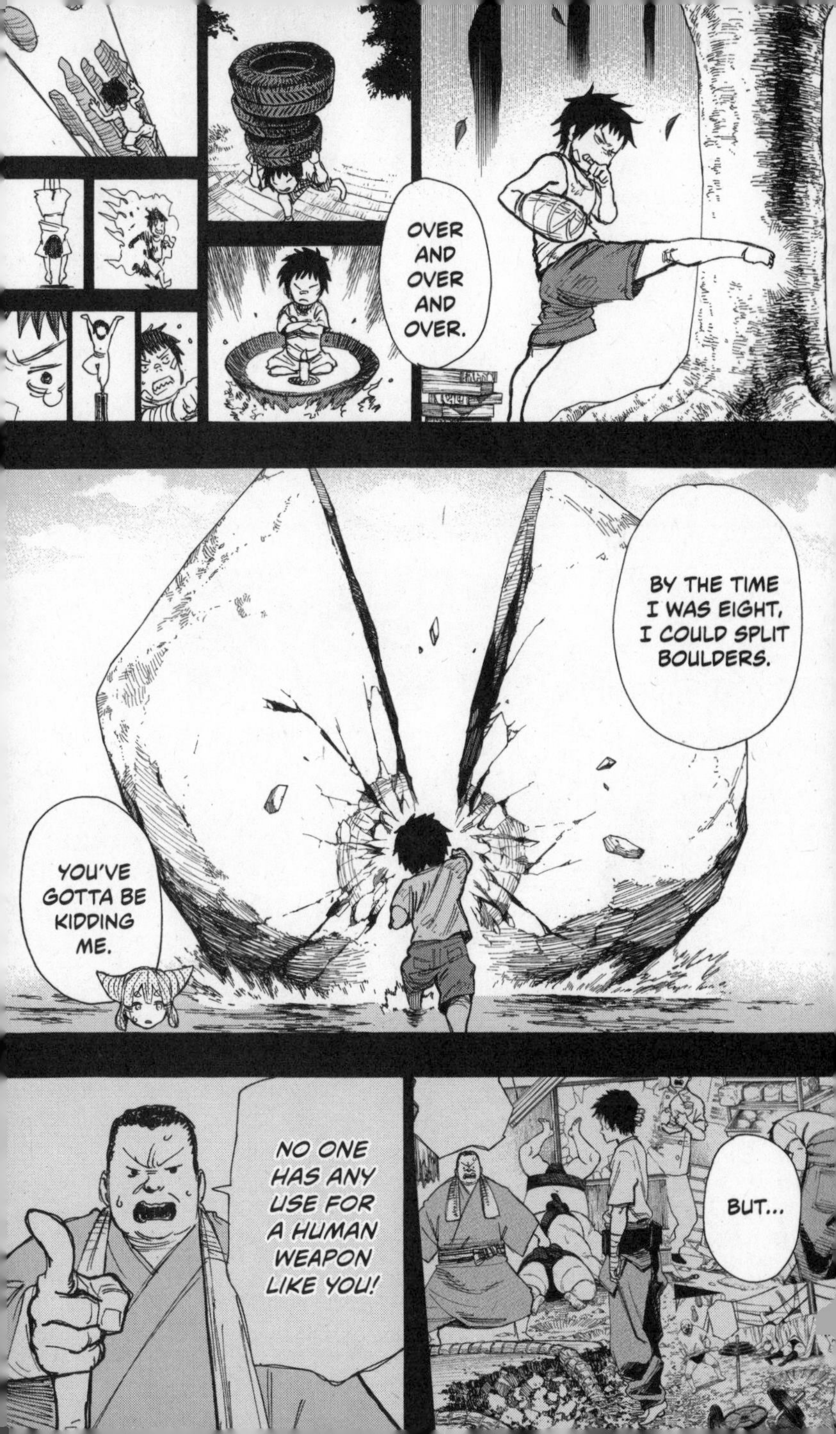
OVER AND OVER AND OVER.
BY THE TIME I WAS EIGHT, I COULD SPLIT BOULDERS.
YOU'VE GOTTA BE KIDDING ME.
BUT...
NO ONE HAS ANY USE FOR A HUMAN WEAPON LIKE YOU!

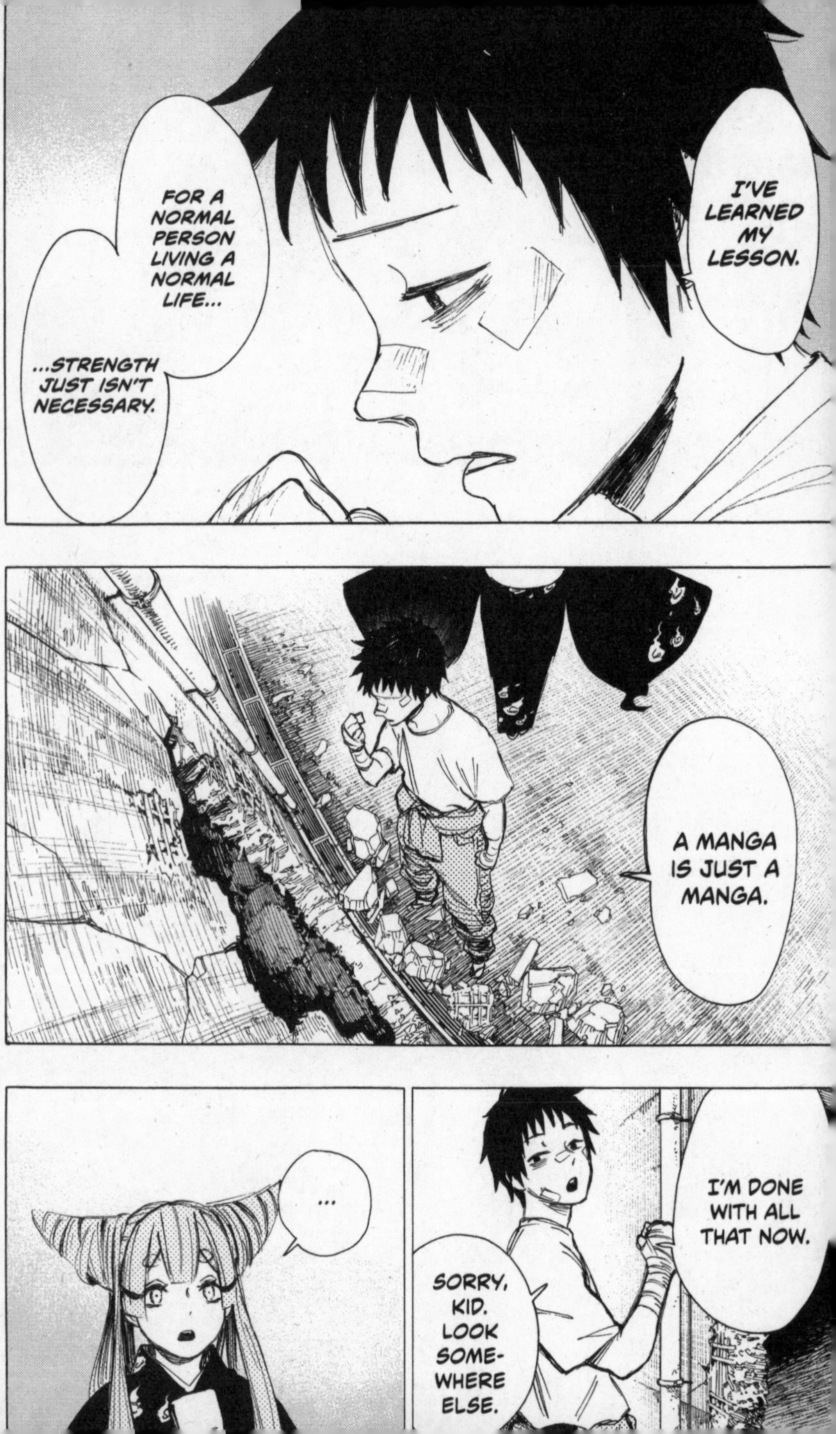
I'VE LEARNED MY LESSON.
FOR A NORMAL PERSON LIVING A NORMAL LIFE...
...STRENGTH JUST ISN'T NECESSARY.
A MANGA IS JUST A MANGA.
I'M DONE WITH ALL THAT NOW.
SORRY, KID. LOOK SOME-WHERE ELSE.
...

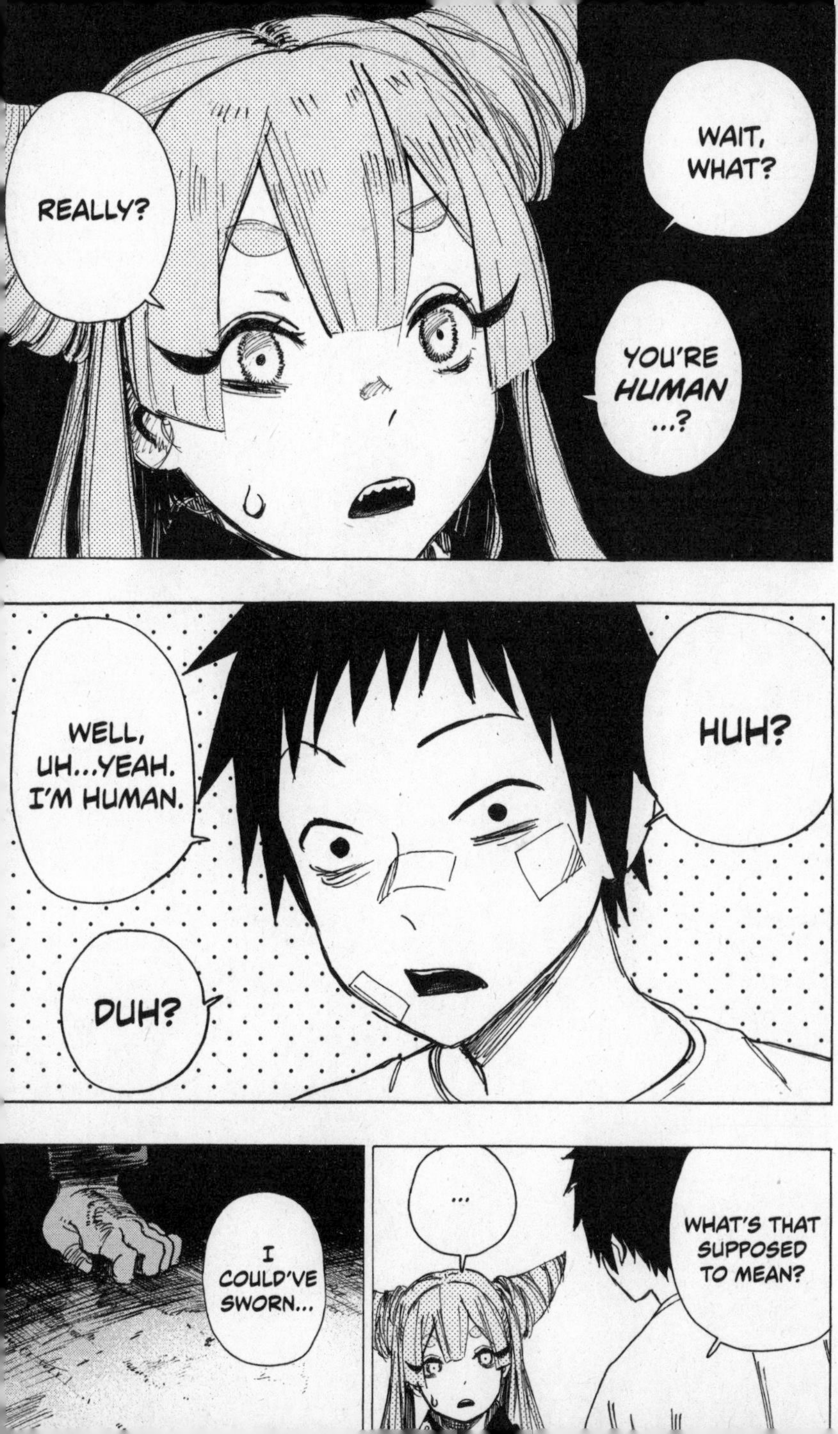
WAIT, WHAT?
YOU'RE *HUMAN* ...?
REALLY?
HUH?
WELL, UH...YEAH. I'M HUMAN.
DUH?
WHAT'S THAT SUPPOSED TO MEAN?
...
I COULD'VE SWORN...

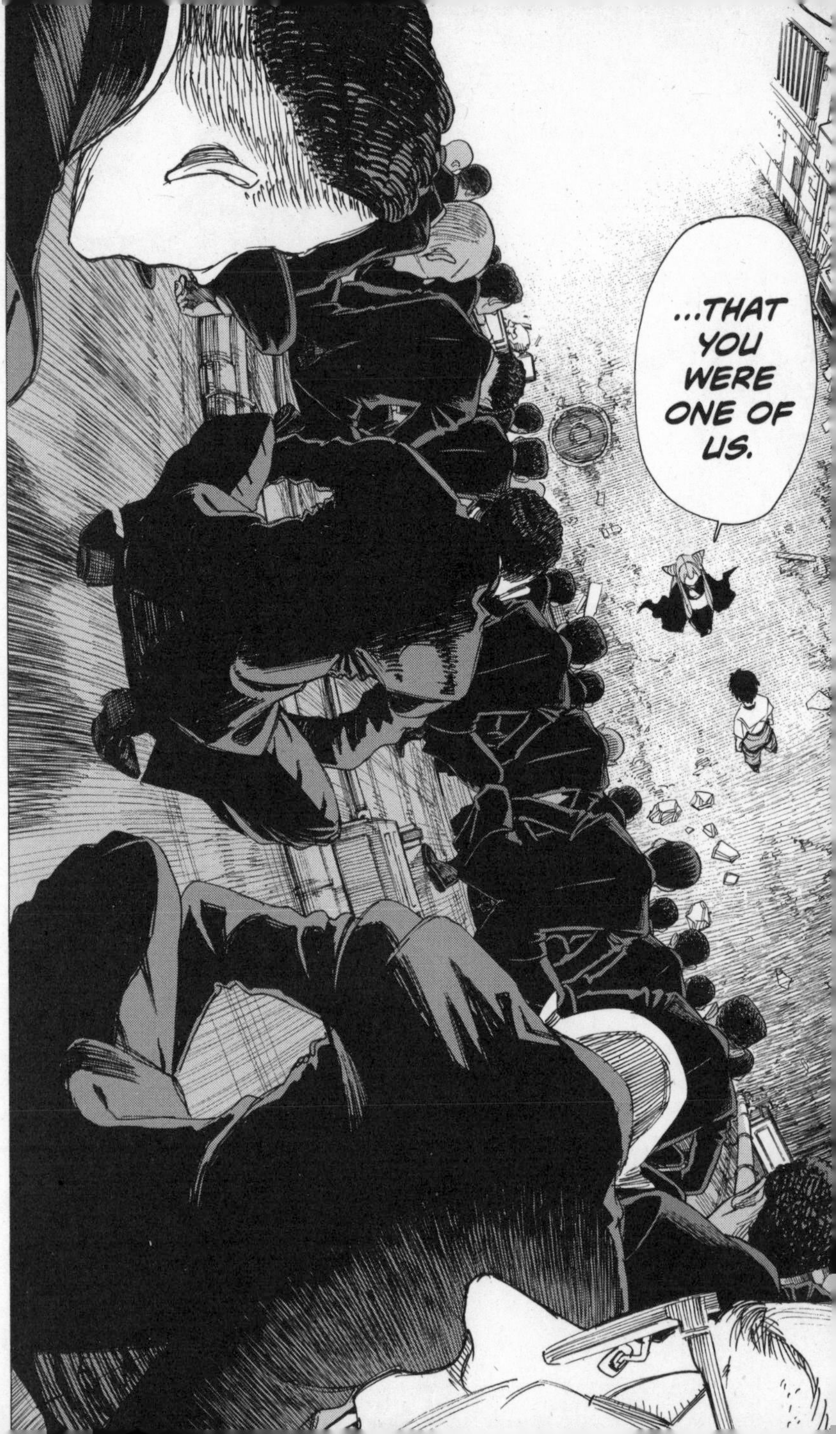
...THAT YOU WERE ONE OF US.

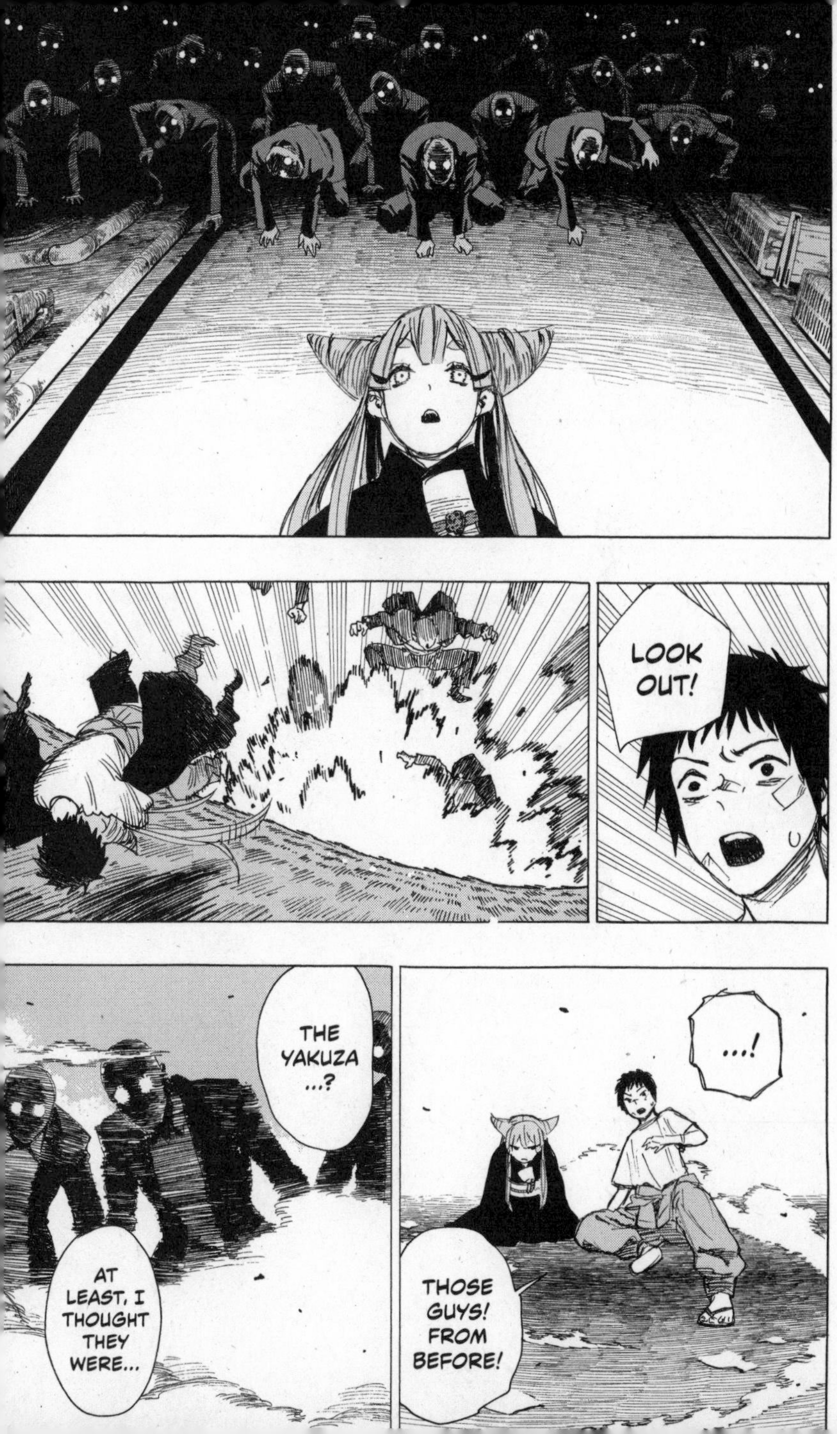
LOOK OUT!
...!
THOSE GUYS! FROM BEFORE!
THE YAKUZA ...?
AT LEAST, I THOUGHT THEY WERE...

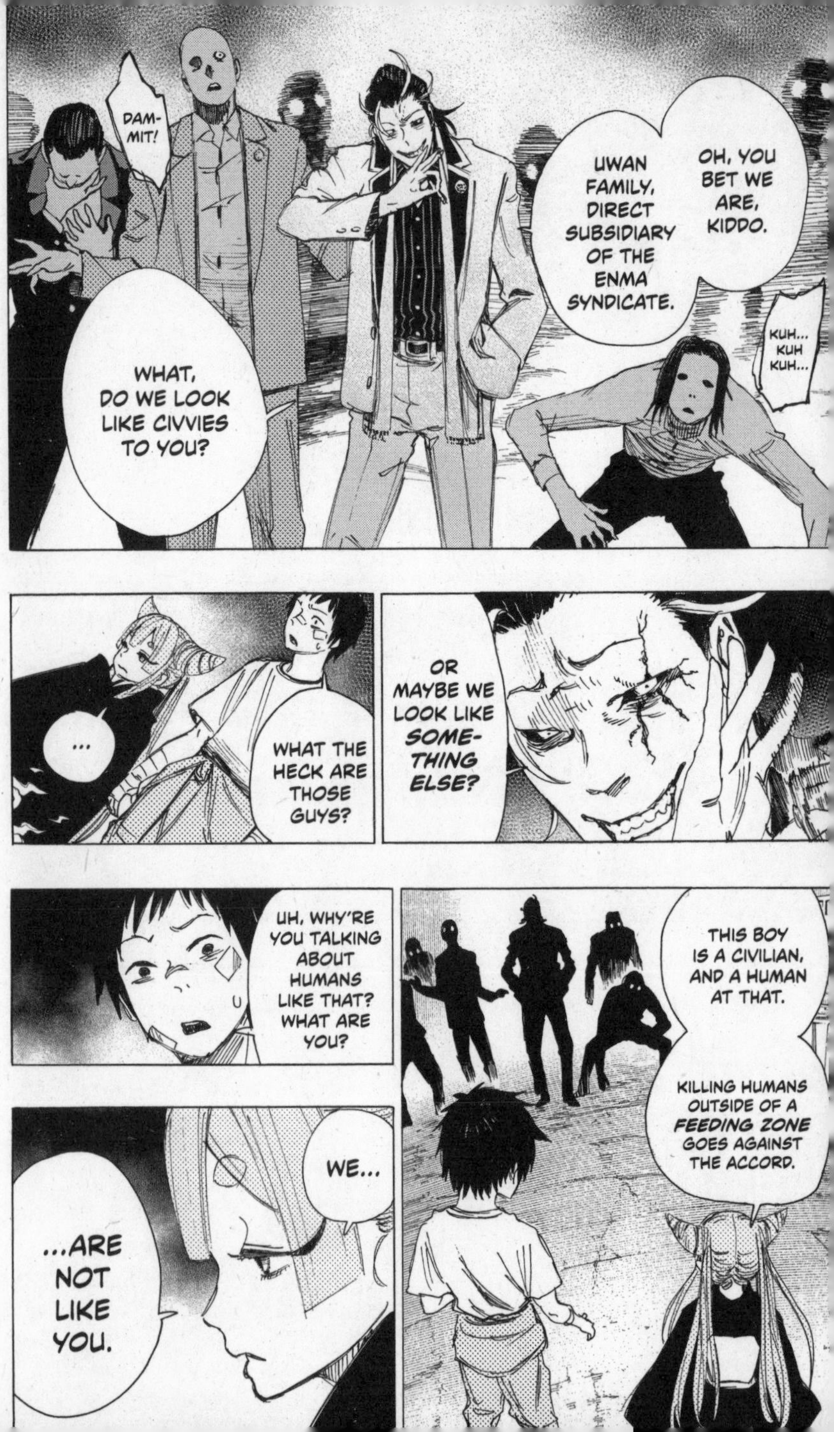
OH, YOU BET WE ARE, KIDDO.
UWAN FAMILY, DIRECT SUBSIDIARY OF THE ENMA SYNDICATE.
KUH... KUH KUH...
DAM-MIT!
WHAT, DO WE LOOK LIKE CIVVIES TO YOU?
OR MAYBE WE LOOK LIKE SOMETHING ELSE?
WHAT THE HECK ARE THOSE GUYS?
...
THIS BOY IS A CIVILIAN, AND A HUMAN AT THAT.
KILLING HUMANS OUTSIDE OF A FEEDING ZONE GOES AGAINST THE ACCORD.
UH, WHY'RE YOU TALKING ABOUT HUMANS LIKE THAT? WHAT ARE YOU?
WE...
...ARE NOT LIKE YOU.

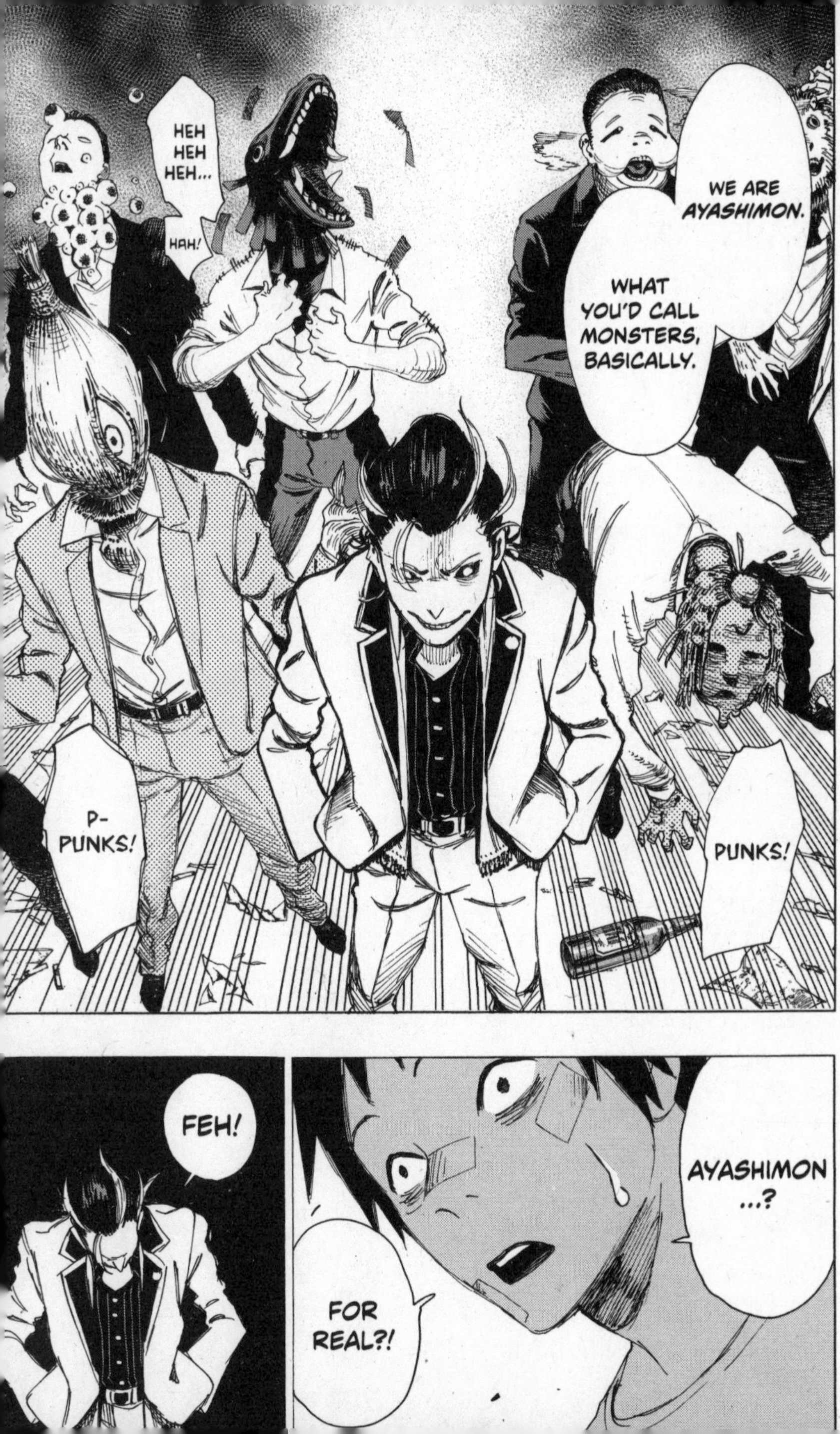
WE ARE AYASHIMON.
WHAT YOU'D CALL MONSTERS, BASICALLY.
HEH HEH HEH...
HAH!
PUNKS!
P-PUNKS!
AYASHIMON ...?
FOR REAL?!
FEH!

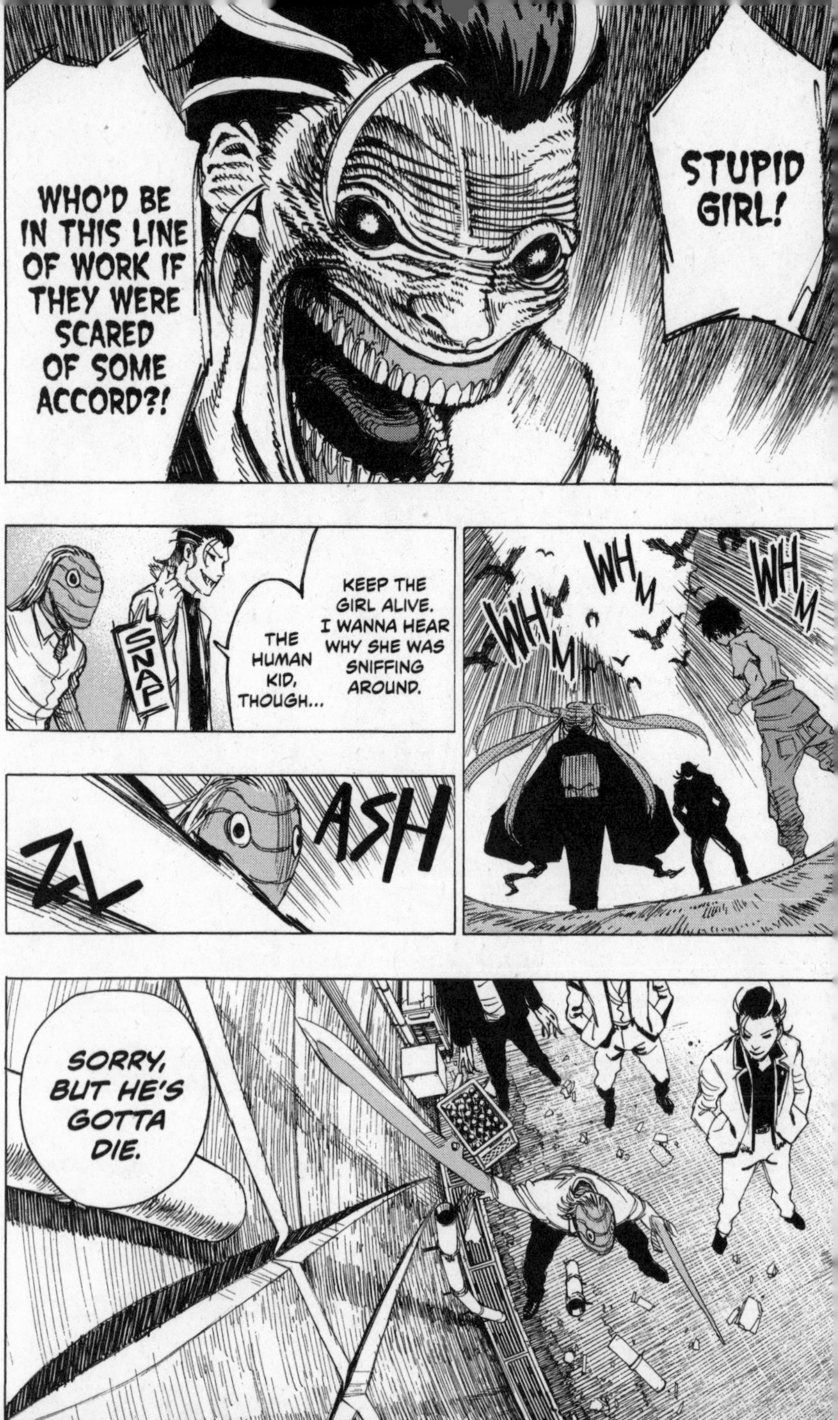
STUPID GIRL!
WHO'D BE IN THIS LINE OF WORK IF THEY WERE SCARED OF SOME ACCORD?!
WHM
WHM
WHM
KEEP THE GIRL ALIVE. I WANNA HEAR WHY SHE WAS SNIFFING AROUND.
THE HUMAN KID, THOUGH...
SNAP
ASH
ZZ
SORRY, BUT HE'S GOTTA DIE.

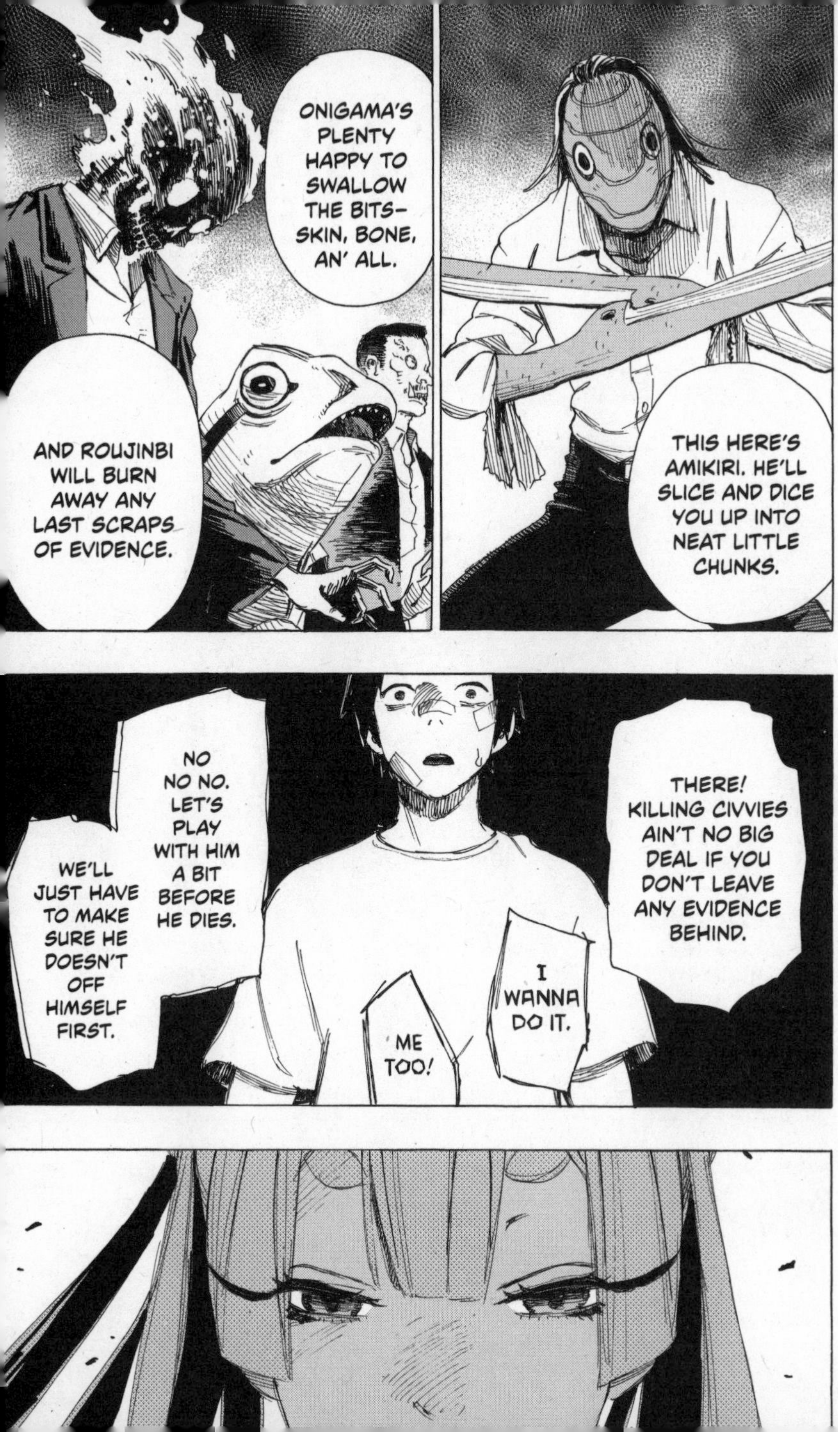
THIS HERE'S AMIKIRI. HE'LL SLICE AND DICE YOU UP INTO NEAT LITTLE CHUNKS.
ONIGAMA'S PLENTY HAPPY TO SWALLOW THE BITS-SKIN, BONE, AN' ALL.
AND ROUJINBI WILL BURN AWAY ANY LAST SCRAPS OF EVIDENCE.
THERE! KILLING CIVVIES AIN'T NO BIG DEAL IF YOU DON'T LEAVE ANY EVIDENCE BEHIND.
I WANNA DO IT.
ME TOO!
NO NO NO. LET'S PLAY WITH HIM A BIT BEFORE HE DIES.
WE'LL JUST HAVE TO MAKE SURE HE DOESN'T OFF HIMSELF FIRST.

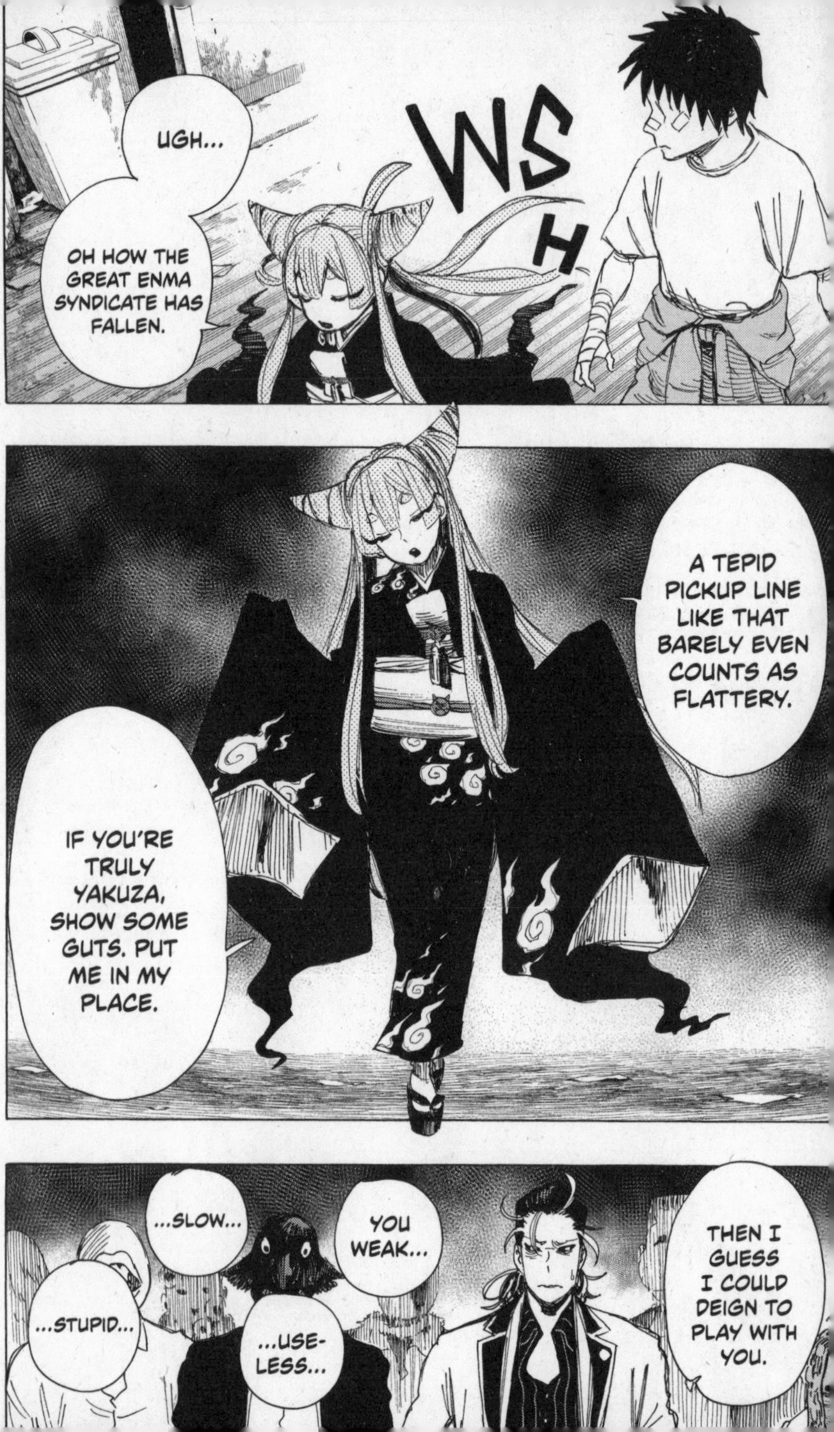
WSH
UGH...
OH HOW THE GREAT ENMA SYNDICATE HAS FALLEN.
A TEPID PICKUP LINE LIKE THAT BARELY EVEN COUNTS AS FLATTERY.
IF YOU'RE TRULY YAKUZA, SHOW SOME GUTS. PUT ME IN MY PLACE.
THEN I GUESS I COULD DEIGN TO PLAY WITH YOU.
YOU WEAK...
...SLOW...
...USE-LESS...
...STUPID...

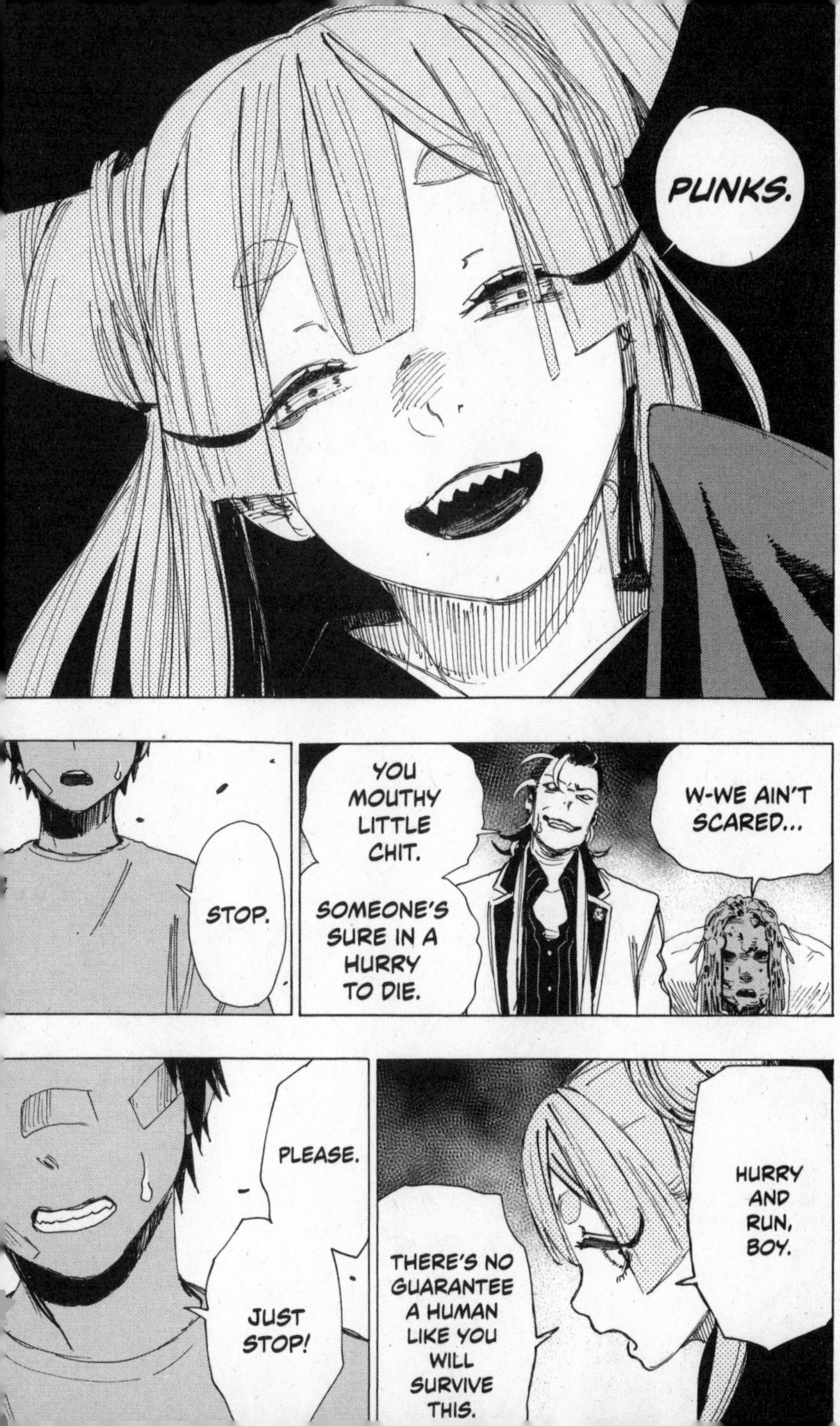
PUNKS.
W-WE AIN'T SCARED...
YOU MOUTHY LITTLE CHIT.
SOMEONE'S SURE IN A HURRY TO DIE.
STOP.
HURRY AND RUN, BOY.
THERE'S NO GUARANTEE A HUMAN LIKE YOU WILL SURVIVE THIS.
PLEASE.
JUST STOP!

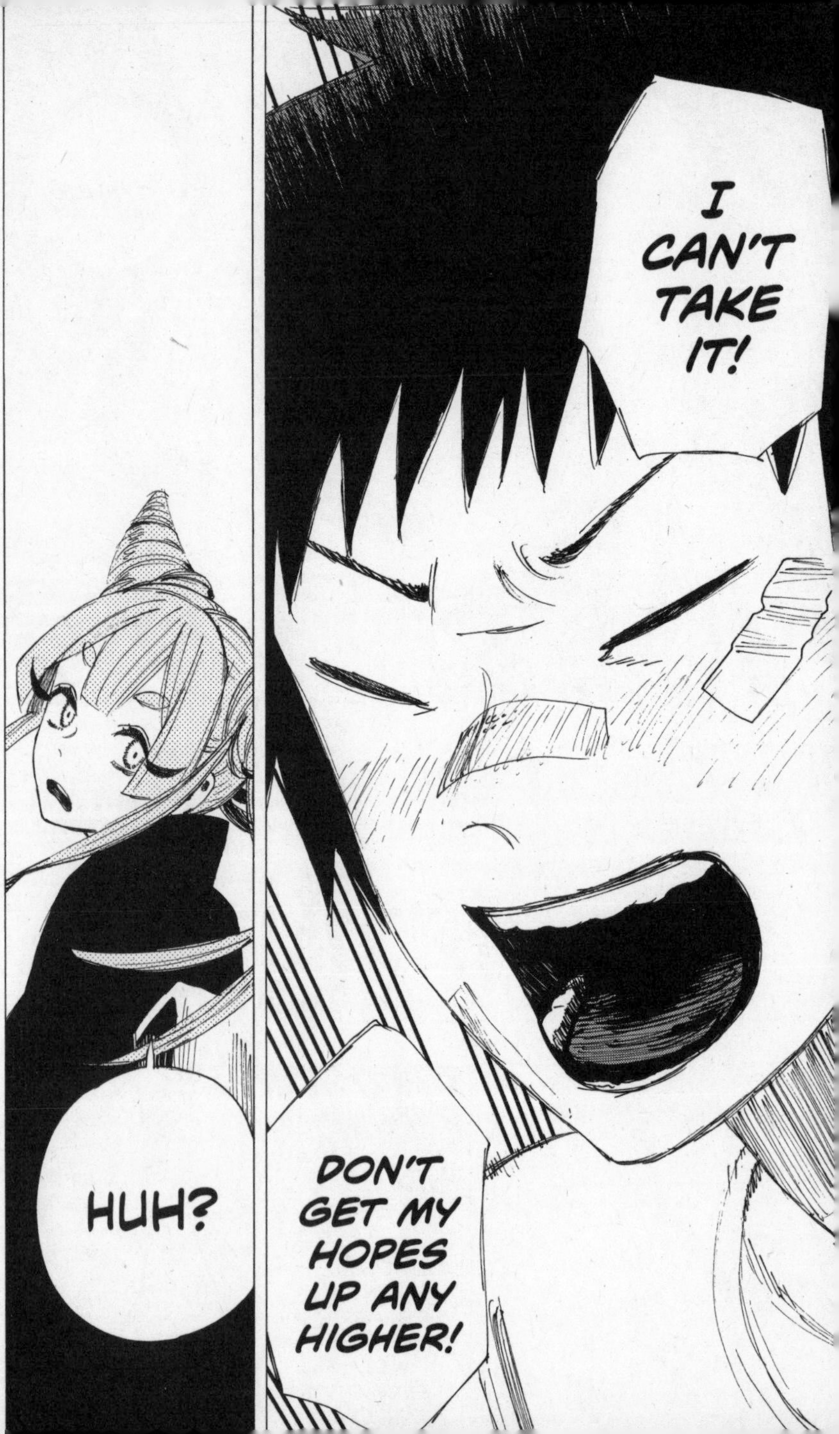
I CAN'T TAKE IT!
DON'T GET MY HOPES UP ANY HIGHER!
HUH?

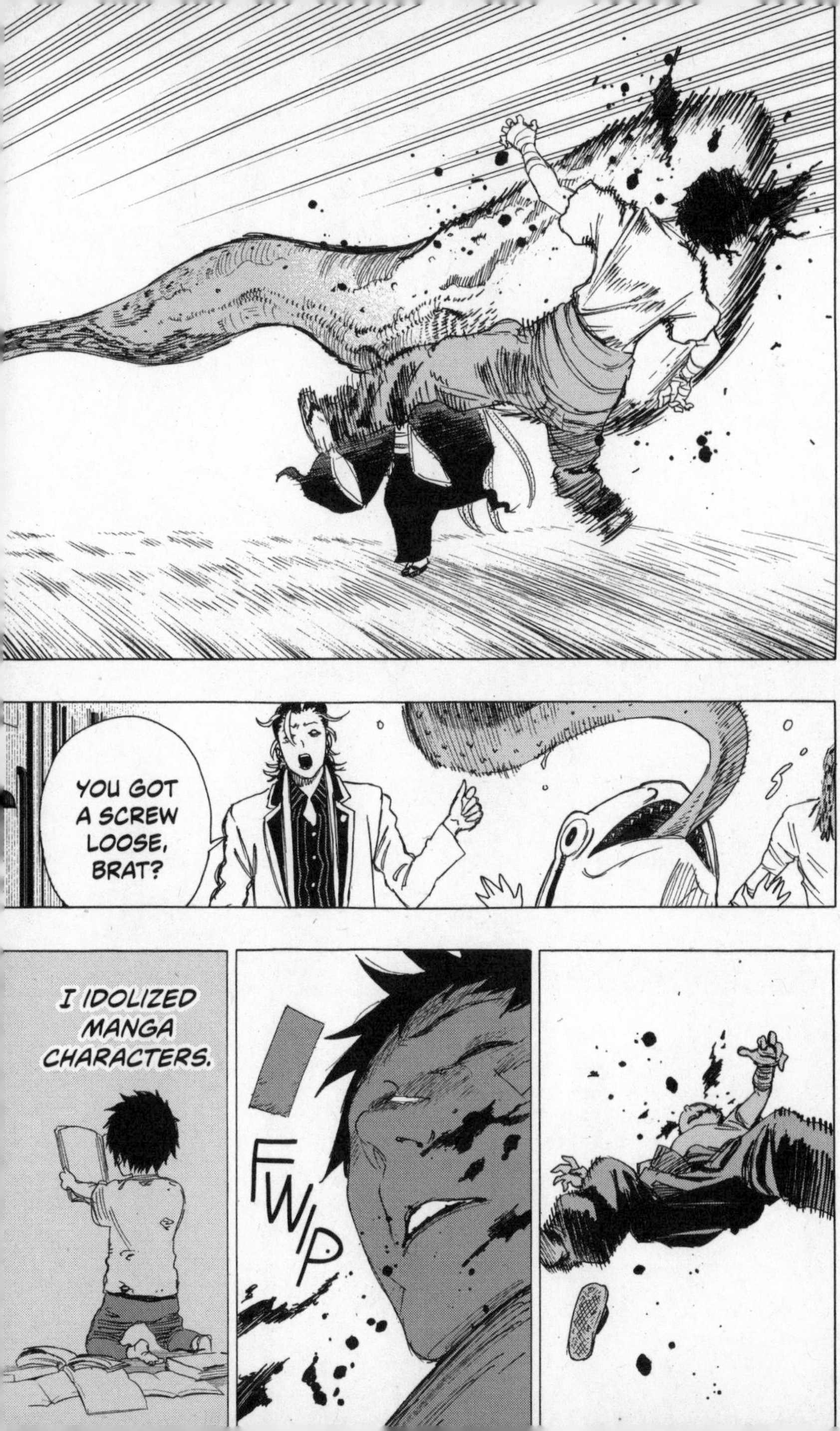
YOU GOT A SCREW LOOSE, BRAT?
FWIP
I IDOLIZED MANGA CHARACTERS.

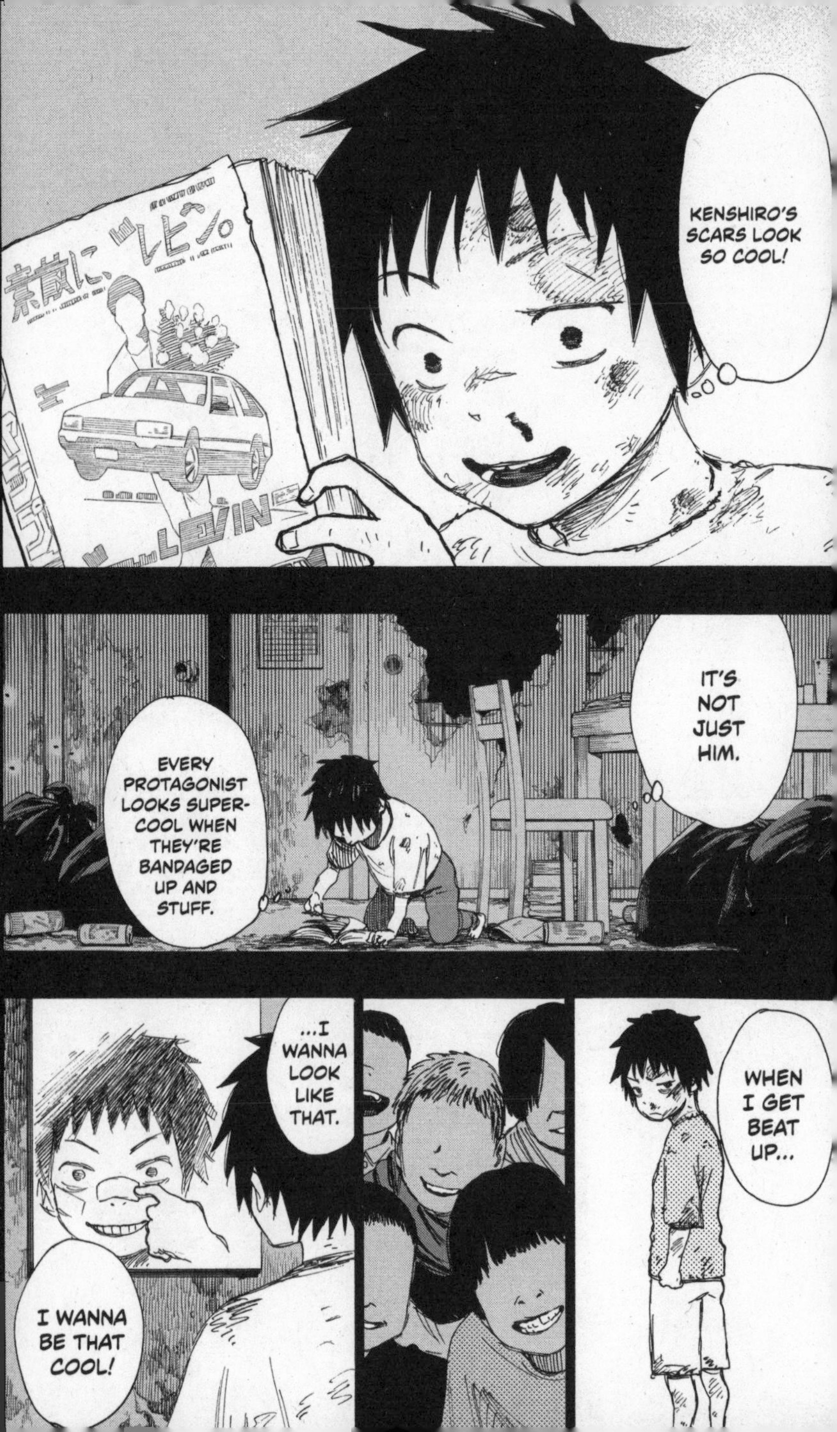
KENSHIRO'S SCARS LOOK SO COOL!
素敵に、レビンへ。
LEVIN
IT'S NOT JUST HIM.
EVERY PROTAGONIST LOOKS SUPER-COOL WHEN THEY'RE BANDAGED UP AND STUFF.
WHEN I GET BEAT UP...
...I WANNA LOOK LIKE THAT.
I WANNA BE THAT COOL!

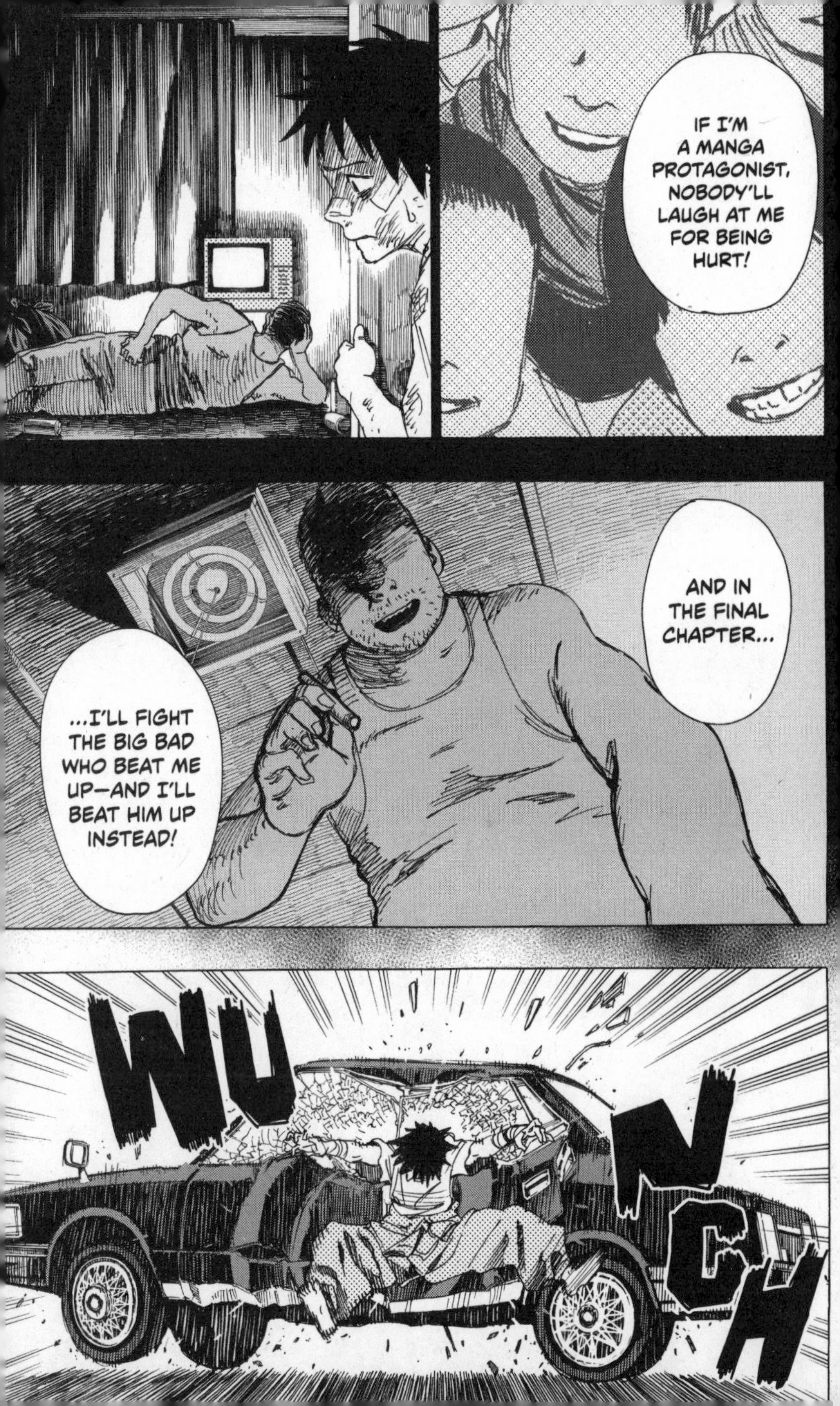
IF I'M A MANGA PROTAGONIST, NOBODY'LL LAUGH AT ME FOR BEING HURT!
AND IN THE FINAL CHAPTER...
...I'LL FIGHT THE BIG BAD WHO BEAT ME UP—AND I'LL BEAT HIM UP INSTEAD!
WUNCH

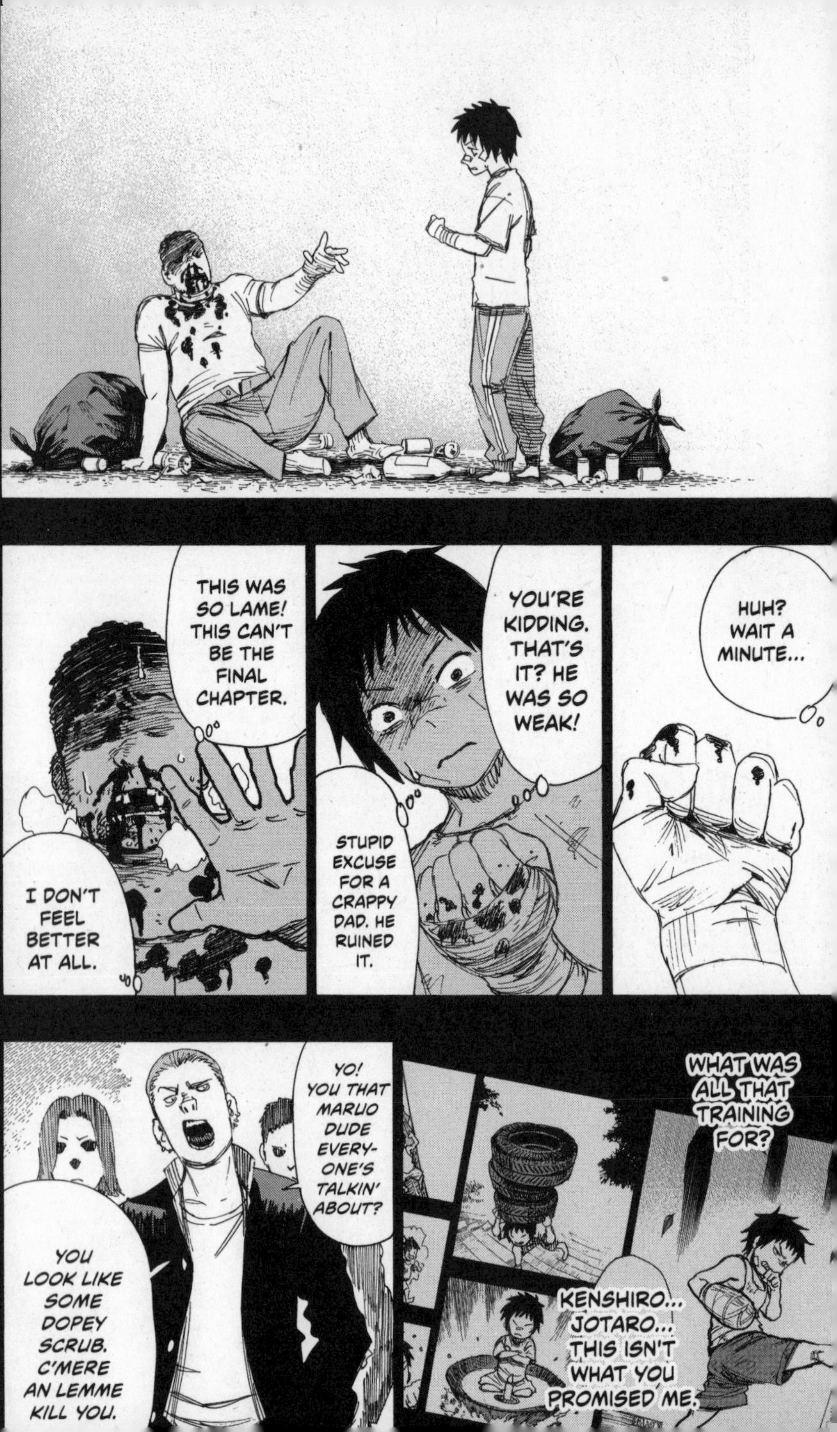
HUH? WAIT A MINUTE...
YOU'RE KIDDING. THAT'S IT? HE WAS SO WEAK!
STUPID EXCUSE FOR A CRAPPY DAD. HE RUINED IT.
THIS WAS SO LAME! THIS CAN'T BE THE FINAL CHAPTER.
I DON'T FEEL BETTER AT ALL.
WHAT WAS ALL THAT TRAINING FOR?
KENSHIRO... JOTARO... THIS ISN'T WHAT YOU PROMISED ME.
YO! YOU THAT MARUO DUDE EVERY-ONE'S TALKIN' ABOUT?
YOU LOOK LIKE SOME DOPEY SCRUB. C'MERE AN LEMME KILL YOU.

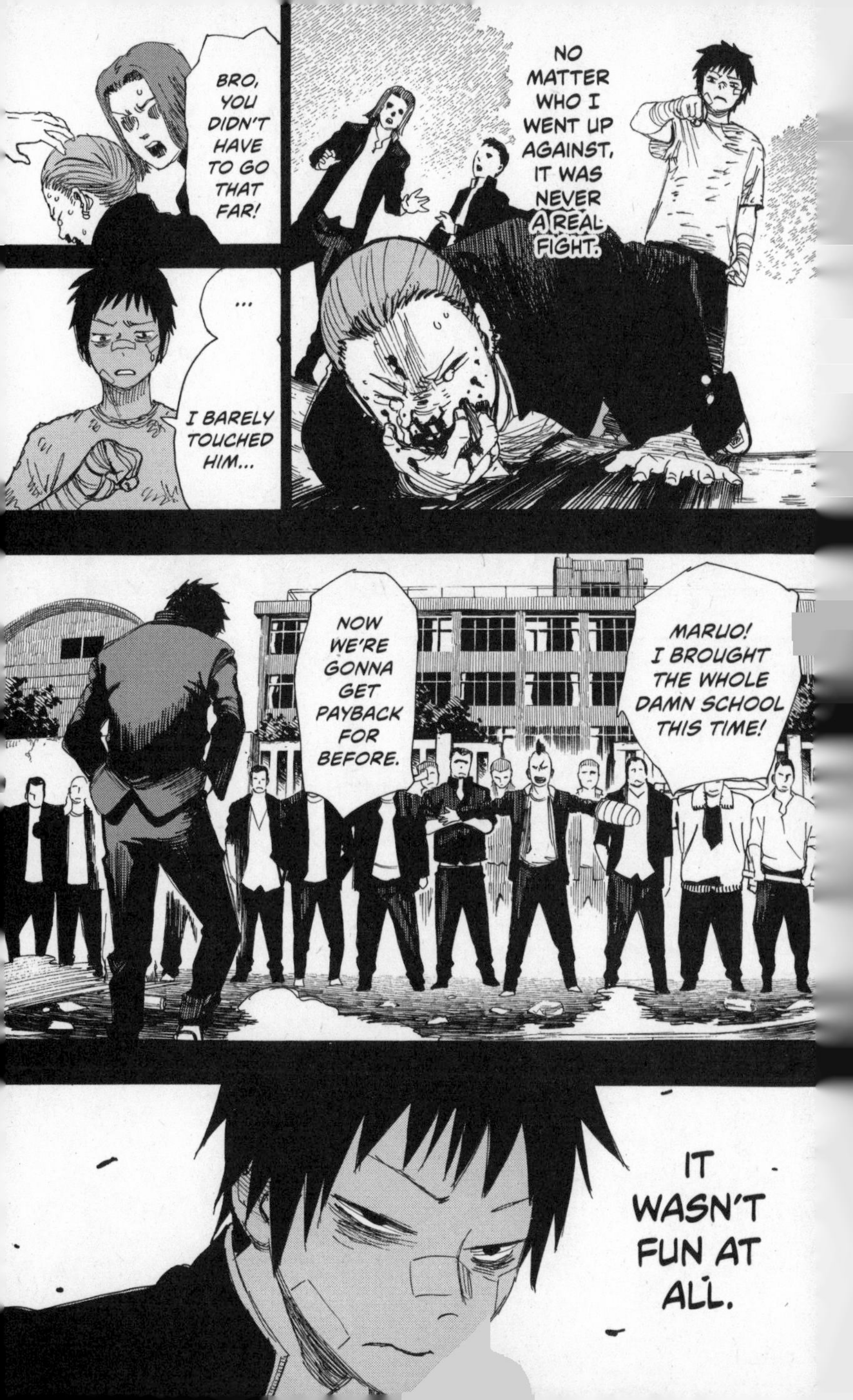
NO MATTER WHO I WENT UP AGAINST, IT WAS NEVER A REAL FIGHT.
BRO, YOU DIDN'T HAVE TO GO THAT FAR!
...
I BARELY TOUCHED HIM...
MARUO! I BROUGHT THE WHOLE DAMN SCHOOL THIS TIME!
NOW WE'RE GONNA GET PAYBACK FOR BEFORE.
IT WASN'T FUN AT ALL.

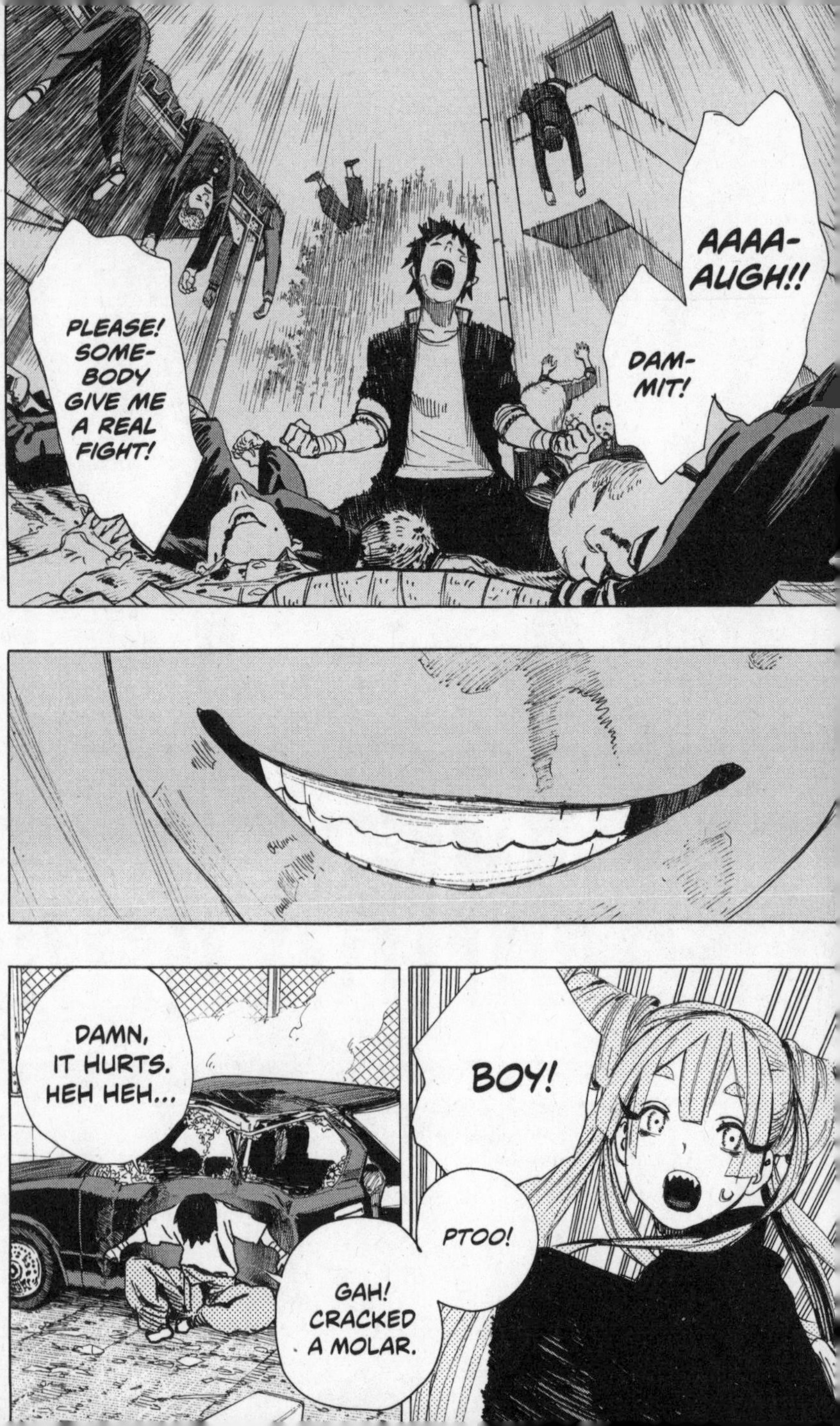
AAAA-AUGH!!
DAM-MIT!
PLEASE! SOME-BODY GIVE ME A REAL FIGHT!
BOY!
DAMN, IT HURTS. HEH HEH...
PTOO!
GAH! CRACKED A MOLAR.

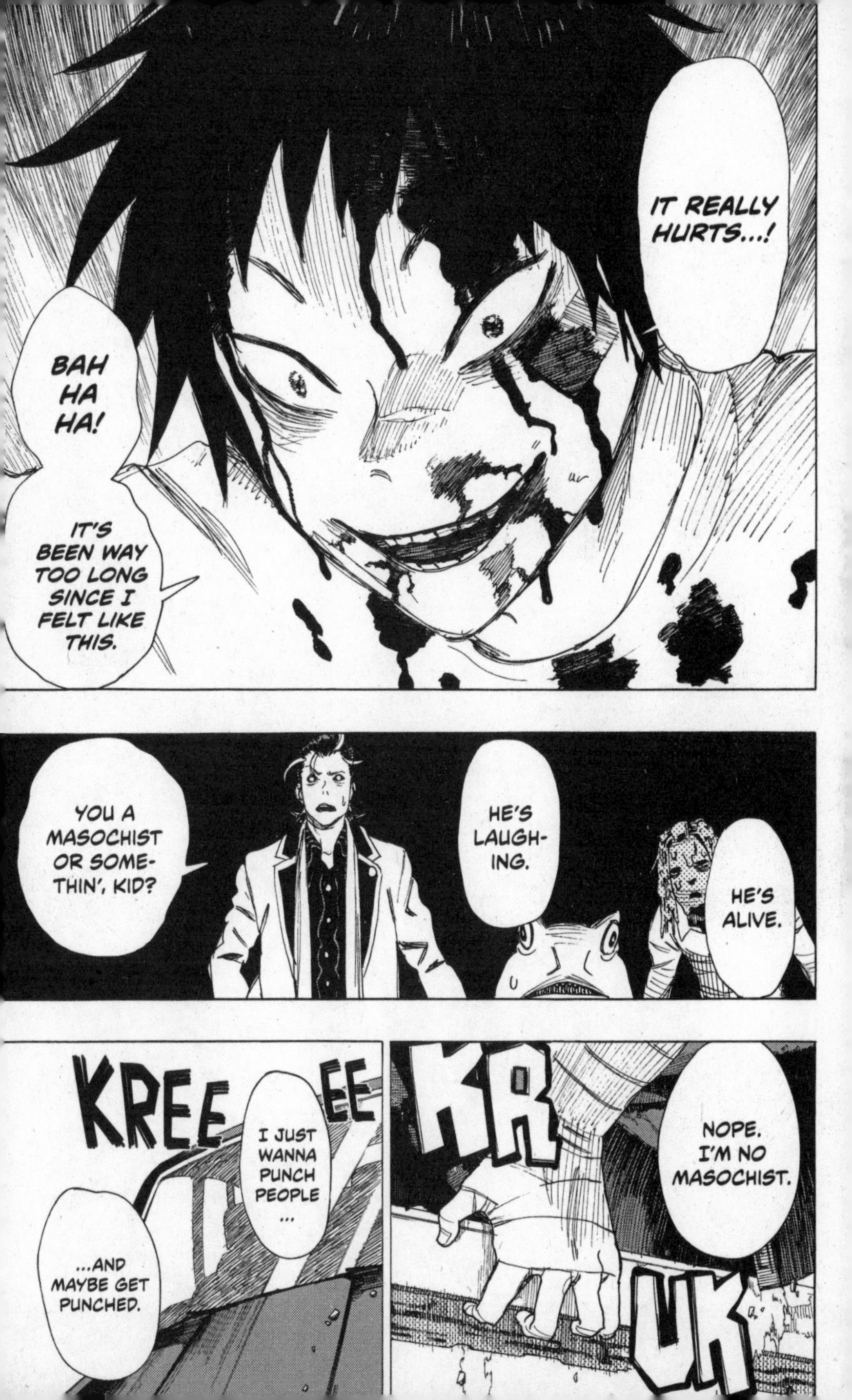
IT REALLY HURTS...!
BAH HA HA!
IT'S BEEN WAY TOO LONG SINCE I FELT LIKE THIS.
HE'S ALIVE.
HE'S LAUGH-ING.
YOU A MASOCHIST OR SOME-THIN', KID?
KR
UK
NOPE. I'M NO MASOCHIST.
KREE
EE
I JUST WANNA PUNCH PEOPLE ...
...AND MAYBE GET PUNCHED.

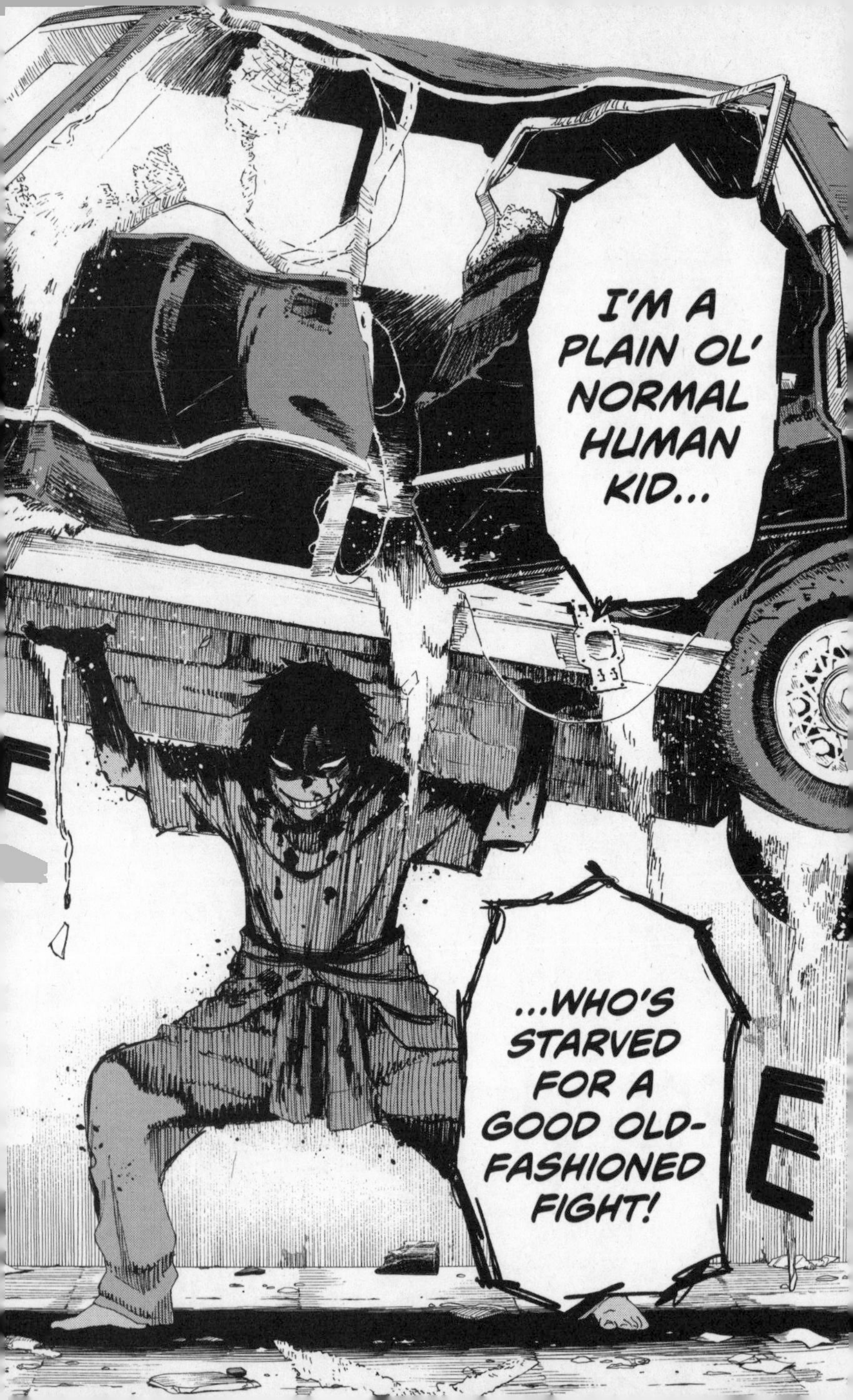
I'M A PLAIN OL' NORMAL HUMAN KID...
...WHO'S STARVED FOR A GOOD OLD-FASHIONED FIGHT!

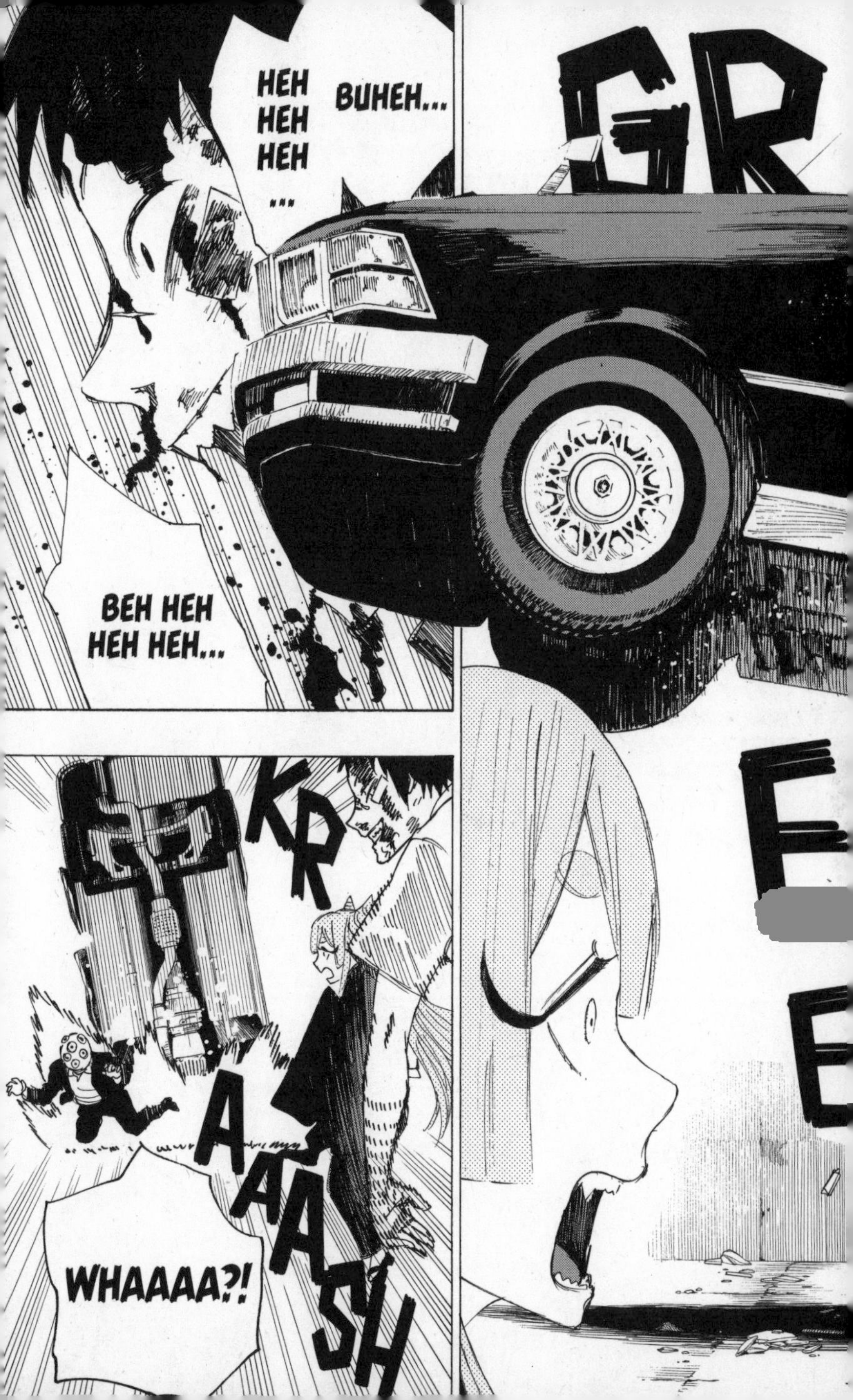
GR
EEE
BUHEH...
HEH HEH HEH ...
BEH HEH HEH HEH...
KR
AAASH
WHAAAA?!

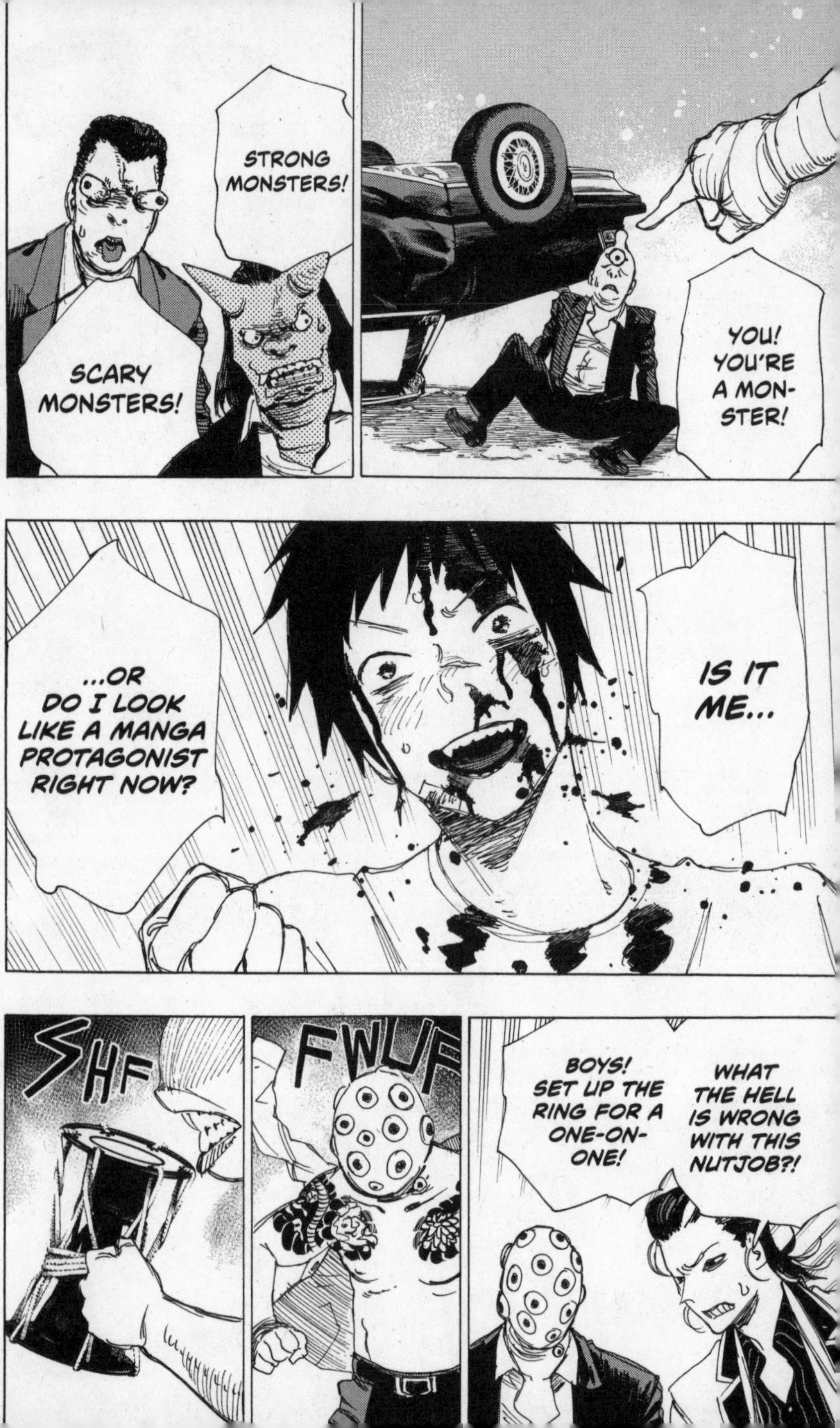
YOU! YOU'RE A MON-STER!
STRONG MONSTERS!
SCARY MONSTERS!
IS IT ME...
...OR DO I LOOK LIKE A MANGA PROTAGONIST RIGHT NOW?
WHAT THE HELL IS WRONG WITH THIS NUTJOB?!
BOYS! SET UP THE RING FOR A ONE-ON-ONE!
FWUF
SHF

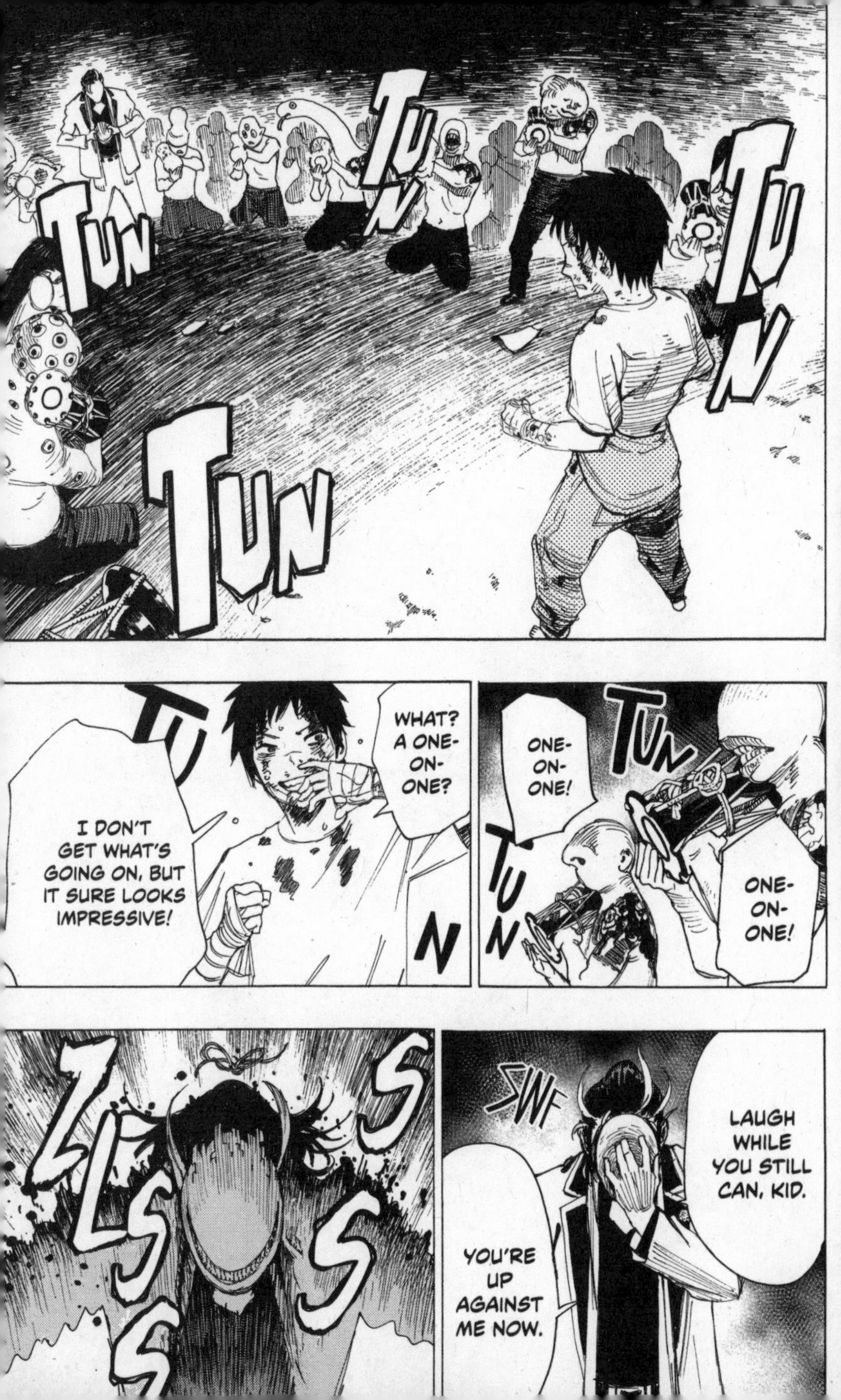
TUN
TUN
TUN
TUN
TUN
ONE-ON-ONE!
ONE-ON-ONE!
TUN
WHAT? A ONE-ON-ONE?
I DON'T GET WHAT'S GOING ON, BUT IT SURE LOOKS IMPRESSIVE!
TUN
SWF
LAUGH WHILE YOU STILL CAN, KID.
YOU'RE UP AGAINST ME NOW.

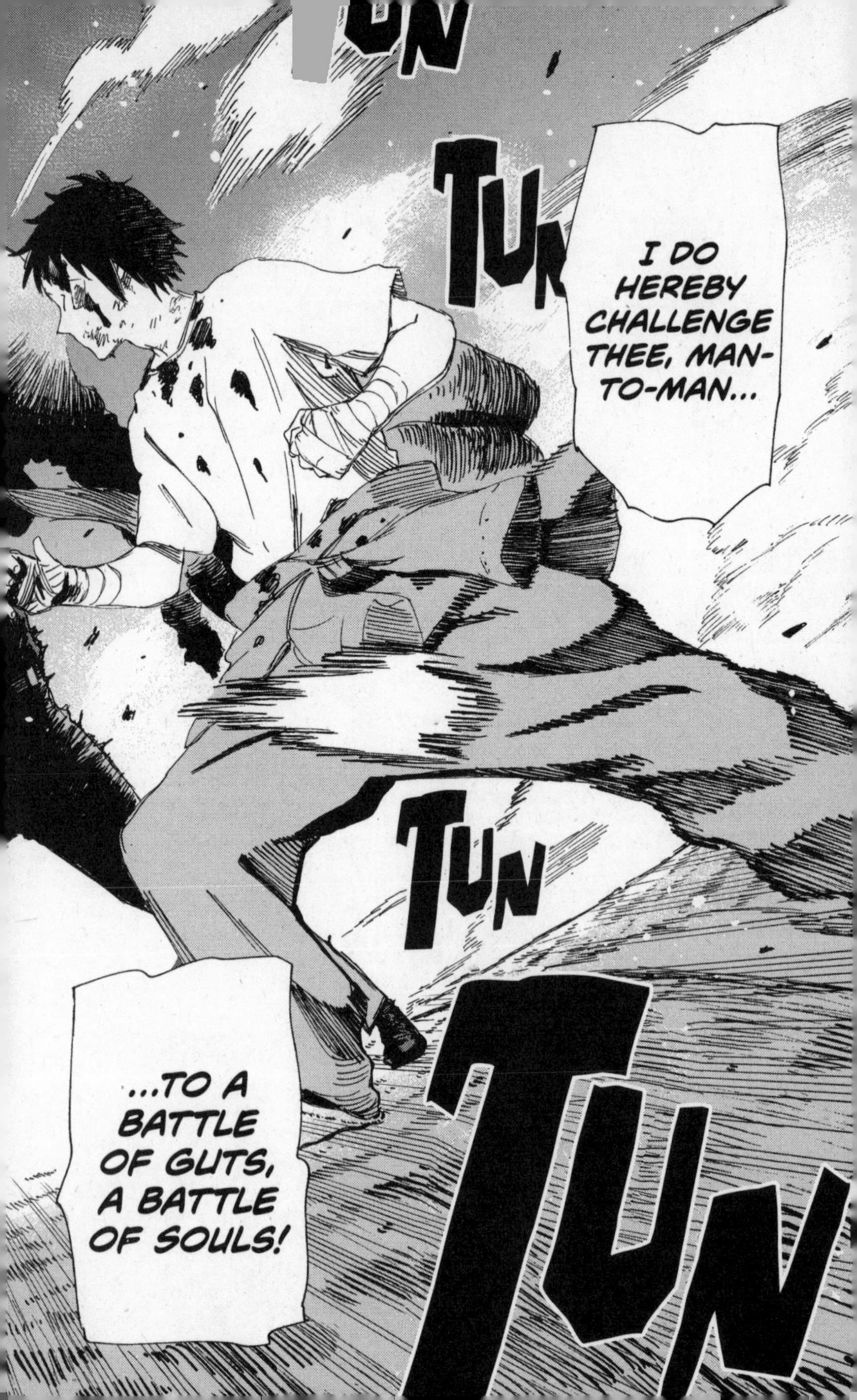
UN
TUN
I DO HEREBY CHALLENGE THEE, MAN-TO-MAN...
TUN
TUN
...TO A BATTLE OF GUTS, A BATTLE OF SOULS!

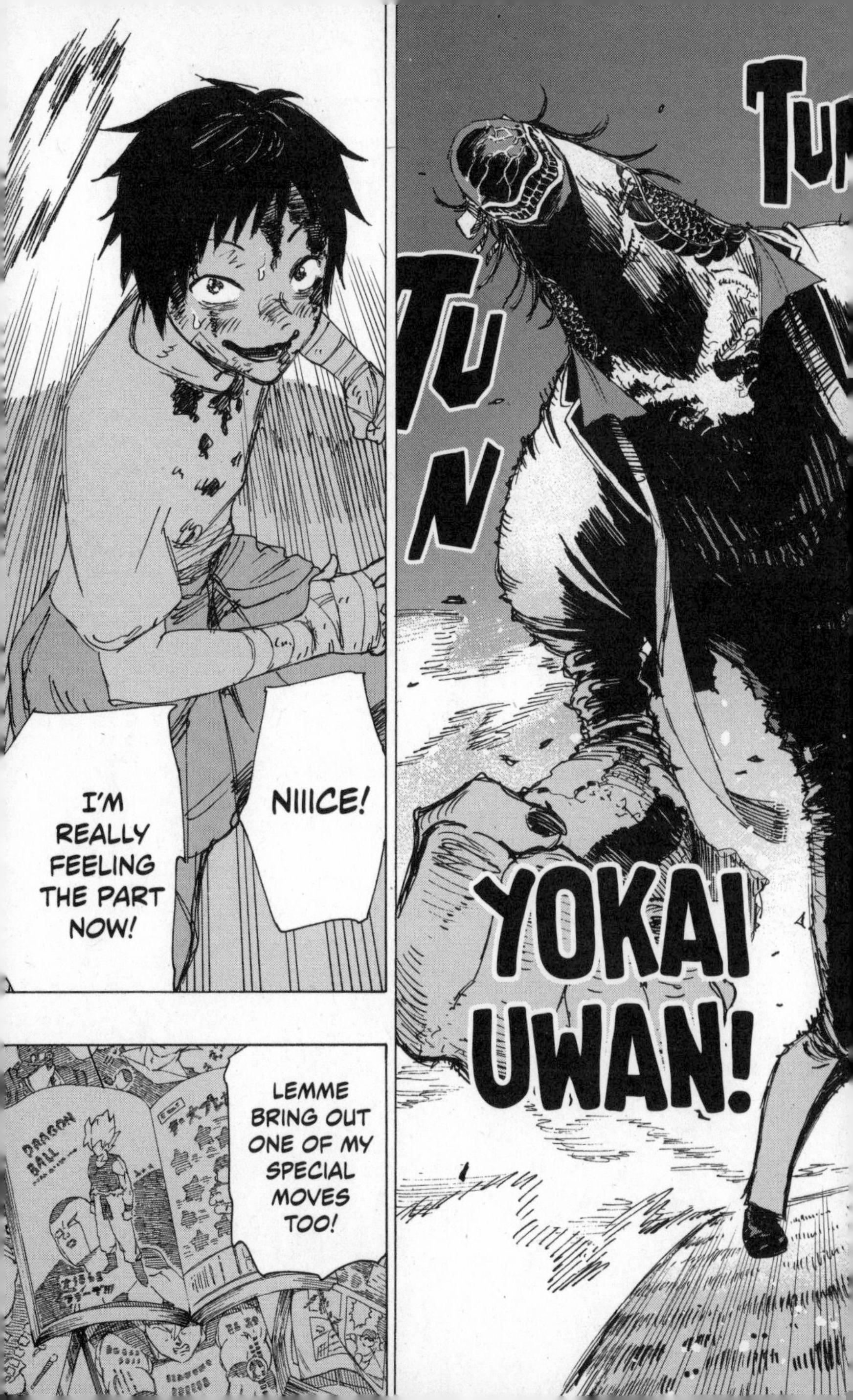
TUN
YOKAI UWAN!
NIIICE!
I'M REALLY FEELING THE PART NOW!
LEMME BRING OUT ONE OF MY SPECIAL MOVES TOO!

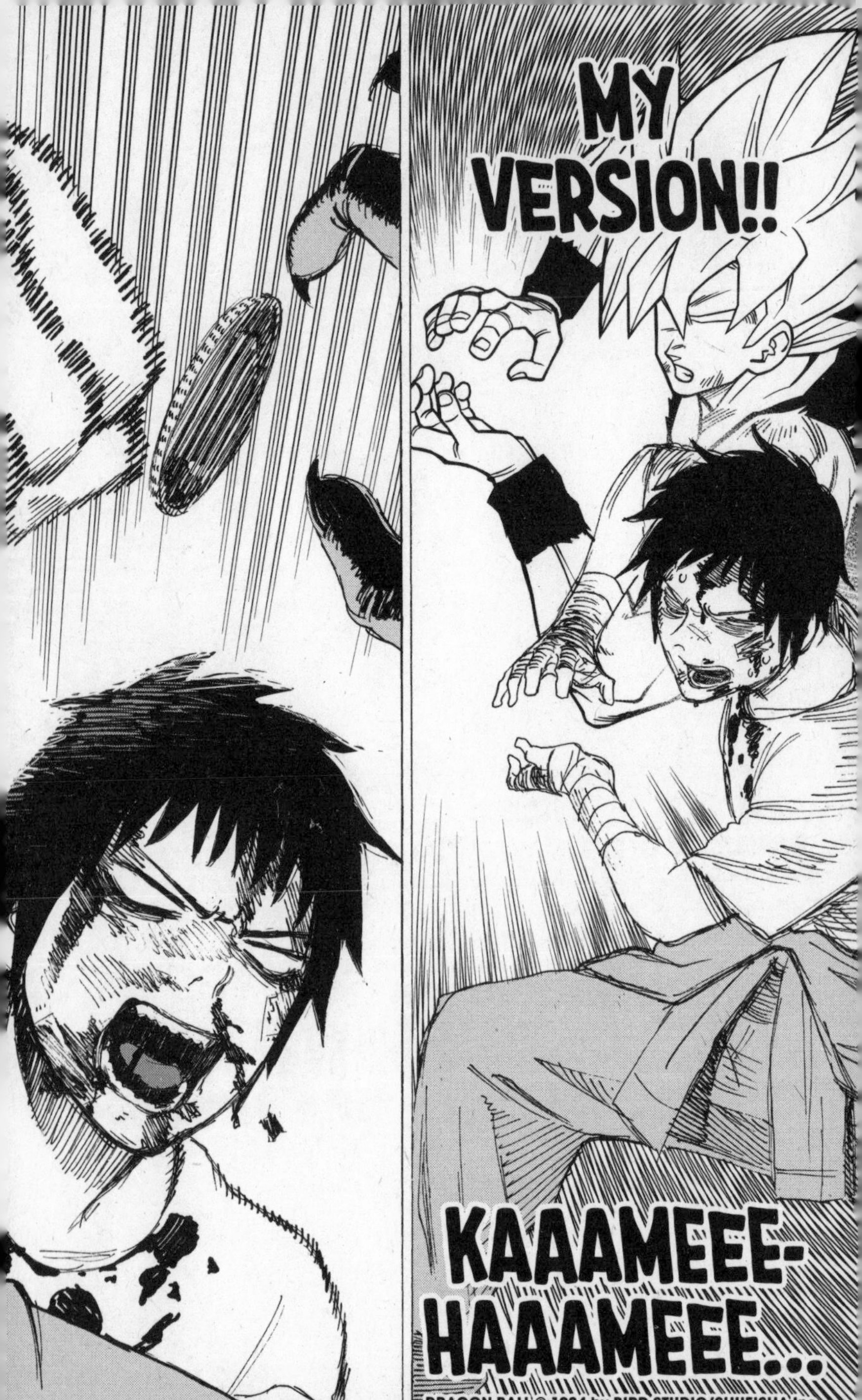
MY VERSION!!
KAAAMEEE-HAAAMEEE...

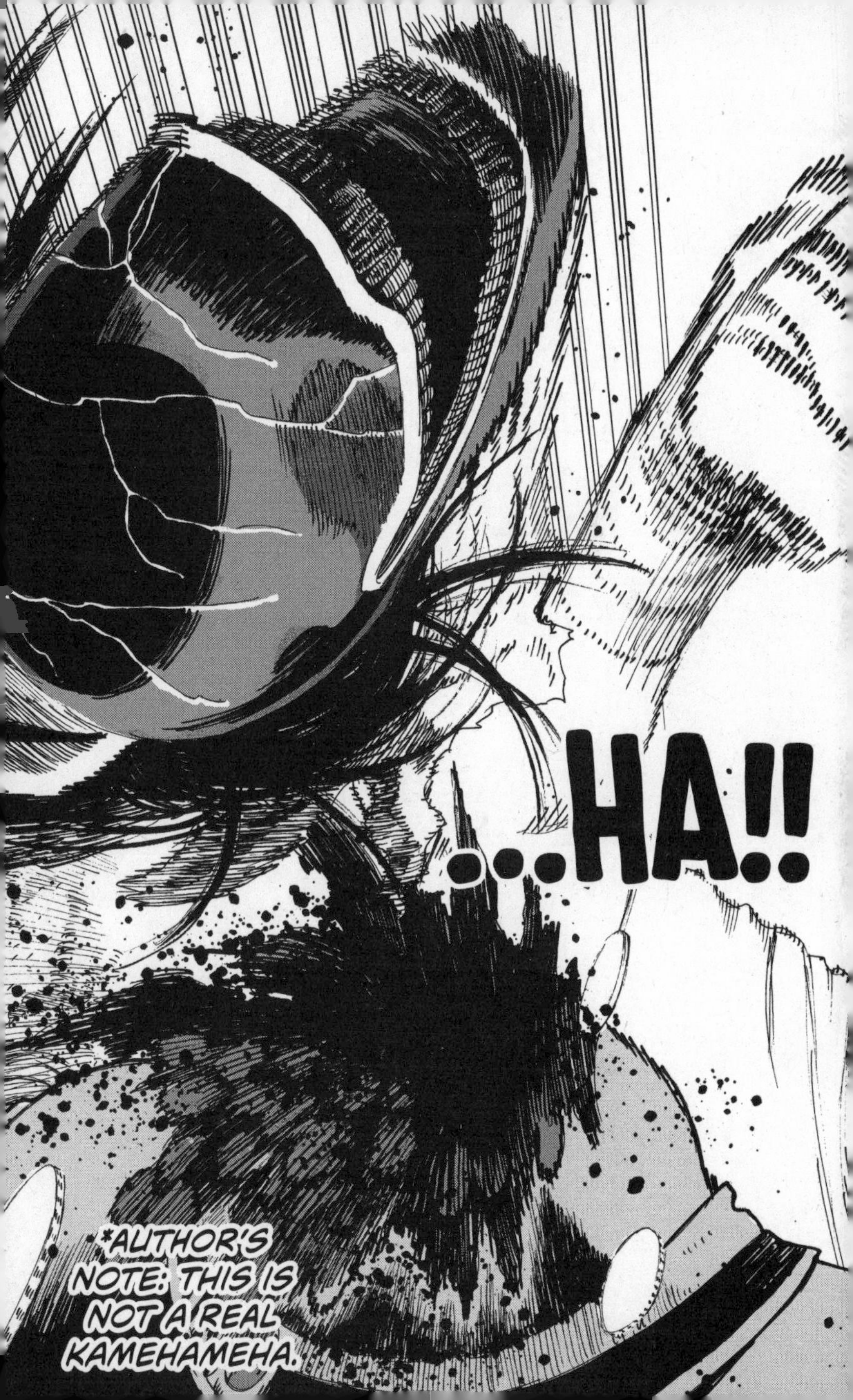
...HA!!
*AUTHOR'S NOTE: THIS IS NOT A REAL KAMEHAMEHA.

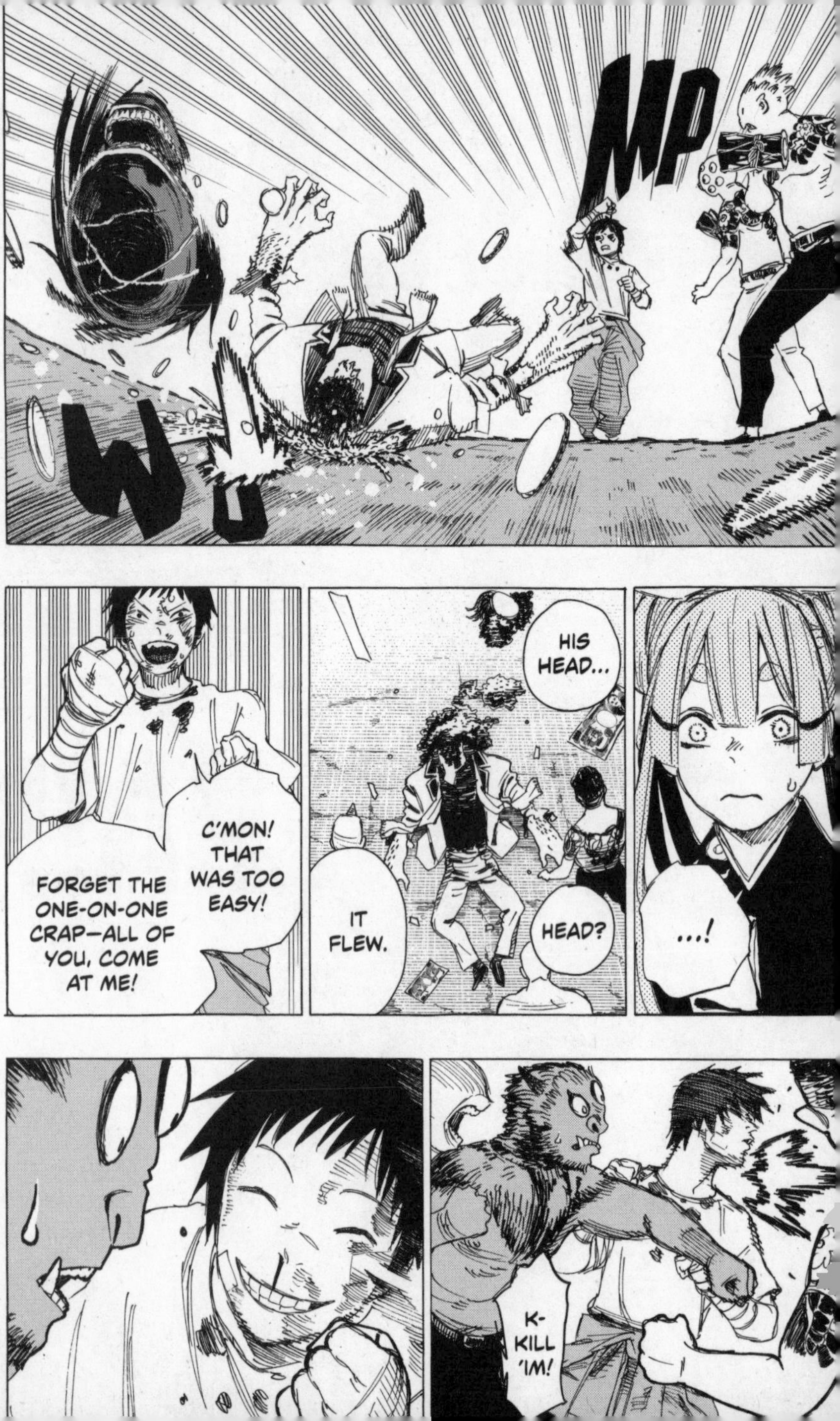
WHUMP
...!
HIS HEAD...
HEAD?
IT FLEW.
C'MON! THAT WAS TOO EASY!
FORGET THE ONE-ON-ONE CRAP—ALL OF YOU, COME AT ME!
K-KILL 'IM!

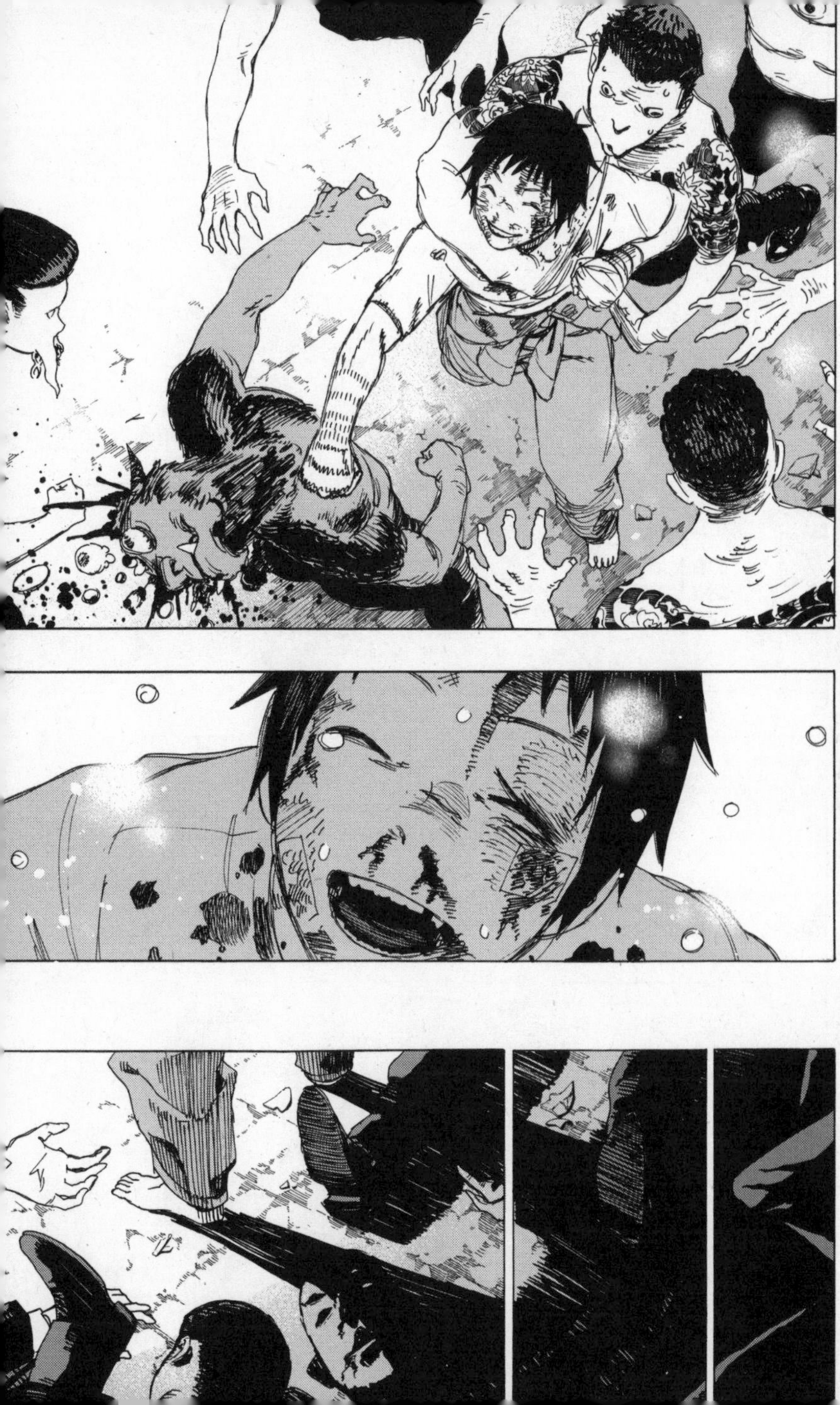

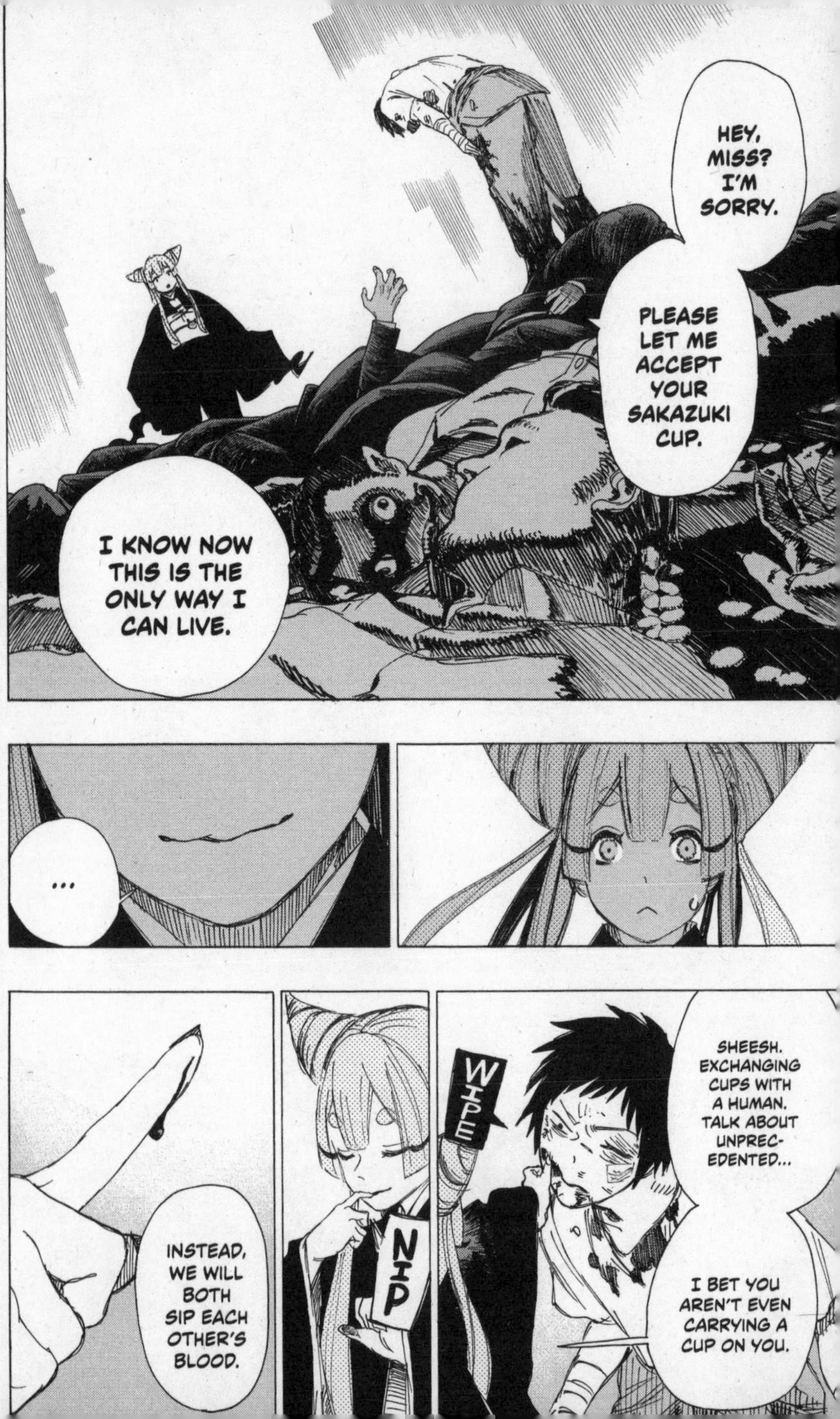
HEY, MISS? I'M SORRY.
PLEASE LET ME ACCEPT YOUR SAKAZUKI CUP.
I KNOW NOW THIS IS THE ONLY WAY I CAN LIVE.
...
SHEESH. EXCHANGING CUPS WITH A HUMAN. TALK ABOUT UNPREC-EDENTED...
WIPE
I BET YOU AREN'T EVEN CARRYING A CUP ON YOU.
NIP
INSTEAD, WE WILL BOTH SIP EACH OTHER'S BLOOD.

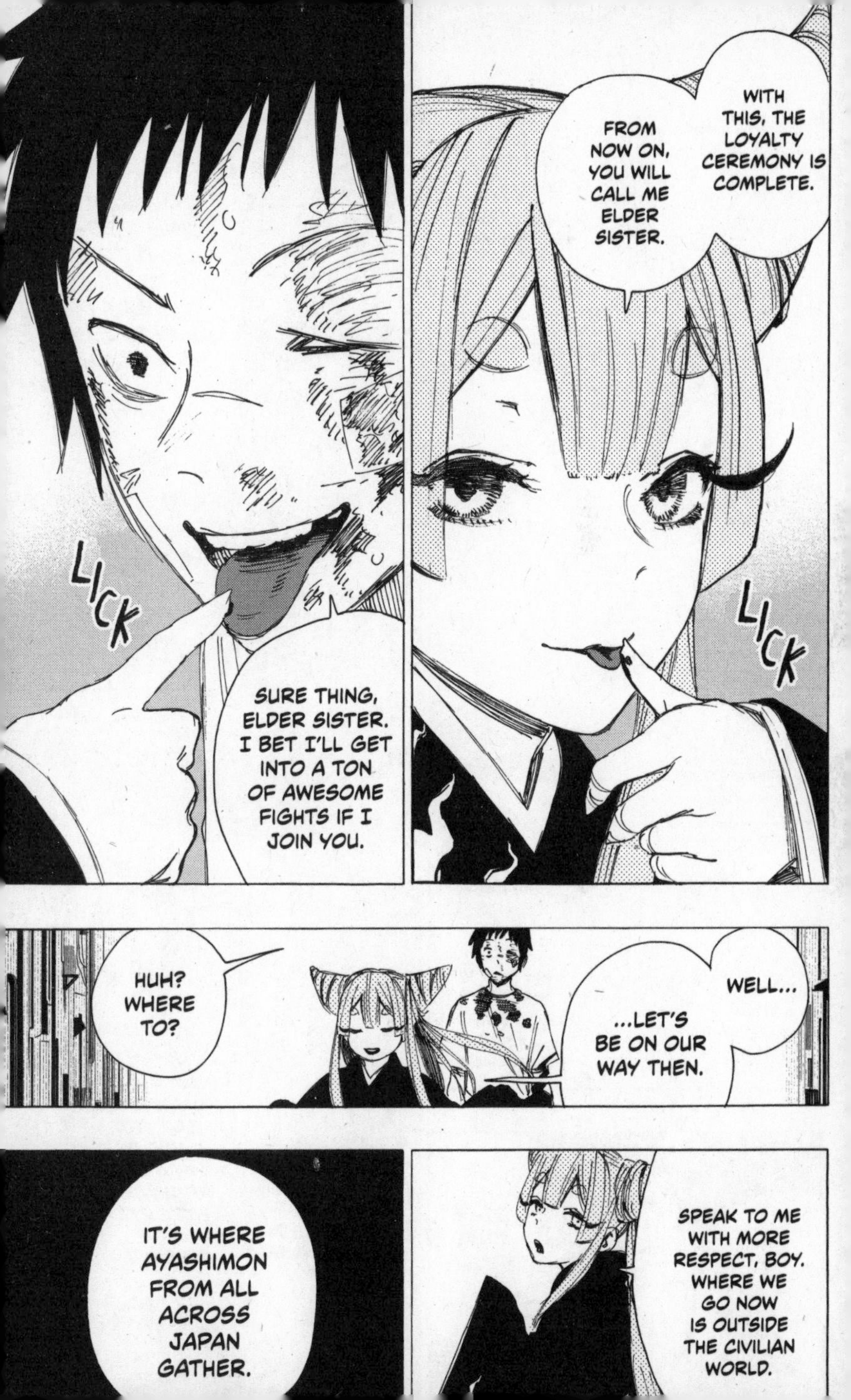
WITH THIS, THE LOYALTY CEREMONY IS COMPLETE.
FROM NOW ON, YOU WILL CALL ME ELDER SISTER.
LICK
LICK
SURE THING, ELDER SISTER. I BET I'LL GET INTO A TON OF AWESOME FIGHTS IF I JOIN YOU.
WELL...
...LET'S BE ON OUR WAY THEN.
HUH? WHERE TO?
SPEAK TO ME WITH MORE RESPECT, BOY. WHERE WE GO NOW IS OUTSIDE THE CIVILIAN WORLD.
IT'S WHERE AYASHIMON FROM ALL ACROSS JAPAN GATHER.

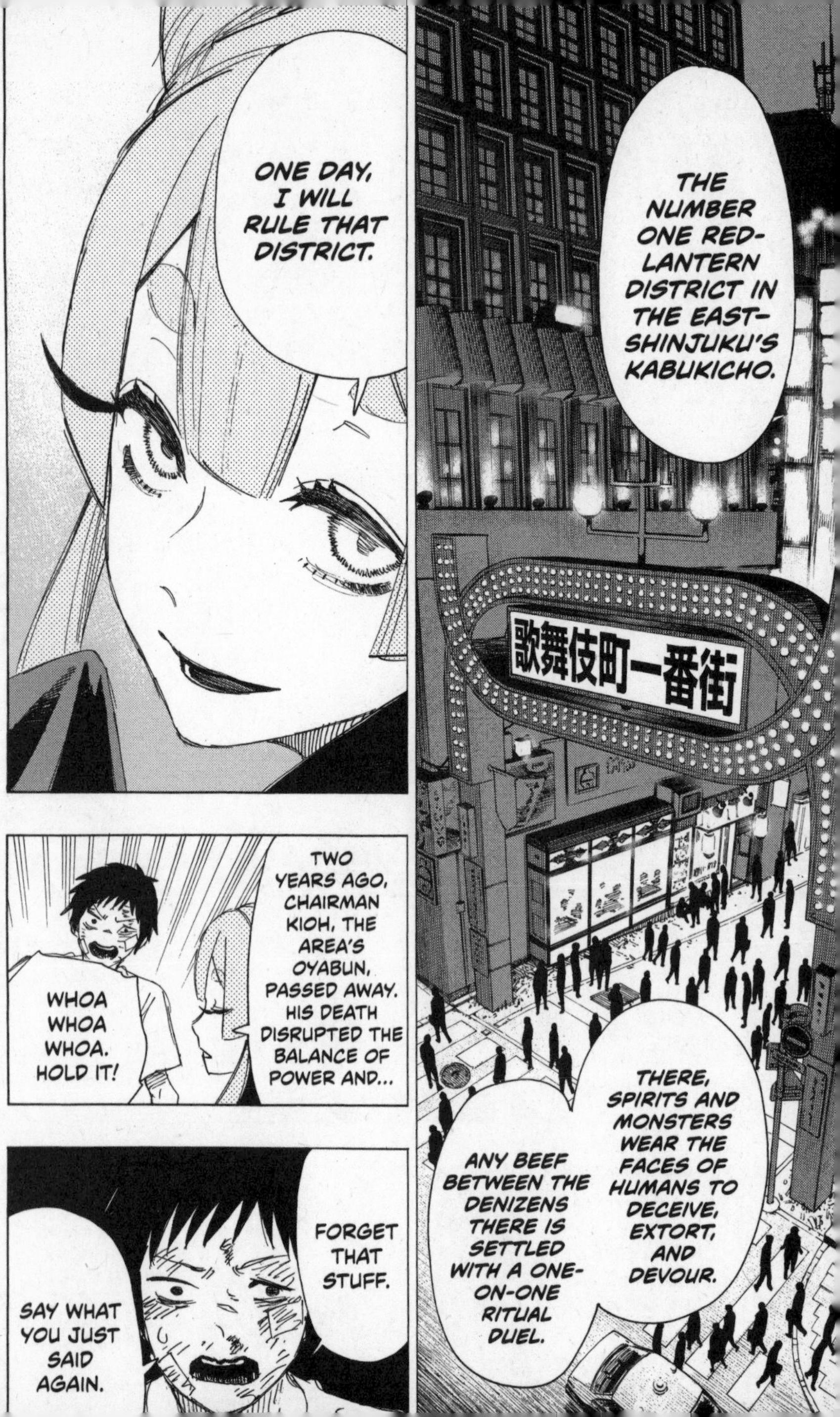
THE NUMBER ONE RED-LANTERN DISTRICT IN THE EAST-SHINJUKU'S KABUKICHO.
歌舞伎町一番街
THERE, SPIRITS AND MONSTERS WEAR THE FACES OF HUMANS TO DECEIVE, EXTORT, AND DEVOUR.
ANY BEEF BETWEEN THE DENIZENS THERE IS SETTLED WITH A ONE-ON-ONE RITUAL DUEL.
ONE DAY, I WILL RULE THAT DISTRICT.
TWO YEARS AGO, CHAIRMAN KIOH, THE AREA'S OYABUN, PASSED AWAY. HIS DEATH DISRUPTED THE BALANCE OF POWER AND...
WHOA WHOA WHOA. HOLD IT!
FORGET THAT STUFF.
SAY WHAT YOU JUST SAID AGAIN.

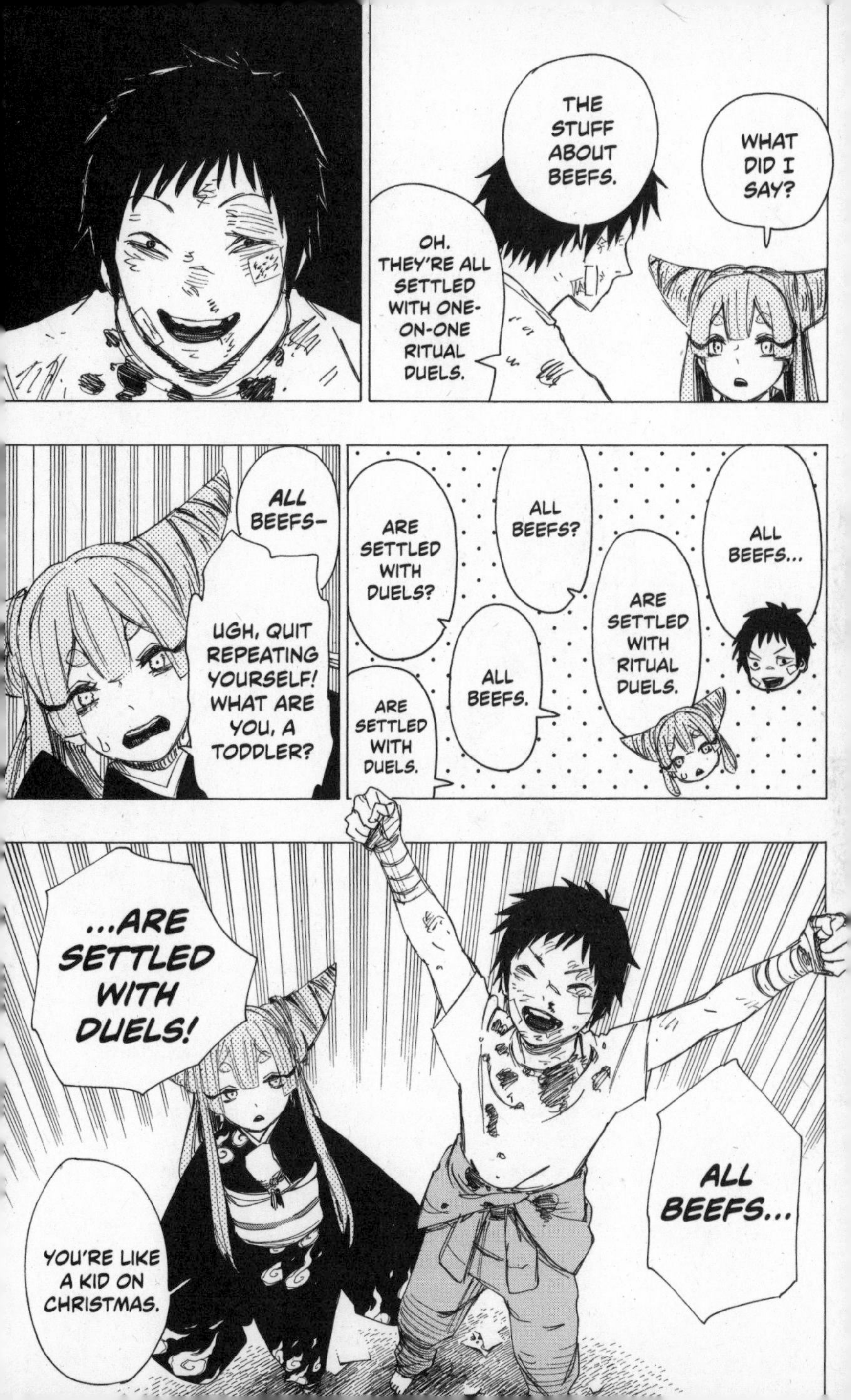
WHAT DID I SAY?
THE STUFF ABOUT BEEFS.
OH. THEY'RE ALL SETTLED WITH ONE-ON-ONE RITUAL DUELS.
ALL BEEFS...
ARE SETTLED WITH RITUAL DUELS.
ALL BEEFS?
ARE SETTLED WITH DUELS?
ALL BEEFS.
ARE SETTLED WITH DUELS.
ALL BEEFS–
UGH, QUIT REPEATING YOURSELF! WHAT ARE YOU, A TODDLER?
ALL BEEFS...
...ARE SETTLED WITH DUELS!
YOU'RE LIKE A KID ON CHRISTMAS.

KABUKICHO MONSTER MANUAL

Maruo Kaido

His gaze isn't particularly nasty, but it can be disturbingly fixed. His most notable features include the pattern of broadaxes and straw ropes on his shirt, his taped wrists, and the bandages on his face. A man was walking along a riverbank in Tokyo when he heard a haunting voice. "Anybody lookin' for a fight? Who's the strongest around?" He turned around and saw a punk kid in a bad mood. The man quickly fled for his life...

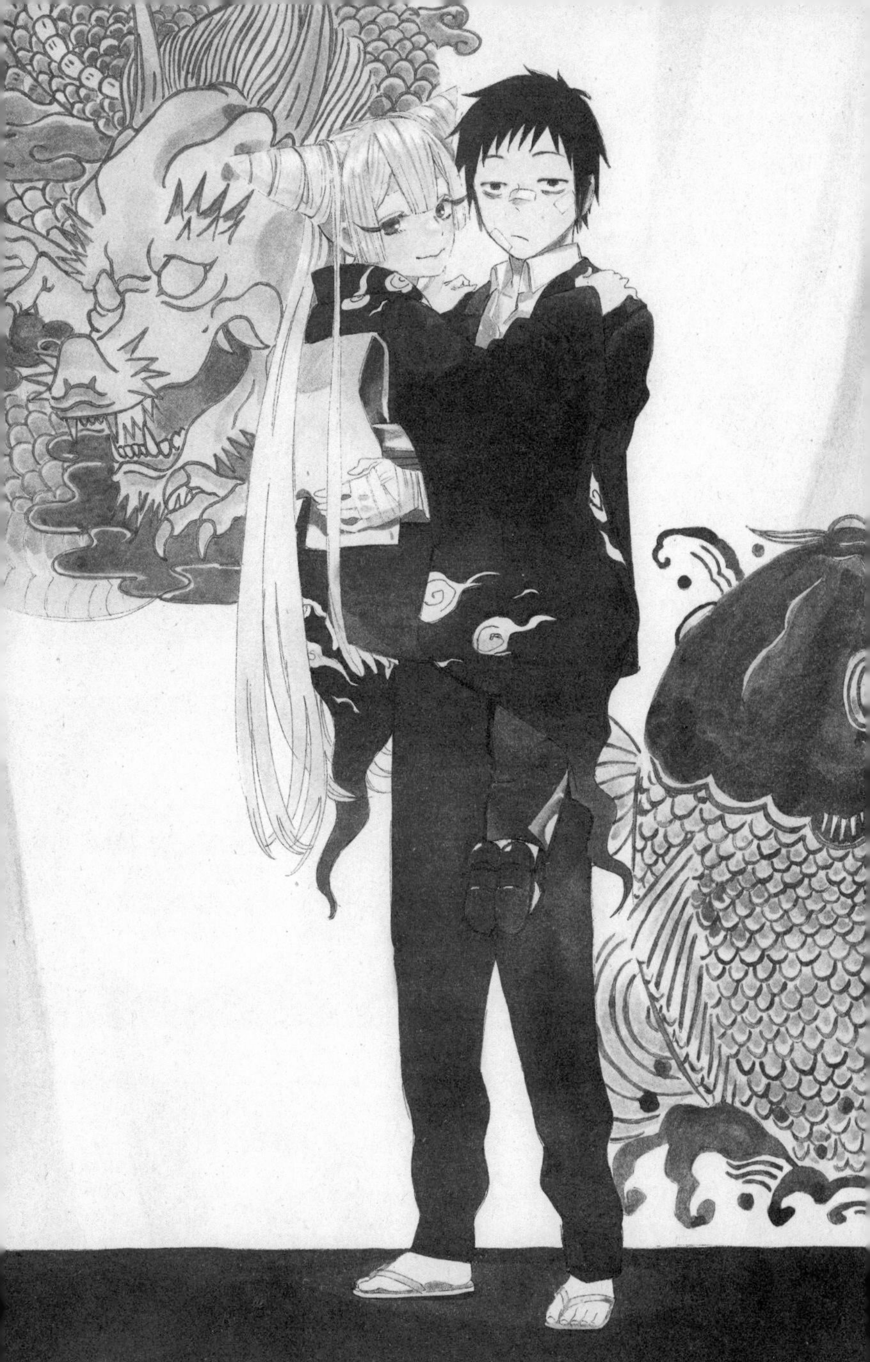

Chapter 2: This Monster-Battle Stuff Is Intense!

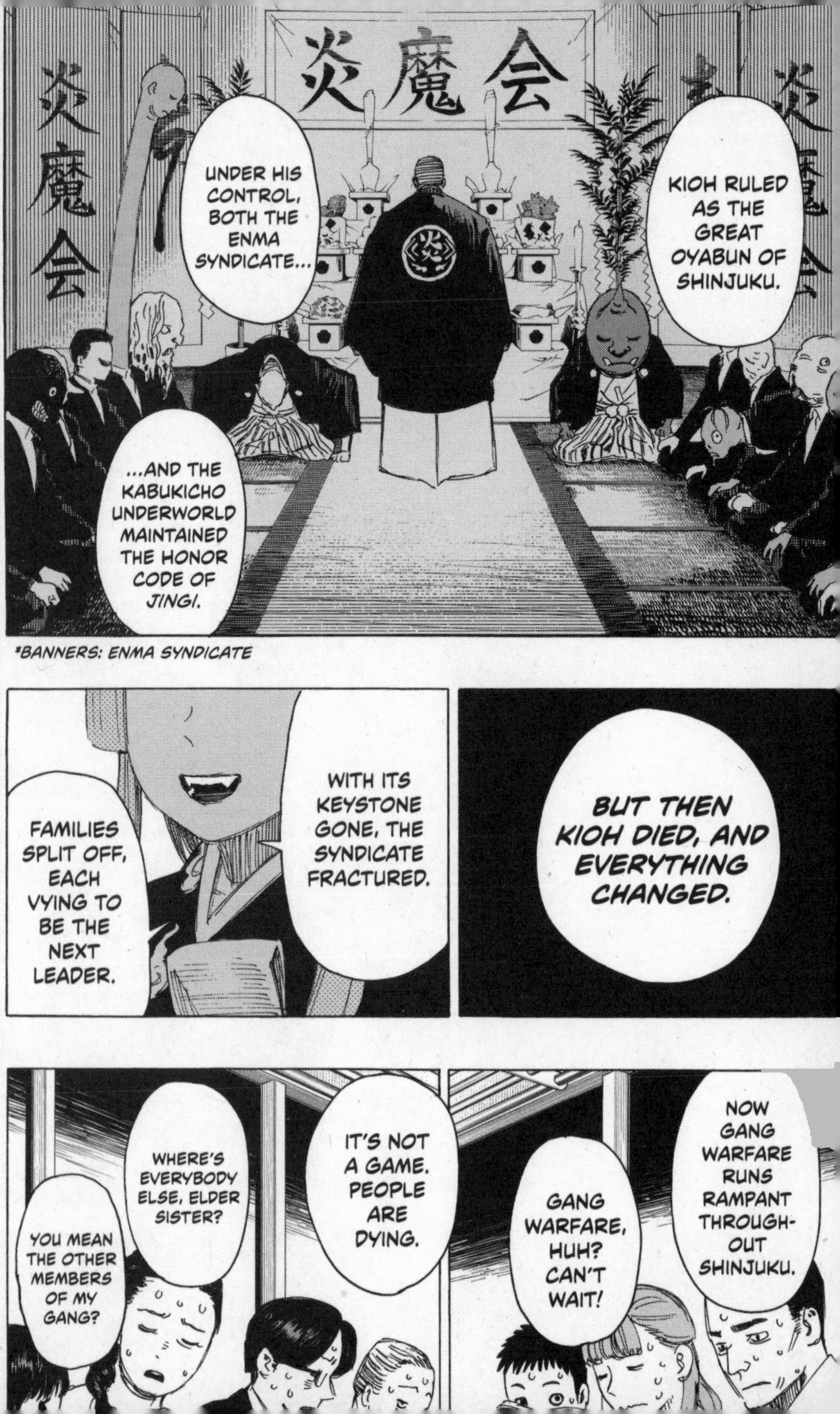
炎魔会
KIOH RULED AS THE GREAT OYABUN OF SHINJUKU.
UNDER HIS CONTROL, BOTH THE ENMA SYNDICATE...
...AND THE KABUKICHO UNDERWORLD MAINTAINED THE HONOR CODE OF JINGI.
*BANNERS: ENMA SYNDICATE
BUT THEN KIOH DIED, AND EVERYTHING CHANGED.
WITH ITS KEYSTONE GONE, THE SYNDICATE FRACTURED.
FAMILIES SPLIT OFF, EACH VYING TO BE THE NEXT LEADER.
NOW GANG WARFARE RUNS RAMPANT THROUGH-OUT SHINJUKU.
GANG WARFARE, HUH? CAN'T WAIT!
IT'S NOT A GAME. PEOPLE ARE DYING.
WHERE'S EVERYBODY ELSE, ELDER SISTER?
YOU MEAN THE OTHER MEMBERS OF MY GANG?

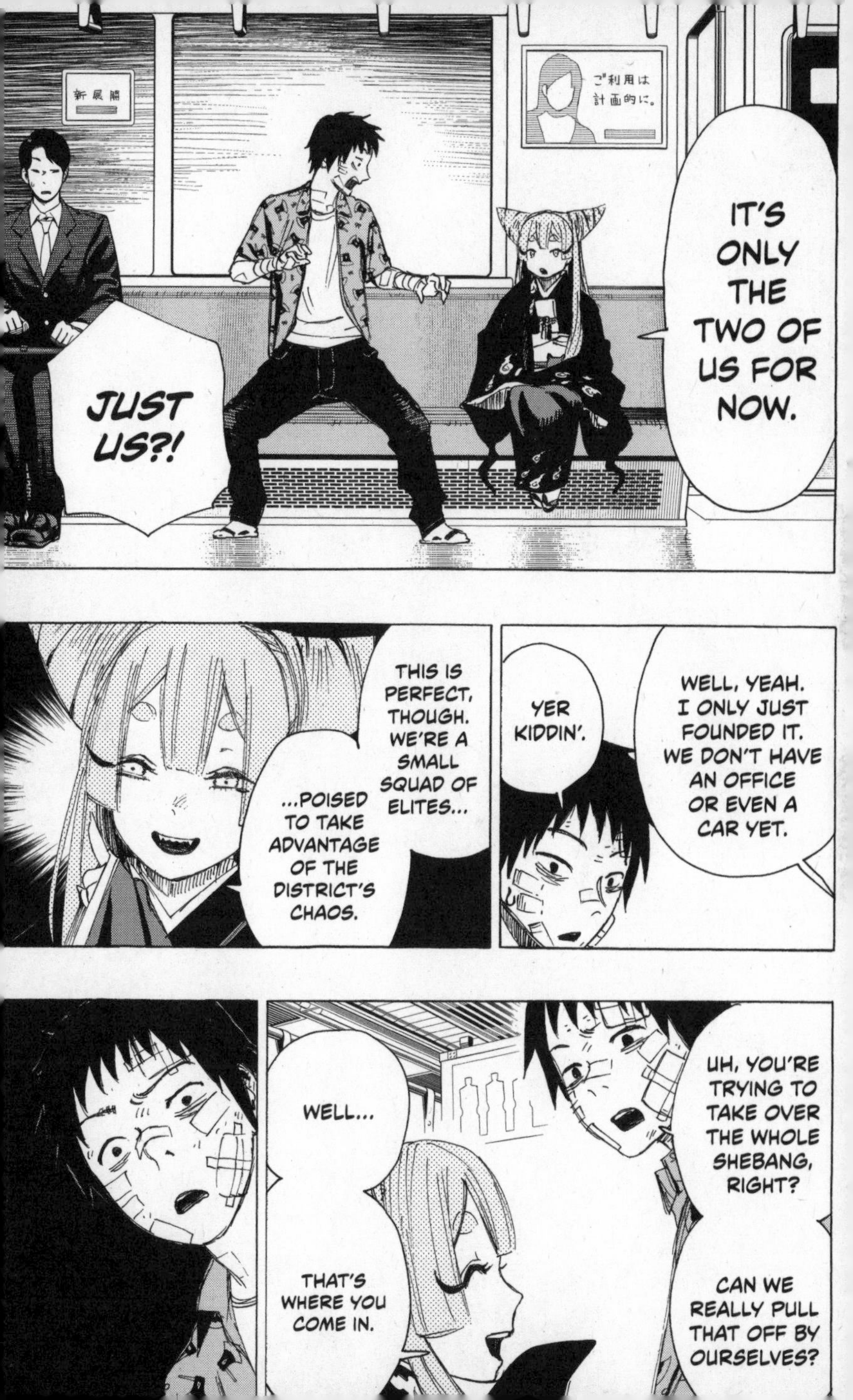
ご利用は計画的に。
新展開
IT'S ONLY THE TWO OF US FOR NOW.
JUST US?!
WELL, YEAH. I ONLY JUST FOUNDED IT. WE DON'T HAVE AN OFFICE OR EVEN A CAR YET.
YER KIDDIN'.
THIS IS PERFECT, THOUGH. WE'RE A SMALL SQUAD OF ELITES...
...POISED TO TAKE ADVANTAGE OF THE DISTRICT'S CHAOS.
UH, YOU'RE TRYING TO TAKE OVER THE WHOLE SHEBANG, RIGHT?
CAN WE REALLY PULL THAT OFF BY OURSELVES?
WELL...
THAT'S WHERE YOU COME IN.

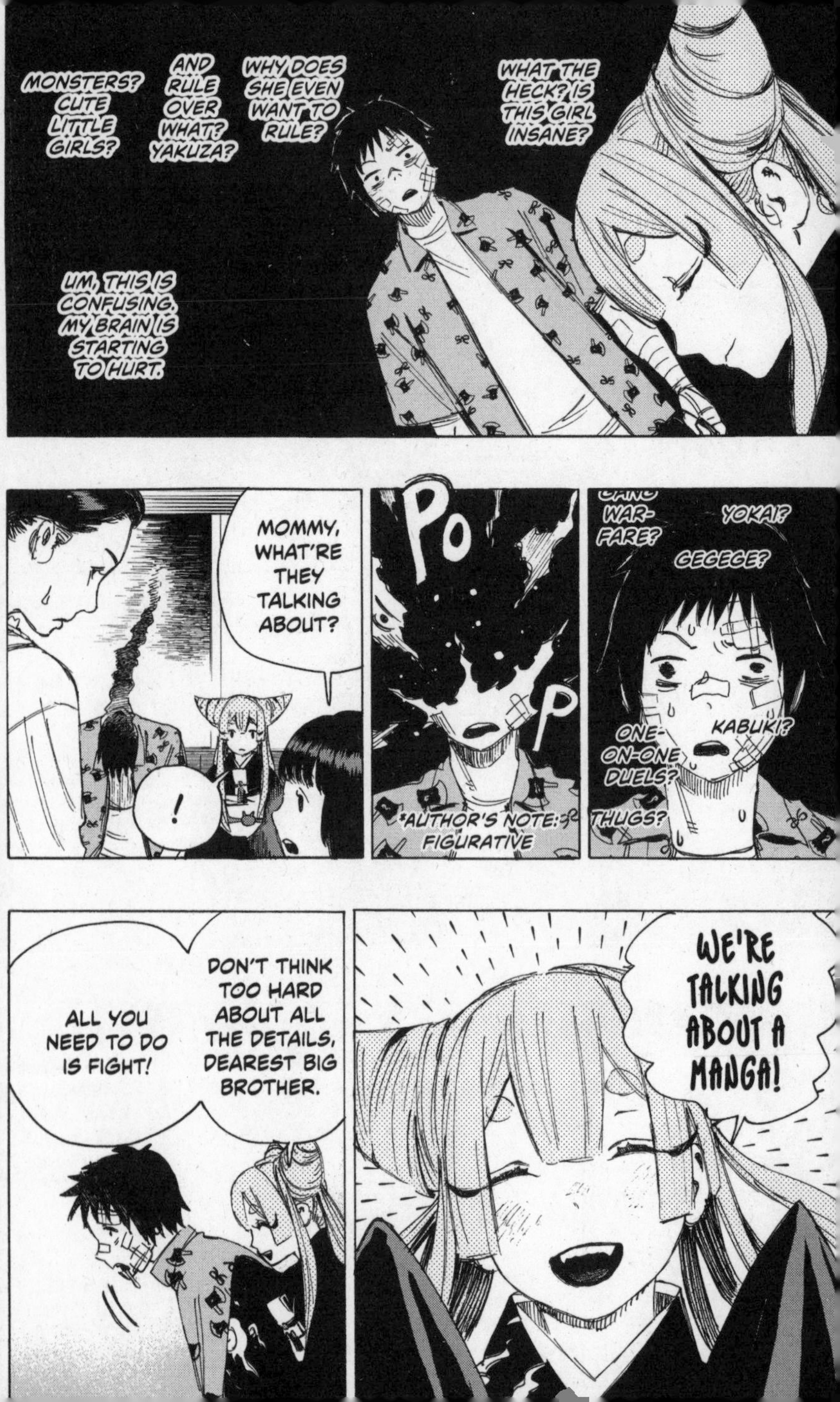
WHAT THE HECK? IS THIS GIRL INSANE?
WHY DOES SHE EVEN WANT TO RULE?
AND RULE OVER WHAT? YAKUZA?
MONSTERS? CUTE LITTLE GIRLS?
UM, THIS IS CONFUSING. MY BRAIN IS STARTING TO HURT.
YOKAI?
WAR-FARE?
GEGEGE?
KABUKI?
ONE-ON-ONE DUELS?
THUGS?
POP
*AUTHOR'S NOTE: FIGURATIVE
MOMMY, WHAT'RE THEY TALKING ABOUT?
!
WE'RE TALKING ABOUT A MANGA!
DON'T THINK TOO HARD ABOUT ALL THE DETAILS, DEAREST BIG BROTHER.
ALL YOU NEED TO DO IS FIGHT!

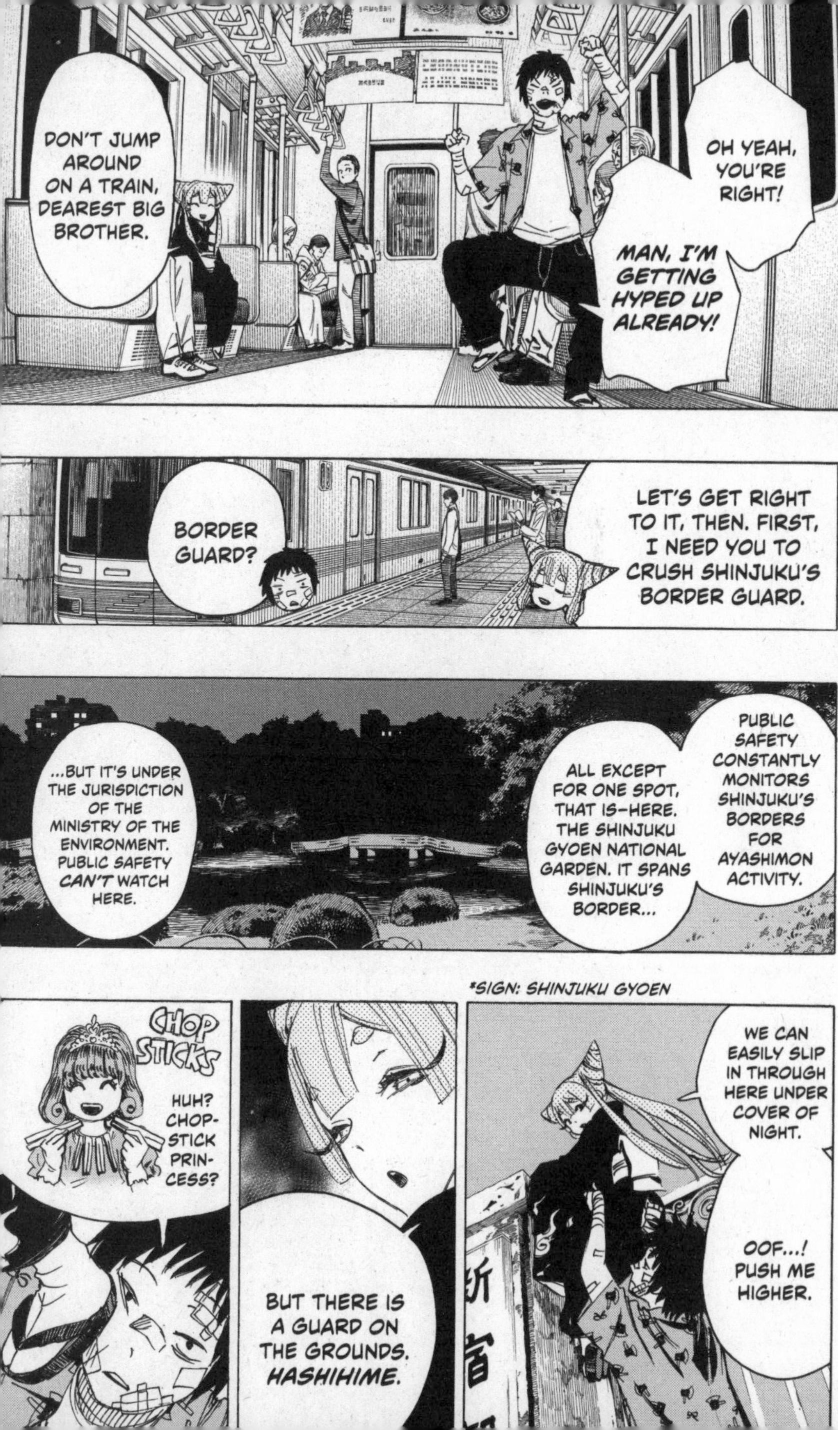
DON'T JUMP AROUND ON A TRAIN, DEAREST BIG BROTHER.
OH YEAH, YOU'RE RIGHT!
MAN, I'M GETTING HYPED UP ALREADY!
LET'S GET RIGHT TO IT, THEN. FIRST, I NEED YOU TO CRUSH SHINJUKU'S BORDER GUARD.
BORDER GUARD?
PUBLIC SAFETY CONSTANTLY MONITORS SHINJUKU'S BORDERS FOR AYASHIMON ACTIVITY.
ALL EXCEPT FOR ONE SPOT, THAT IS—HERE. THE SHINJUKU GYOEN NATIONAL GARDEN. IT SPANS SHINJUKU'S BORDER...
...BUT IT'S UNDER THE JURISDICTION OF THE MINISTRY OF THE ENVIRONMENT. PUBLIC SAFETY CAN'T WATCH HERE.
*SIGN: SHINJUKU GYOEN
WE CAN EASILY SLIP IN THROUGH HERE UNDER COVER OF NIGHT.
OOF...! PUSH ME HIGHER.
BUT THERE IS A GUARD ON THE GROUNDS. HASHIHIME.
CHOP STICKS
HUH? CHOP-STICK PRIN-CESS?

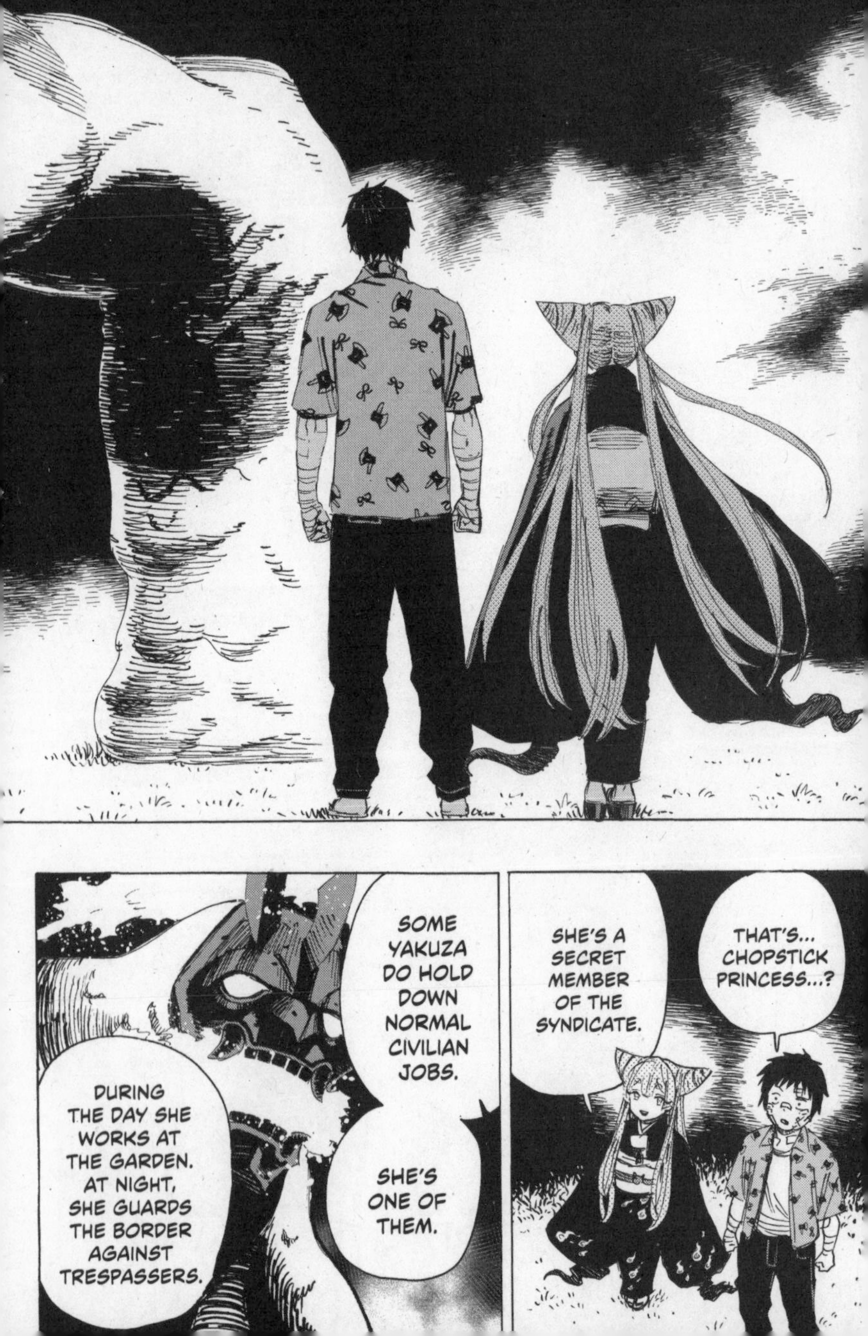
THAT'S... CHOPSTICK PRINCESS...?
SHE'S A SECRET MEMBER OF THE SYNDICATE.
SOME YAKUZA DO HOLD DOWN NORMAL CIVILIAN JOBS.
SHE'S ONE OF THEM.
DURING THE DAY SHE WORKS AT THE GARDEN. AT NIGHT, SHE GUARDS THE BORDER AGAINST TRESPASSERS.

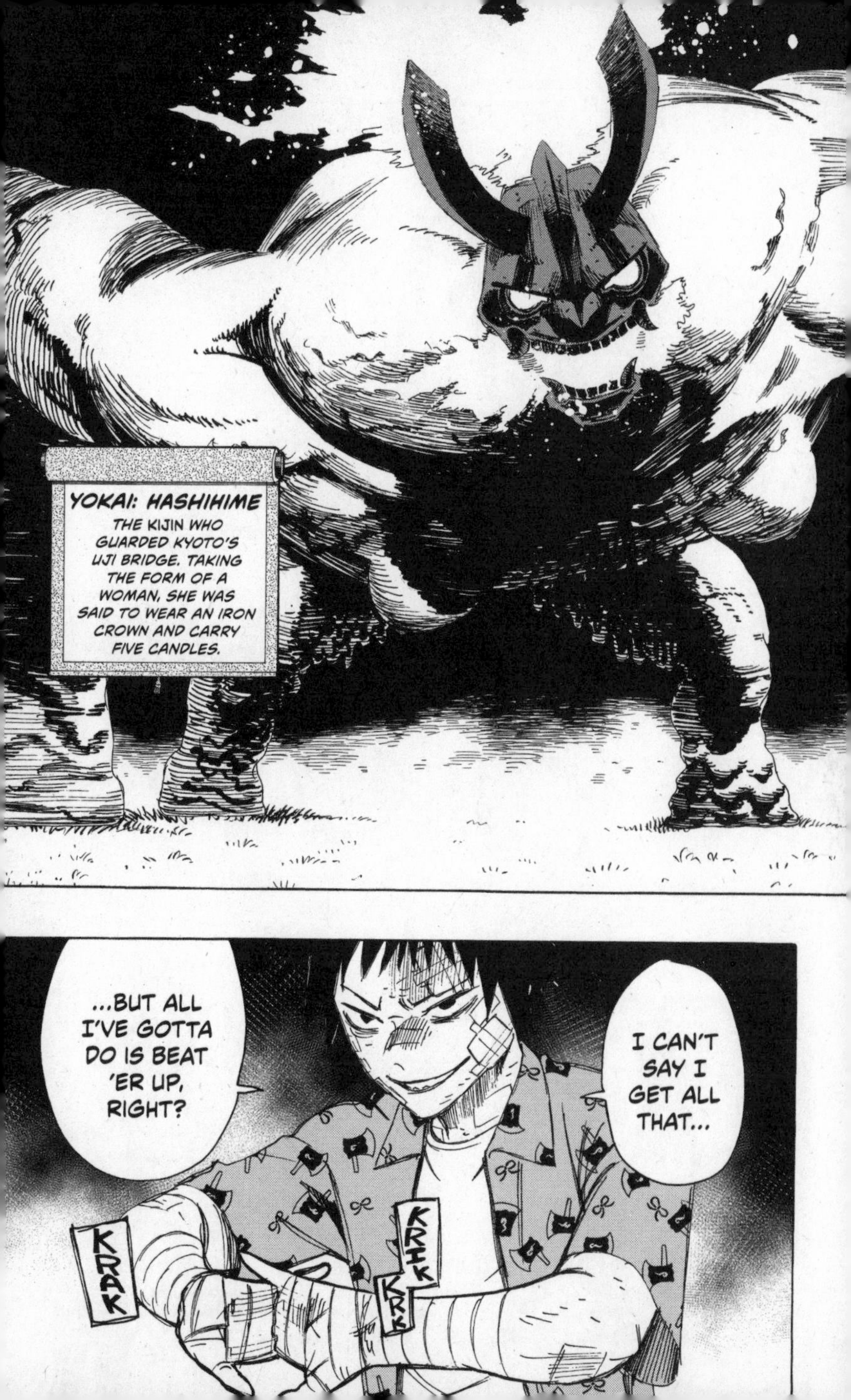
YOKAI: HASHIHIME
THE KIJIN WHO GUARDED KYOTO'S UJI BRIDGE. TAKING THE FORM OF A WOMAN, SHE WAS SAID TO WEAR AN IRON CROWN AND CARRY FIVE CANDLES.
I CAN'T SAY I GET ALL THAT...
...BUT ALL I'VE GOTTA DO IS BEAT 'ER UP, RIGHT?
KRIK
KRK
KRAK

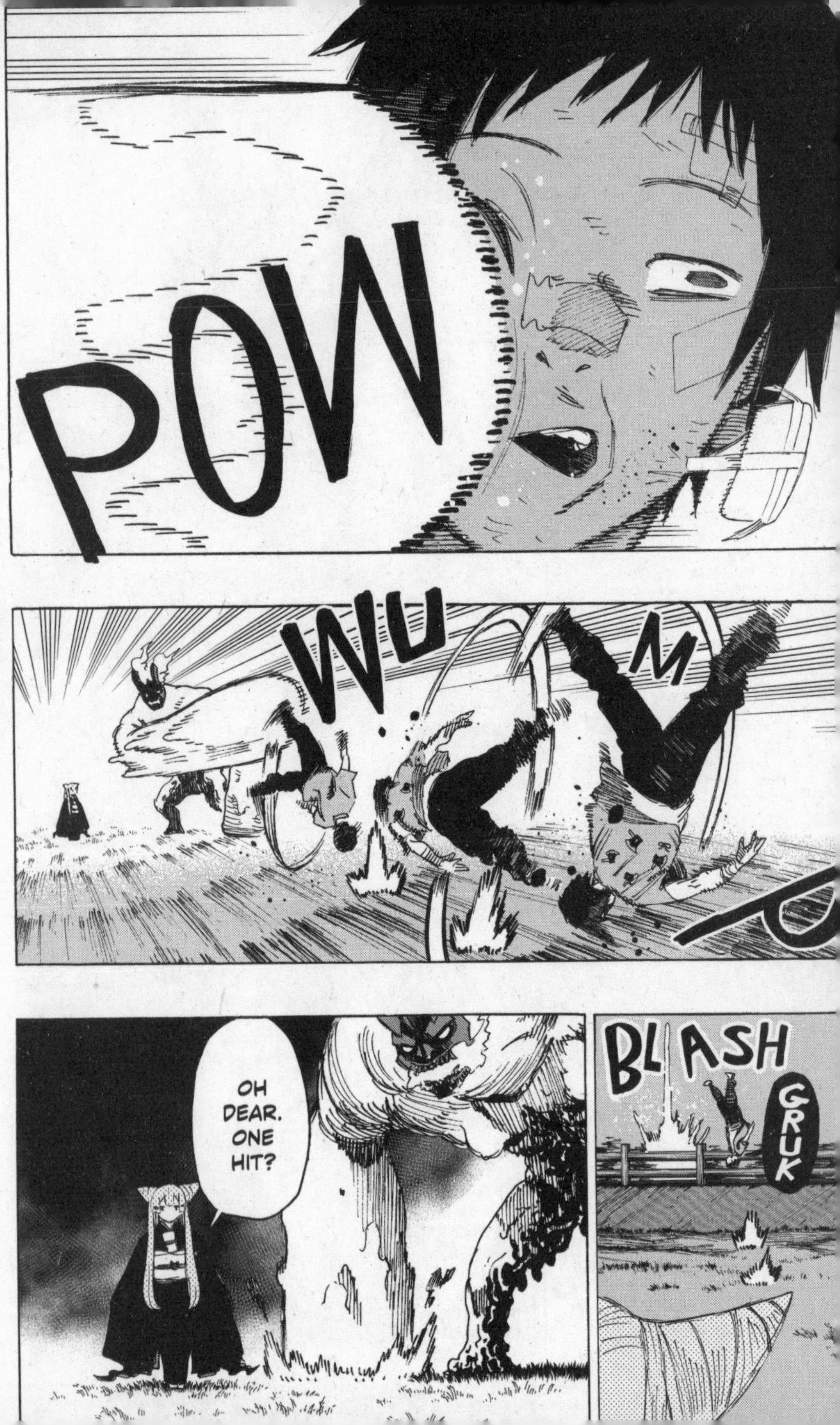
POW
WUMP
BLASH
GRUK
OH DEAR. ONE HIT?

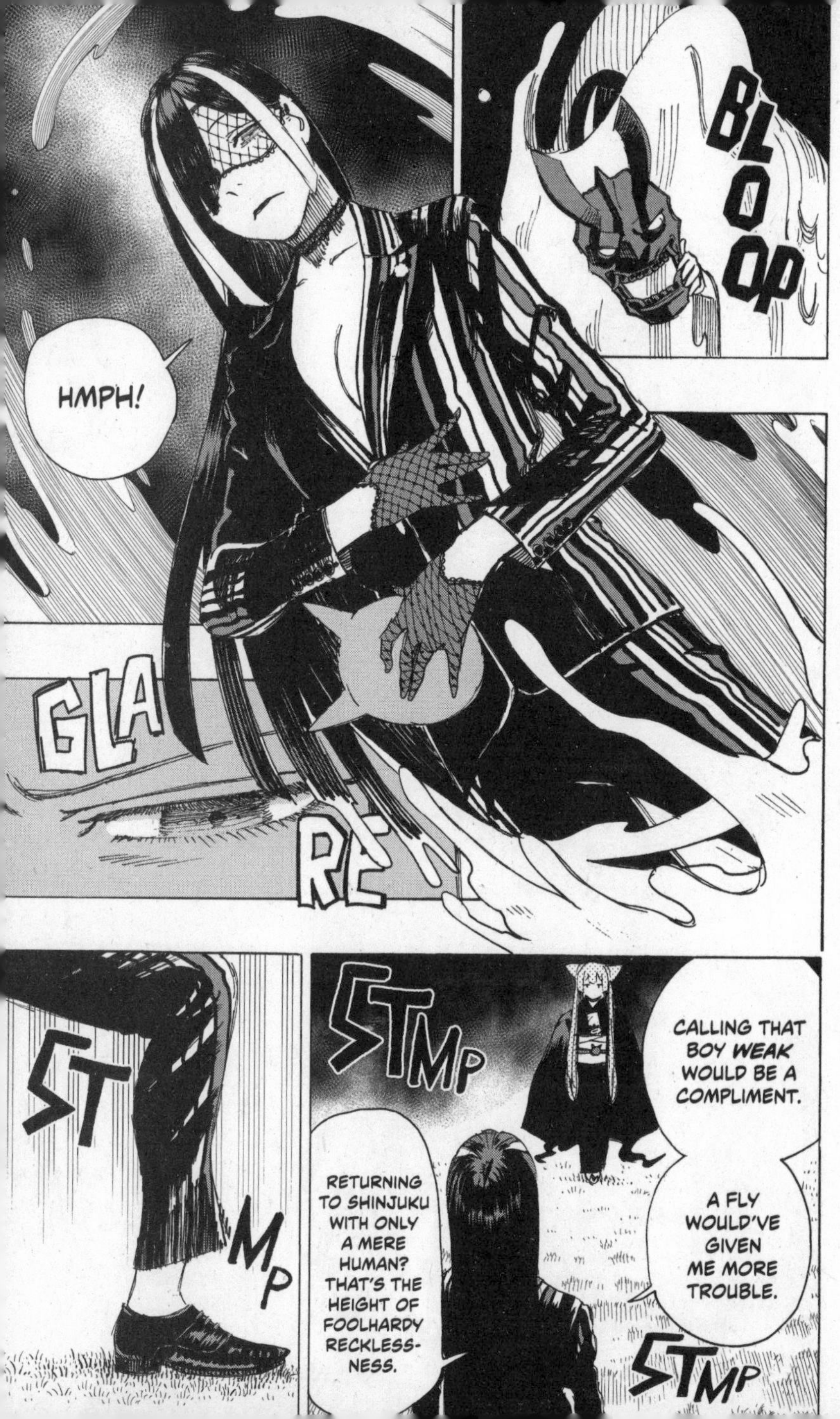
BLOOOP
HMPH!
GLARE
CALLING THAT BOY WEAK WOULD BE A COMPLIMENT.
A FLY WOULD'VE GIVEN ME MORE TROUBLE.
STMP
RETURNING TO SHINJUKU WITH ONLY A MERE HUMAN? THAT'S THE HEIGHT OF FOOLHARDY RECKLESS-NESS.
STMP
STMP

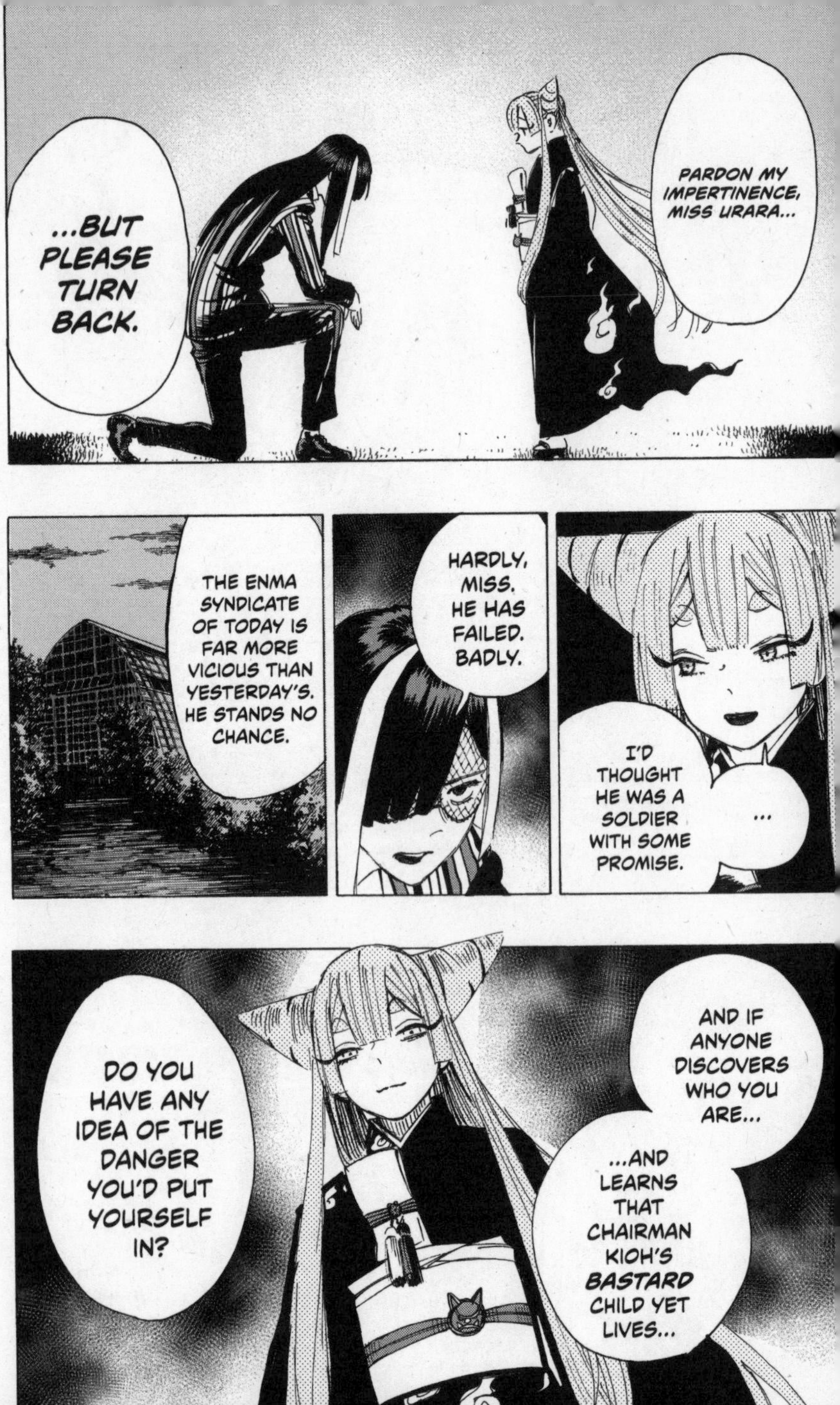
PARDON MY IMPERTINENCE, MISS URARA...
...BUT PLEASE TURN BACK.
...
I'D THOUGHT HE WAS A SOLDIER WITH SOME PROMISE.
HARDLY, MISS. HE HAS FAILED. BADLY.
THE ENMA SYNDICATE OF TODAY IS FAR MORE VICIOUS THAN YESTERDAY'S. HE STANDS NO CHANCE.
AND IF ANYONE DISCOVERS WHO YOU ARE...
...AND LEARNS THAT CHAIRMAN KIOH'S *BASTARD* CHILD YET LIVES...
DO YOU HAVE ANY IDEA OF THE DANGER YOU'D PUT YOURSELF IN?

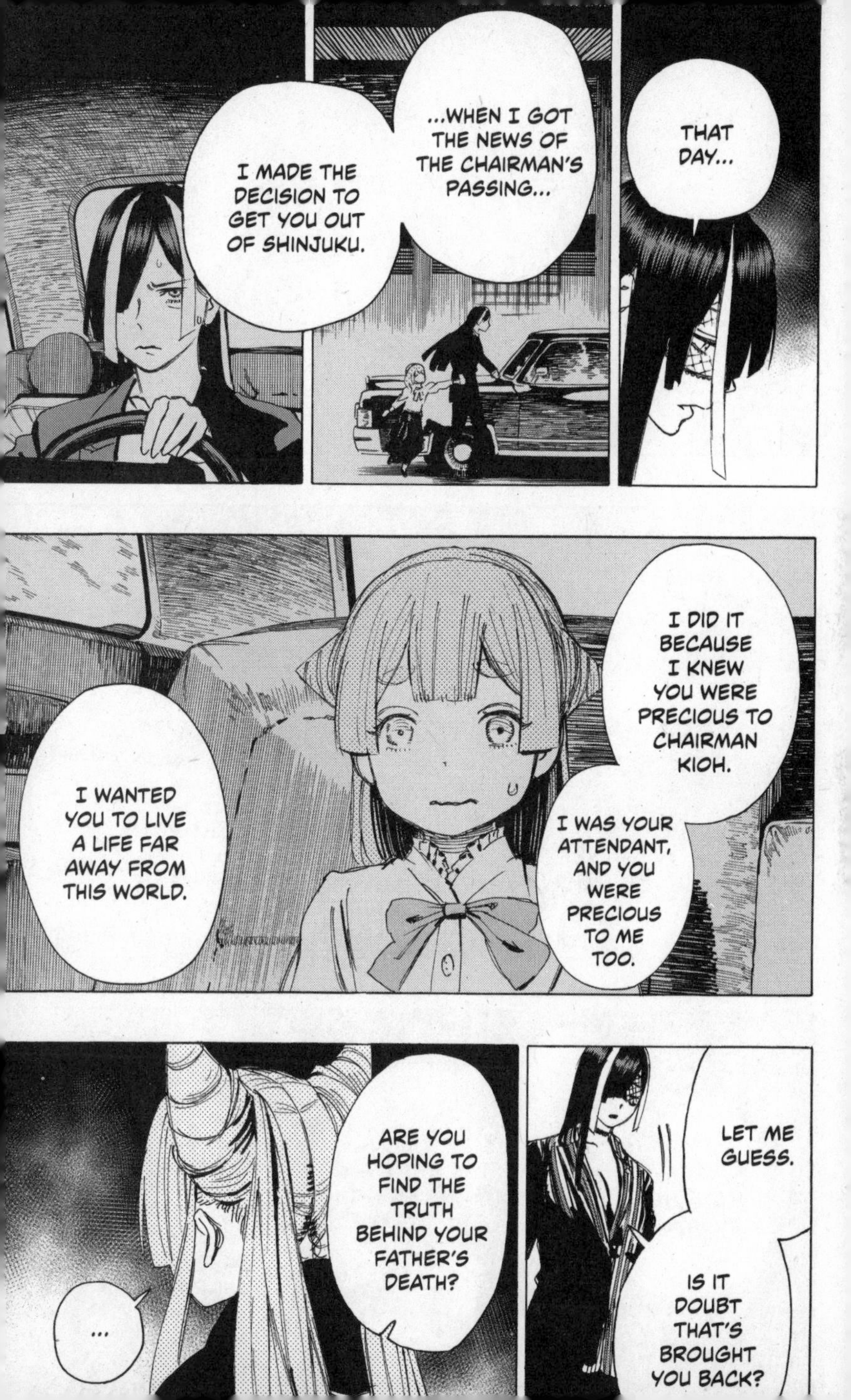
THAT DAY...
...WHEN I GOT THE NEWS OF THE CHAIRMAN'S PASSING...
I MADE THE DECISION TO GET YOU OUT OF SHINJUKU.
I DID IT BECAUSE I KNEW YOU WERE PRECIOUS TO CHAIRMAN KIOH.
I WAS YOUR ATTENDANT, AND YOU WERE PRECIOUS TO ME TOO.
I WANTED YOU TO LIVE A LIFE FAR AWAY FROM THIS WORLD.
LET ME GUESS.
IS IT DOUBT THAT'S BROUGHT YOU BACK?
ARE YOU HOPING TO FIND THE TRUTH BEHIND YOUR FATHER'S DEATH?
...

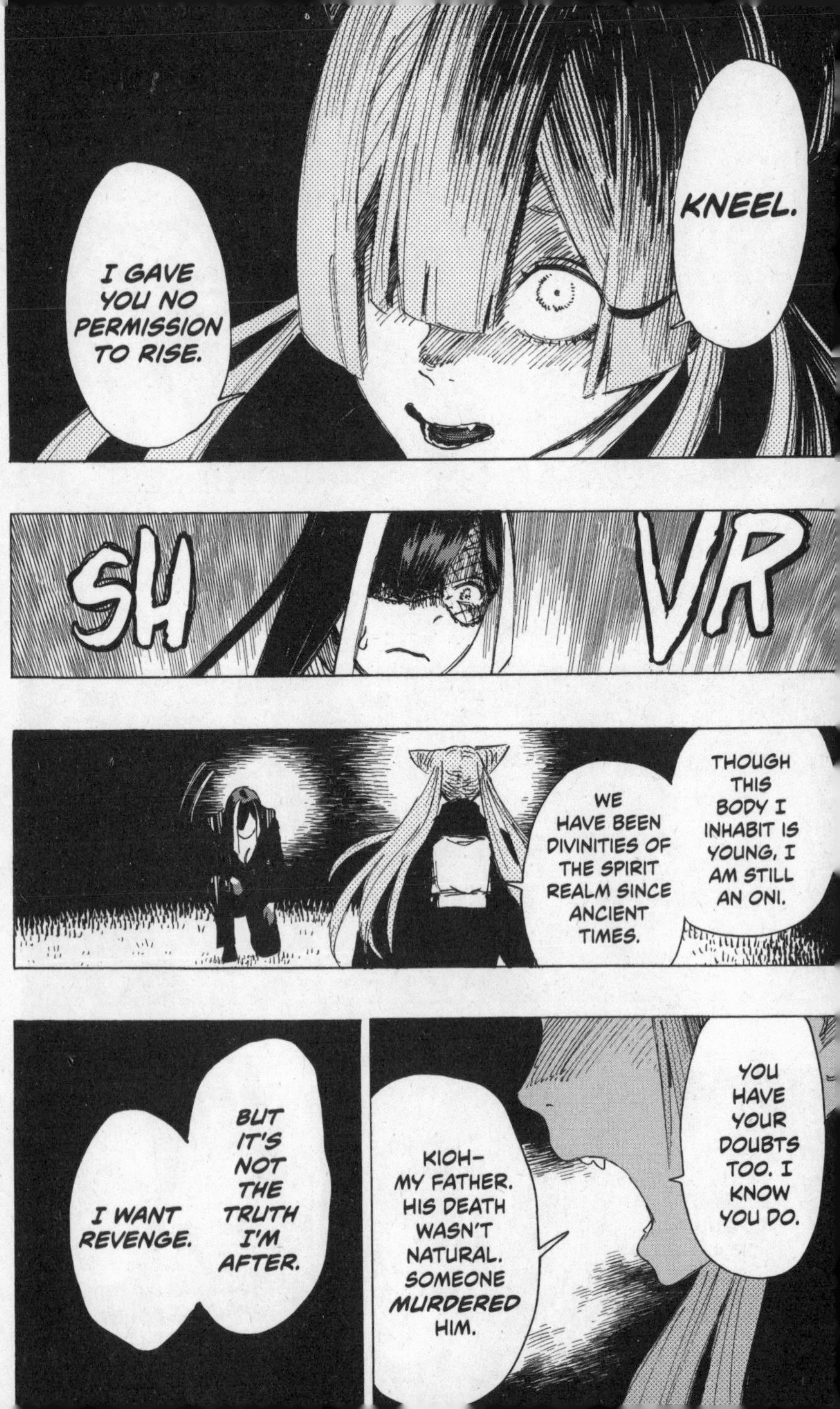
KNEEL.
I GAVE YOU NO PERMISSION TO RISE.
SH VR
THOUGH THIS BODY I INHABIT IS YOUNG, I AM STILL AN ONI.
WE HAVE BEEN DIVINITIES OF THE SPIRIT REALM SINCE ANCIENT TIMES.
YOU HAVE YOUR DOUBTS TOO. I KNOW YOU DO.
KIOH— MY FATHER. HIS DEATH WASN'T NATURAL. SOMEONE MURDERED HIM.
BUT IT'S NOT THE TRUTH I'M AFTER.
I WANT REVENGE.

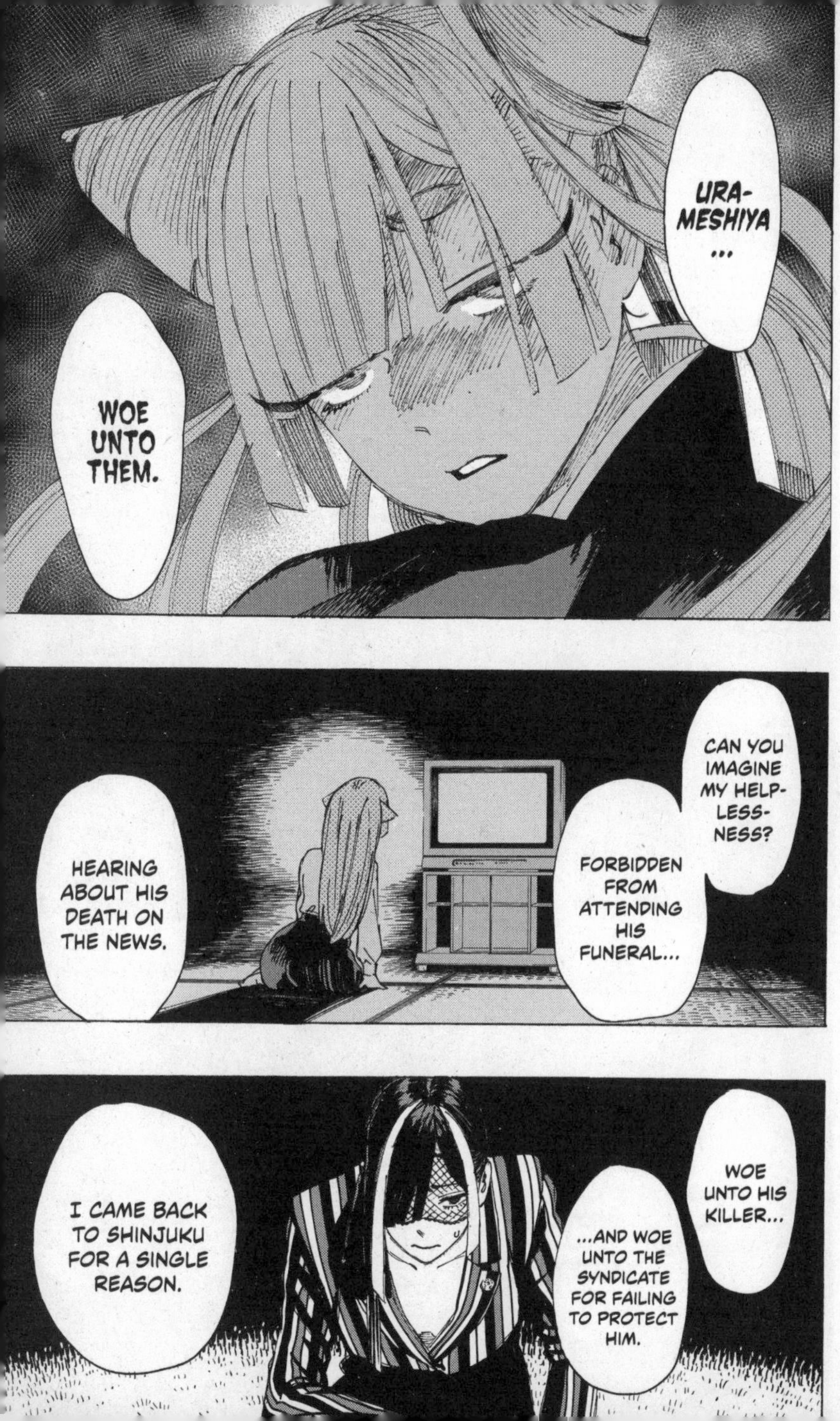
URA-MESHIYA...
WOE UNTO THEM.
CAN YOU IMAGINE MY HELP-LESS-NESS?
FORBIDDEN FROM ATTENDING HIS FUNERAL...
HEARING ABOUT HIS DEATH ON THE NEWS.
WOE UNTO HIS KILLER...
...AND WOE UNTO THE SYNDICATE FOR FAILING TO PROTECT HIM.
I CAME BACK TO SHINJUKU FOR A SINGLE REASON.

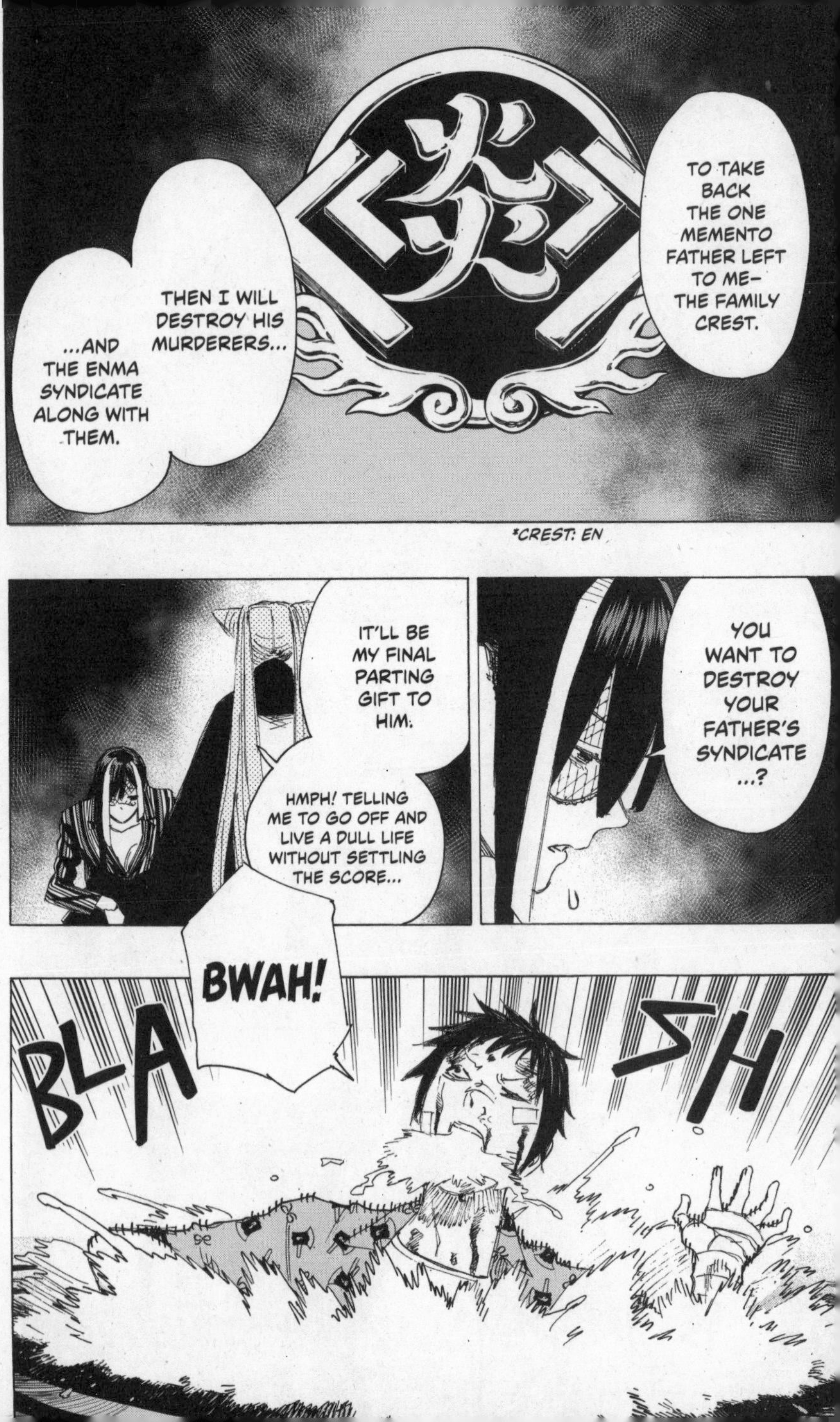
TO TAKE BACK THE ONE MEMENTO FATHER LEFT TO ME— THE FAMILY CREST.
THEN I WILL DESTROY HIS MURDERERS...
...AND THE ENMA SYNDICATE ALONG WITH THEM.
*CREST: EN
YOU WANT TO DESTROY YOUR FATHER'S SYNDICATE ...?
IT'LL BE MY FINAL PARTING GIFT TO HIM.
HMPH! TELLING ME TO GO OFF AND LIVE A DULL LIFE WITHOUT SETTLING THE SCORE...
BWAH!
BLASH

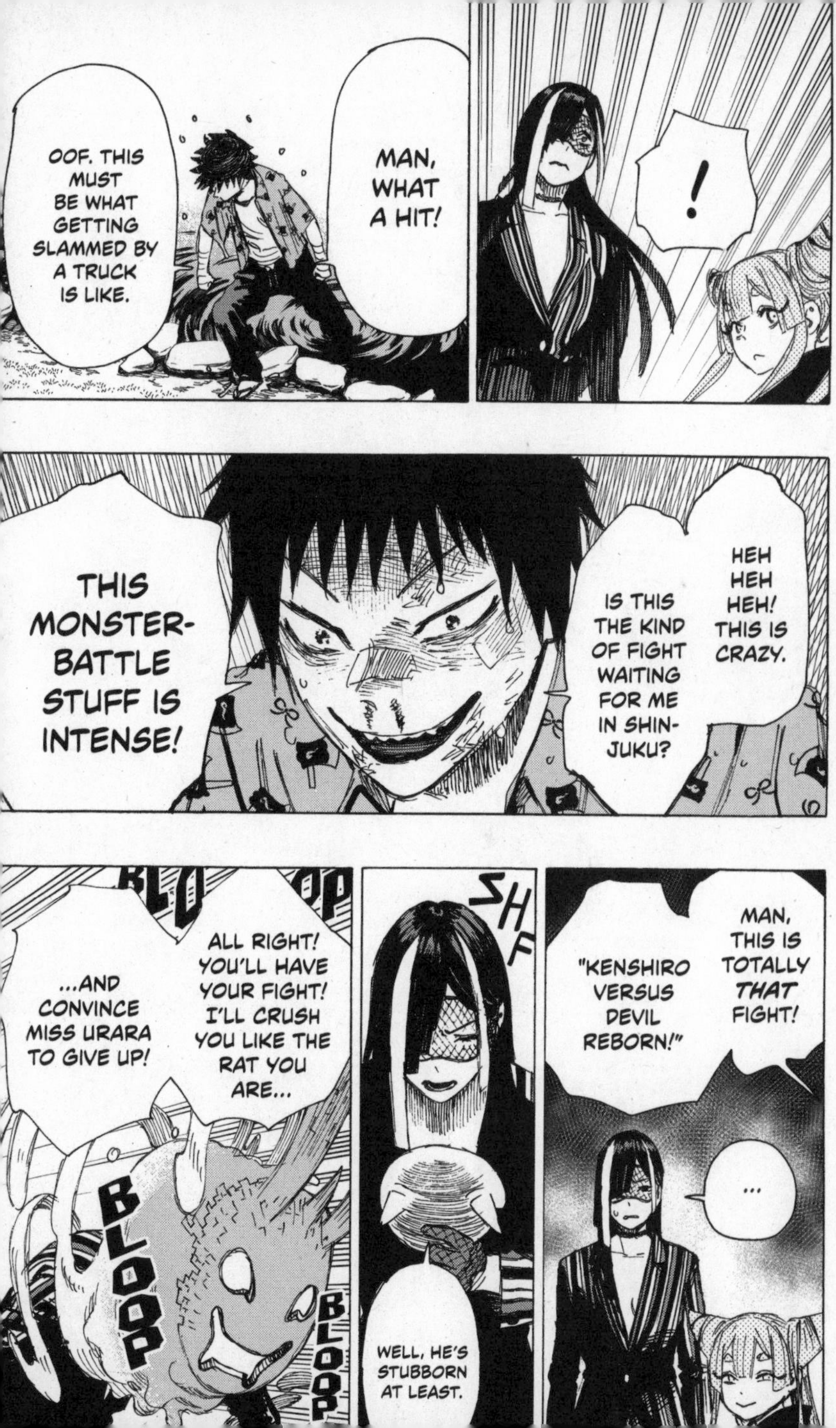
!
MAN, WHAT A HIT!
OOF. THIS MUST BE WHAT GETTING SLAMMED BY A TRUCK IS LIKE.
HEH HEH HEH! THIS IS CRAZY.
IS THIS THE KIND OF FIGHT WAITING FOR ME IN SHIN-JUKU?
THIS MONSTER-BATTLE STUFF IS INTENSE!
MAN, THIS IS TOTALLY *THAT* FIGHT!
"KENSHIRO VERSUS DEVIL REBORN!"
...
SHF
WELL, HE'S STUBBORN AT LEAST.
ALL RIGHT! YOU'LL HAVE YOUR FIGHT! I'LL CRUSH YOU LIKE THE RAT YOU ARE...
...AND CONVINCE MISS URARA TO GIVE UP!
BLOOP
BLOOP

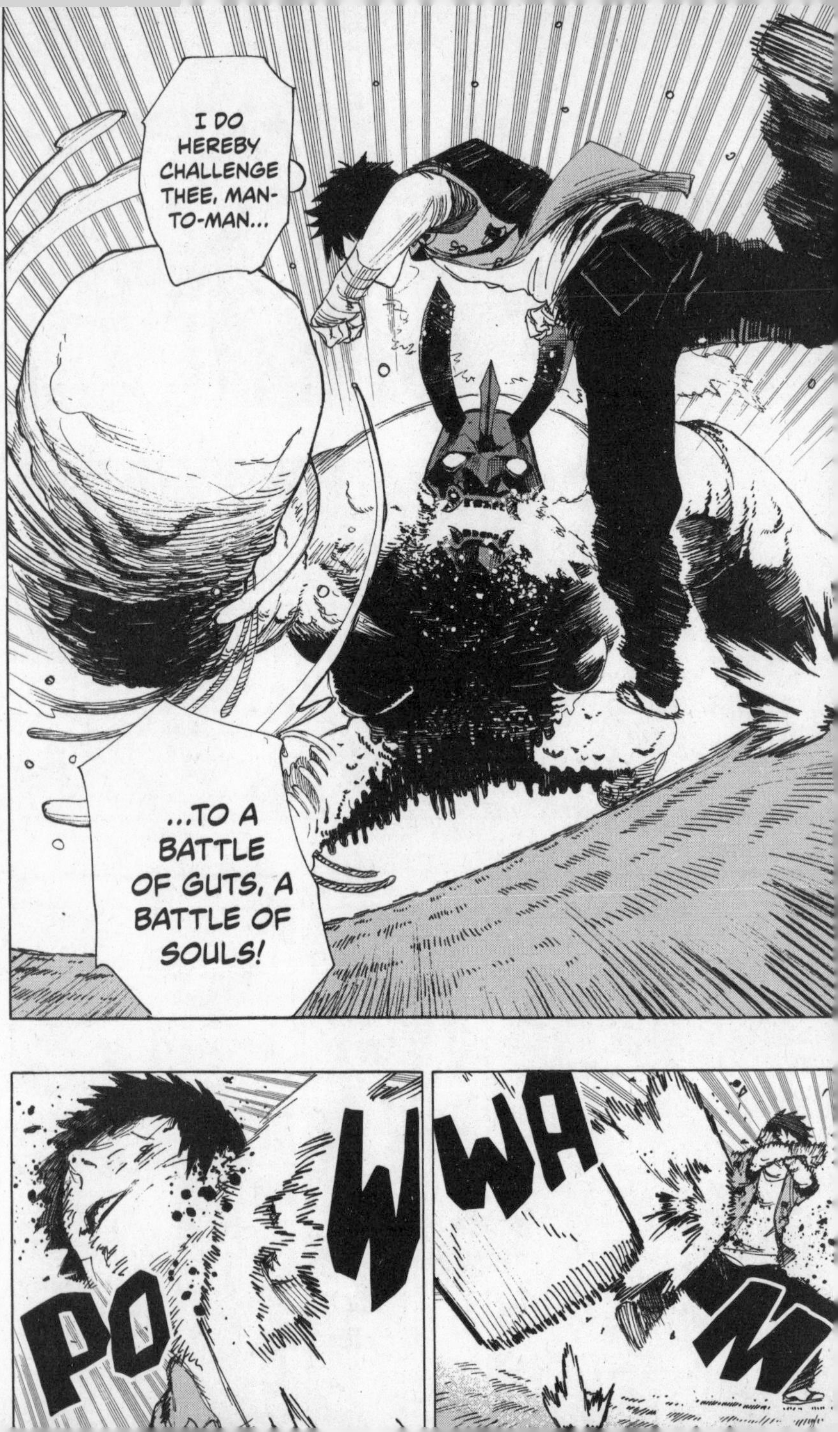
I DO HEREBY CHALLENGE THEE, MAN-TO-MAN...
...TO A BATTLE OF GUTS, A BATTLE OF SOULS!
POWWAM

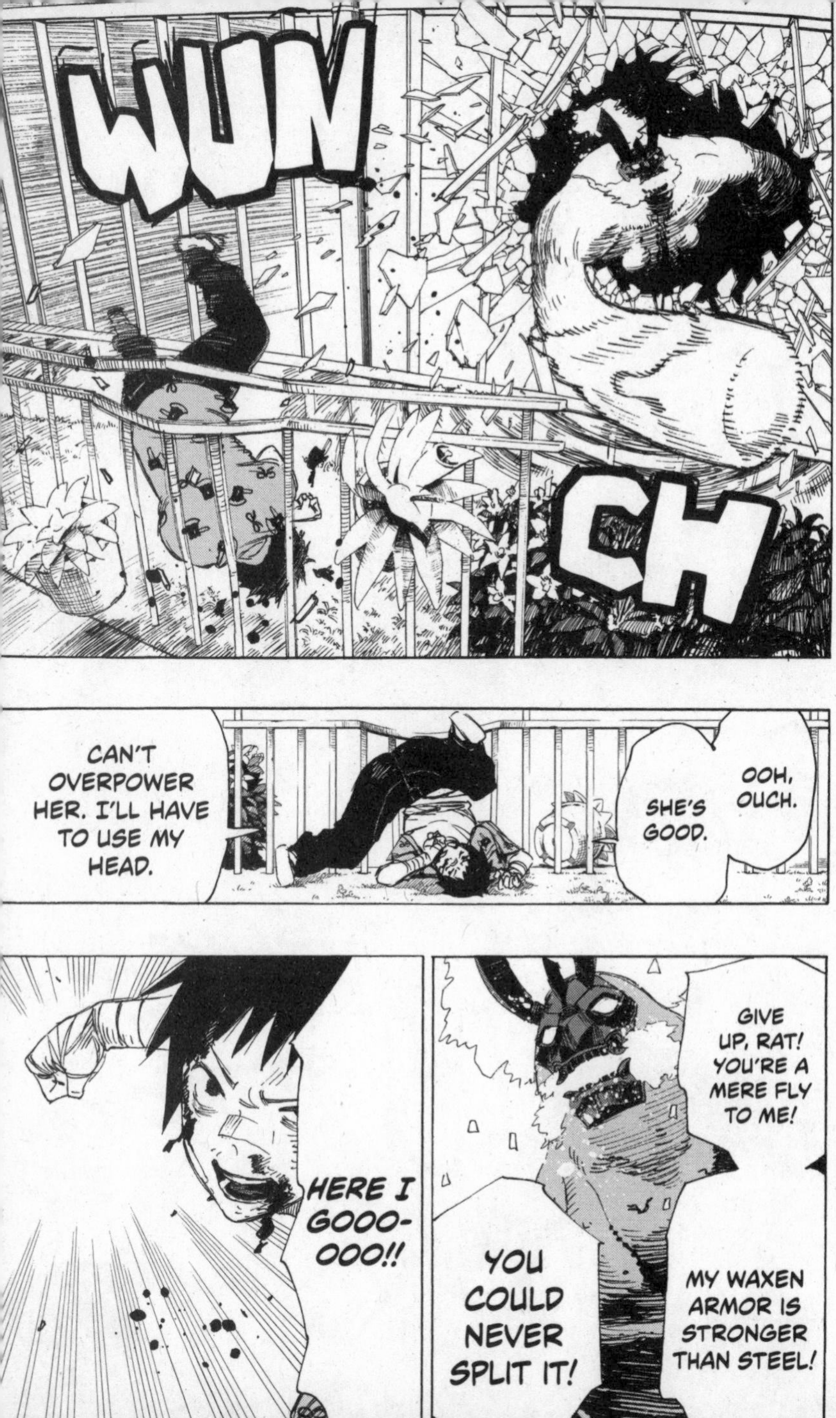
WUN
CH
OOH, OUCH.
SHE'S GOOD.
CAN'T OVERPOWER HER. I'LL HAVE TO USE MY HEAD.
GIVE UP, RAT! YOU'RE A MERE FLY TO ME!
MY WAXEN ARMOR IS STRONGER THAN STEEL!
YOU COULD NEVER SPLIT IT!
HERE I GOOOO-OOO!!

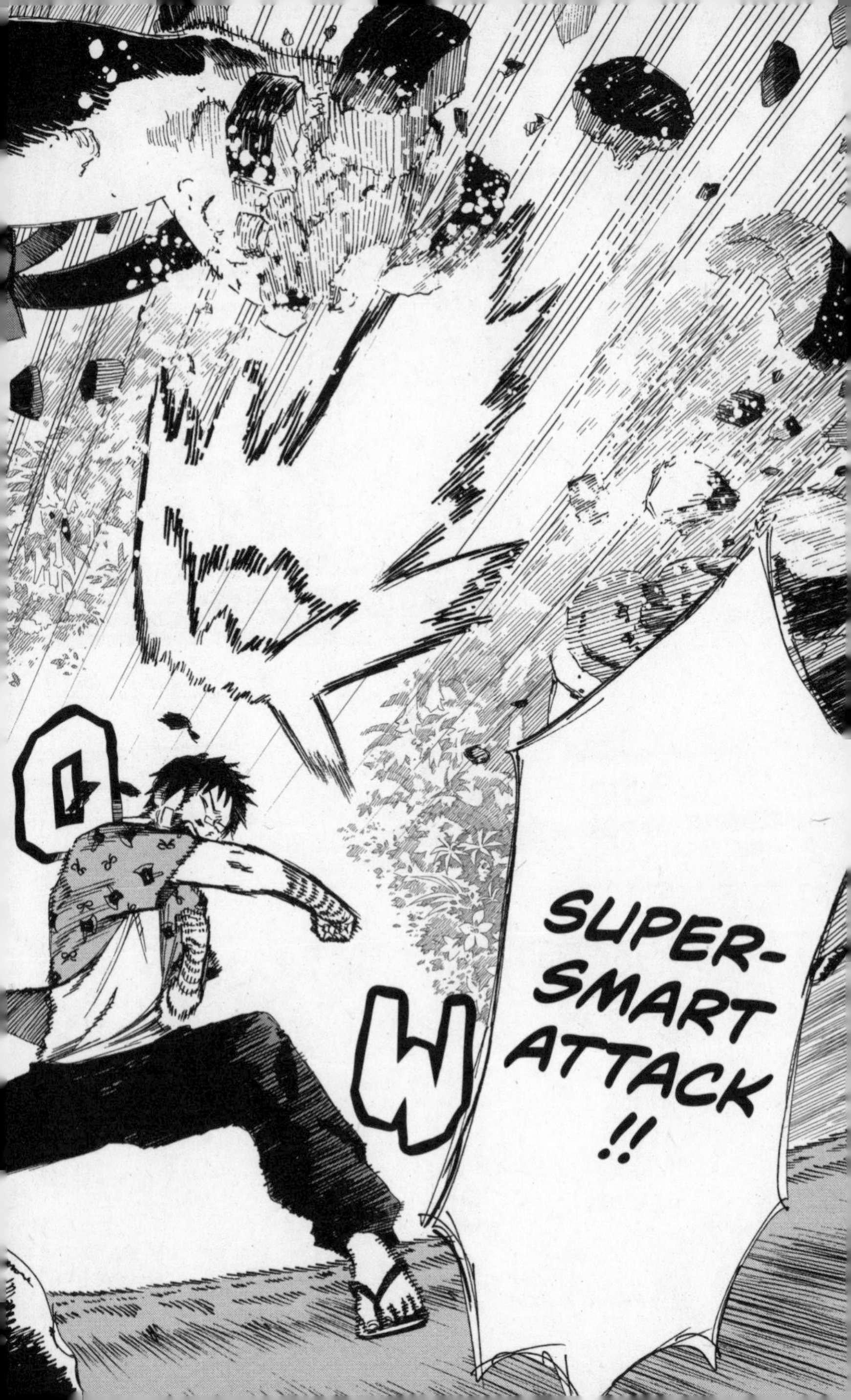
SUPER-
SMART
ATTACK
!!

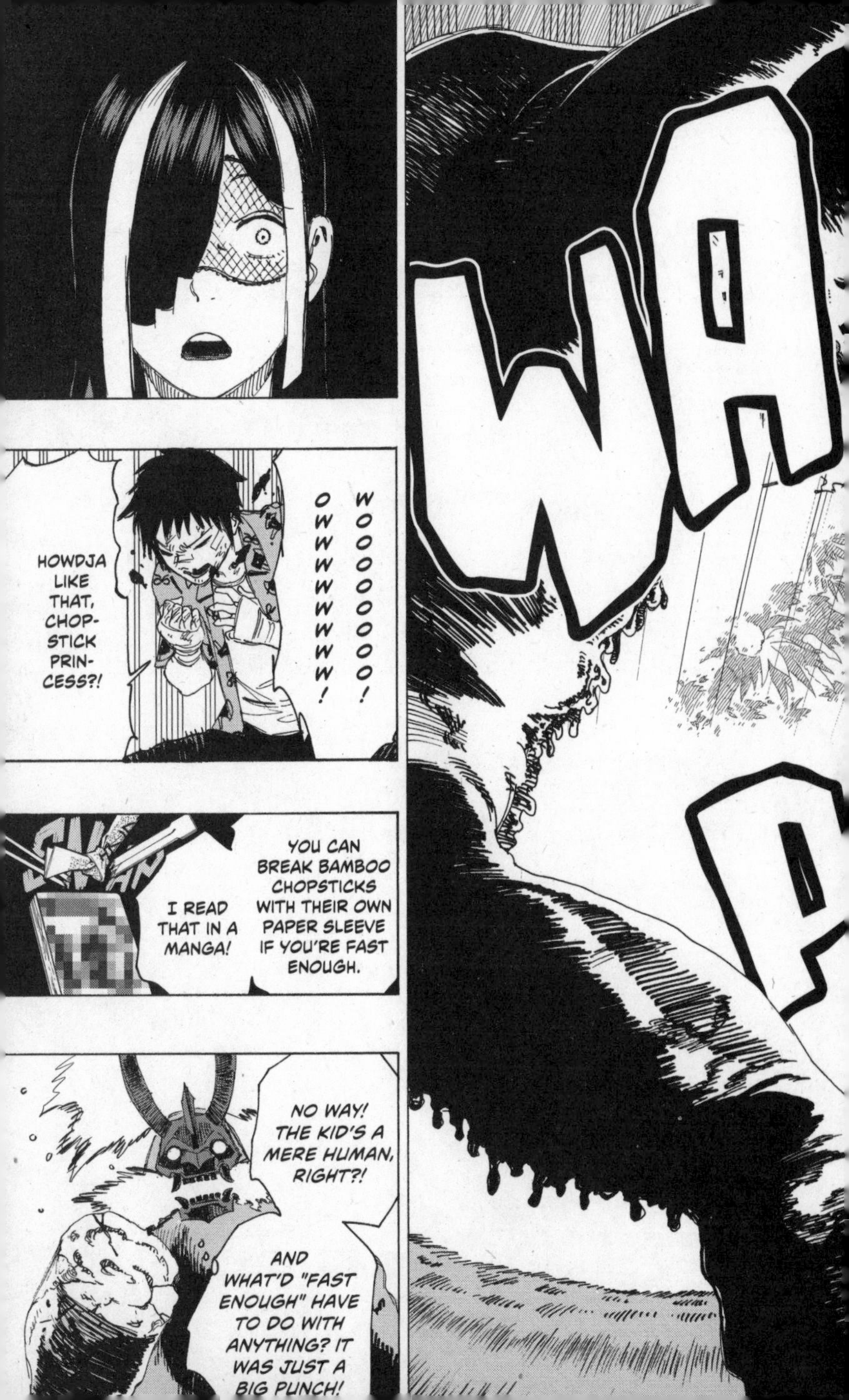
WOOOOOOOO!
OWWWWWWWW!
HOWDJA LIKE THAT, CHOP-STICK PRIN-CESS?!
YOU CAN BREAK BAMBOO CHOPSTICKS WITH THEIR OWN PAPER SLEEVE IF YOU'RE FAST ENOUGH.
I READ THAT IN A MANGA!
NO WAY! THE KID'S A MERE HUMAN, RIGHT?!
AND WHAT'D "FAST ENOUGH" HAVE TO DO WITH ANYTHING? IT WAS JUST A BIG PUNCH!

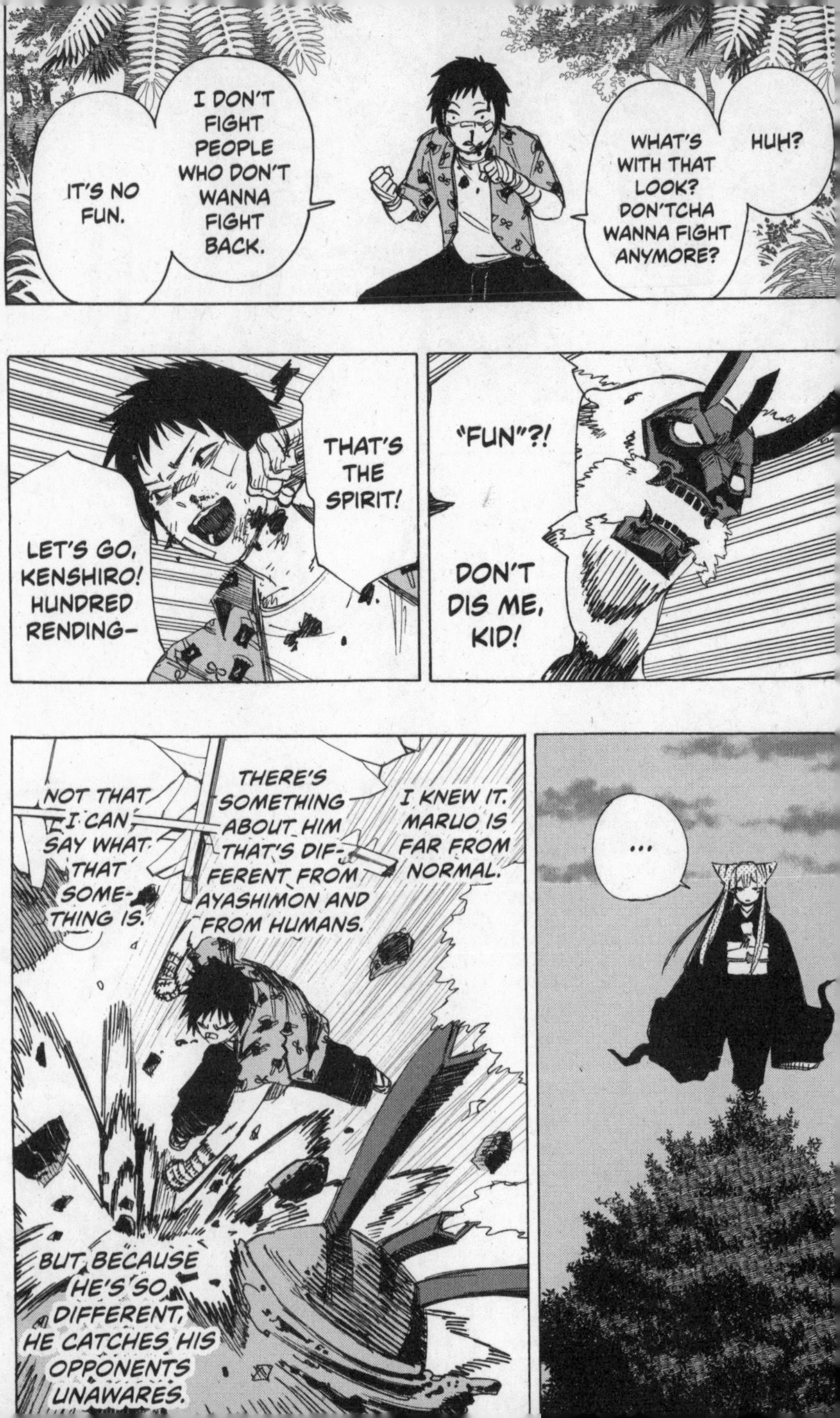
HUH?
WHAT'S WITH THAT LOOK? DON'TCHA WANNA FIGHT ANYMORE?
I DON'T FIGHT PEOPLE WHO DON'T WANNA FIGHT BACK.
IT'S NO FUN.
"FUN"?!
DON'T DIS ME, KID!
THAT'S THE SPIRIT!
LET'S GO, KENSHIRO! HUNDRED RENDING-
...
I KNEW IT. MARUO IS FAR FROM NORMAL.
THERE'S SOMETHING ABOUT HIM THAT'S DIF-FERENT FROM AYASHIMON AND FROM HUMANS.
NOT THAT I CAN SAY WHAT THAT SOME-THING IS.
BUT BECAUSE HE'S SO DIFFERENT, HE CATCHES HIS OPPONENTS UNAWARES.

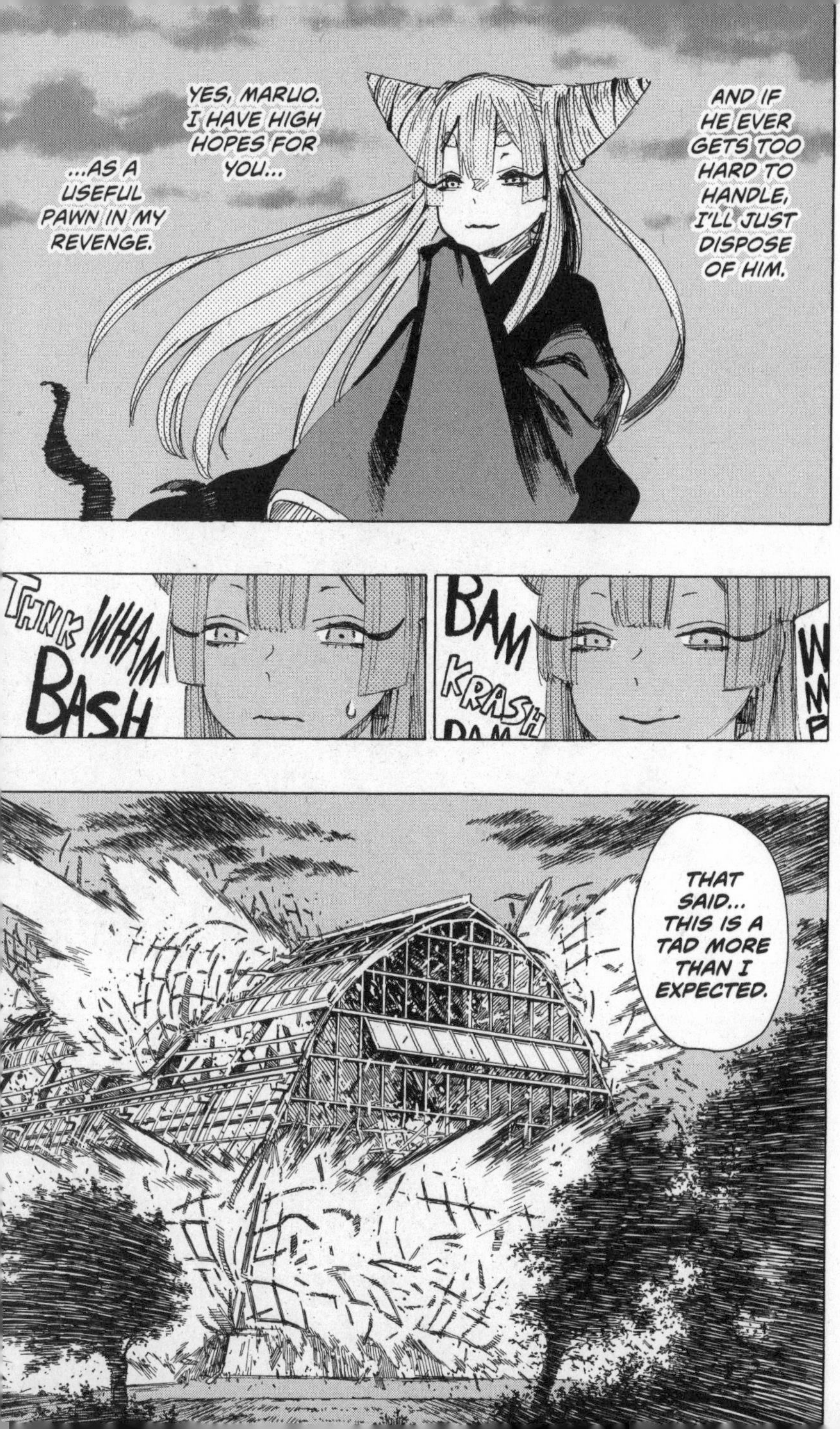
AND IF HE EVER GETS TOO HARD TO HANDLE, I'LL JUST DISPOSE OF HIM.
YES, MARUO. I HAVE HIGH HOPES FOR YOU...
...AS A USEFUL PAWN IN MY REVENGE.
BAM
KRASH
WMP
THNK
WHAM
BASH
THAT SAID... THIS IS A TAD MORE THAN I EXPECTED.

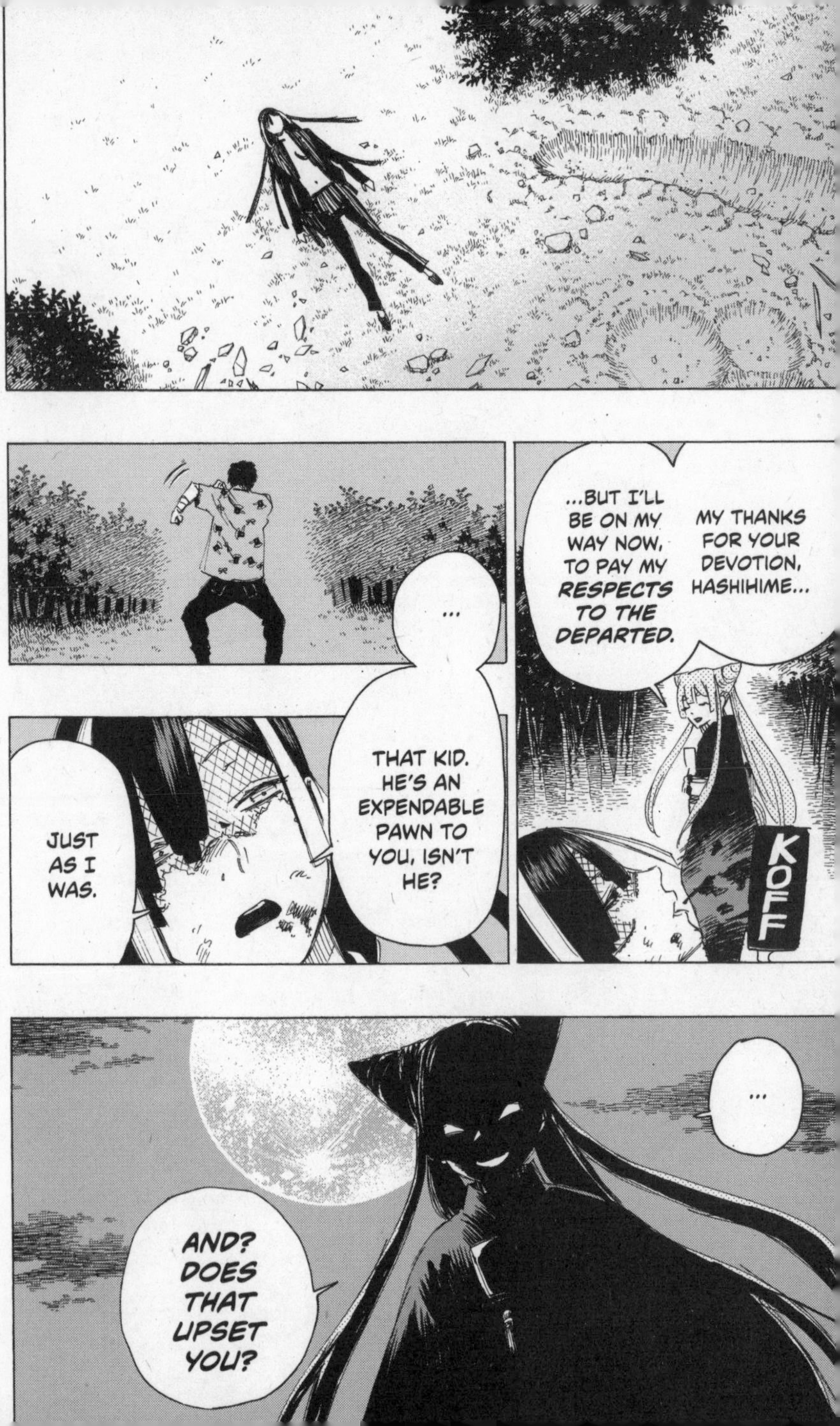
MY THANKS FOR YOUR DEVOTION, HASHIHIME...
...BUT I'LL BE ON MY WAY NOW, TO PAY MY RESPECTS TO THE DEPARTED.
KOFF
...
THAT KID. HE'S AN EXPENDABLE PAWN TO YOU, ISN'T HE?
JUST AS I WAS.
...
AND? DOES THAT UPSET YOU?

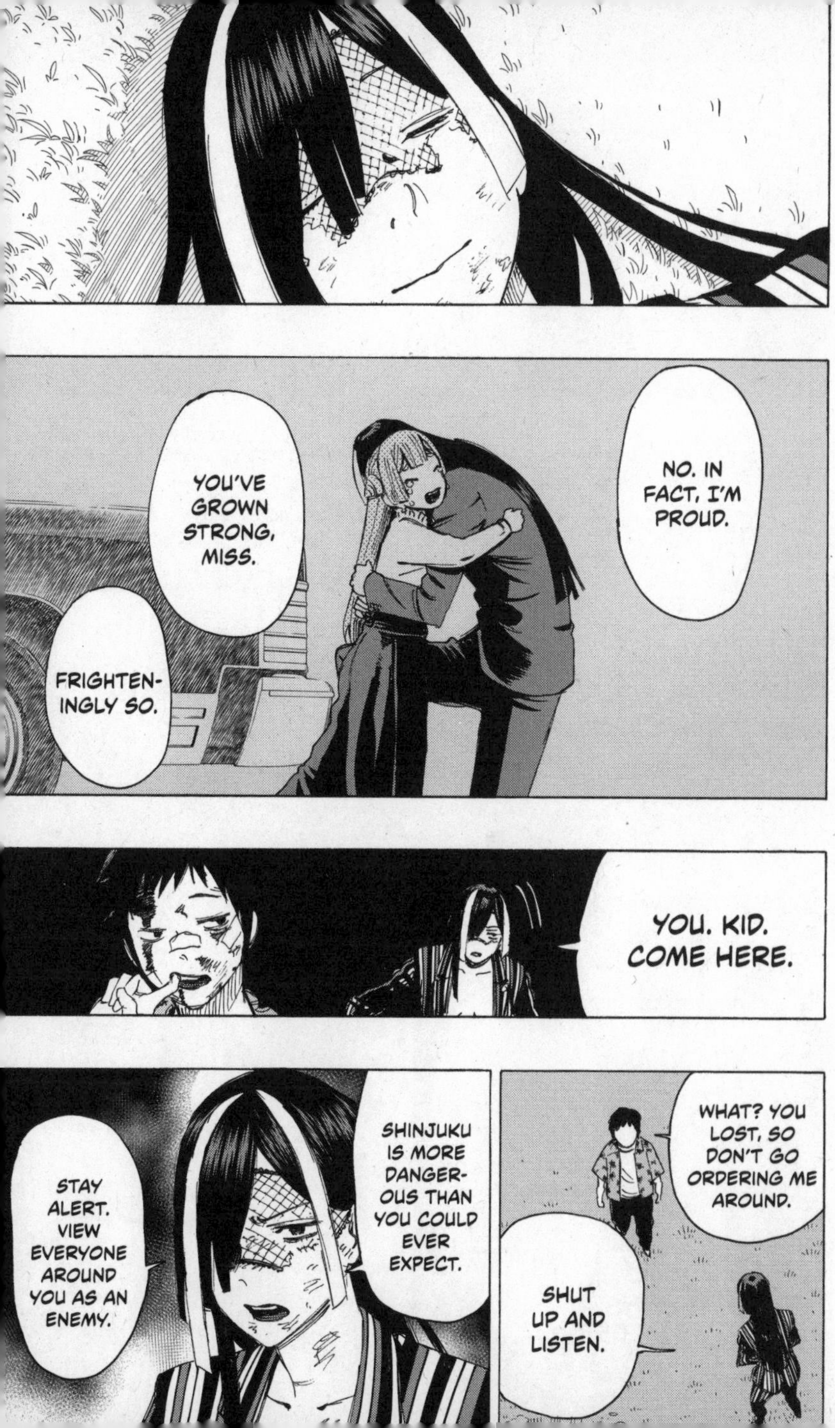
NO. IN FACT, I'M PROUD.
YOU'VE GROWN STRONG, MISS.
FRIGHTEN-INGLY SO.
YOU. KID. COME HERE.
WHAT? YOU LOST, SO DON'T GO ORDERING ME AROUND.
SHUT UP AND LISTEN.
SHINJUKU IS MORE DANGER-OUS THAN YOU COULD EVER EXPECT.
STAY ALERT. VIEW EVERYONE AROUND YOU AS AN ENEMY.

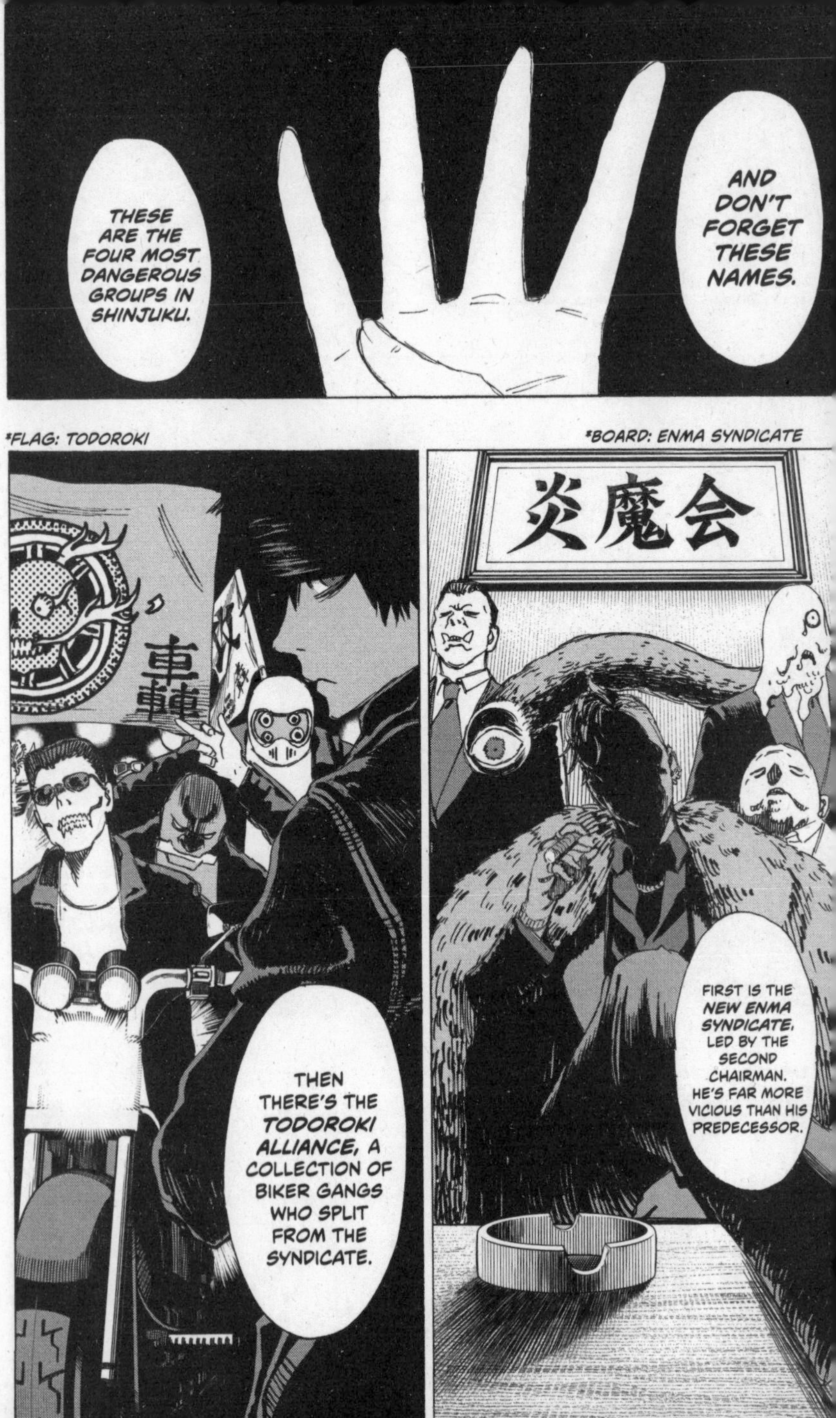
AND DON'T FORGET THESE NAMES.
THESE ARE THE FOUR MOST DANGEROUS GROUPS IN SHINJUKU.
*BOARD: ENMA SYNDICATE
炎魔会
FIRST IS THE NEW ENMA SYNDICATE, LED BY THE SECOND CHAIRMAN. HE'S FAR MORE VICIOUS THAN HIS PREDECESSOR.
*FLAG: TODOROKI
THEN THERE'S THE TODOROKI ALLIANCE, A COLLECTION OF BIKER GANGS WHO SPLIT FROM THE SYNDICATE.

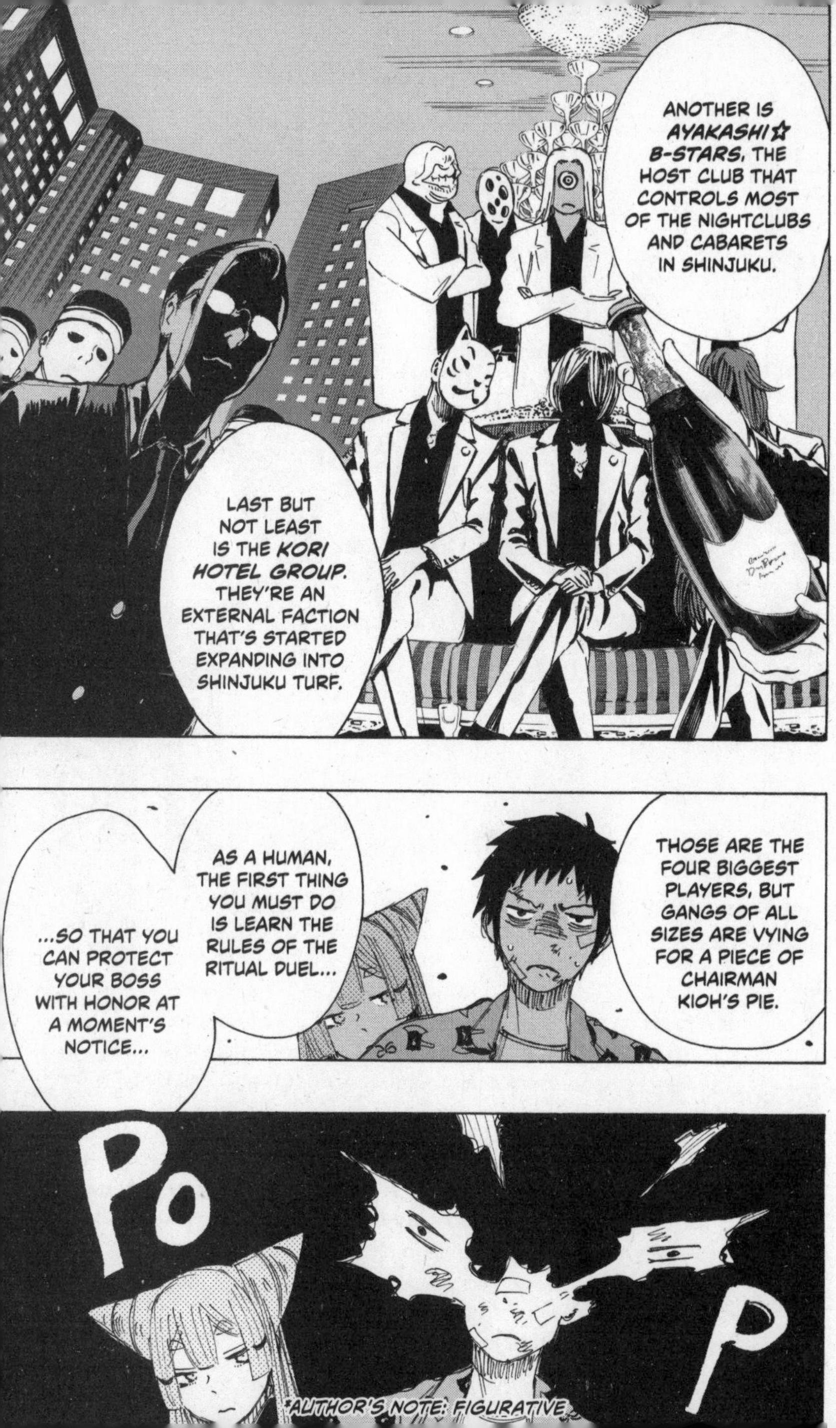
ANOTHER IS AYAKASHI☆ B-STARS, THE HOST CLUB THAT CONTROLS MOST OF THE NIGHTCLUBS AND CABARETS IN SHINJUKU.
LAST BUT NOT LEAST IS THE KORI HOTEL GROUP. THEY'RE AN EXTERNAL FACTION THAT'S STARTED EXPANDING INTO SHINJUKU TURF.
THOSE ARE THE FOUR BIGGEST PLAYERS, BUT GANGS OF ALL SIZES ARE VYING FOR A PIECE OF CHAIRMAN KIOH'S PIE.
AS A HUMAN, THE FIRST THING YOU MUST DO IS LEARN THE RULES OF THE RITUAL DUEL...
...SO THAT YOU CAN PROTECT YOUR BOSS WITH HONOR AT A MOMENT'S NOTICE...
POP
*AUTHOR'S NOTE: FIGURATIVE

AYASHIMON

KABUKICHO MONSTER MANUAL

Urara

The buns on her head resemble horns, and she wears a *hitodama*-patterned kimono with sleeves too long for her arms. She keeps a ceremonial dagger tucked in her obi, which has a clasp shaped like an oni's face. Her tastes are childlike, as she prefers sweet things and dislikes anything bitter or spicy.

One day, a man travelling through a train station overheard a conductor arguing with someone overpaying their fare. Strangely, it was a child demanding to pay full price. "I'm no child," she insisted. "I am a yokai!" But to all appearances, she could be no older than a child...

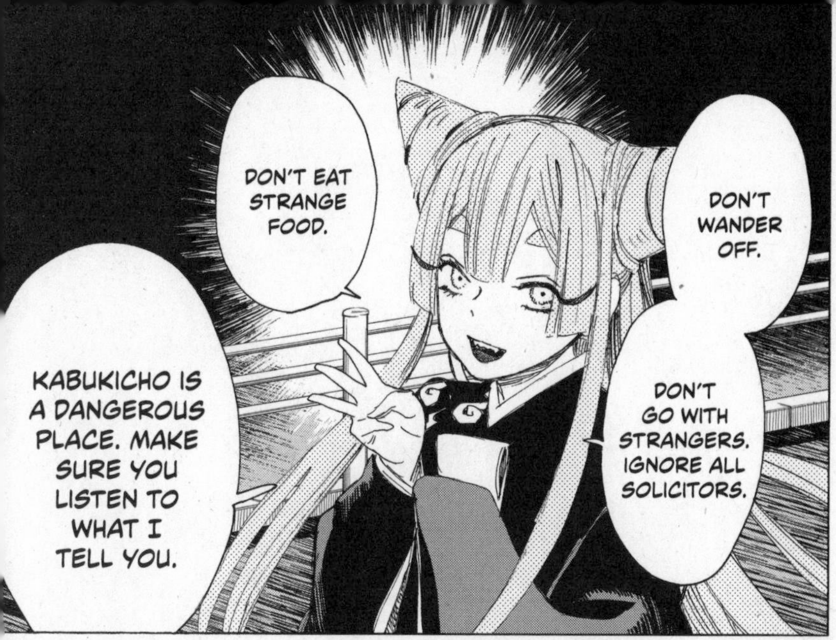
DON'T WANDER OFF.
DON'T EAT STRANGE FOOD.
DON'T GO WITH STRANGERS. IGNORE ALL SOLICITORS.
KABUKICHO IS A DANGEROUS PLACE. MAKE SURE YOU LISTEN TO WHAT I TELL YOU.

Chapter 3

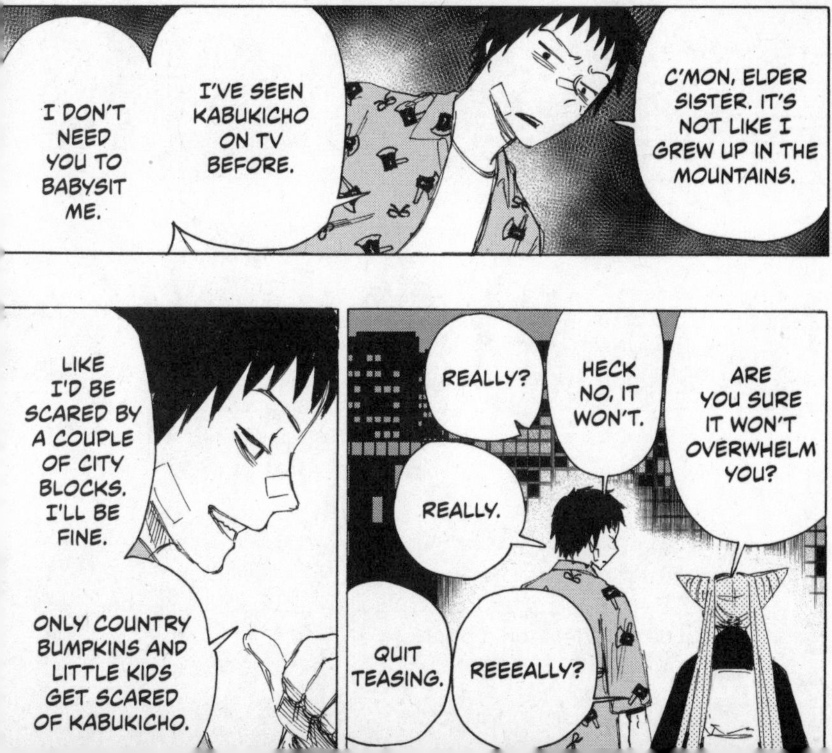
C'MON, ELDER SISTER. IT'S NOT LIKE I GREW UP IN THE MOUNTAINS.
I'VE SEEN KABUKICHO ON TV BEFORE.
I DON'T NEED YOU TO BABYSIT ME.
ARE YOU SURE IT WON'T OVERWHELM YOU?
HECK NO, IT WON'T.
REALLY?
REALLY.
REEEALLY?
QUIT TEASING.
LIKE I'D BE SCARED BY A COUPLE OF CITY BLOCKS. I'LL BE FINE.
ONLY COUNTRY BUMPKINS AND LITTLE KIDS GET SCARED OF KABUKICHO.

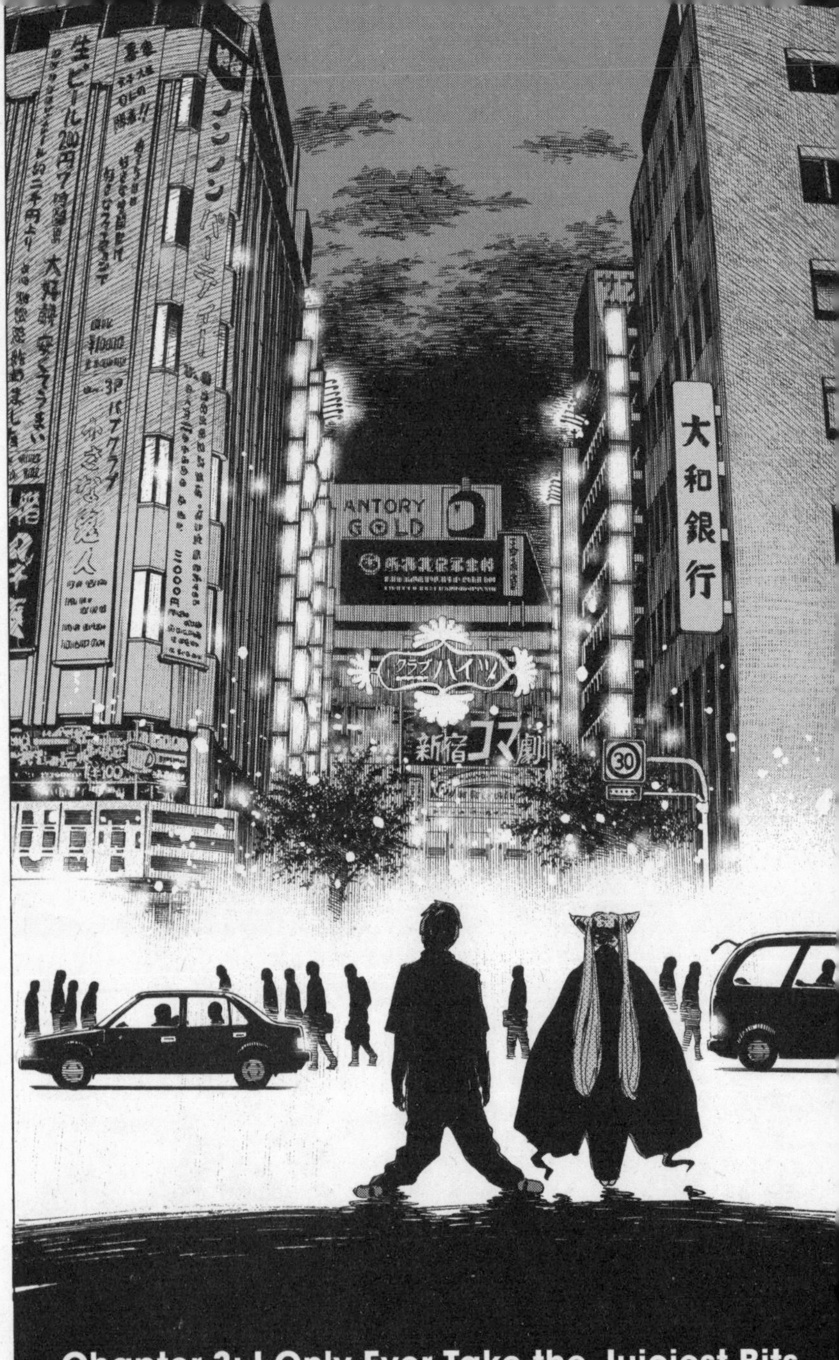

大和銀行
ANTORY GOLD
クラブハイツ
新宿コマ劇
30

Chapter 3: I Only Ever Take the Juiciest Bits

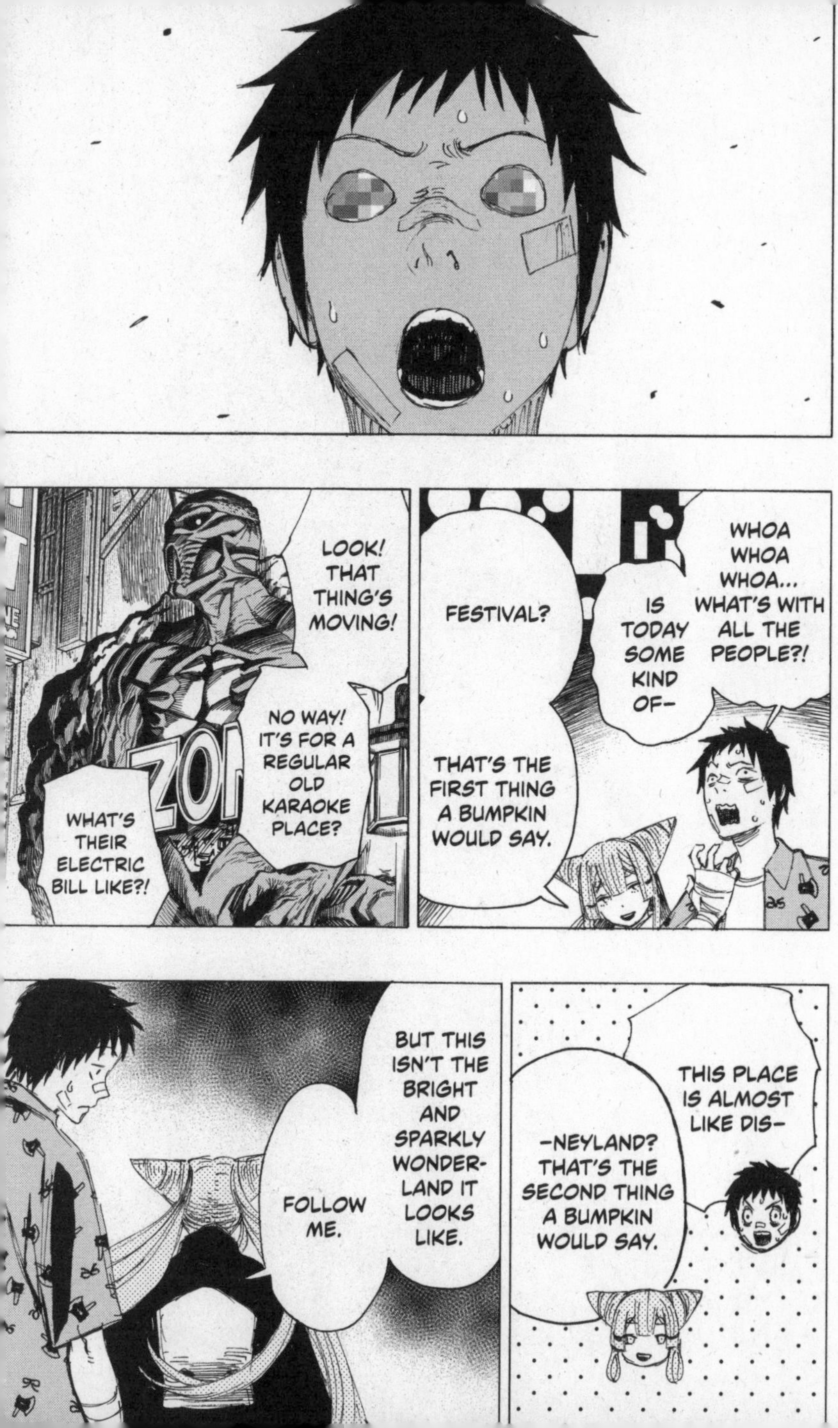
WHOA WHOA WHOA... WHAT'S WITH ALL THE PEOPLE?!
IS TODAY SOME KIND OF-
FESTIVAL?
THAT'S THE FIRST THING A BUMPKIN WOULD SAY.
LOOK! THAT THING'S MOVING!
NO WAY! IT'S FOR A REGULAR OLD KARAOKE PLACE?
WHAT'S THEIR ELECTRIC BILL LIKE?!
THIS PLACE IS ALMOST LIKE DIS-
-NEYLAND? THAT'S THE SECOND THING A BUMPKIN WOULD SAY.
BUT THIS ISN'T THE BRIGHT AND SPARKLY WONDERLAND IT LOOKS LIKE.
FOLLOW ME.

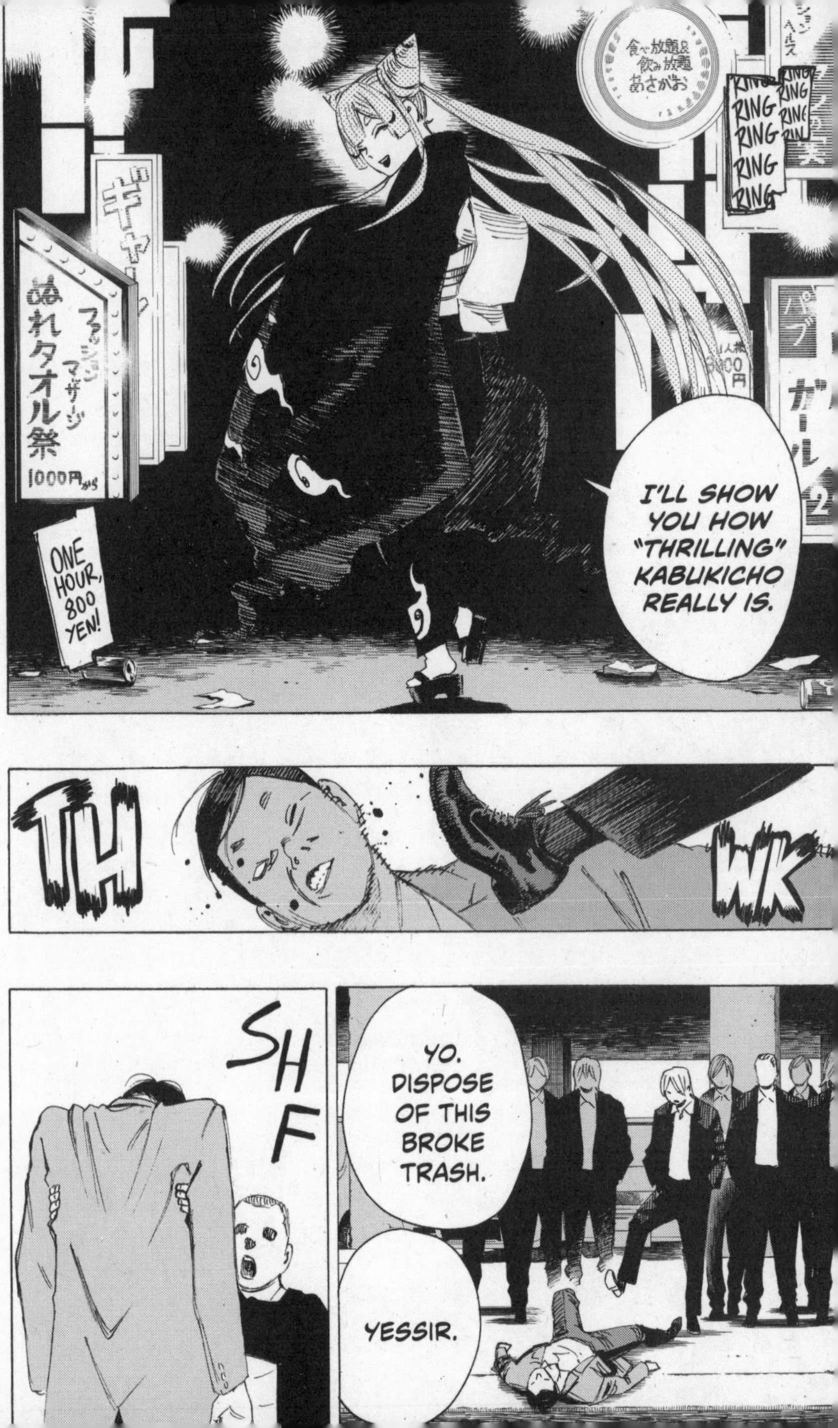

食べ放題&飲み放題 あさがお
RING RING RING RING RING RING
RING RING RING
ファッションマッサージ ぬれタオル祭 1000円から
ONE HOUR, 800 YEN!
I'LL SHOW YOU HOW "THRILLING" KABUKICHO REALLY IS.
THWK
YO. DISPOSE OF THIS BROKE TRASH.
YESSIR.
SHF

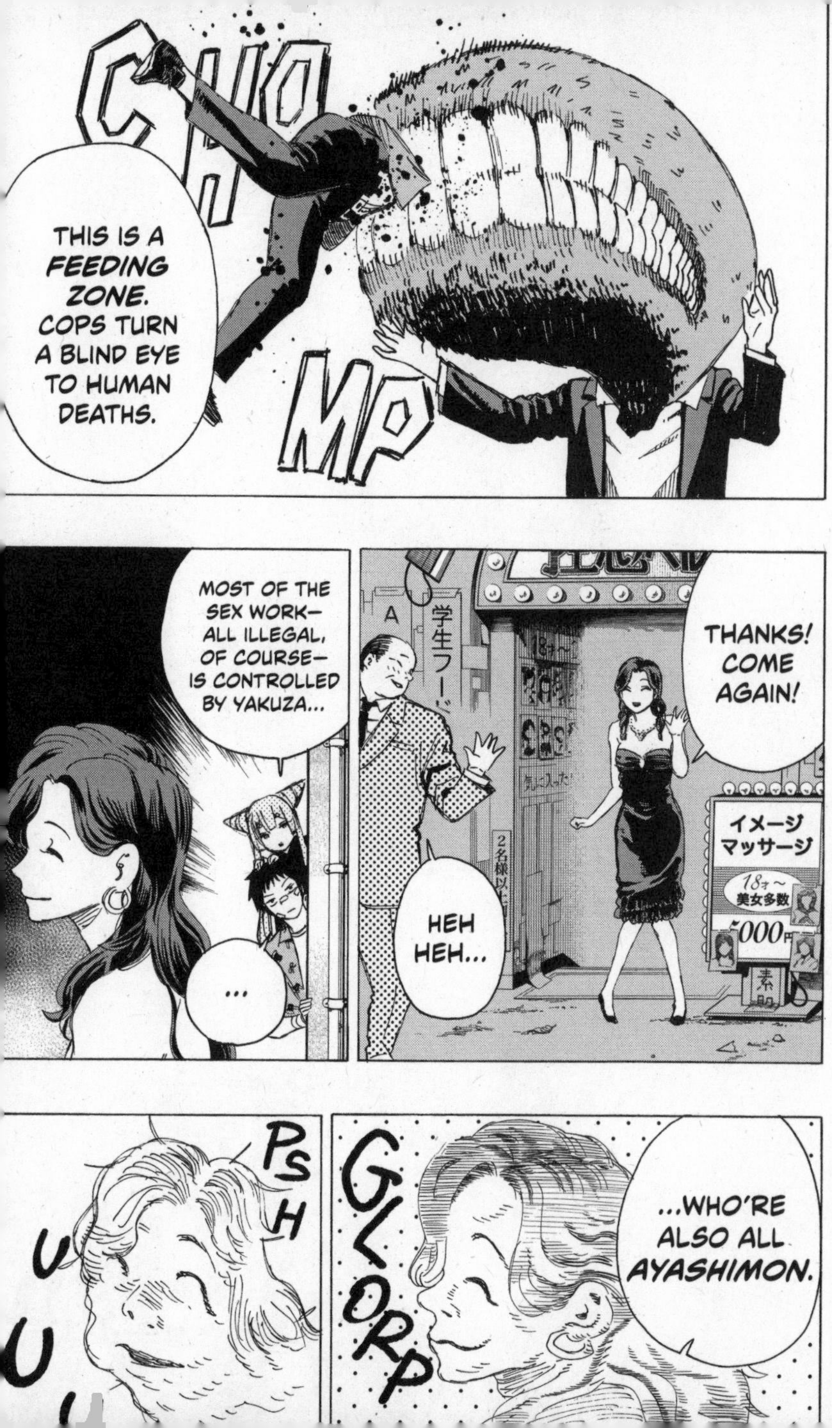
CHOMP
THIS IS A FEEDING ZONE. COPS TURN A BLIND EYE TO HUMAN DEATHS.
THANKS! COME AGAIN!
イメージ マッサージ
18才～ 美女多数
HEH HEH...
MOST OF THE SEX WORK—ALL ILLEGAL, OF COURSE—IS CONTROLLED BY YAKUZA...
...
...WHO'RE ALSO ALL AYASHIMON.
GLORP
PSH
UU

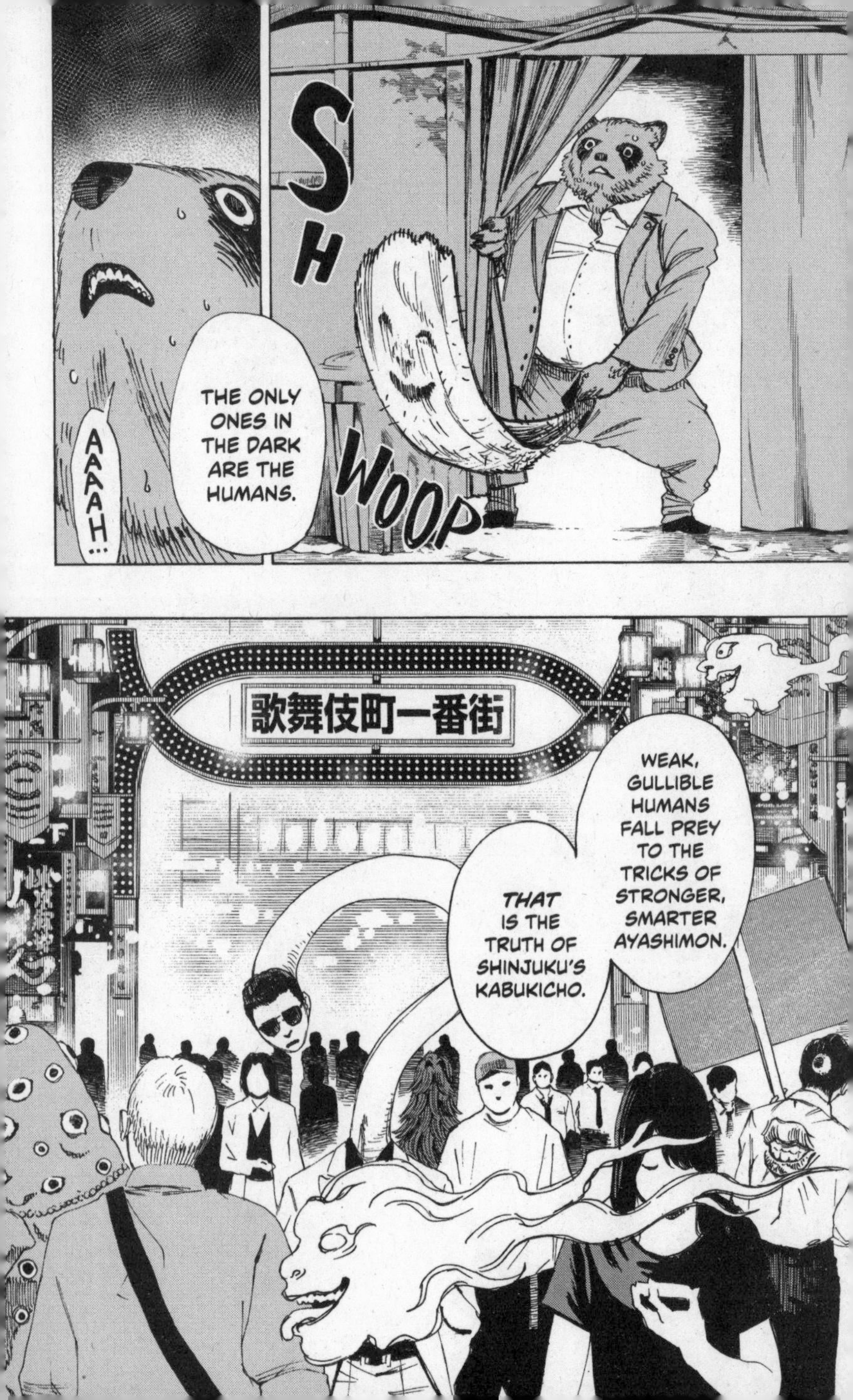

SHWOOP
THE ONLY ONES IN THE DARK ARE THE HUMANS.
AAAAH...
歌舞伎町一番街
WEAK, GULLIBLE HUMANS FALL PREY TO THE TRICKS OF STRONGER, SMARTER AYASHIMON.
THAT IS THE TRUTH OF SHINJUKU'S KABUKICHO.

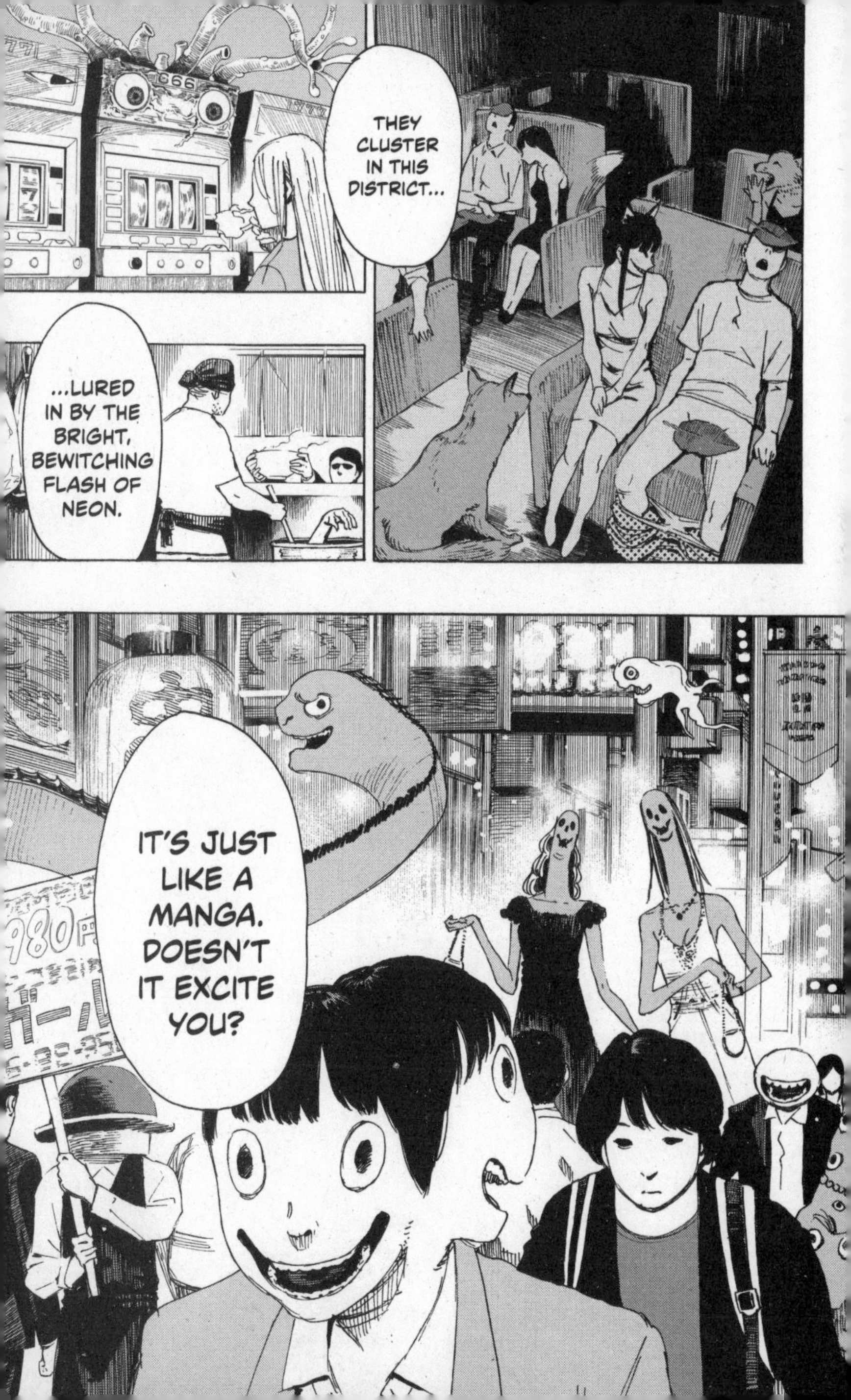
THEY CLUSTER IN THIS DISTRICT...
...LURED IN BY THE BRIGHT, BEWITCHING FLASH OF NEON.
IT'S JUST LIKE A MANGA. DOESN'T IT EXCITE YOU?

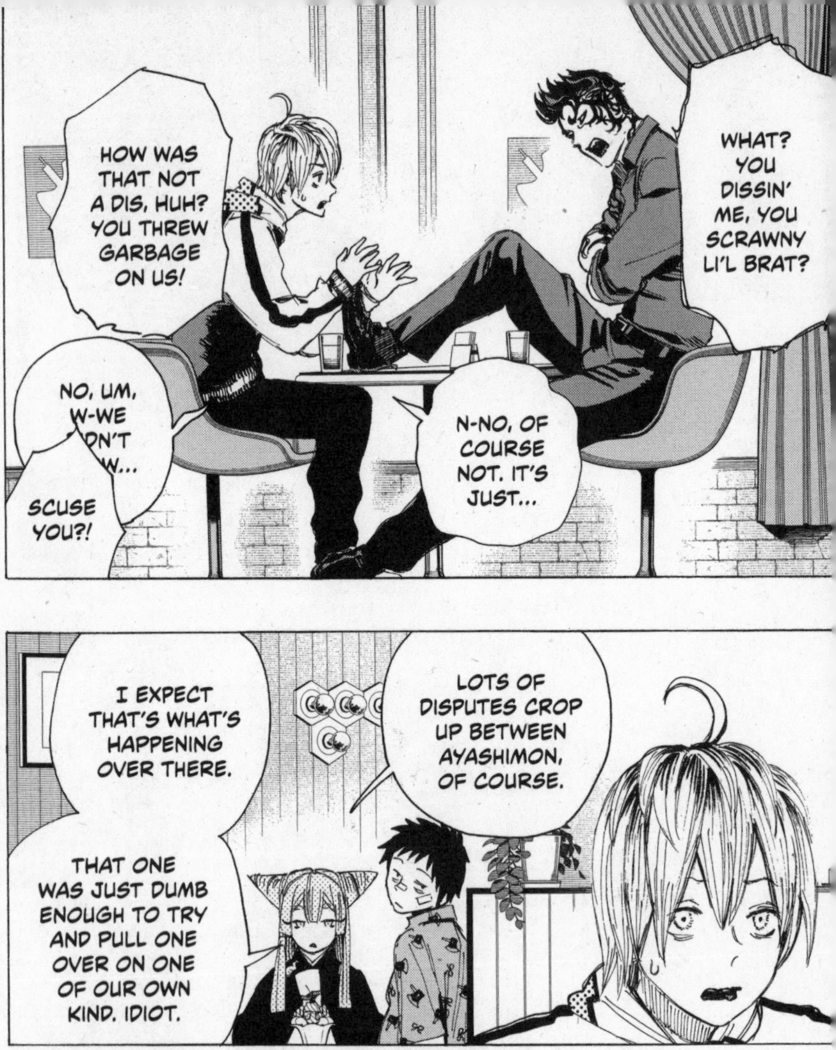
WHAT? YOU DISSIN' ME, YOU SCRAWNY LI'L BRAT?
HOW WAS THAT NOT A DIS, HUH? YOU THREW GARBAGE ON US!
N-NO, OF COURSE NOT. IT'S JUST...
NO, UM, W-WE
SCUSE YOU?!
LOTS OF DISPUTES CROP UP BETWEEN AYASHIMON, OF COURSE.
I EXPECT THAT'S WHAT'S HAPPENING OVER THERE.
THAT ONE WAS JUST DUMB ENOUGH TO TRY AND PULL ONE OVER ON ONE OF OUR OWN KIND. IDIOT.

*PHONE SCAMMERS HAVE THEIR OWN JARGON AND BASES OF OPERATIONS, BUT THEY AREN'T ACTUALLY YAKUZA.

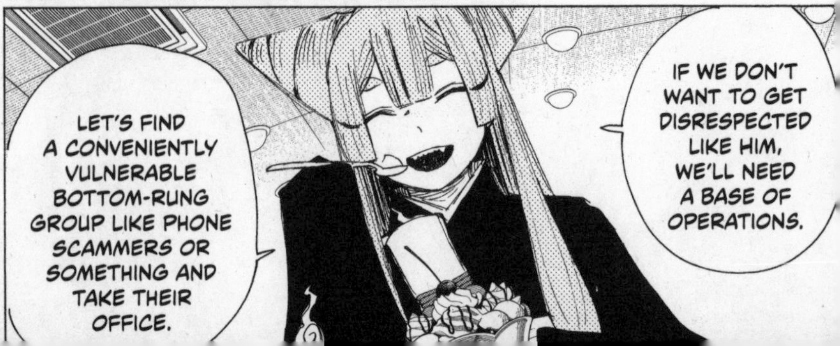
IF WE DON'T WANT TO GET DISRESPECTED LIKE HIM, WE'LL NEED A BASE OF OPERATIONS.
LET'S FIND A CONVENIENTLY VULNERABLE BOTTOM-RUNG GROUP LIKE PHONE SCAMMERS OR SOMETHING AND TAKE THEIR OFFICE.

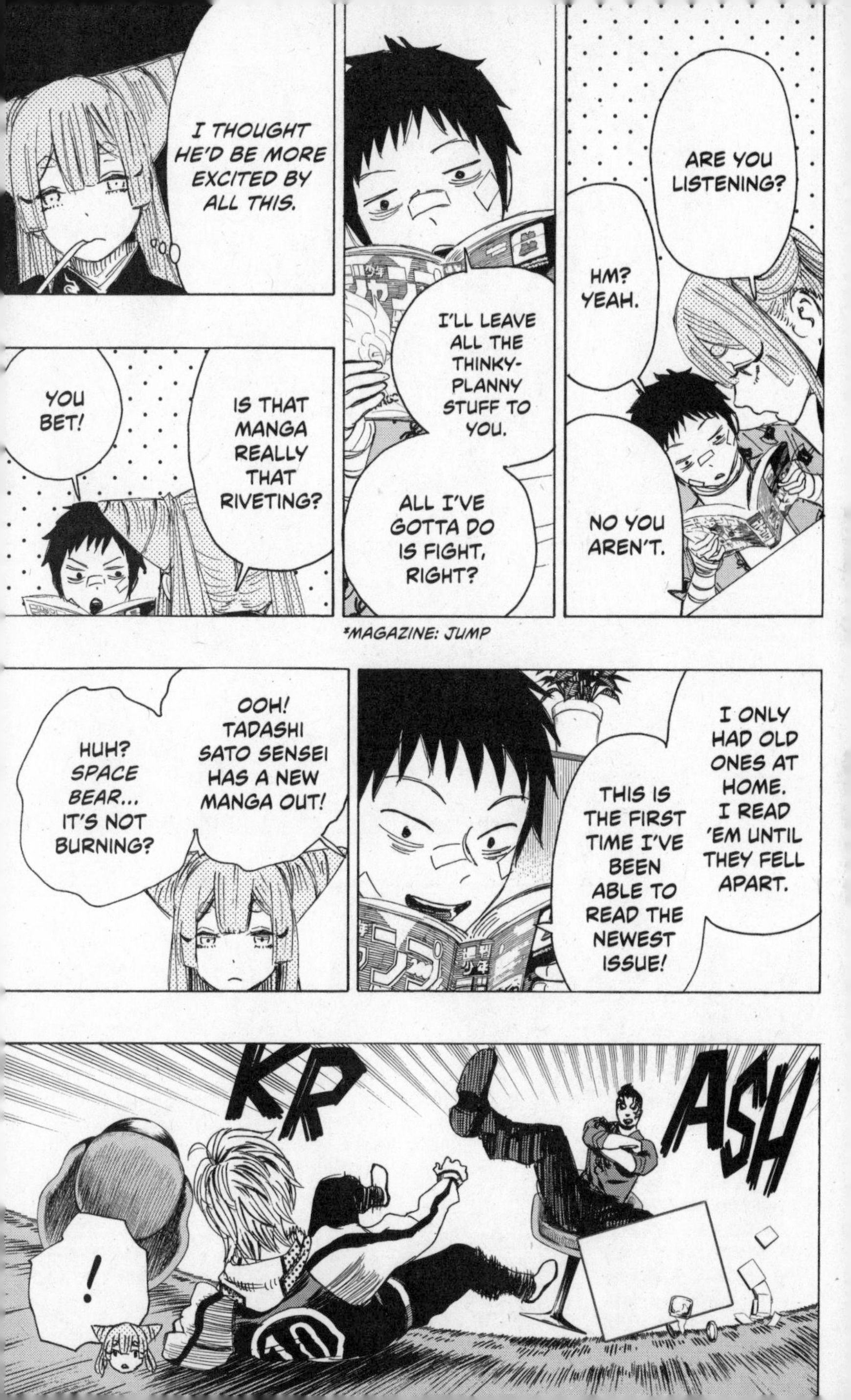
ARE YOU LISTENING?
HM? YEAH.
NO YOU AREN'T.
I'LL LEAVE ALL THE THINKY-PLANNY STUFF TO YOU.
ALL I'VE GOTTA DO IS FIGHT, RIGHT?
I THOUGHT HE'D BE MORE EXCITED BY ALL THIS.
IS THAT MANGA REALLY THAT RIVETING?
YOU BET!
*MAGAZINE: JUMP
I ONLY HAD OLD ONES AT HOME. I READ 'EM UNTIL THEY FELL APART.
THIS IS THE FIRST TIME I'VE BEEN ABLE TO READ THE NEWEST ISSUE!
OOH! TADASHI SATO SENSEI HAS A NEW MANGA OUT!
HUH? SPACE BEAR... IT'S NOT BURNING?
KRASH
!

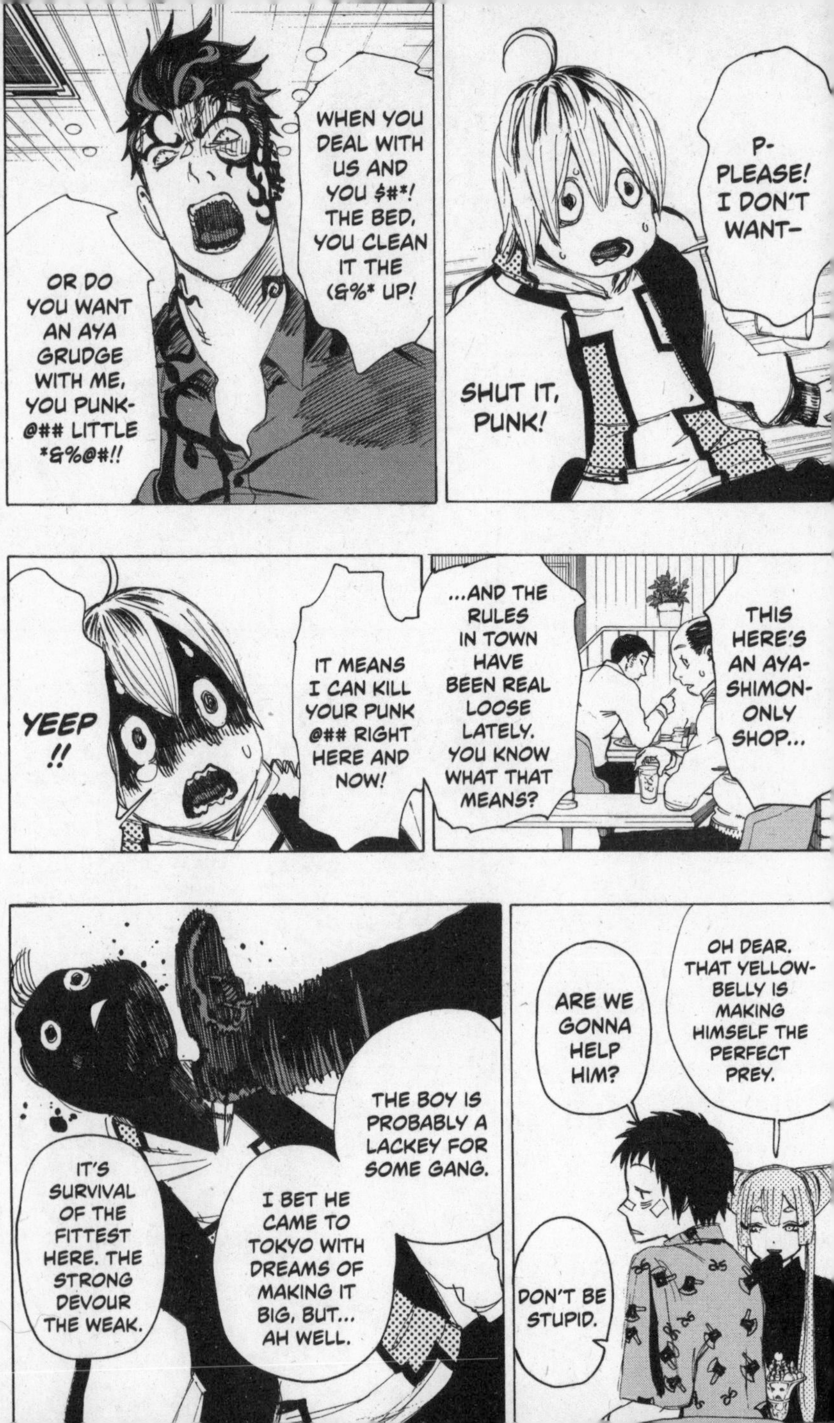
P-PLEASE! I DON'T WANT-
SHUT IT, PUNK!
WHEN YOU DEAL WITH US AND YOU $#*! THE BED, YOU CLEAN IT THE (&%* UP!
OR DO YOU WANT AN AYA GRUDGE WITH ME, YOU PUNK-@## LITTLE *&%@#!!
THIS HERE'S AN AYA-SHIMON-ONLY SHOP...
...AND THE RULES IN TOWN HAVE BEEN REAL LOOSE LATELY. YOU KNOW WHAT THAT MEANS?
IT MEANS I CAN KILL YOUR PUNK @## RIGHT HERE AND NOW!
YEEP!!
OH DEAR. THAT YELLOW-BELLY IS MAKING HIMSELF THE PERFECT PREY.
ARE WE GONNA HELP HIM?
DON'T BE STUPID.
THE BOY IS PROBABLY A LACKEY FOR SOME GANG.
I BET HE CAME TO TOKYO WITH DREAMS OF MAKING IT BIG, BUT... AH WELL.
IT'S SURVIVAL OF THE FITTEST HERE. THE STRONG DEVOUR THE WEAK.

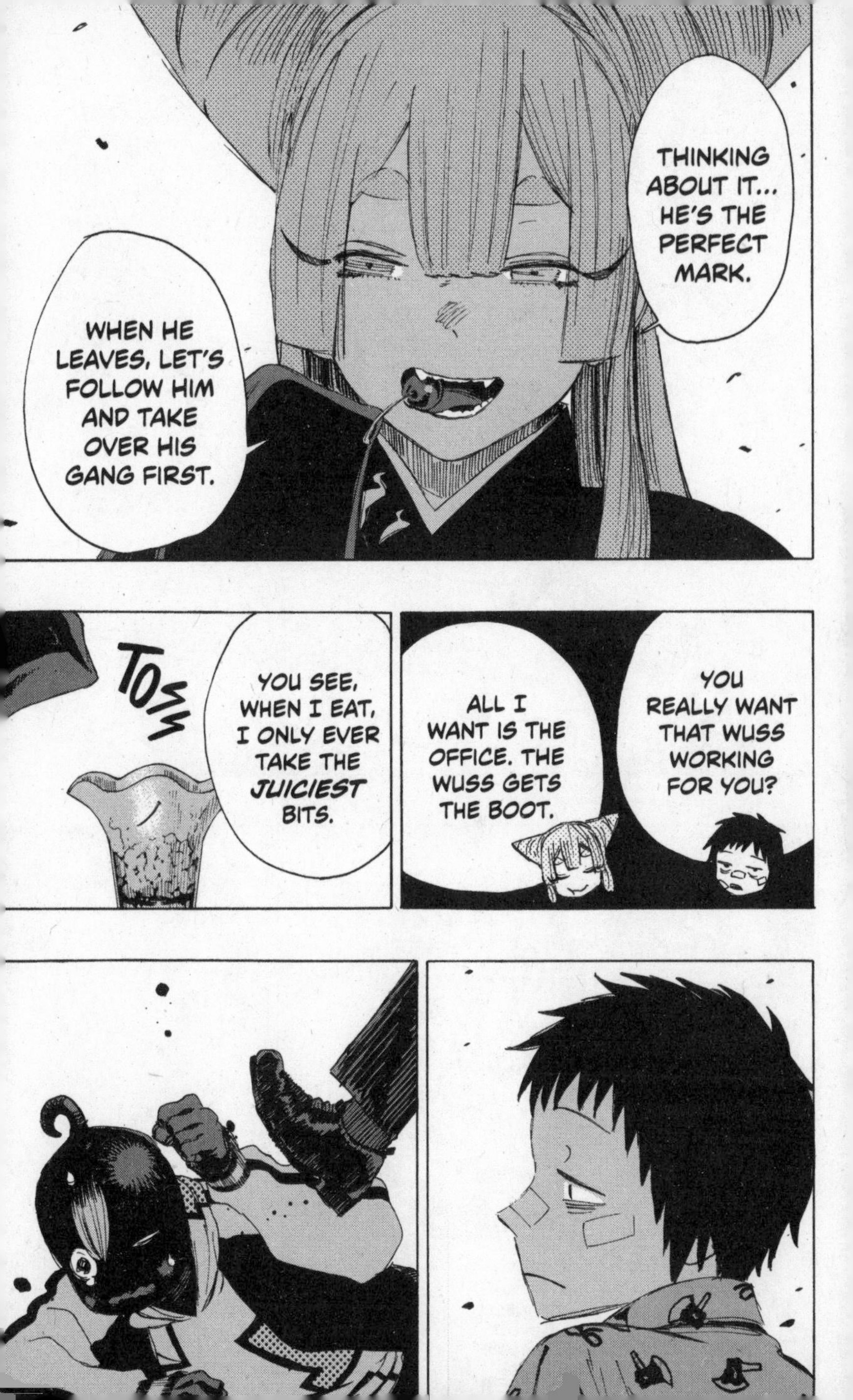
THINKING ABOUT IT... HE'S THE PERFECT MARK.
WHEN HE LEAVES, LET'S FOLLOW HIM AND TAKE OVER HIS GANG FIRST.
YOU REALLY WANT THAT WUSS WORKING FOR YOU?
ALL I WANT IS THE OFFICE. THE WUSS GETS THE BOOT.
YOU SEE, WHEN I EAT, I ONLY EVER TAKE THE *JUICIEST* BITS.
TOSS

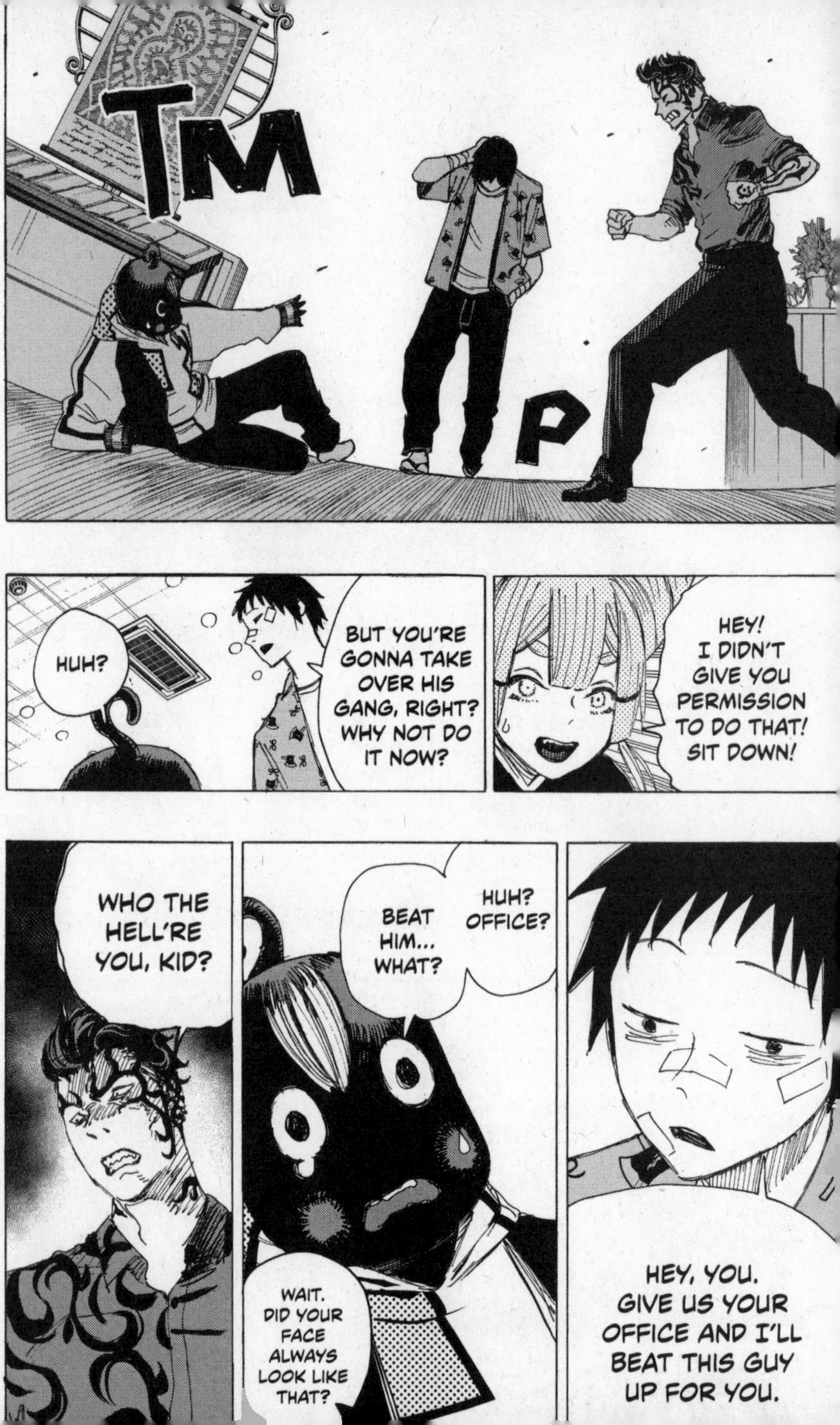
TMP
HEY! I DIDN'T GIVE YOU PERMISSION TO DO THAT! SIT DOWN!
BUT YOU'RE GONNA TAKE OVER HIS GANG, RIGHT? WHY NOT DO IT NOW?
HUH?
HEY, YOU. GIVE US YOUR OFFICE AND I'LL BEAT THIS GUY UP FOR YOU.
HUH? OFFICE?
BEAT HIM... WHAT?
WAIT. DID YOUR FACE ALWAYS LOOK LIKE THAT?
WHO THE HELL'RE YOU, KID?

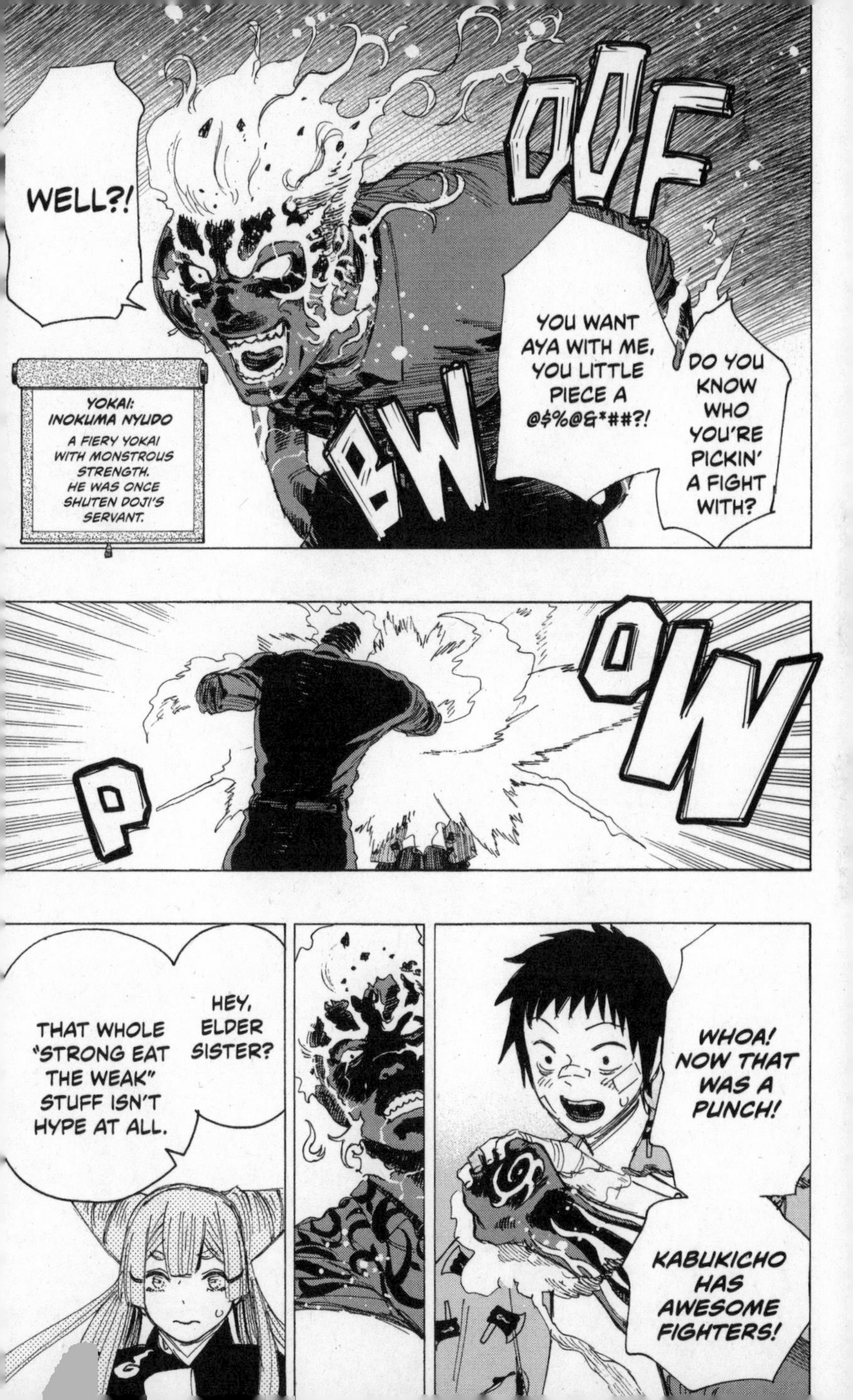
DOOF
YOU WANT AYA WITH ME, YOU LITTLE PIECE A @$%@&*##?!
DO YOU KNOW WHO YOU'RE PICKIN' A FIGHT WITH?
BW
WELL?!
YOKAI: INOKUMA NYUDO
A FIERY YOKAI WITH MONSTROUS STRENGTH. HE WAS ONCE SHUTEN DOJI'S SERVANT.
POW
WHOA! NOW THAT WAS A PUNCH!
KABUKICHO HAS AWESOME FIGHTERS!
HEY, ELDER SISTER?
THAT WHOLE "STRONG EAT THE WEAK" STUFF ISN'T HYPE AT ALL.

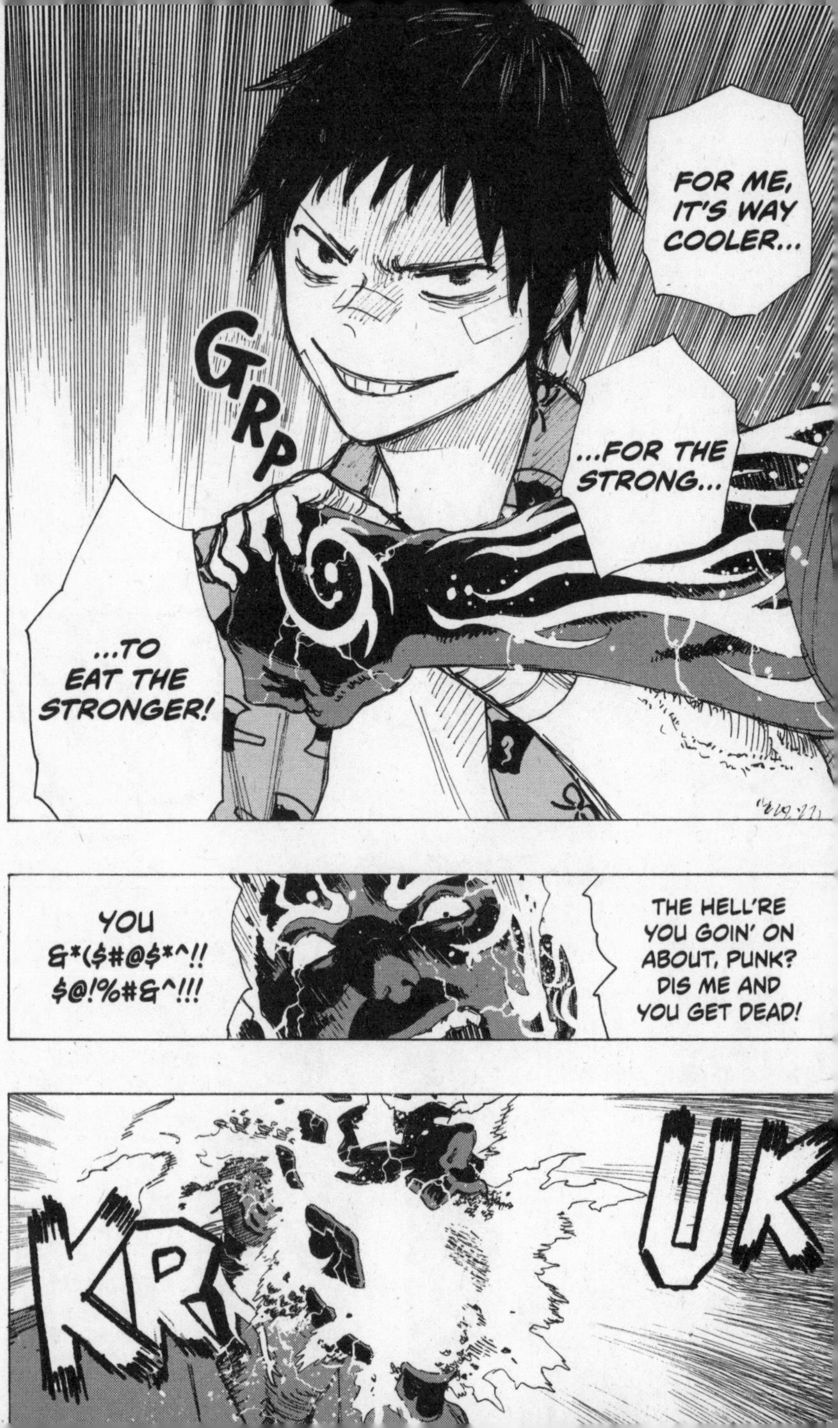
FOR ME, IT'S WAY COOLER...
GRP
...FOR THE STRONG...
...TO EAT THE STRONGER!
THE HELL'RE YOU GOIN' ON ABOUT, PUNK? DIS ME AND YOU GET DEAD!
YOU &*($#@$*^!! $@!%#&^!!!
KR
UK

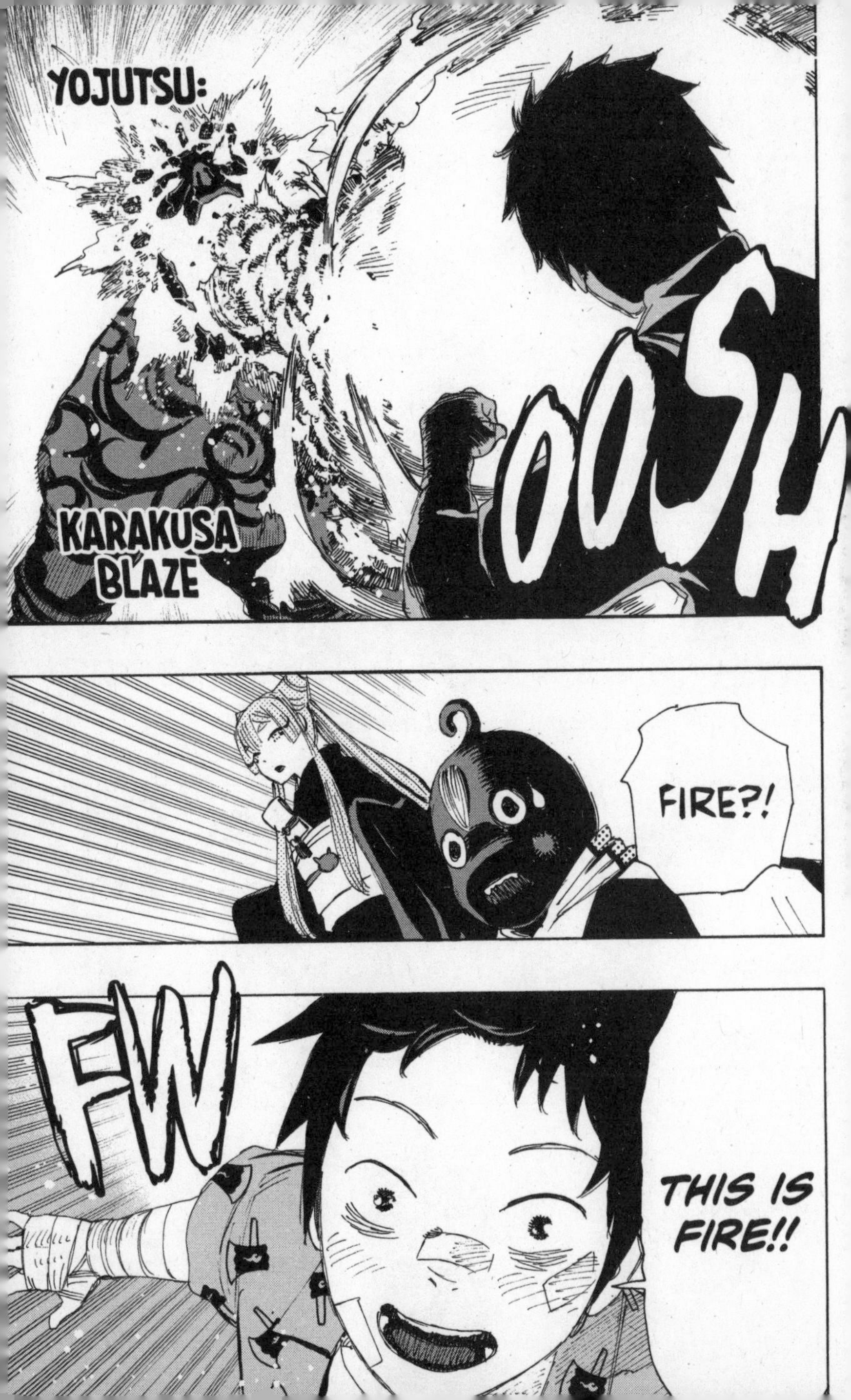
YOJUTSU:
KARAKUSA BLAZE
OOSH
FIRE?!
FW
THIS IS FIRE!!

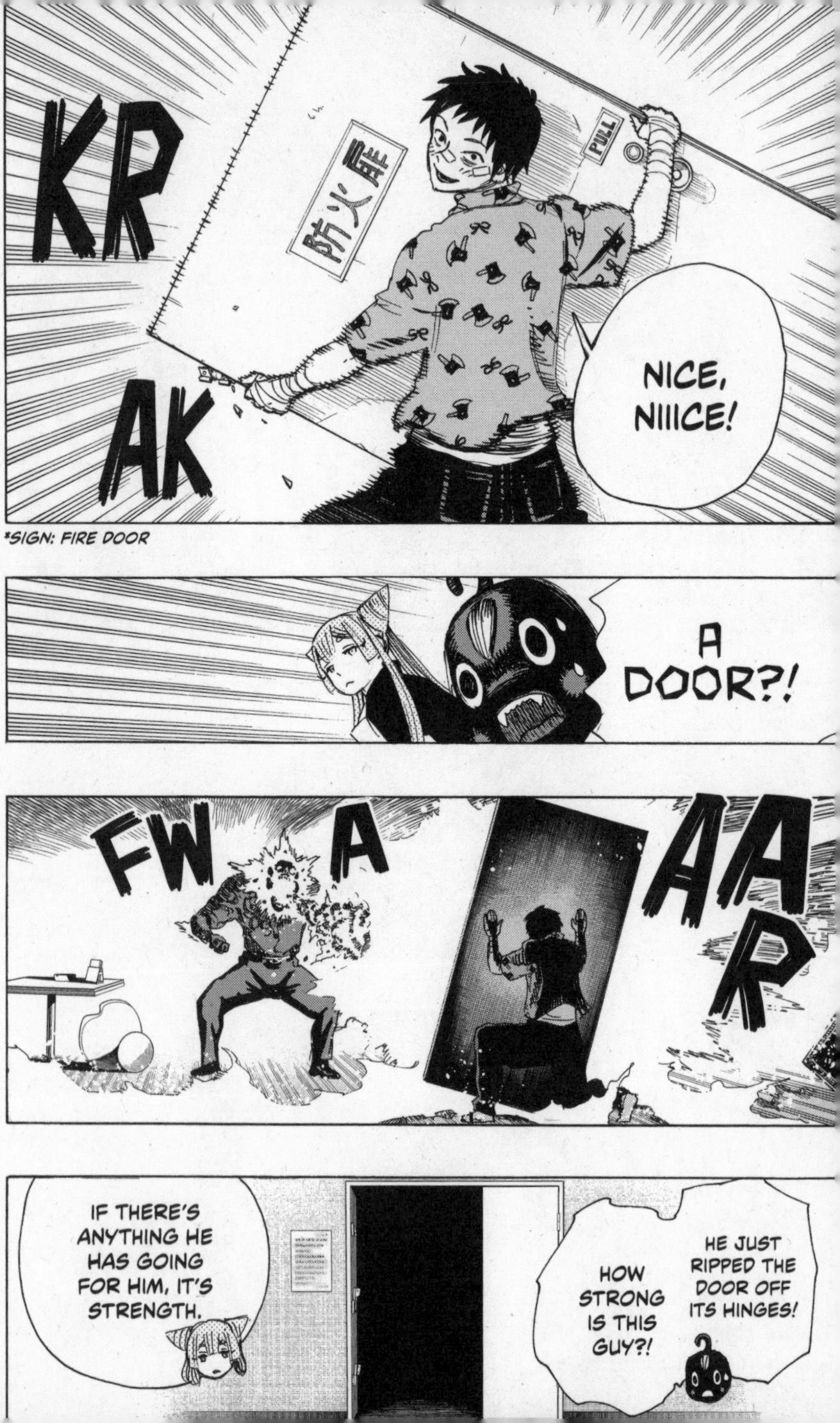
KRAK
防火扉
PULL
NICE, NIIICE!
*SIGN: FIRE DOOR
A DOOR?!
FWAAAR
HE JUST RIPPED THE DOOR OFF ITS HINGES!
HOW STRONG IS THIS GUY?!
IF THERE'S ANYTHING HE HAS GOING FOR HIM, IT'S STRENGTH.

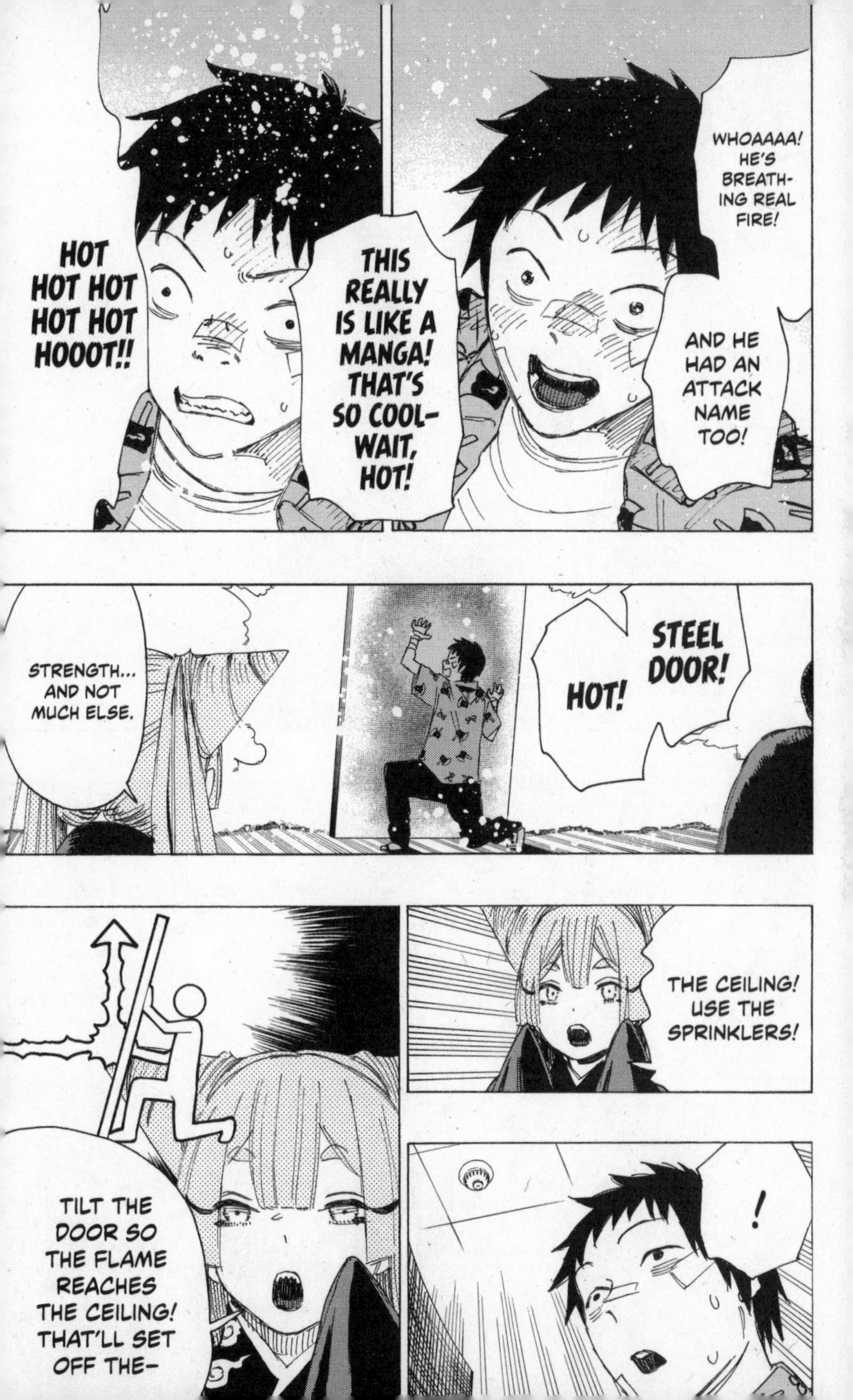
WHOAAAA! HE'S BREATHING REAL FIRE!
AND HE HAD AN ATTACK NAME TOO!
THIS REALLY IS LIKE A MANGA! THAT'S SO COOL- WAIT, HOT!
HOT HOT HOT HOT HOT HOOOT!!
STEEL DOOR!
HOT!
STRENGTH... AND NOT MUCH ELSE.
THE CEILING! USE THE SPRINKLERS!
!
TILT THE DOOR SO THE FLAME REACHES THE CEILING! THAT'LL SET OFF THE-

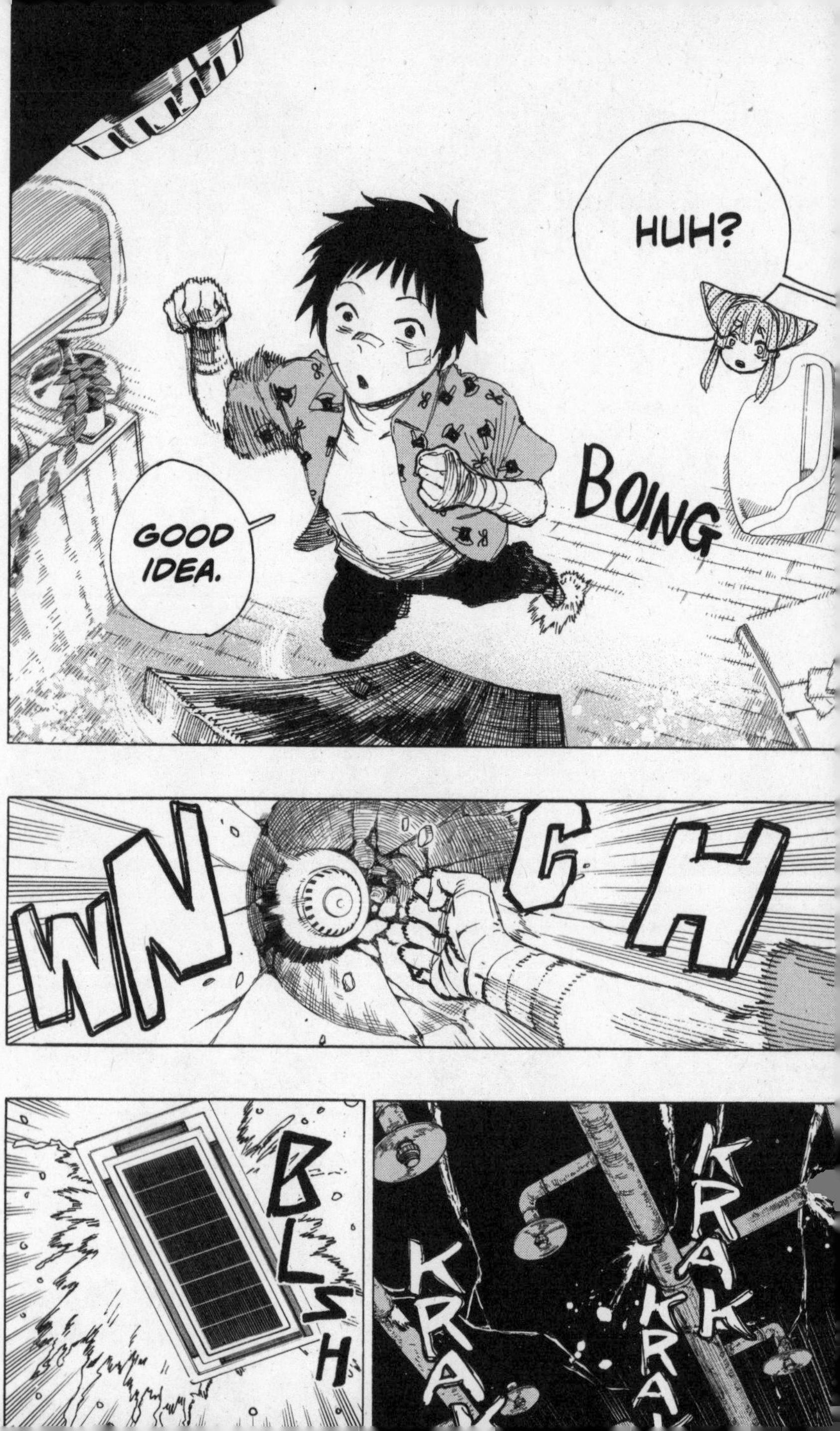
HUH?
BOING
GOOD IDEA.
WNCH
KRAK
KRA
KRA
BLSH

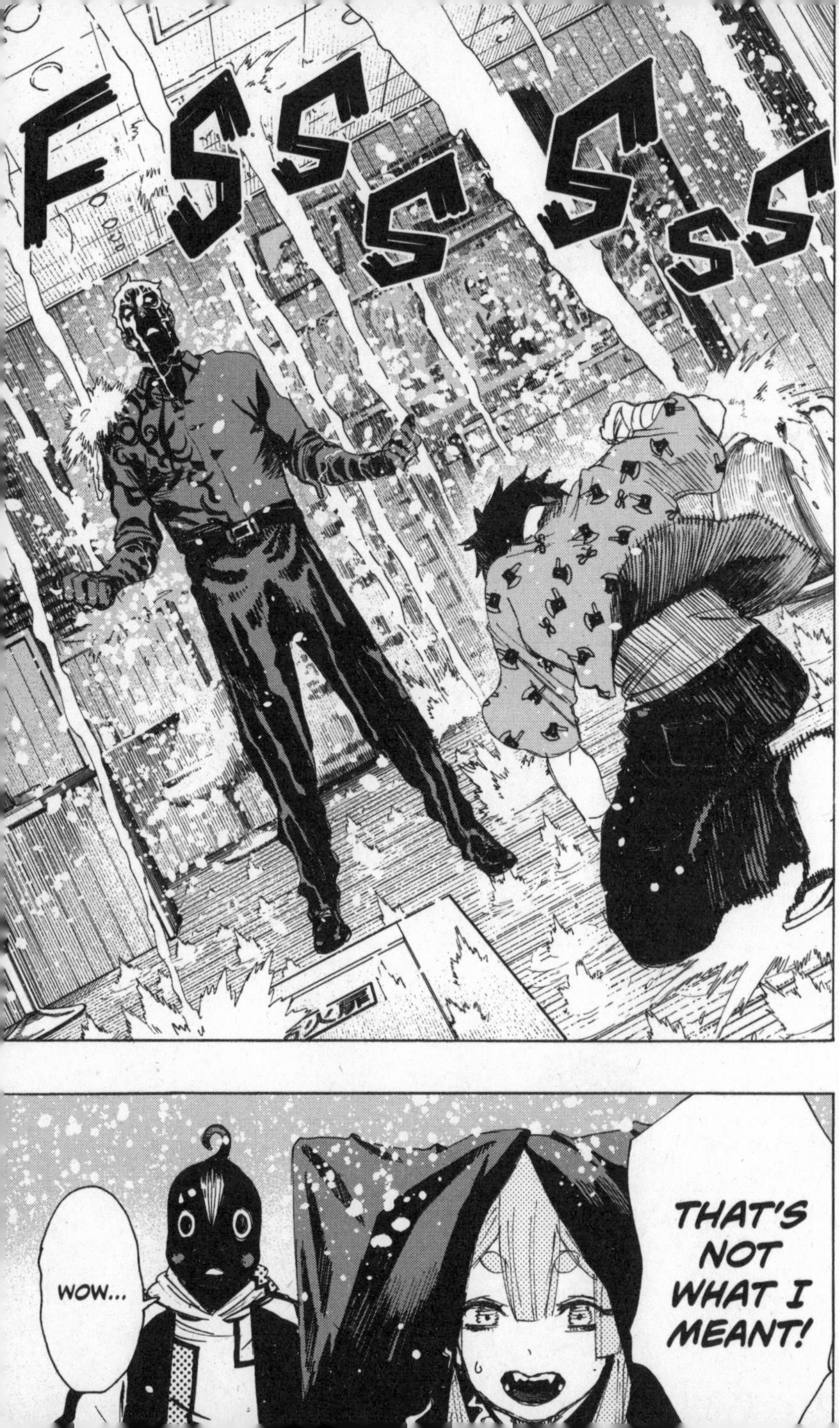
FSSSSSS
THAT'S NOT WHAT I MEANT!
WOW...

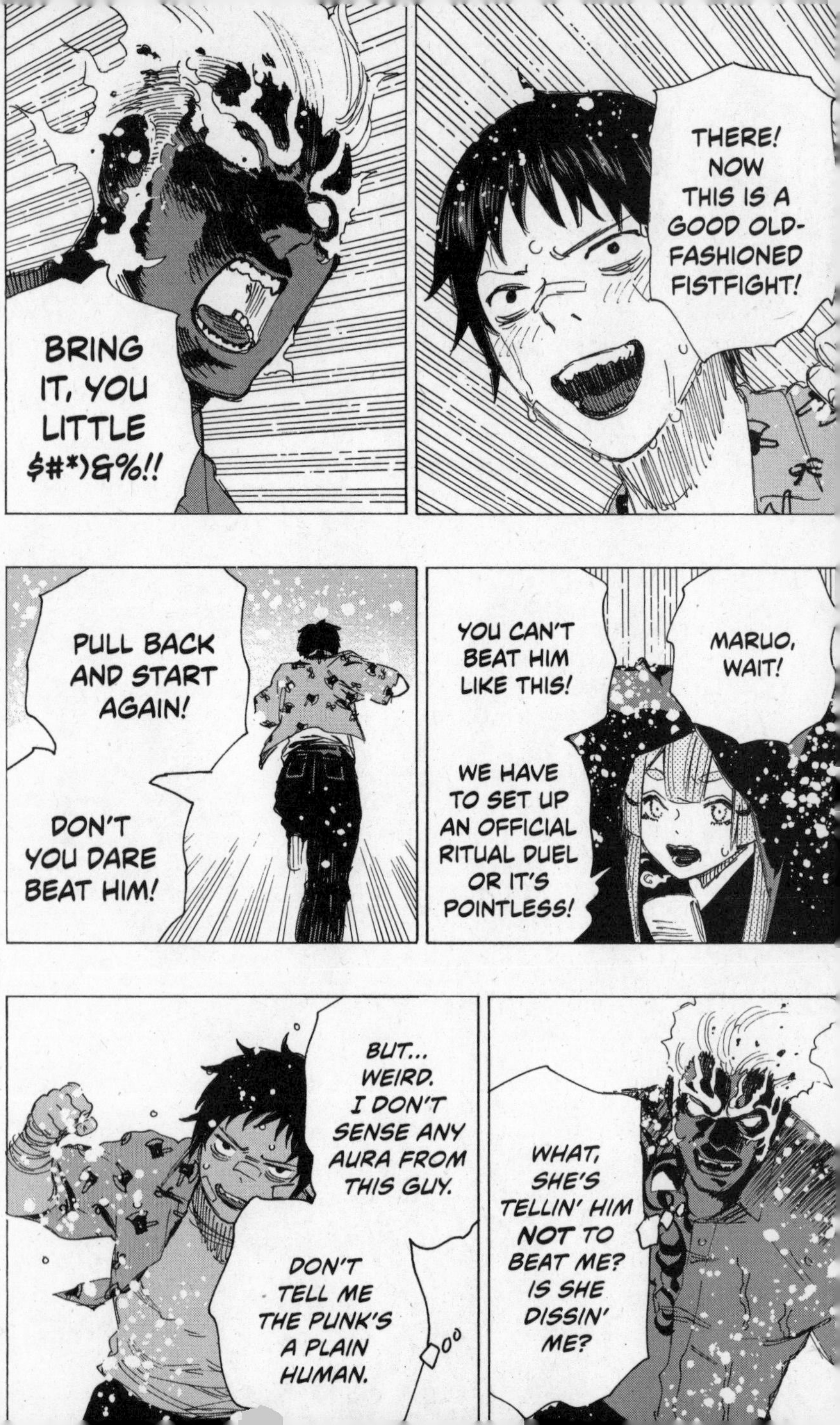
THERE! NOW THIS IS A GOOD OLD-FASHIONED FISTFIGHT!
BRING IT, YOU LITTLE $#*)&%!!
MARUO, WAIT!
YOU CAN'T BEAT HIM LIKE THIS!
WE HAVE TO SET UP AN OFFICIAL RITUAL DUEL OR IT'S POINTLESS!
PULL BACK AND START AGAIN!
DON'T YOU DARE BEAT HIM!
WHAT, SHE'S TELLIN' HIM **NOT** TO BEAT ME? IS SHE DISSIN' ME?
BUT... WEIRD. I DON'T SENSE ANY AURA FROM THIS GUY.
DON'T TELL ME THE PUNK'S A PLAIN HUMAN.

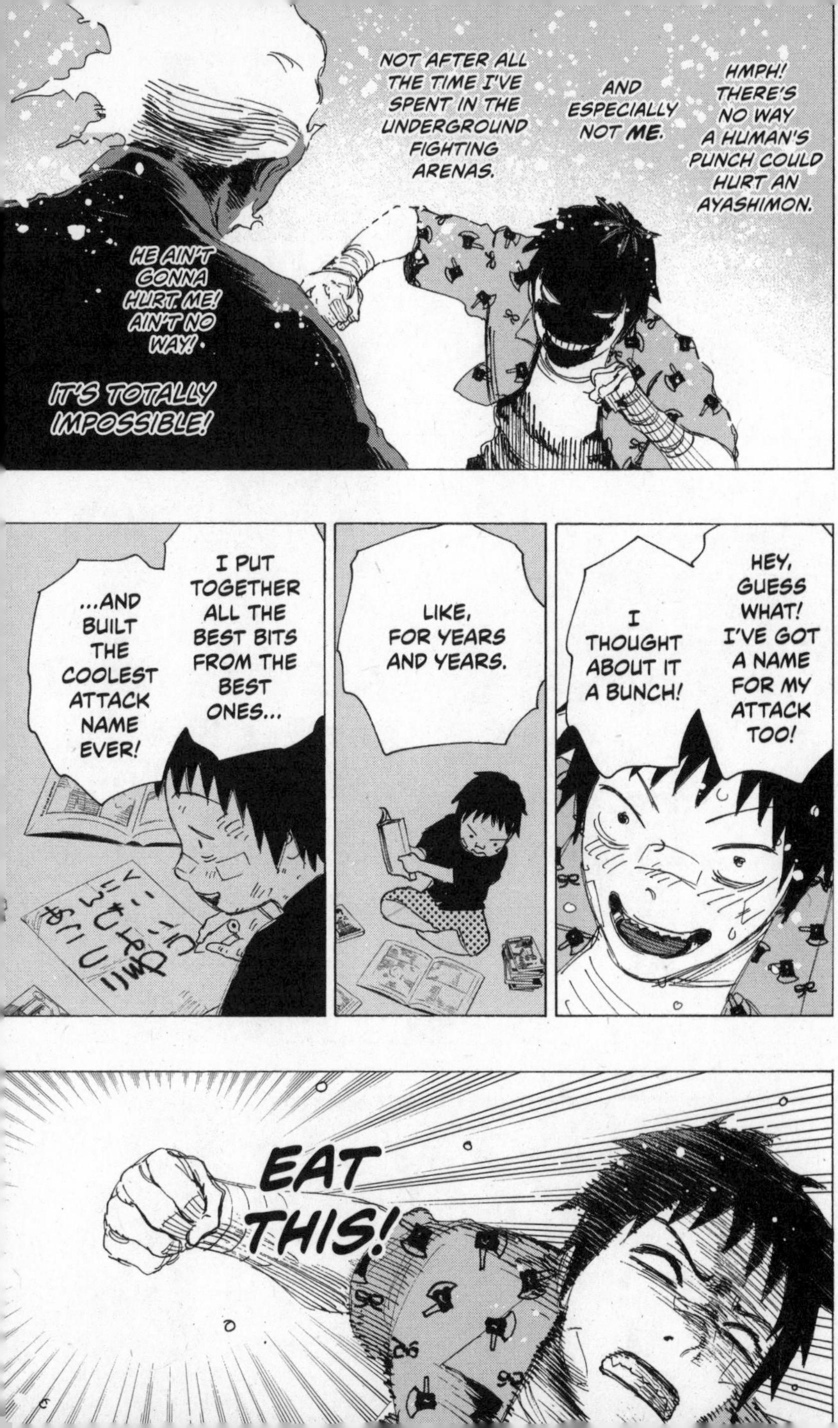
HMPH! THERE'S NO WAY A HUMAN'S PUNCH COULD HURT AN AYASHIMON.
AND ESPECIALLY NOT ME.
NOT AFTER ALL THE TIME I'VE SPENT IN THE UNDERGROUND FIGHTING ARENAS.
HE AIN'T GONNA HURT ME! AIN'T NO WAY!
IT'S TOTALLY IMPOSSIBLE!
HEY, GUESS WHAT! I'VE GOT A NAME FOR MY ATTACK TOO!
I THOUGHT ABOUT IT A BUNCH!
LIKE, FOR YEARS AND YEARS.
I PUT TOGETHER ALL THE BEST BITS FROM THE BEST ONES...
...AND BUILT THE COOLEST ATTACK NAME EVER!
EAT THIS!

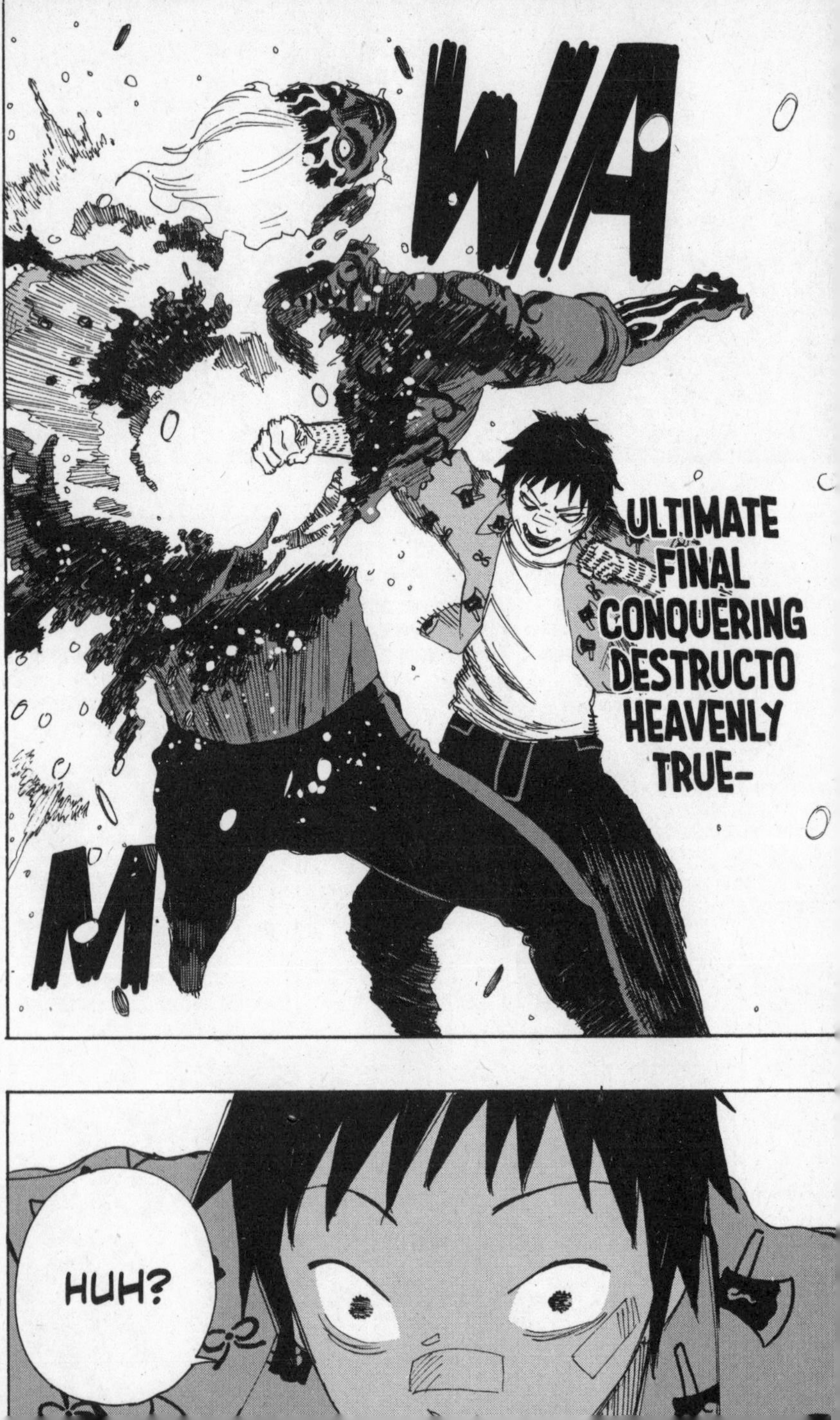
WA
M
ULTIMATE FINAL CONQUERING DESTRUCTO HEAVENLY TRUE-
HUH?

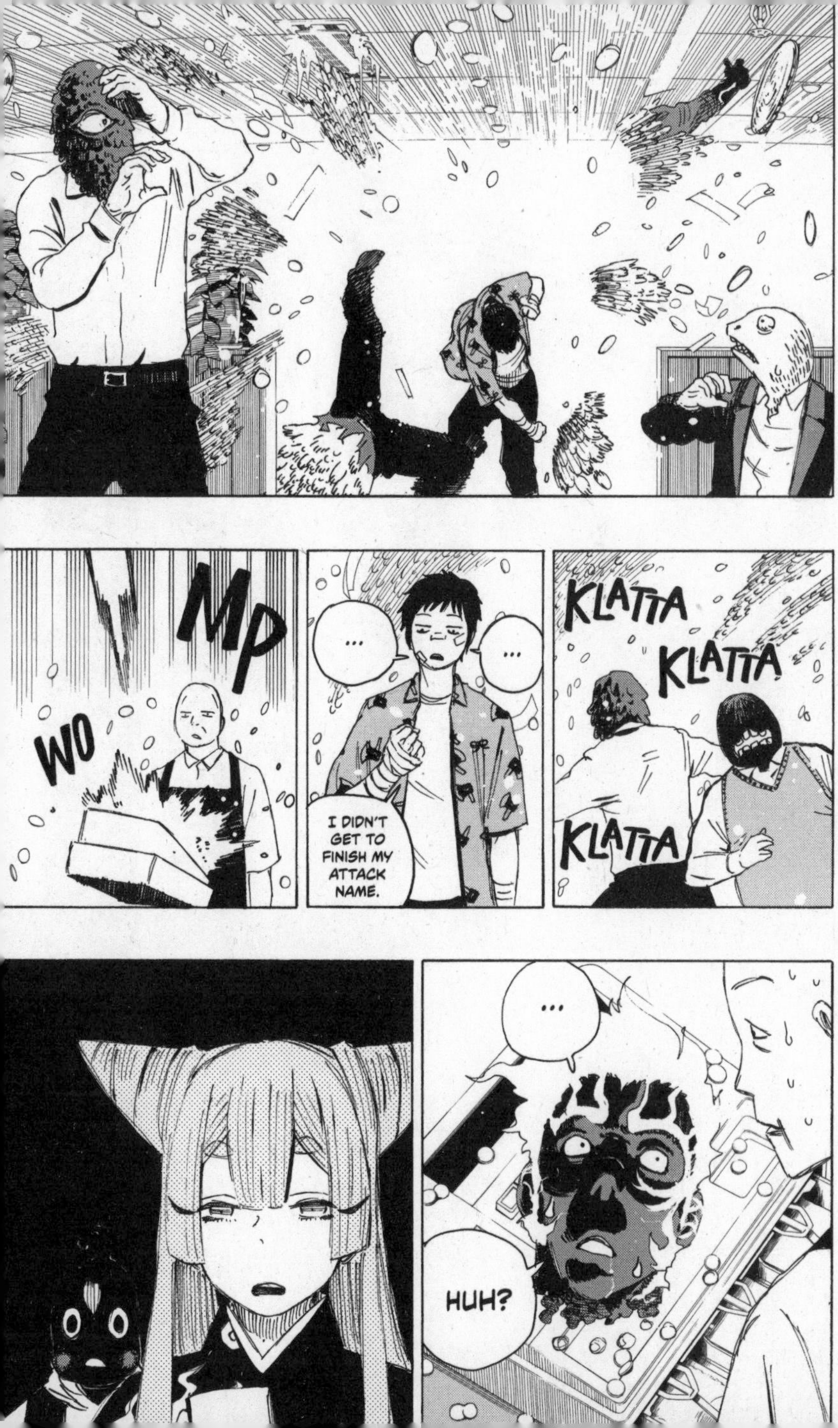
KLATTA
KLATTA
KLATTA
...
...
I DIDN'T GET TO FINISH MY ATTACK NAME.
WOMP
...
HUH?

KABUKICHO MONSTER MANUAL

Yokai: Hashihime

Even in the most casual of situations, she can always be found wearing a suit. Her lace veil and gloves are signs of mourning for the late Chairman Kioh. She is so massively fond of sweets that she always keeps a pack of matcha-flavored pudding cups in the break-room fridge.

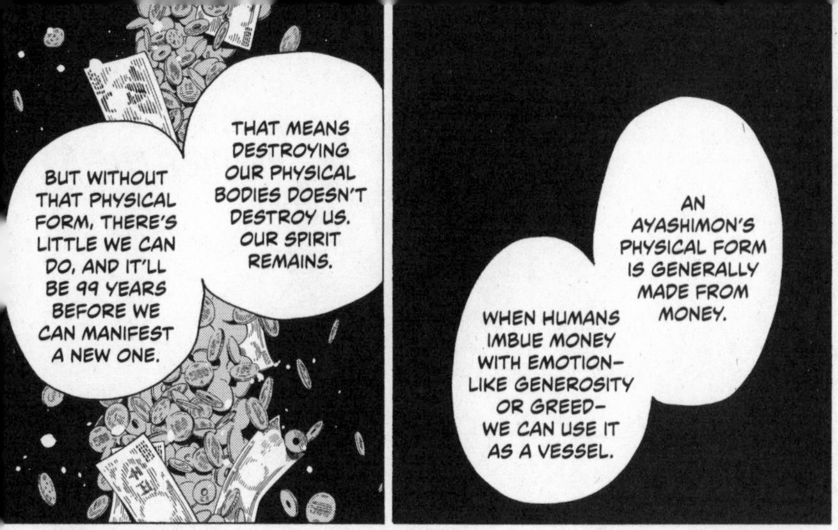
AN AYASHIMON'S PHYSICAL FORM IS GENERALLY MADE FROM MONEY.
WHEN HUMANS IMBUE MONEY WITH EMOTION—LIKE GENEROSITY OR GREED—WE CAN USE IT AS A VESSEL.
THAT MEANS DESTROYING OUR PHYSICAL BODIES DOESN'T DESTROY US. OUR SPIRIT REMAINS.
BUT WITHOUT THAT PHYSICAL FORM, THERE'S LITTLE WE CAN DO, AND IT'LL BE 99 YEARS BEFORE WE CAN MANIFEST A NEW ONE.

Chapter 4

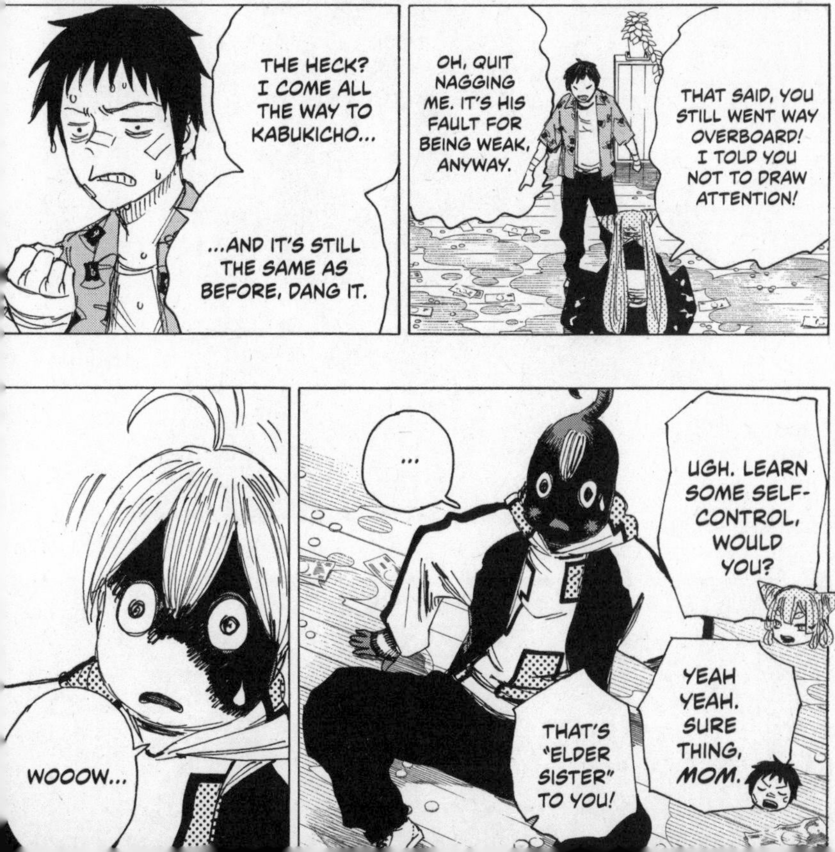
THAT SAID, YOU STILL WENT WAY OVERBOARD! I TOLD YOU NOT TO DRAW ATTENTION!
OH, QUIT NAGGING ME. IT'S HIS FAULT FOR BEING WEAK, ANYWAY.
THE HECK? I COME ALL THE WAY TO KABUKICHO...
...AND IT'S STILL THE SAME AS BEFORE, DANG IT.
UGH. LEARN SOME SELF-CONTROL, WOULD YOU?
...
YEAH YEAH. SURE THING, *MOM.*
THAT'S "ELDER SISTER" TO YOU!
WOOOW...

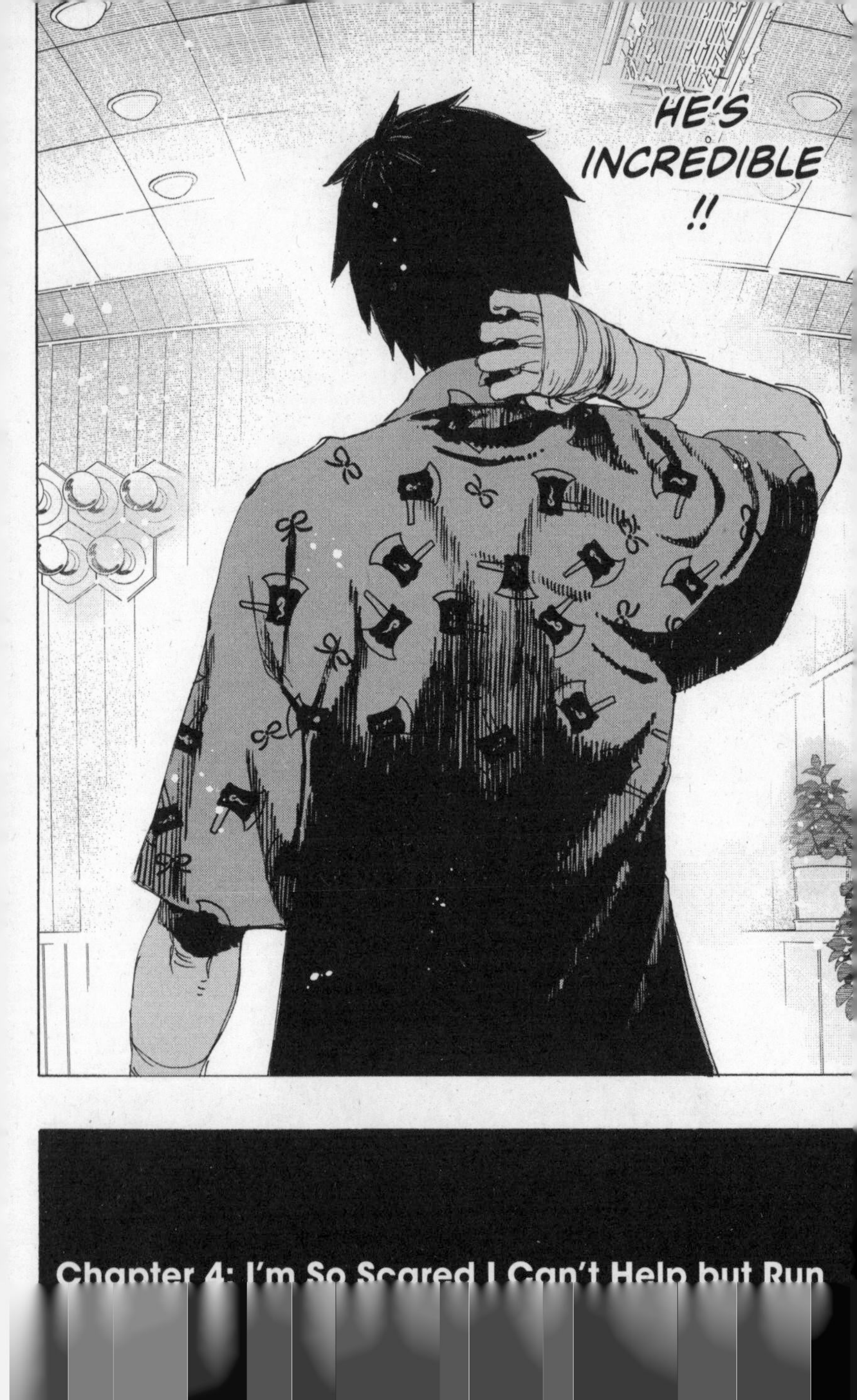
HE'S INCREDIBLE !!

Chapter 4: I'm So Scared I Can't Help but Run

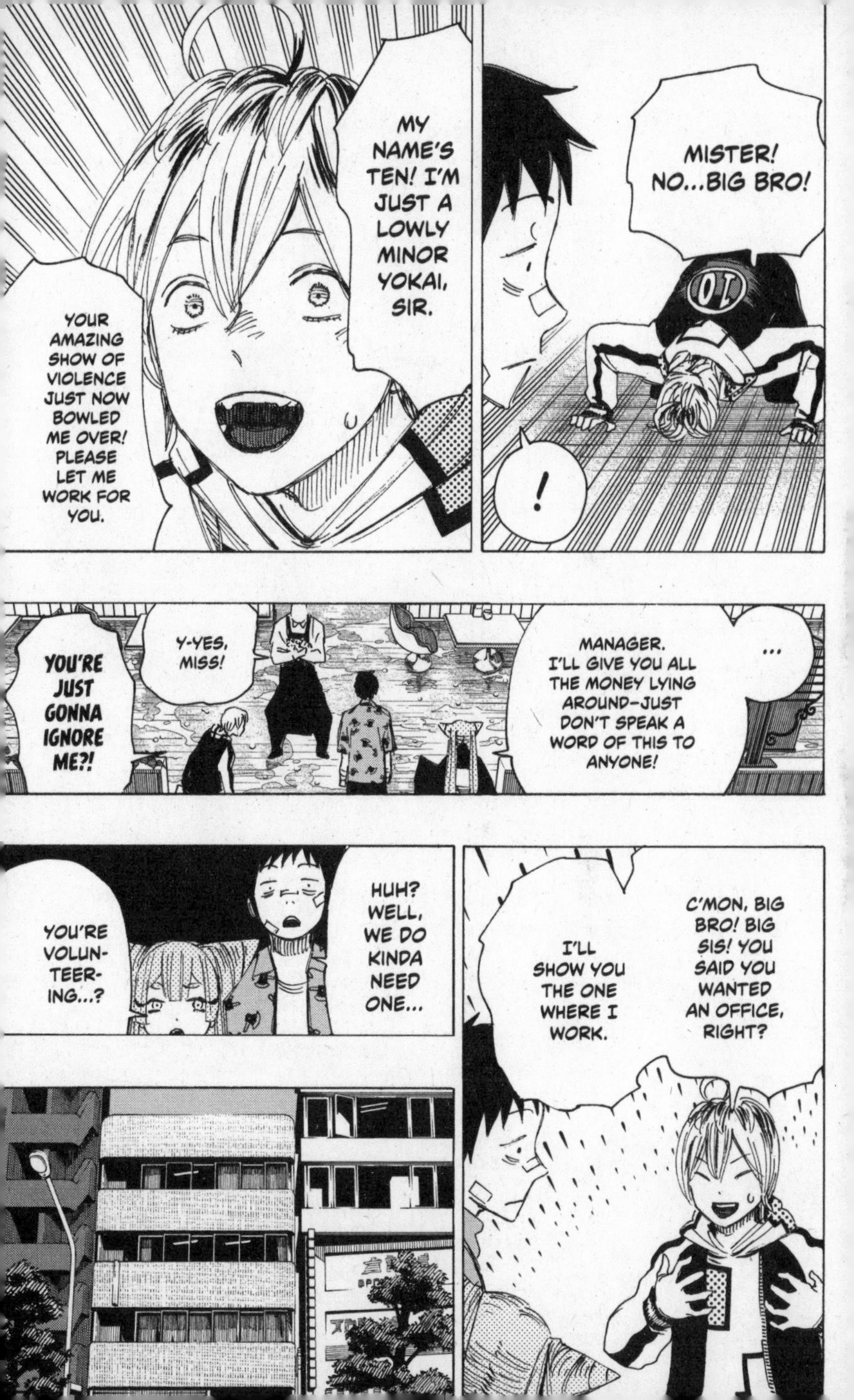
MISTER! NO...BIG BRO!
!
MY NAME'S TEN! I'M JUST A LOWLY MINOR YOKAI, SIR.
YOUR AMAZING SHOW OF VIOLENCE JUST NOW BOWLED ME OVER! PLEASE LET ME WORK FOR YOU.
...
MANAGER. I'LL GIVE YOU ALL THE MONEY LYING AROUND—JUST DON'T SPEAK A WORD OF THIS TO ANYONE!
Y-YES, MISS!
YOU'RE JUST GONNA IGNORE ME?!
C'MON, BIG BRO! BIG SIS! YOU SAID YOU WANTED AN OFFICE, RIGHT?
I'LL SHOW YOU THE ONE WHERE I WORK.
HUH? WELL, WE DO KINDA NEED ONE...
YOU'RE VOLUN-TEER-ING...?

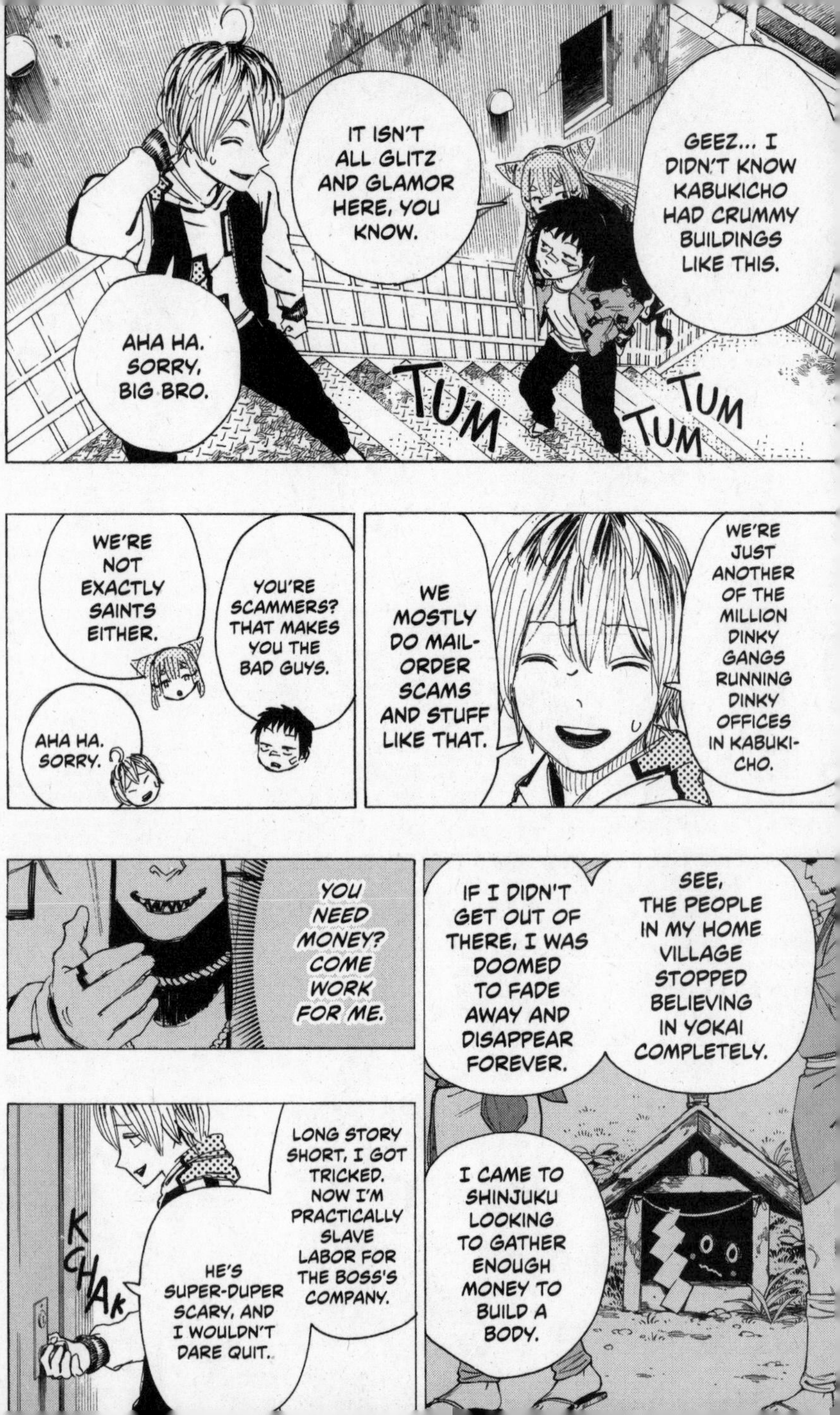
GEEZ... I DIDN'T KNOW KABUKICHO HAD CRUMMY BUILDINGS LIKE THIS.
IT ISN'T ALL GLITZ AND GLAMOR HERE, YOU KNOW.
AHA HA. SORRY, BIG BRO.
TUM TUM TUM
WE'RE JUST ANOTHER OF THE MILLION DINKY GANGS RUNNING DINKY OFFICES IN KABUKI-CHO.
WE MOSTLY DO MAIL-ORDER SCAMS AND STUFF LIKE THAT.
YOU'RE SCAMMERS? THAT MAKES YOU THE BAD GUYS.
WE'RE NOT EXACTLY SAINTS EITHER.
AHA HA. SORRY.
SEE, THE PEOPLE IN MY HOME VILLAGE STOPPED BELIEVING IN YOKAI COMPLETELY.
IF I DIDN'T GET OUT OF THERE, I WAS DOOMED TO FADE AWAY AND DISAPPEAR FOREVER.
I CAME TO SHINJUKU LOOKING TO GATHER ENOUGH MONEY TO BUILD A BODY.
YOU NEED MONEY? COME WORK FOR ME.
LONG STORY SHORT, I GOT TRICKED. NOW I'M PRACTICALLY SLAVE LABOR FOR THE BOSS'S COMPANY.
HE'S SUPER-DUPER SCARY, AND I WOULDN'T DARE QUIT.
KCHAK

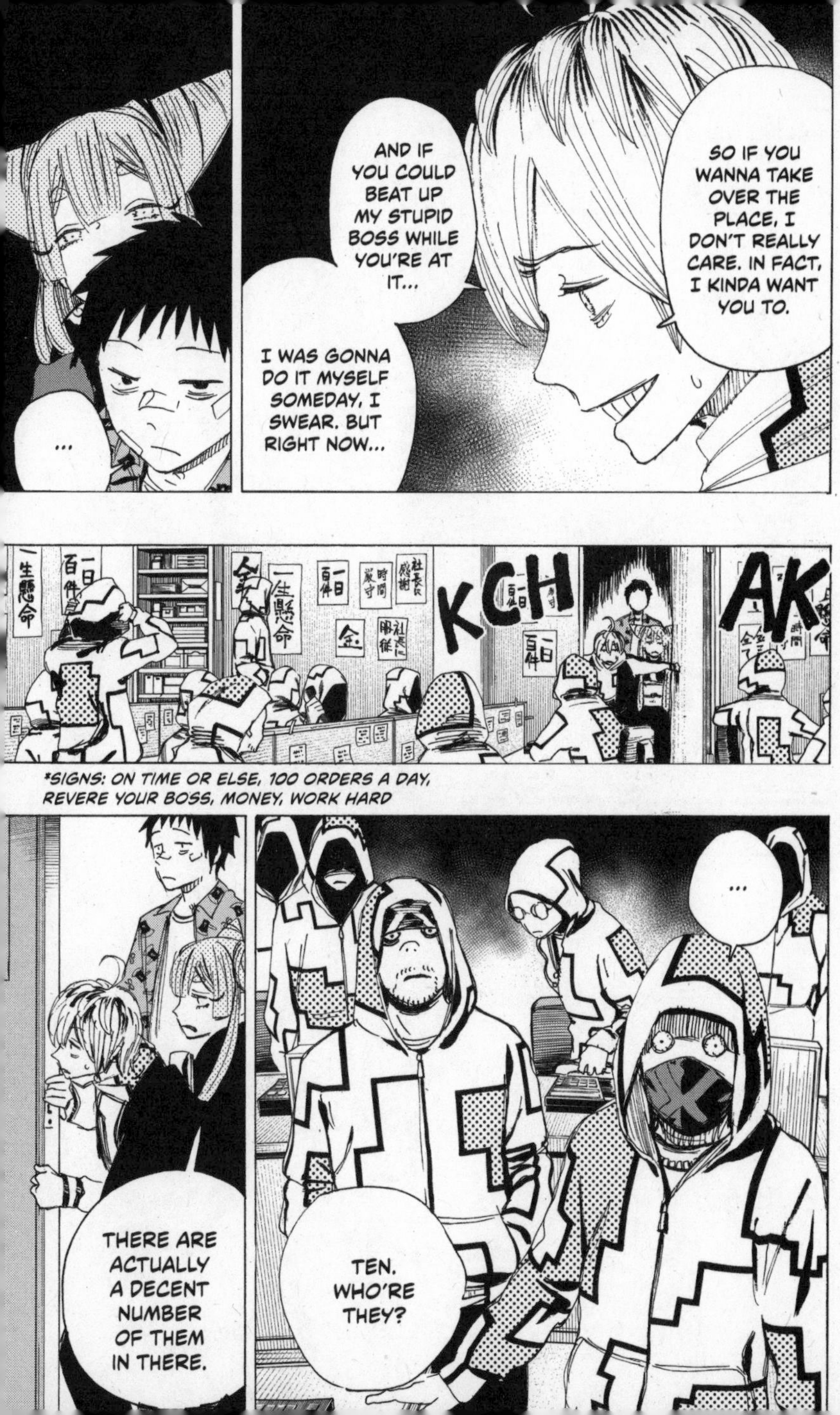
SO IF YOU WANNA TAKE OVER THE PLACE, I DON'T REALLY CARE. IN FACT, I KINDA WANT YOU TO.
AND IF YOU COULD BEAT UP MY STUPID BOSS WHILE YOU'RE AT IT...
I WAS GONNA DO IT MYSELF SOMEDAY, I SWEAR. BUT RIGHT NOW...
...
KCH
AK
*SIGNS: ON TIME OR ELSE, 100 ORDERS A DAY, REVERE YOUR BOSS, MONEY, WORK HARD
...
TEN. WHO'RE THEY?
THERE ARE ACTUALLY A DECENT NUMBER OF THEM IN THERE.

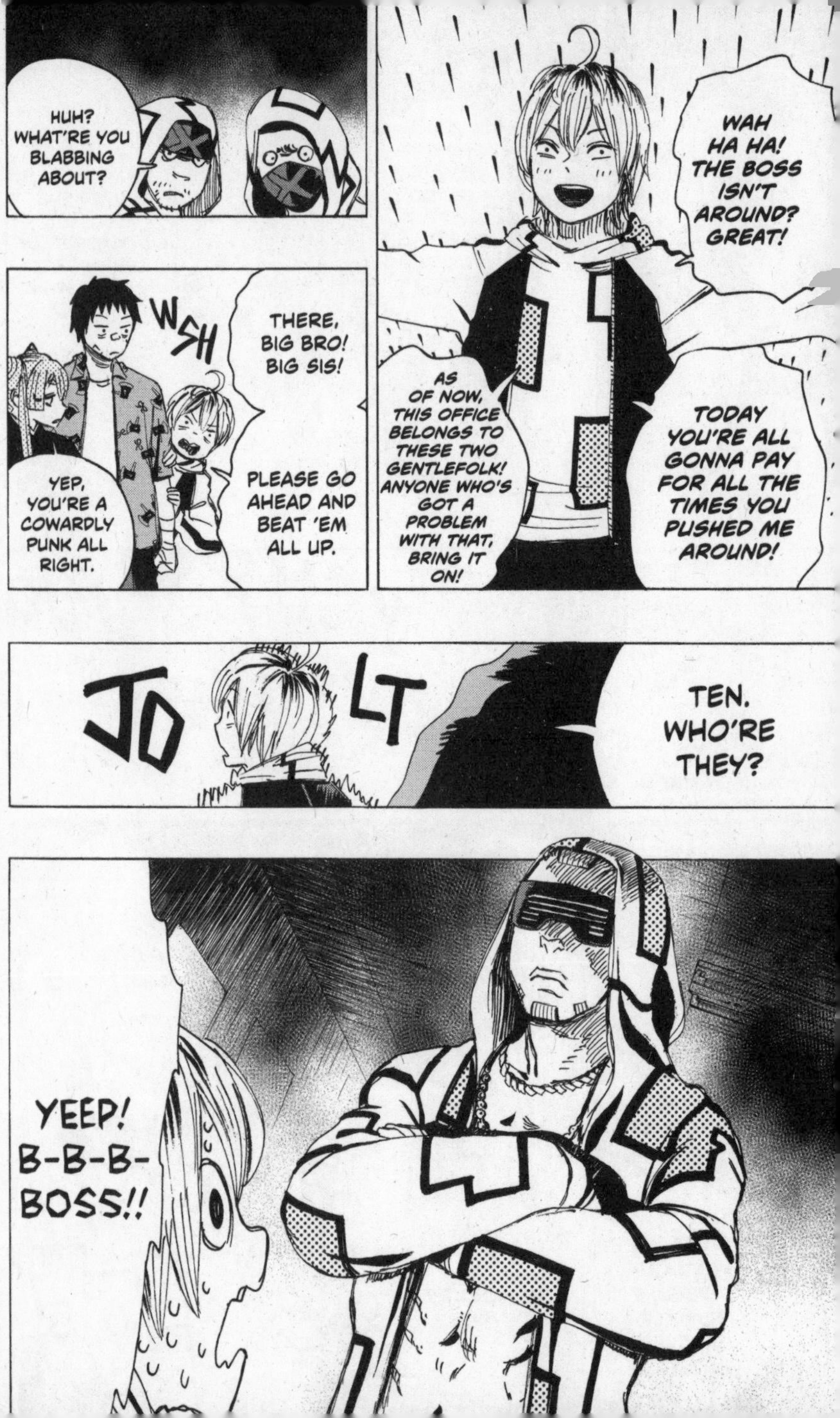
WAH HA HA! THE BOSS ISN'T AROUND? GREAT!
TODAY YOU'RE ALL GONNA PAY FOR ALL THE TIMES YOU PUSHED ME AROUND!
AS OF NOW, THIS OFFICE BELONGS TO THESE TWO GENTLEFOLK! ANYONE WHO'S GOT A PROBLEM WITH THAT, BRING IT ON!
HUH? WHAT'RE YOU BLABBING ABOUT?
THERE, BIG BRO! BIG SIS!
PLEASE GO AHEAD AND BEAT 'EM ALL UP.
WSH
YEP, YOU'RE A COWARDLY PUNK ALL RIGHT.
TEN. WHO'RE THEY?
JOLT
YEEP! B-B-B-BOSS!!

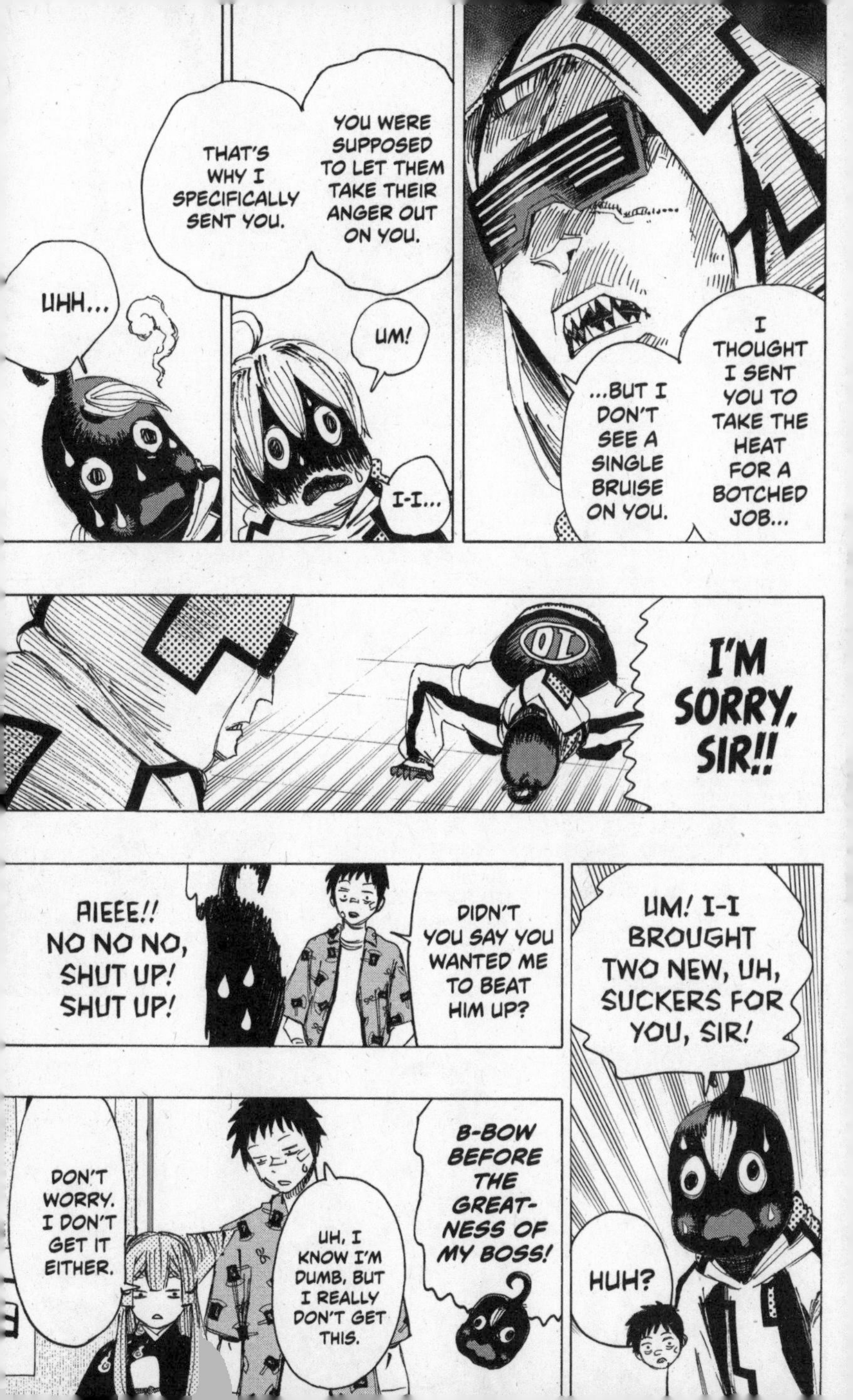
I THOUGHT I SENT YOU TO TAKE THE HEAT FOR A BOTCHED JOB...
...BUT I DON'T SEE A SINGLE BRUISE ON YOU.
YOU WERE SUPPOSED TO LET THEM TAKE THEIR ANGER OUT ON YOU.
THAT'S WHY I SPECIFICALLY SENT YOU.
UM!
I-I...
UHH...
I'M SORRY, SIR!!
UM! I-I BROUGHT TWO NEW, UH, SUCKERS FOR YOU, SIR!
HUH?
DIDN'T YOU SAY YOU WANTED ME TO BEAT HIM UP?
AIEEE!! NO NO NO, SHUT UP! SHUT UP!
B-BOW BEFORE THE GREAT-NESS OF MY BOSS!
UH, I KNOW I'M DUMB, BUT I REALLY DON'T GET THIS.
DON'T WORRY. I DON'T GET IT EITHER.

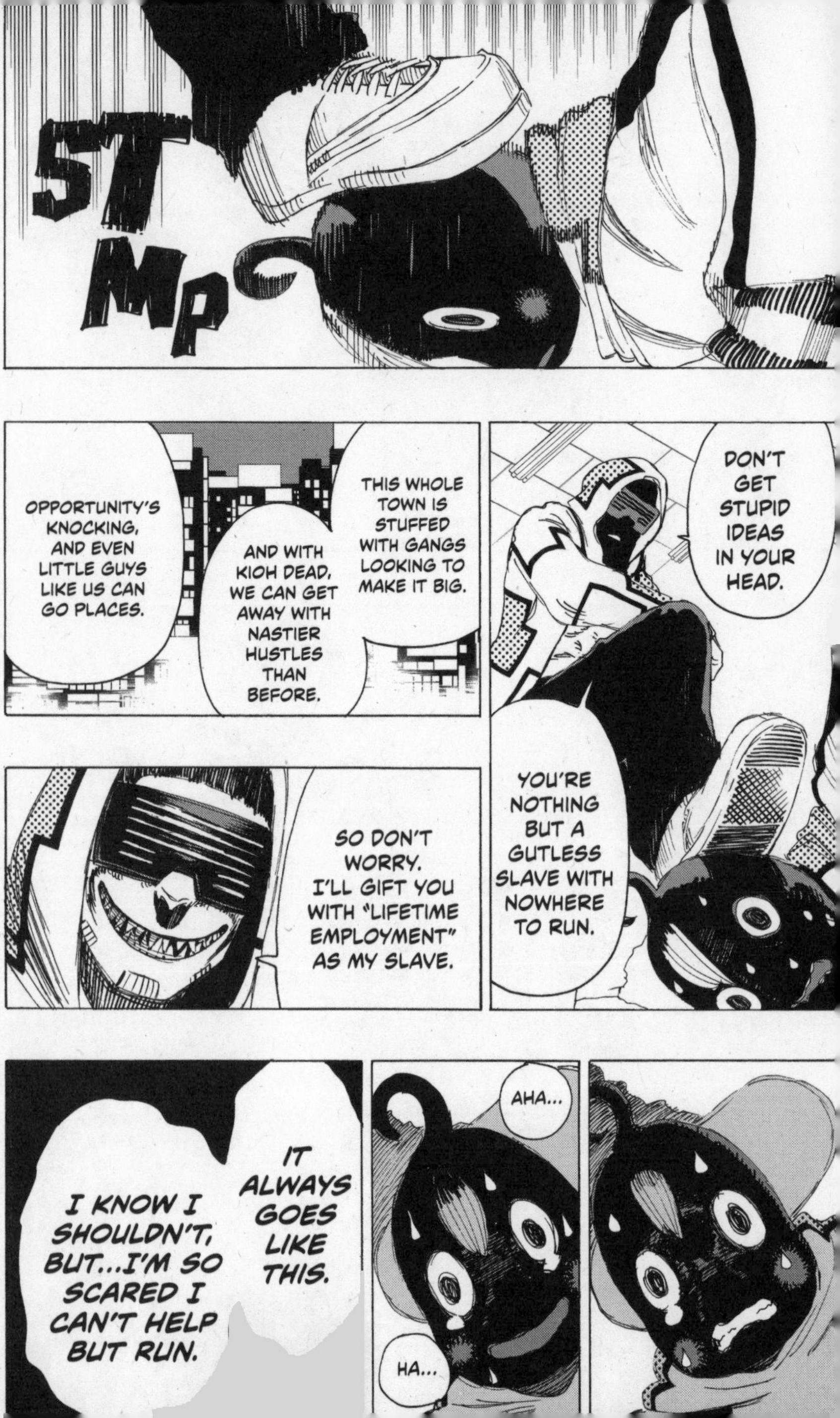
STMP
DON'T GET STUPID IDEAS IN YOUR HEAD.
THIS WHOLE TOWN IS STUFFED WITH GANGS LOOKING TO MAKE IT BIG.
AND WITH KIOH DEAD, WE CAN GET AWAY WITH NASTIER HUSTLES THAN BEFORE.
OPPORTUNITY'S KNOCKING, AND EVEN LITTLE GUYS LIKE US CAN GO PLACES.
YOU'RE NOTHING BUT A GUTLESS SLAVE WITH NOWHERE TO RUN.
SO DON'T WORRY. I'LL GIFT YOU WITH "LIFETIME EMPLOYMENT" AS MY SLAVE.
AHA...
HA...
IT ALWAYS GOES LIKE THIS.
I KNOW I SHOULDN'T, BUT...I'M SO SCARED I CAN'T HELP BUT RUN.

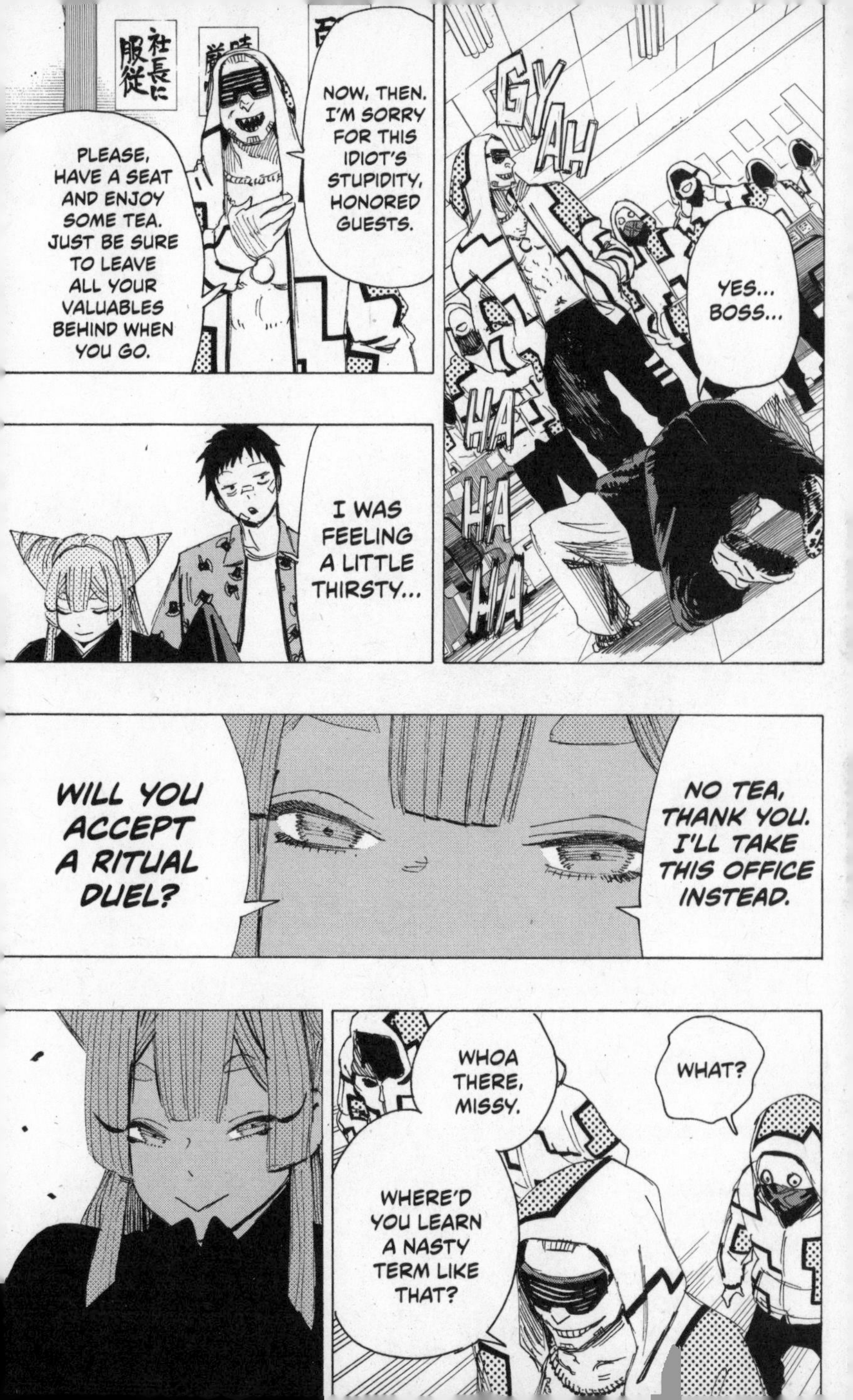
GYAH
YES... BOSS...
HA HA HA
社長に服従
NOW, THEN. I'M SORRY FOR THIS IDIOT'S STUPIDITY, HONORED GUESTS.
PLEASE, HAVE A SEAT AND ENJOY SOME TEA. JUST BE SURE TO LEAVE ALL YOUR VALUABLES BEHIND WHEN YOU GO.
I WAS FEELING A LITTLE THIRSTY...
NO TEA, THANK YOU. I'LL TAKE THIS OFFICE INSTEAD.
WILL YOU ACCEPT A RITUAL DUEL?
WHAT?
WHOA THERE, MISSY.
WHERE'D YOU LEARN A NASTY TERM LIKE THAT?

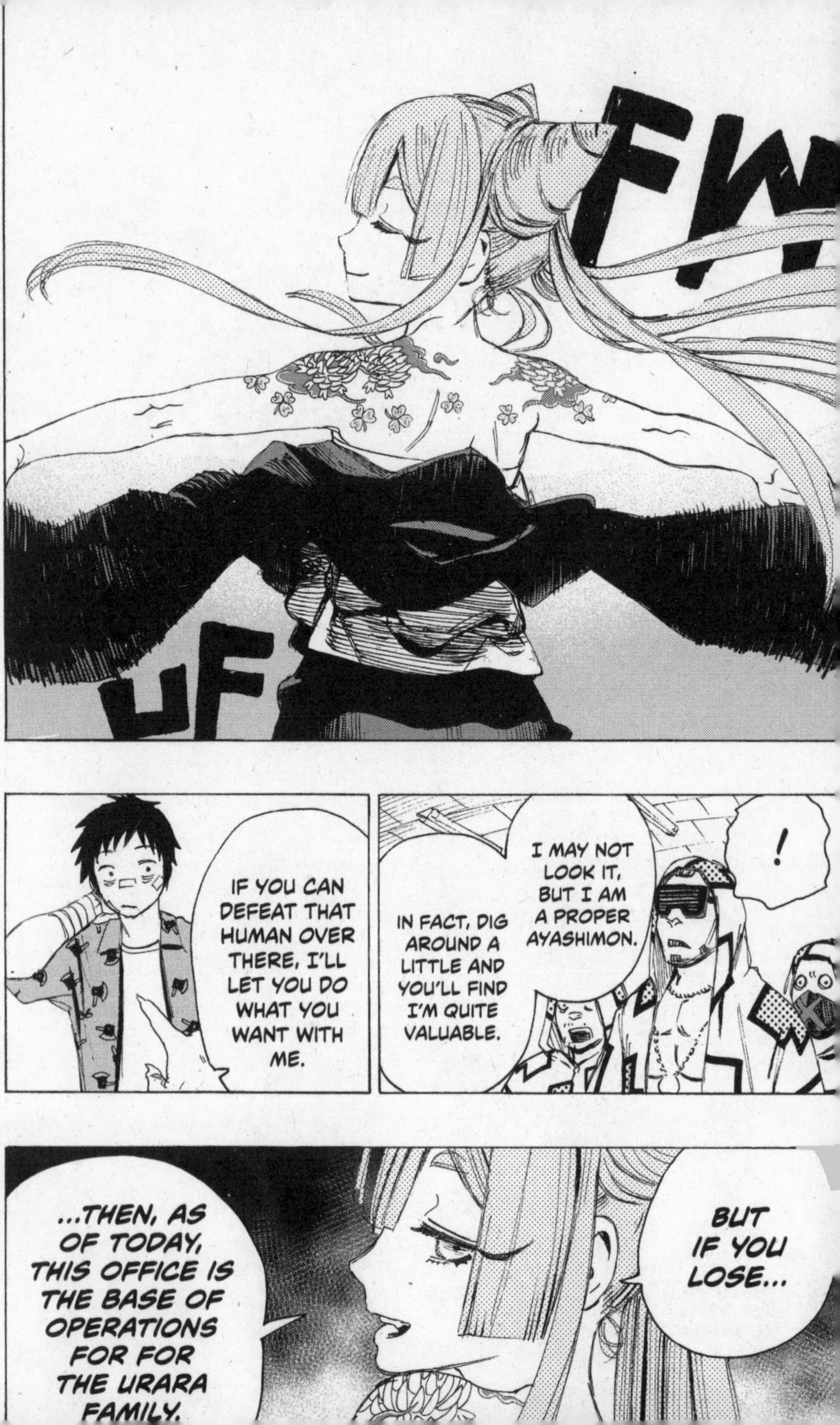
FW
UF
!
I MAY NOT LOOK IT, BUT I AM A PROPER AYASHIMON.
IN FACT, DIG AROUND A LITTLE AND YOU'LL FIND I'M QUITE VALUABLE.
IF YOU CAN DEFEAT THAT HUMAN OVER THERE, I'LL LET YOU DO WHAT YOU WANT WITH ME.
BUT IF YOU LOSE...
...THEN, AS OF TODAY, THIS OFFICE IS THE BASE OF OPERATIONS FOR FOR THE URARA FAMILY.

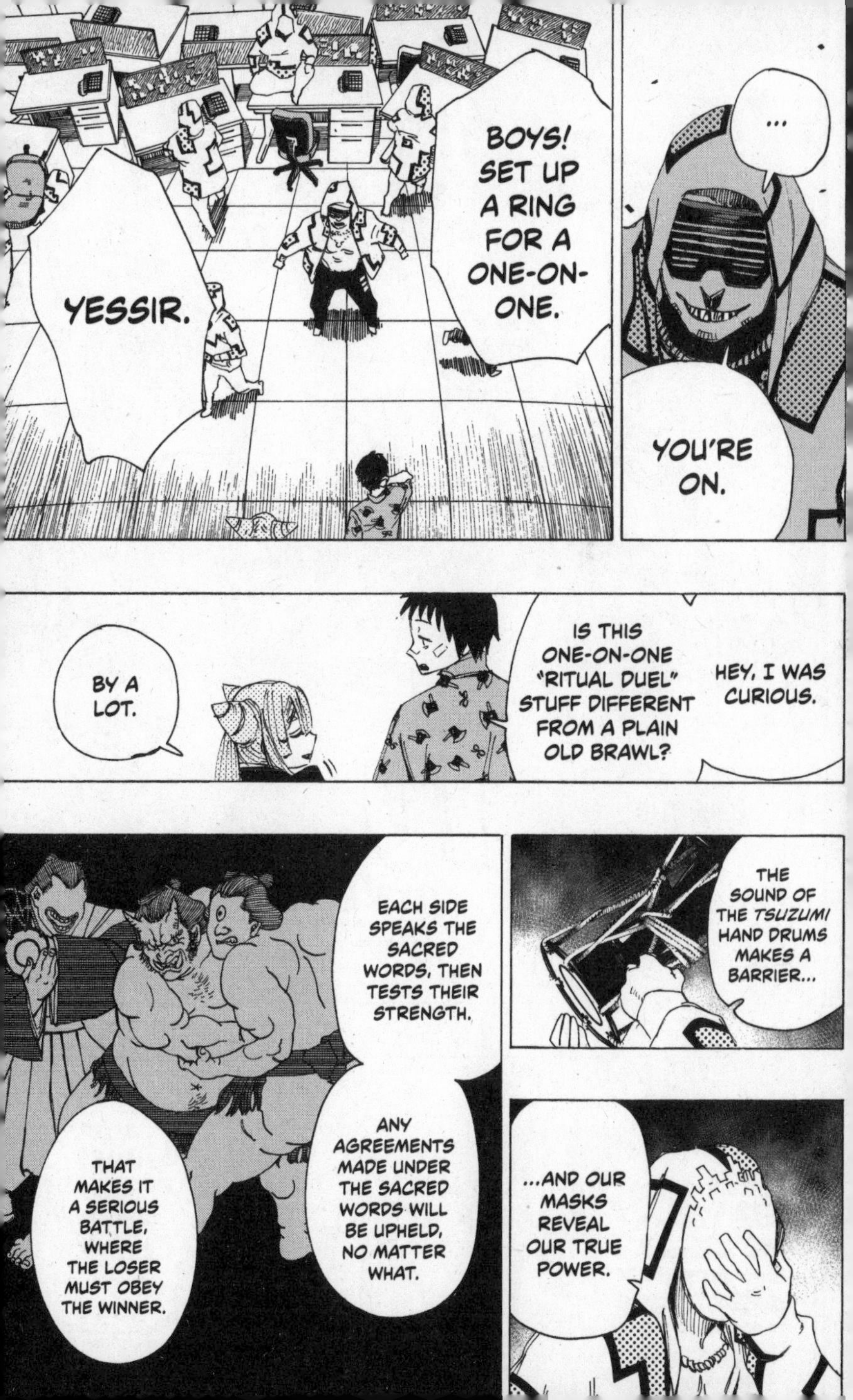
...
YOU'RE ON.
BOYS! SET UP A RING FOR A ONE-ON-ONE.
YESSIR.
HEY, I WAS CURIOUS.
IS THIS ONE-ON-ONE "RITUAL DUEL" STUFF DIFFERENT FROM A PLAIN OLD BRAWL?
BY A LOT.
THE SOUND OF THE *TSUZUMI* HAND DRUMS MAKES A BARRIER...
...AND OUR MASKS REVEAL OUR TRUE POWER.
EACH SIDE SPEAKS THE SACRED WORDS, THEN TESTS THEIR STRENGTH.
ANY AGREEMENTS MADE UNDER THE SACRED WORDS WILL BE UPHELD, NO MATTER WHAT.
THAT MAKES IT A SERIOUS BATTLE, WHERE THE LOSER MUST OBEY THE WINNER.

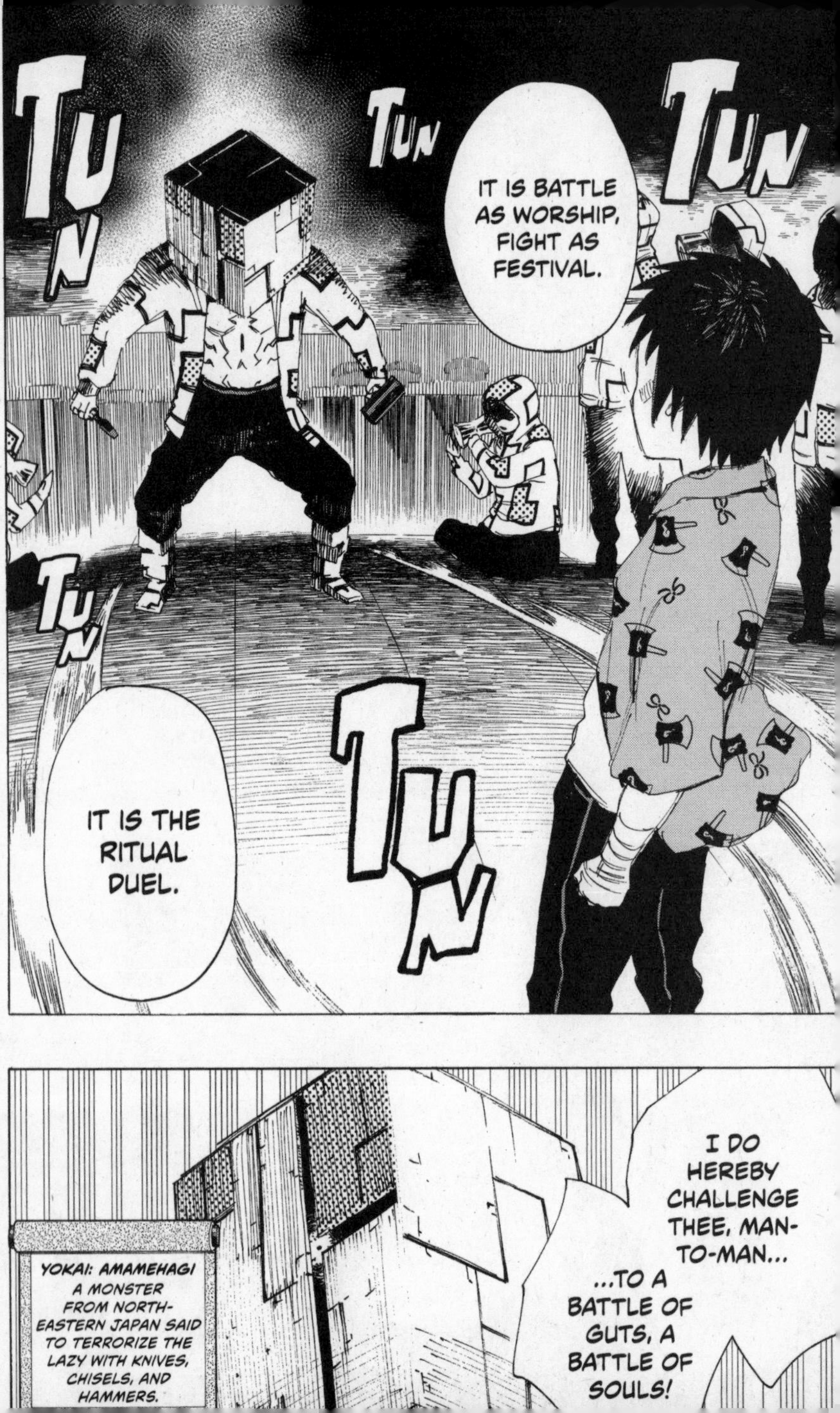
TUN
IT IS BATTLE AS WORSHIP, FIGHT AS FESTIVAL.
TUN
TUN
TUN
TUN
IT IS THE RITUAL DUEL.
I DO HEREBY CHALLENGE THEE, MAN-TO-MAN...
...TO A BATTLE OF GUTS, A BATTLE OF SOULS!
YOKAI: AMAMEHAGI
A MONSTER FROM NORTH-EASTERN JAPAN SAID TO TERRORIZE THE LAZY WITH KNIVES, CHISELS, AND HAMMERS.

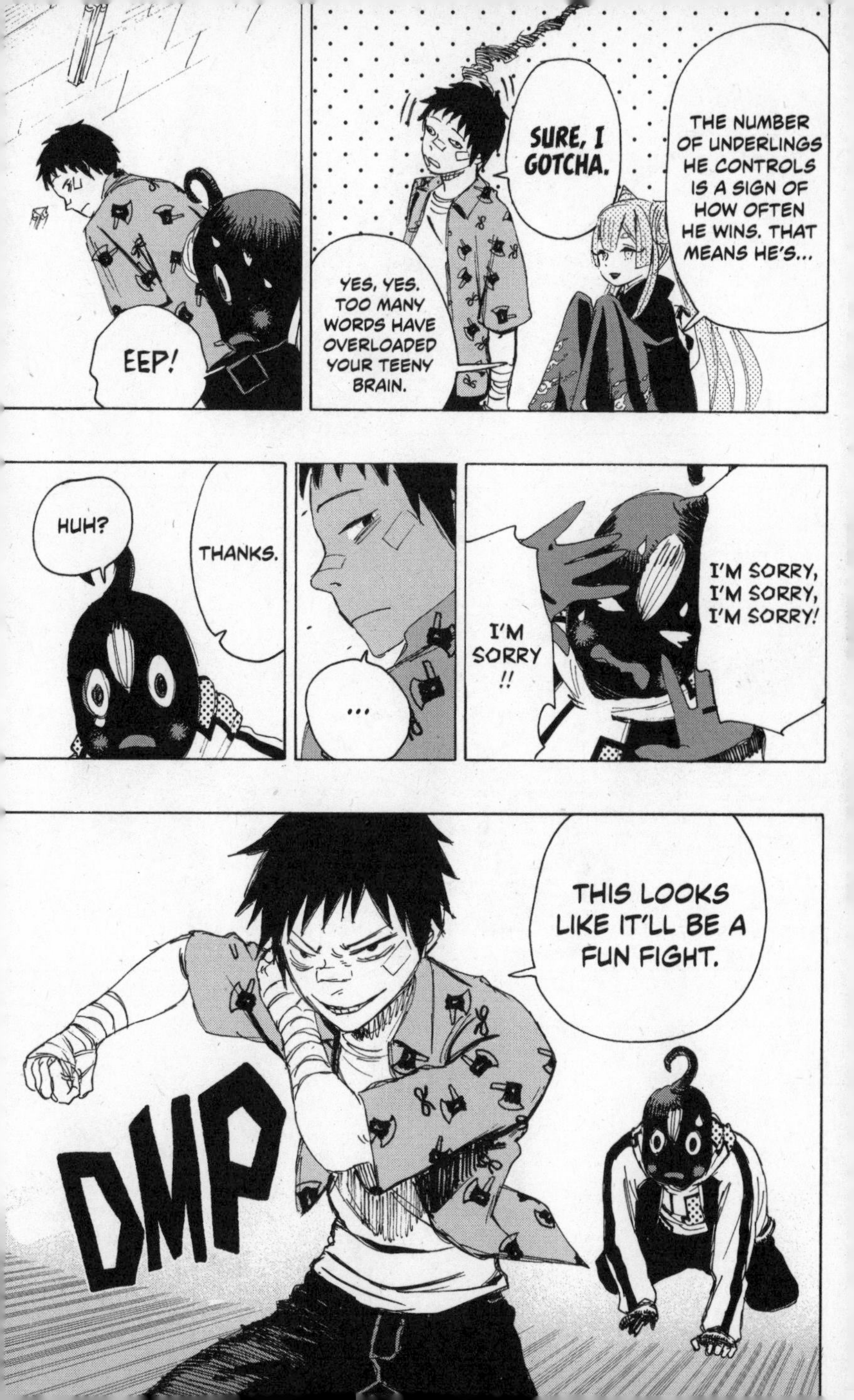
THE NUMBER OF UNDERLINGS HE CONTROLS IS A SIGN OF HOW OFTEN HE WINS. THAT MEANS HE'S...
SURE, I GOTCHA.
YES, YES. TOO MANY WORDS HAVE OVERLOADED YOUR TEENY BRAIN.
EEP!
I'M SORRY, I'M SORRY, I'M SORRY!
I'M SORRY !!
...
THANKS.
HUH?
THIS LOOKS LIKE IT'LL BE A FUN FIGHT.
DMP

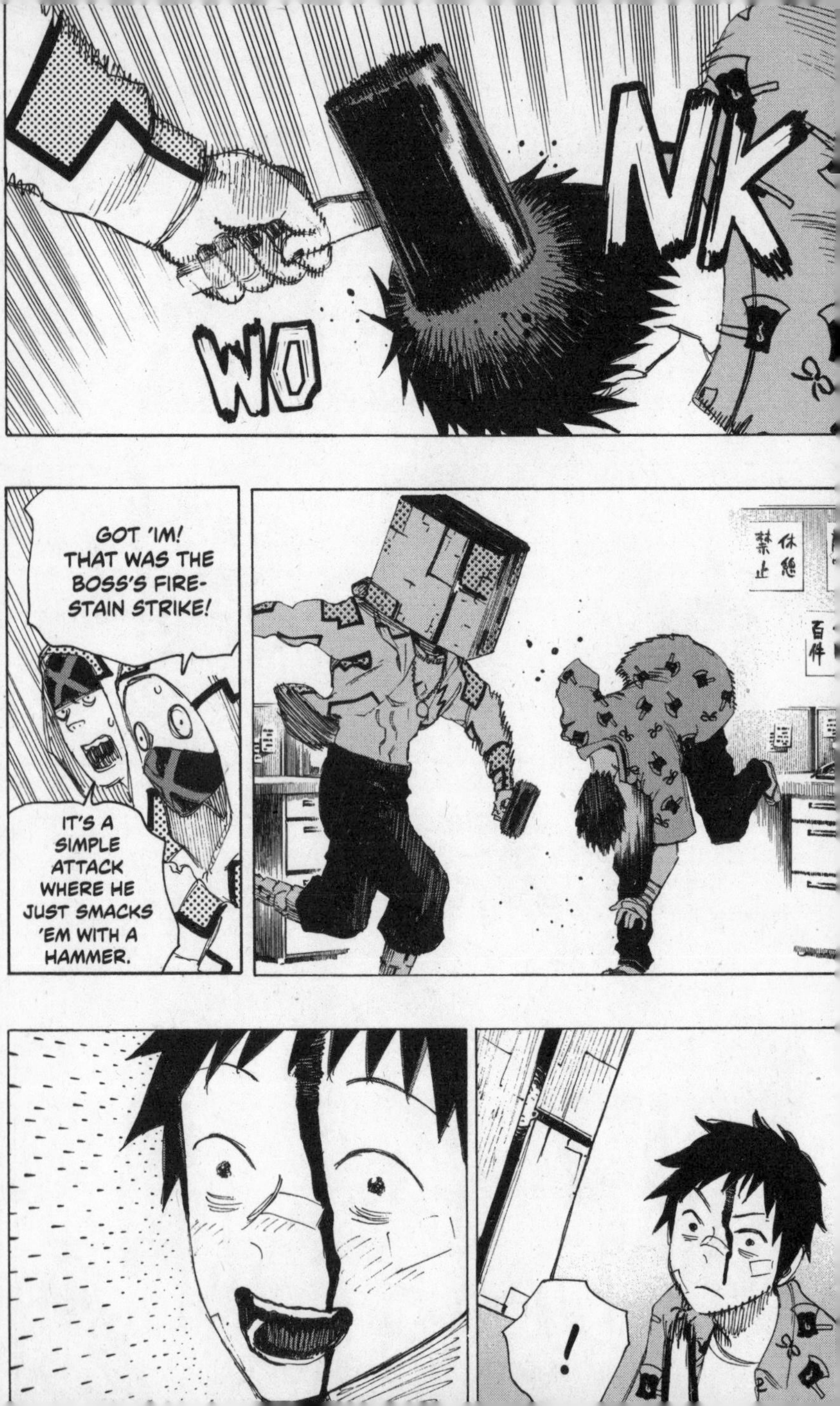
WO
NK
休憩禁止
GOT 'IM! THAT WAS THE BOSS'S FIRE-STAIN STRIKE!
IT'S A SIMPLE ATTACK WHERE HE JUST SMACKS 'EM WITH A HAMMER.
!

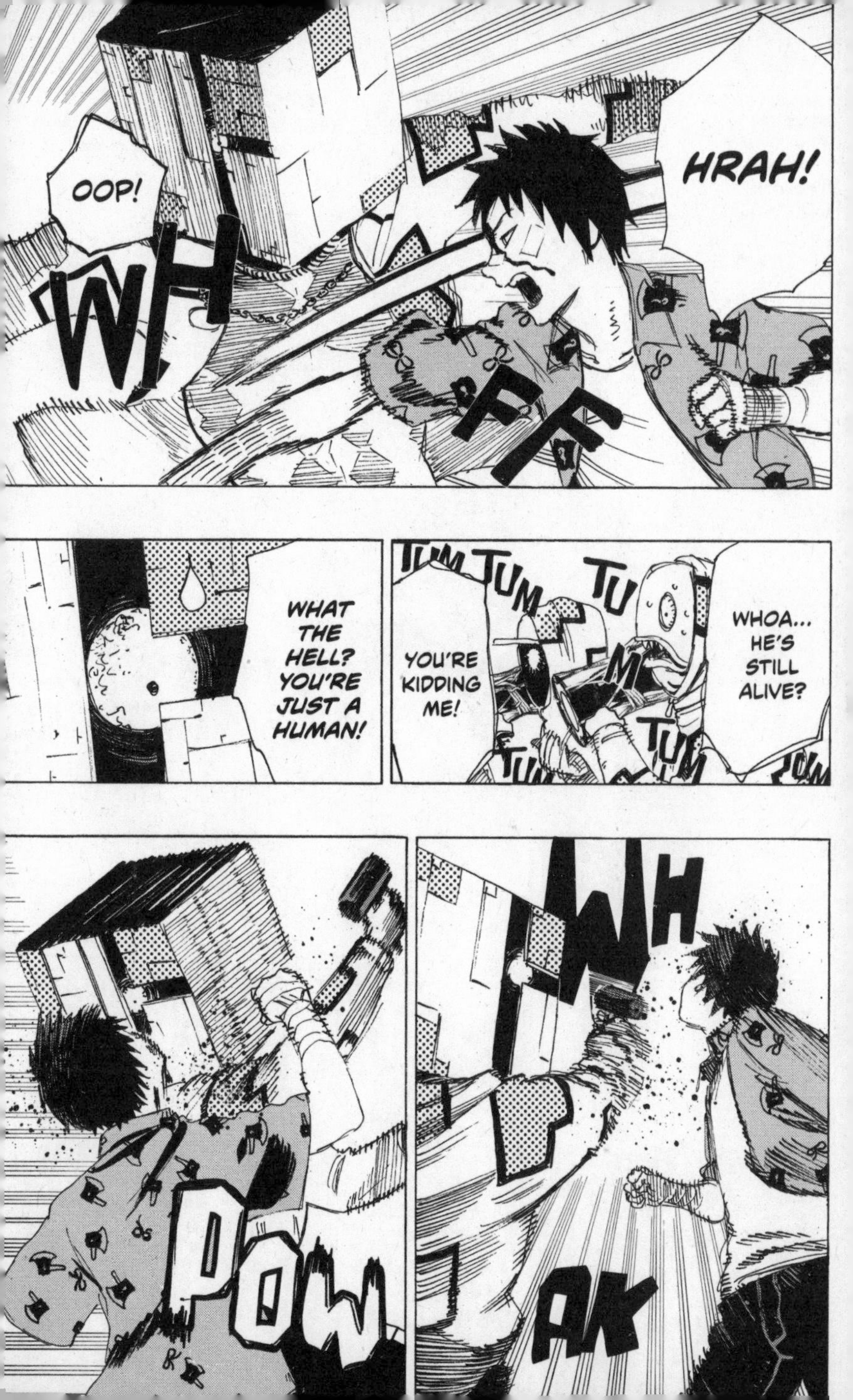
HRAH!
OOP!
WH
FF
WHOA... HE'S STILL ALIVE?
YOU'RE KIDDING ME!
TUM TUM TU
TUM TUM
WHAT THE HELL? YOU'RE JUST A HUMAN!
WH
AK
POW

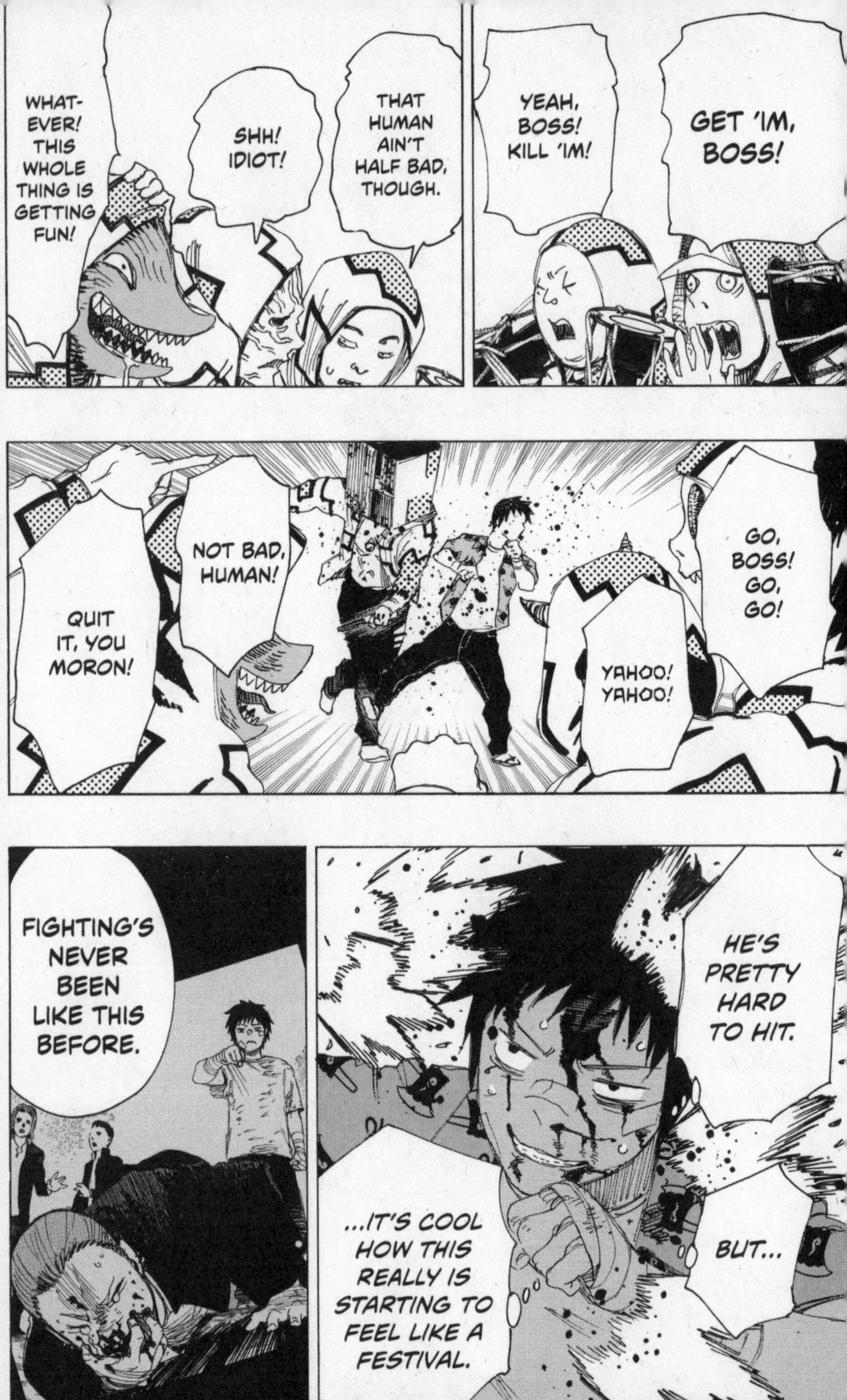
GET 'IM, BOSS!
YEAH, BOSS! KILL 'IM!
THAT HUMAN AIN'T HALF BAD, THOUGH.
SHH! IDIOT!
WHAT-EVER! THIS WHOLE THING IS GETTING FUN!
GO, BOSS! GO, GO!
YAHOO! YAHOO!
NOT BAD, HUMAN!
QUIT IT, YOU MORON!
HE'S PRETTY HARD TO HIT.
BUT...
...IT'S COOL HOW THIS REALLY IS STARTING TO FEEL LIKE A FESTIVAL.
FIGHTING'S NEVER BEEN LIKE THIS BEFORE.

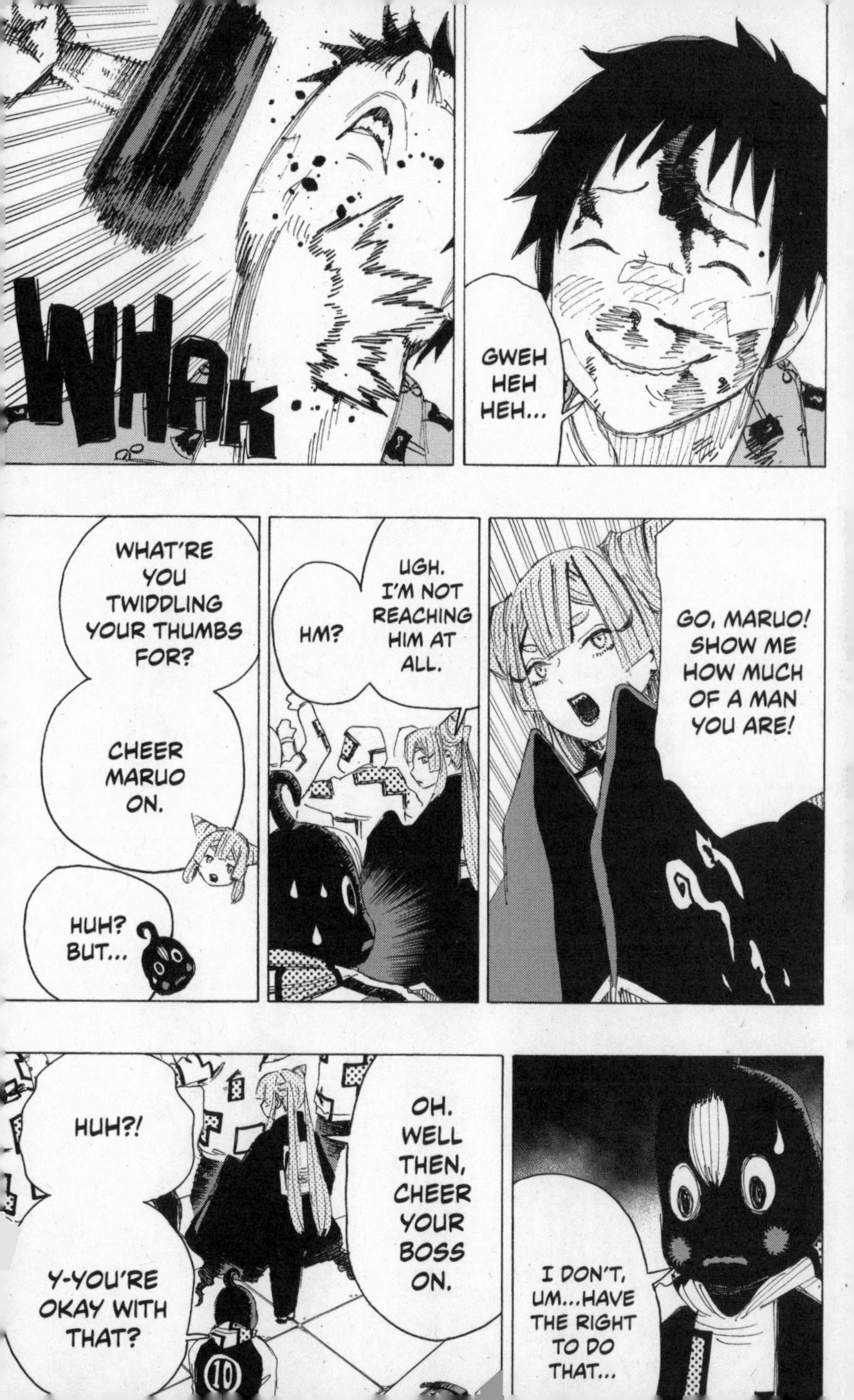
GWEH HEH HEH...
WHAK
GO, MARUO! SHOW ME HOW MUCH OF A MAN YOU ARE!
UGH. I'M NOT REACHING HIM AT ALL.
HM?
WHAT'RE YOU TWIDDLING YOUR THUMBS FOR?
CHEER MARUO ON.
HUH? BUT...
I DON'T, UM...HAVE THE RIGHT TO DO THAT...
OH. WELL THEN, CHEER YOUR BOSS ON.
HUH?!
Y-YOU'RE OKAY WITH THAT?
10

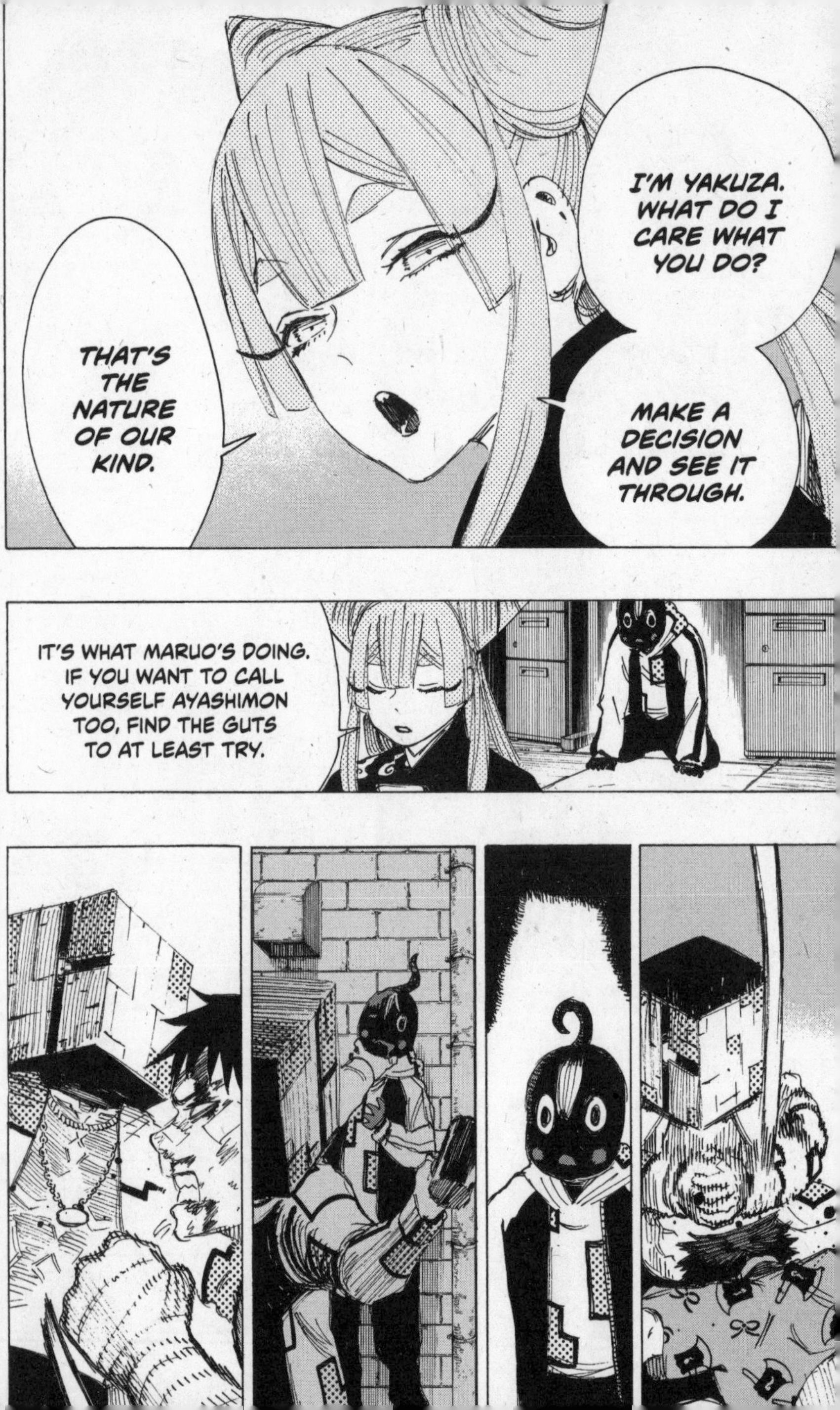
I'M YAKUZA. WHAT DO I CARE WHAT YOU DO?
MAKE A DECISION AND SEE IT THROUGH.
THAT'S THE NATURE OF OUR KIND.
IT'S WHAT MARUO'S DOING. IF YOU WANT TO CALL YOURSELF AYASHIMON TOO, FIND THE GUTS TO AT LEAST TRY.

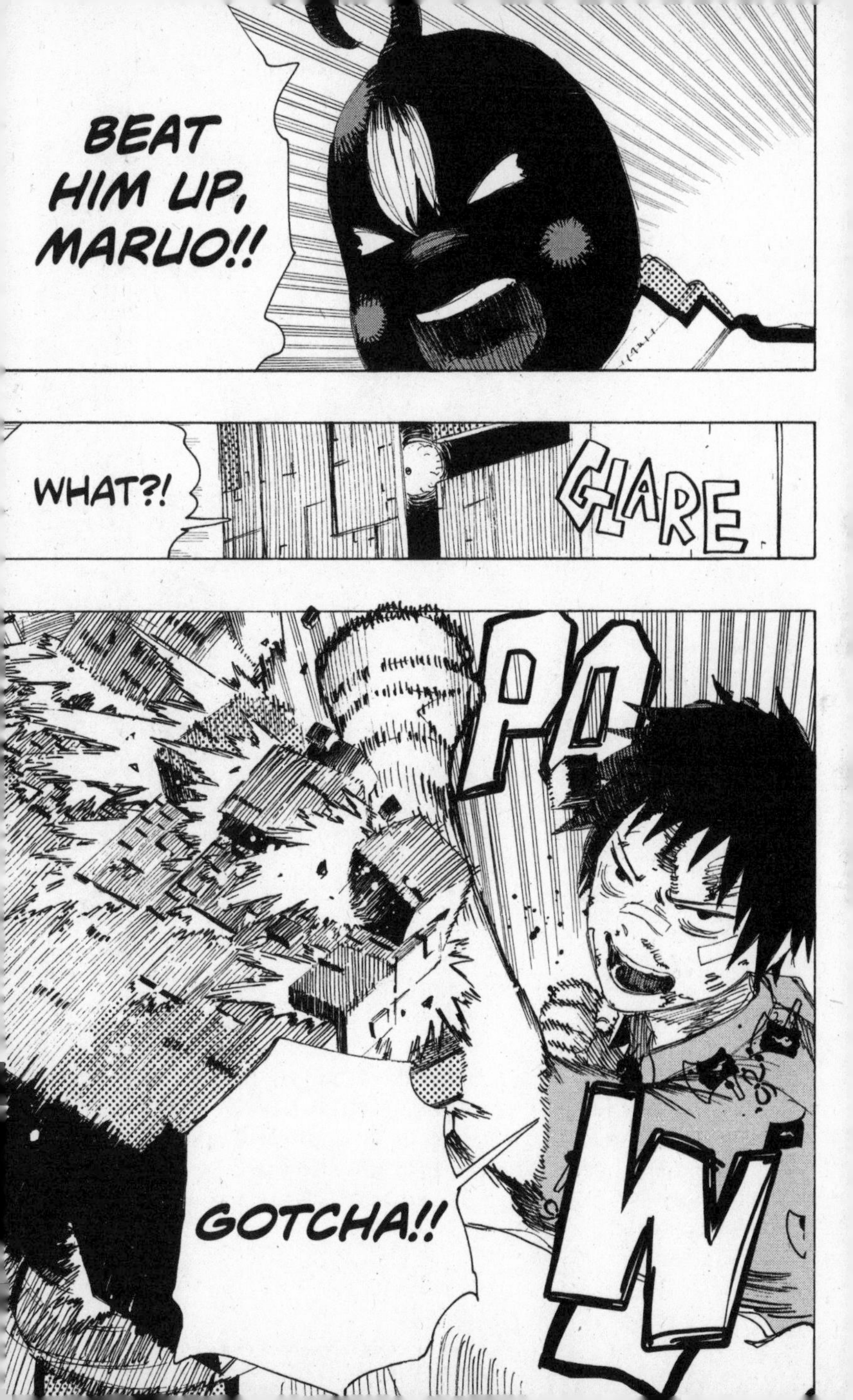
BEAT HIM UP, MARUO!!
GLARE
WHAT?!
POW
GOTCHA!!

KABUKICHO MONSTER MANUAL

Yokai: Uwan

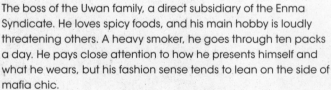

The boss of the Uwan family, a direct subsidiary of the Enma Syndicate. He loves spicy foods, and his main hobby is loudly threatening others. A heavy smoker, he goes through ten packs a day. He pays close attention to how he presents himself and what he wears, but his fashion sense tends to lean on the side of mafia chic.

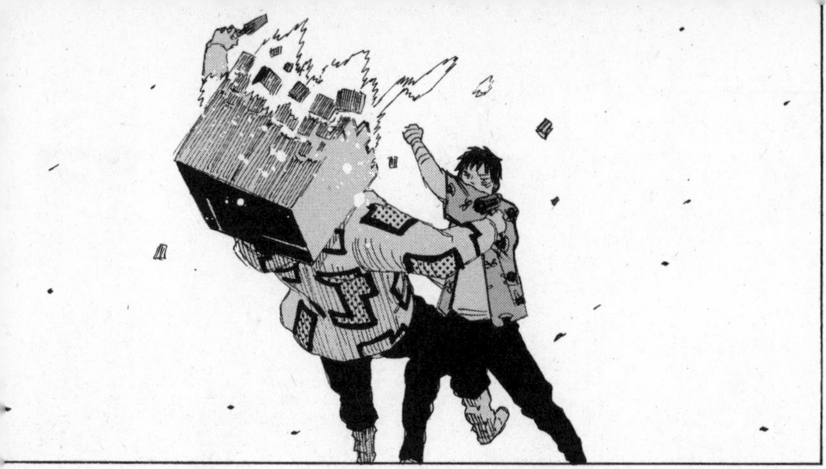

Chapter 5

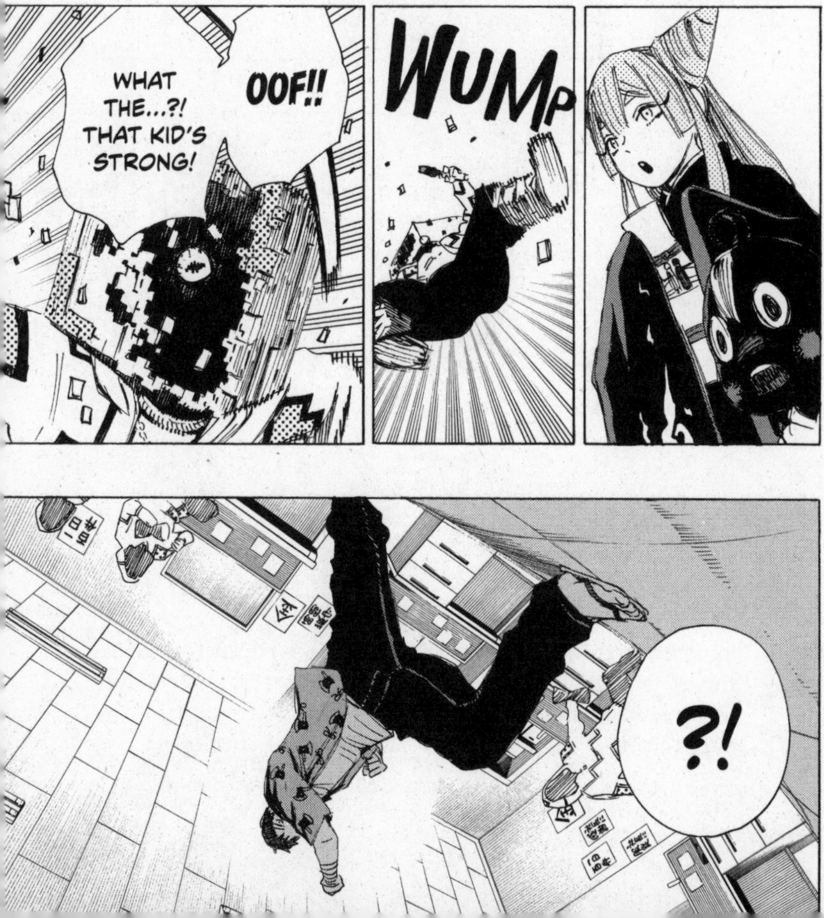
WUMP
OOF!!
WHAT THE...?! THAT KID'S STRONG!
?!

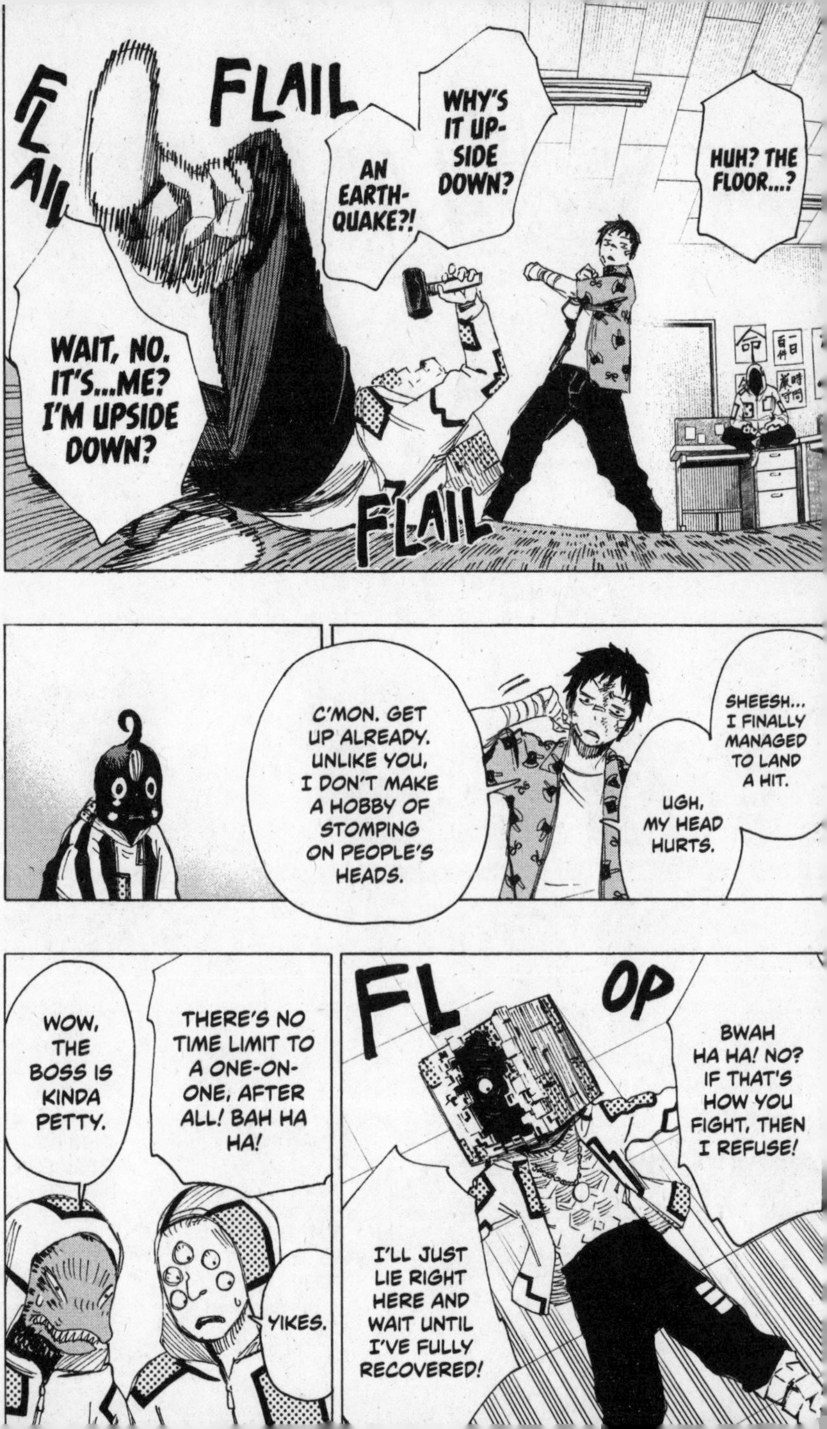
HUH? THE FLOOR...?
WHY'S IT UP-SIDE DOWN?
AN EARTH-QUAKE?!
FLAIL
FLAIL
WAIT, NO. IT'S...ME? I'M UPSIDE DOWN?
FLAIL
SHEESH... I FINALLY MANAGED TO LAND A HIT.
UGH, MY HEAD HURTS.
C'MON. GET UP ALREADY. UNLIKE YOU, I DON'T MAKE A HOBBY OF STOMPING ON PEOPLE'S HEADS.
FLOP
BWAH HA HA! NO? IF THAT'S HOW YOU FIGHT, THEN I REFUSE!
I'LL JUST LIE RIGHT HERE AND WAIT UNTIL I'VE FULLY RECOVERED!
THERE'S NO TIME LIMIT TO A ONE-ON-ONE, AFTER ALL! BAH HA HA!
WOW, THE BOSS IS KINDA PETTY.
YIKES.

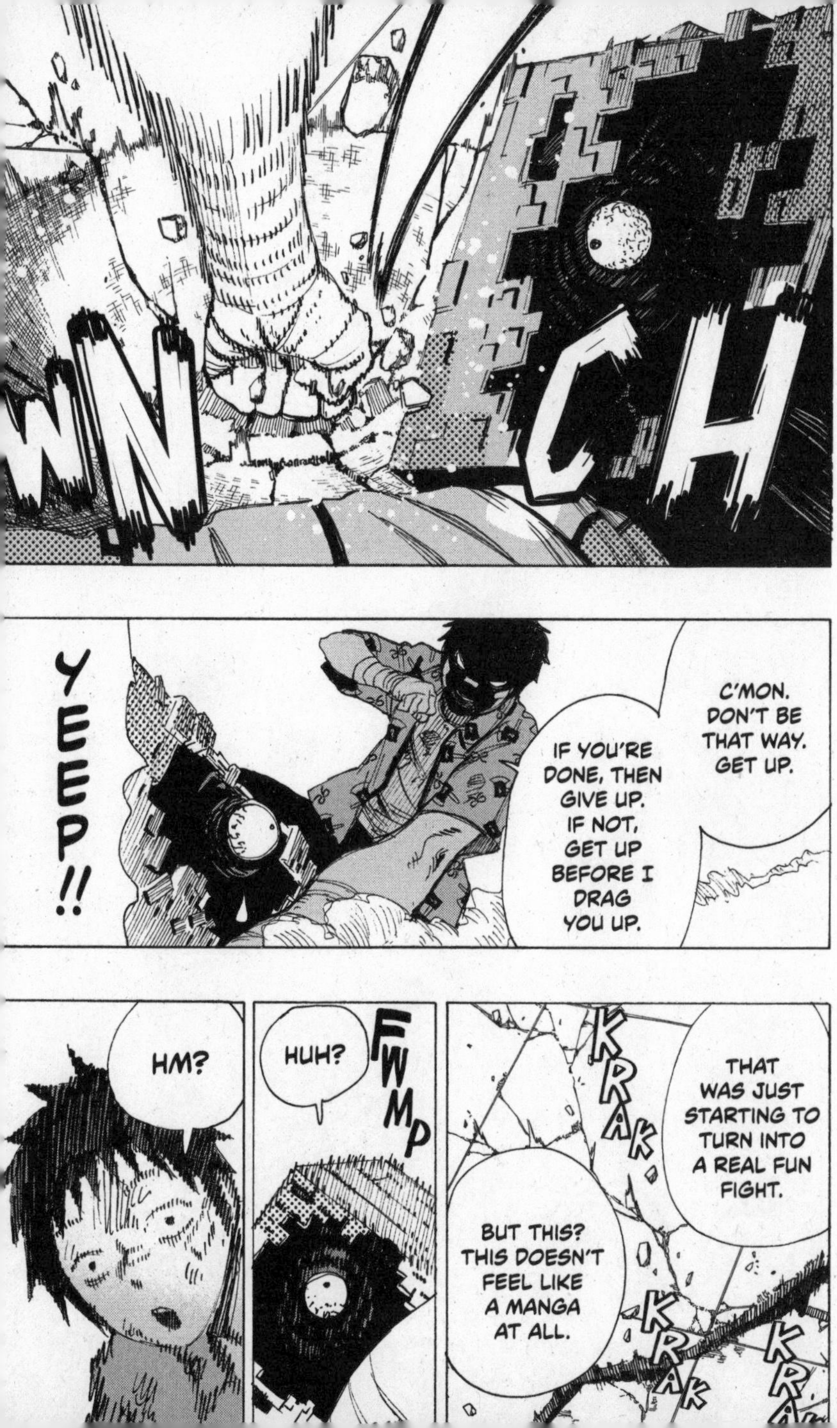
WN
CH
C'MON. DON'T BE THAT WAY. GET UP.
IF YOU'RE DONE, THEN GIVE UP. IF NOT, GET UP BEFORE I DRAG YOU UP.
YEEP!!
THAT WAS JUST STARTING TO TURN INTO A REAL FUN FIGHT.
KRAK
BUT THIS? THIS DOESN'T FEEL LIKE A MANGA AT ALL.
KRAK
KRAK
FWMP
HUH?
HM?

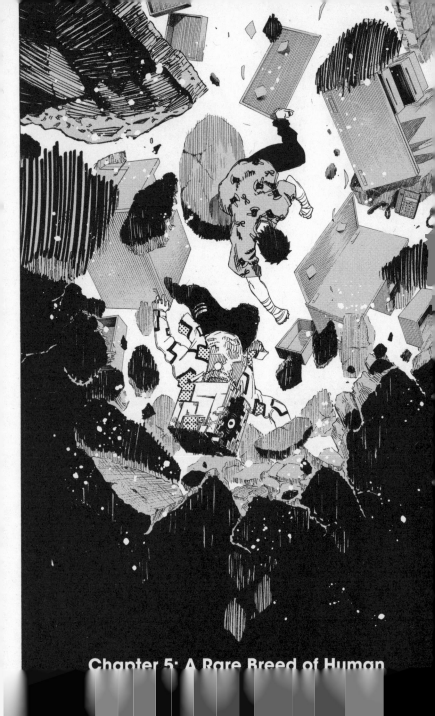

Chapter 5: A Rare Breed of Human

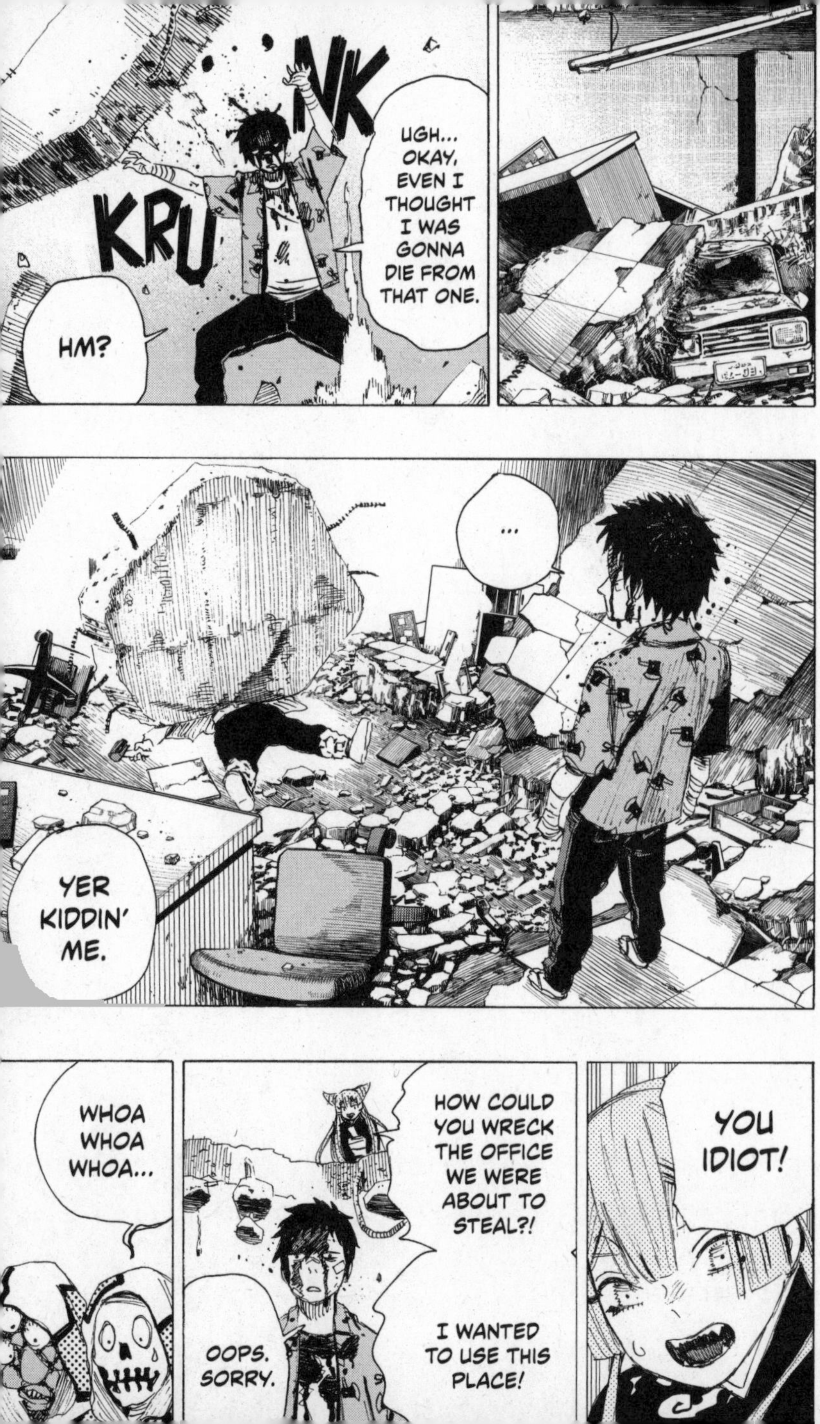
KRUNK
UGH... OKAY, EVEN I THOUGHT I WAS GONNA DIE FROM THAT ONE.
HM?
...
YER KIDDIN' ME.
YOU IDIOT!
HOW COULD YOU WRECK THE OFFICE WE WERE ABOUT TO STEAL?!
I WANTED TO USE THIS PLACE!
OOPS. SORRY.
WHOA WHOA WHOA...

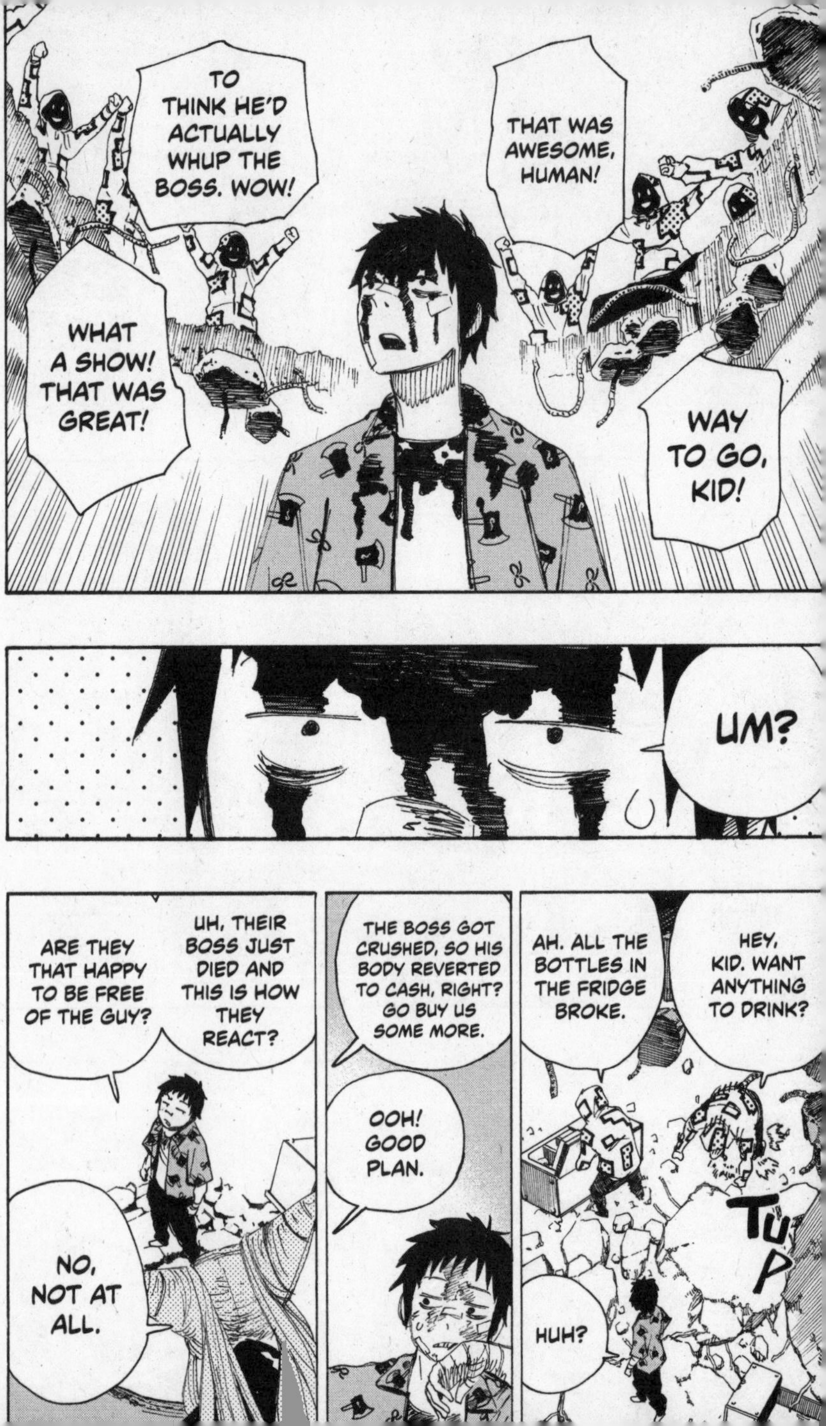
THAT WAS AWESOME, HUMAN!
TO THINK HE'D ACTUALLY WHUP THE BOSS. WOW!
WAY TO GO, KID!
WHAT A SHOW! THAT WAS GREAT!
UM?
HEY, KID. WANT ANYTHING TO DRINK?
AH. ALL THE BOTTLES IN THE FRIDGE BROKE.
TUP
HUH?
THE BOSS GOT CRUSHED, SO HIS BODY REVERTED TO CASH, RIGHT? GO BUY US SOME MORE.
OOH! GOOD PLAN.
UH, THEIR BOSS JUST DIED AND THIS IS HOW THEY REACT?
ARE THEY THAT HAPPY TO BE FREE OF THE GUY?
NO, NOT AT ALL.

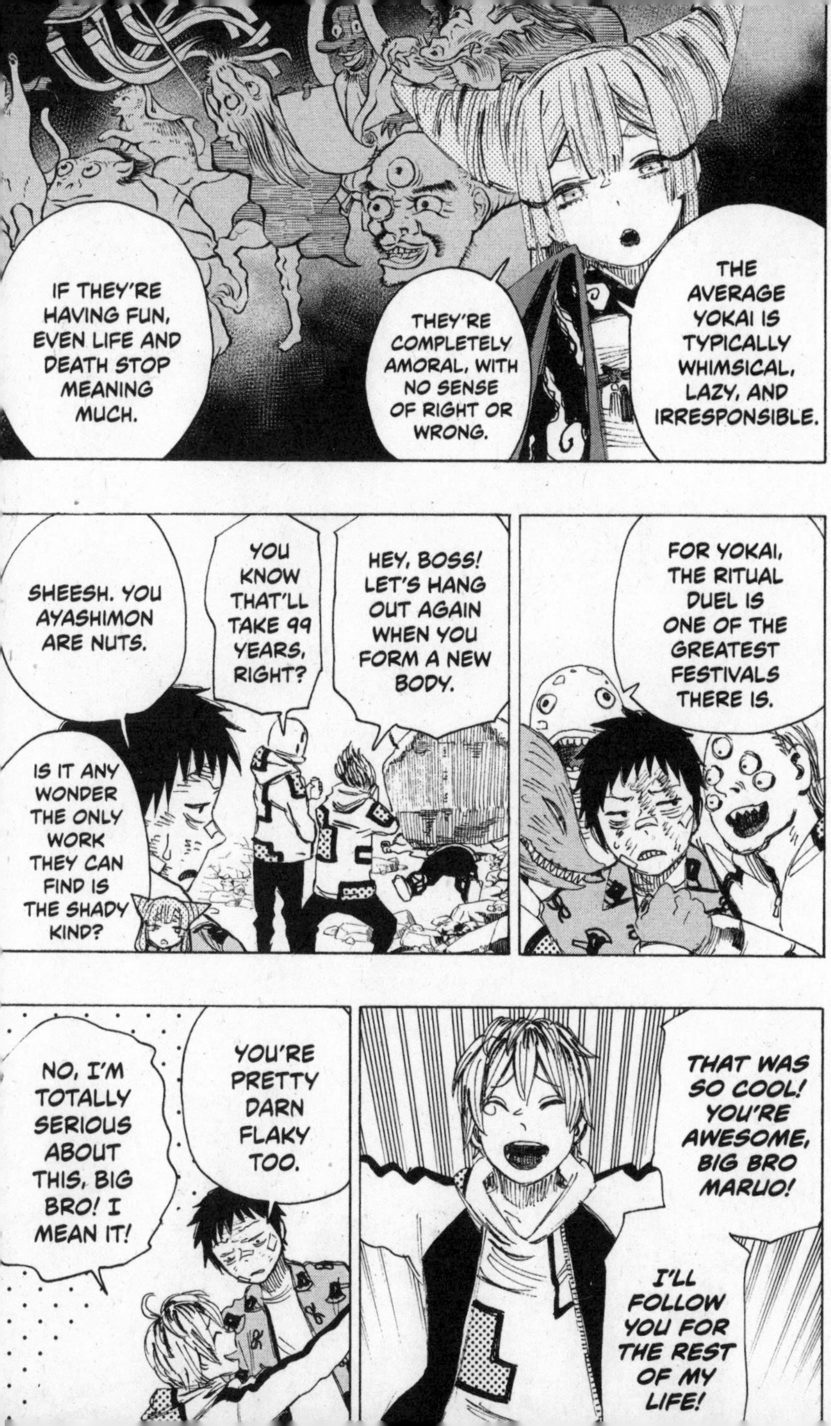
THE AVERAGE YOKAI IS TYPICALLY WHIMSICAL, LAZY, AND IRRESPONSIBLE.
THEY'RE COMPLETELY AMORAL, WITH NO SENSE OF RIGHT OR WRONG.
IF THEY'RE HAVING FUN, EVEN LIFE AND DEATH STOP MEANING MUCH.
FOR YOKAI, THE RITUAL DUEL IS ONE OF THE GREATEST FESTIVALS THERE IS.
HEY, BOSS! LET'S HANG OUT AGAIN WHEN YOU FORM A NEW BODY.
YOU KNOW THAT'LL TAKE 99 YEARS, RIGHT?
SHEESH. YOU AYASHIMON ARE NUTS.
IS IT ANY WONDER THE ONLY WORK THEY CAN FIND IS THE SHADY KIND?
THAT WAS SO COOL! YOU'RE AWESOME, BIG BRO MARUO!
I'LL FOLLOW YOU FOR THE REST OF MY LIFE!
YOU'RE PRETTY DARN FLAKY TOO.
NO, I'M TOTALLY SERIOUS ABOUT THIS, BIG BRO! I MEAN IT!

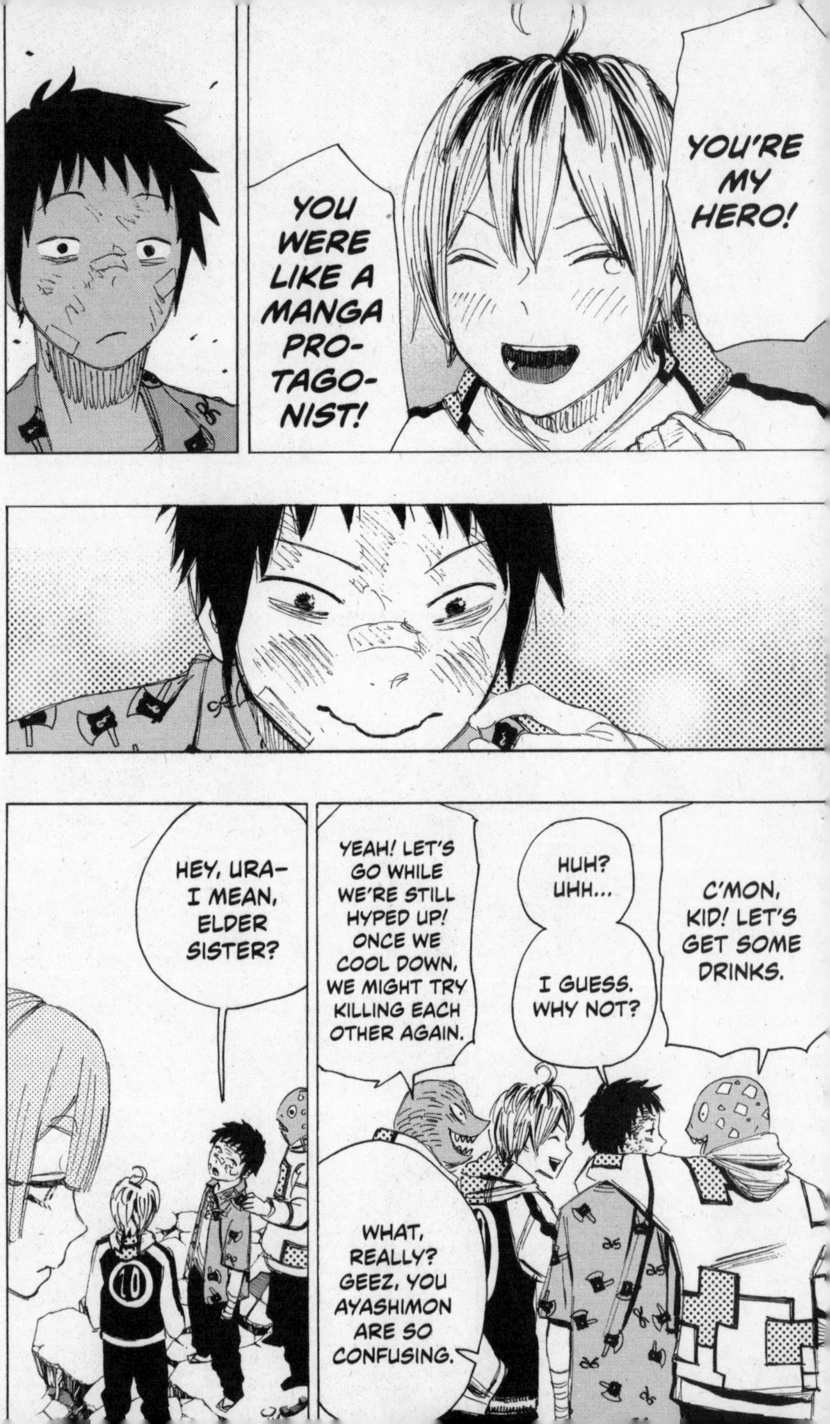
YOU'RE MY HERO!
YOU WERE LIKE A MANGA PRO-TAGO-NIST!
C'MON, KID! LET'S GET SOME DRINKS.
HUH? UHH...
I GUESS. WHY NOT?
YEAH! LET'S GO WHILE WE'RE STILL HYPED UP! ONCE WE COOL DOWN, WE MIGHT TRY KILLING EACH OTHER AGAIN.
WHAT, REALLY? GEEZ, YOU AYASHIMON ARE SO CONFUSING.
HEY, URA– I MEAN, ELDER SISTER?

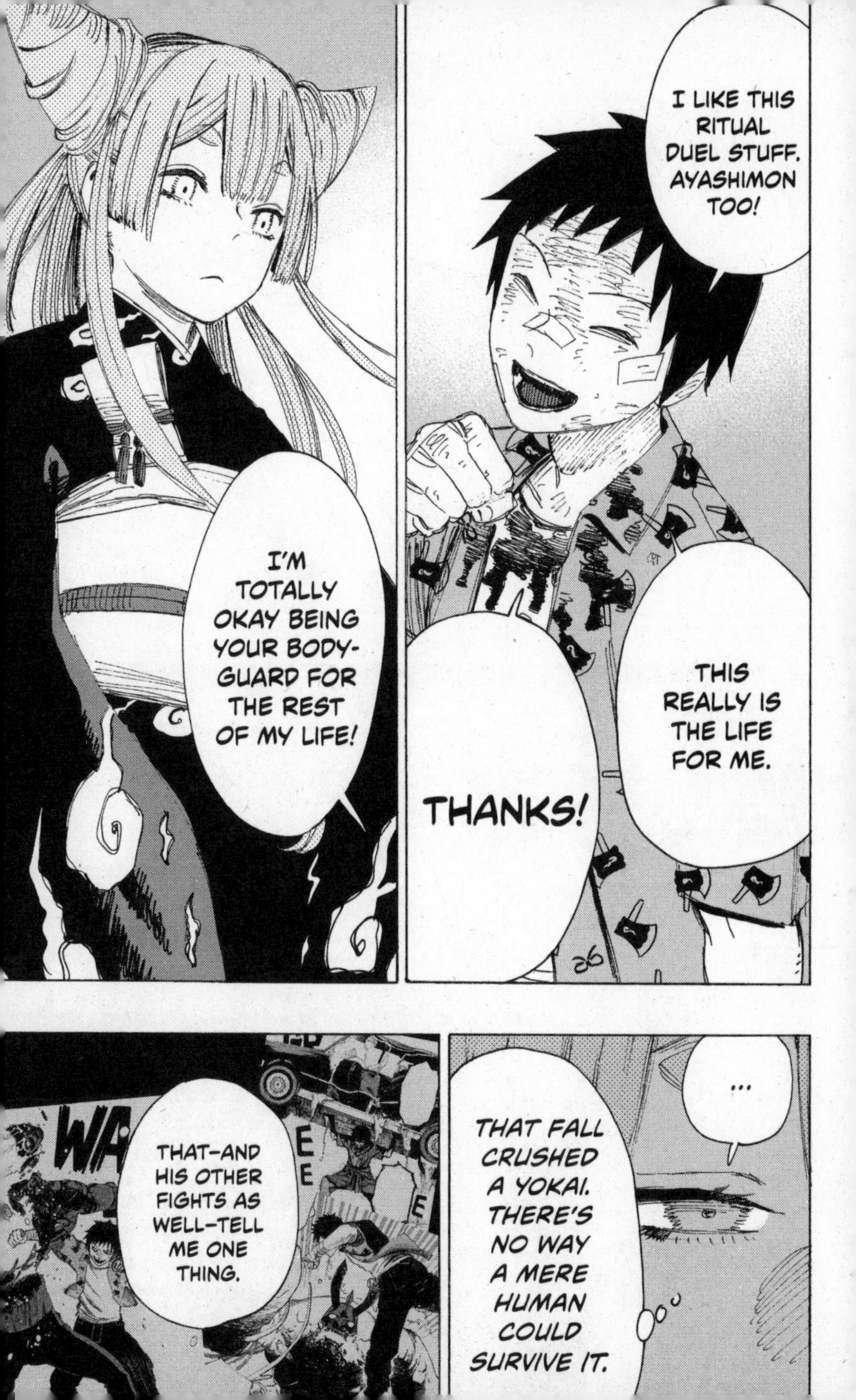
I LIKE THIS RITUAL DUEL STUFF. AYASHIMON TOO!
THIS REALLY IS THE LIFE FOR ME.
THANKS!
I'M TOTALLY OKAY BEING YOUR BODY-GUARD FOR THE REST OF MY LIFE!
...
THAT FALL CRUSHED A YOKAI. THERE'S NO WAY A MERE HUMAN COULD SURVIVE IT.
WA
THAT—AND HIS OTHER FIGHTS AS WELL—TELL ME ONE THING.

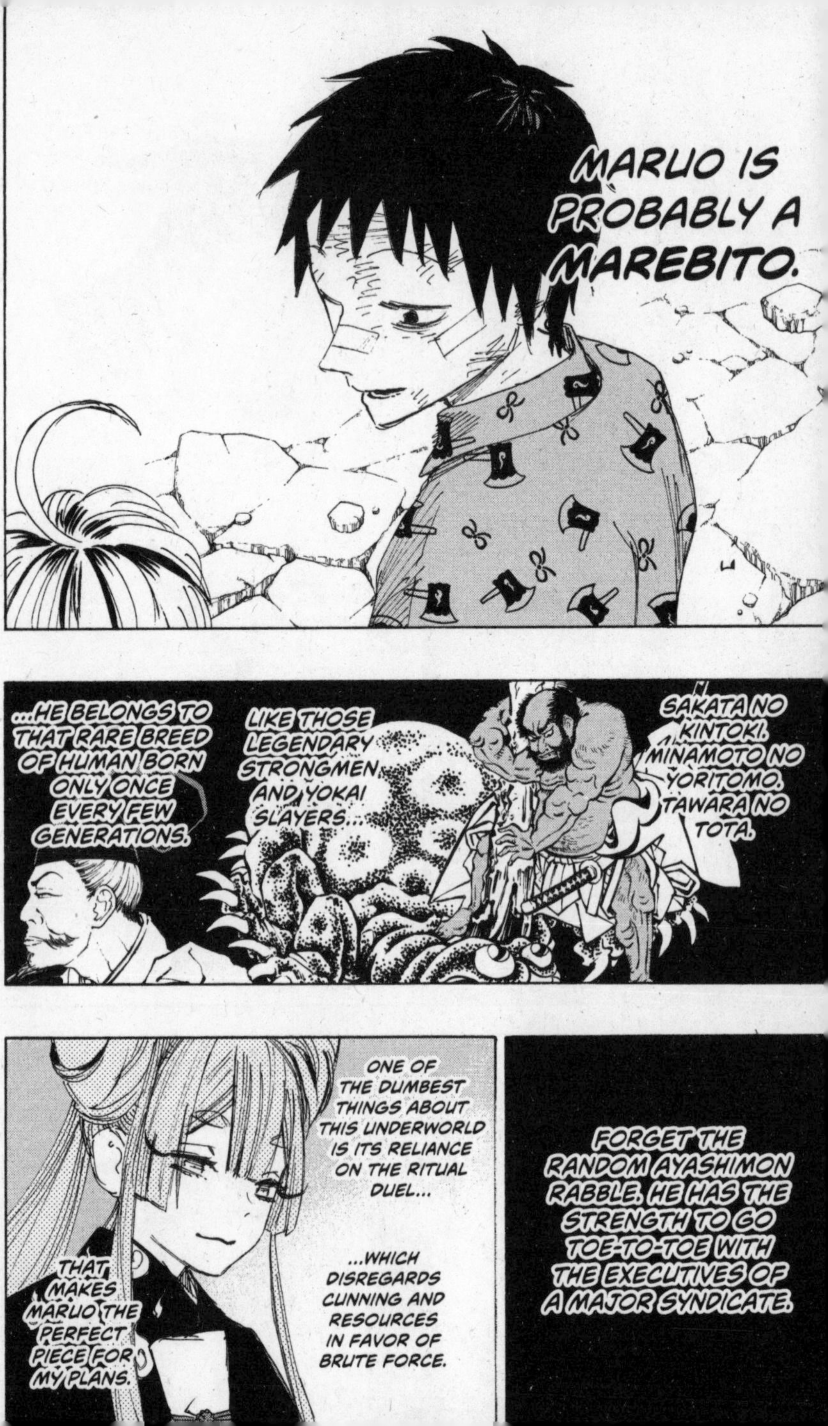
MARUO IS PROBABLY A MAREBITO.
SAKATA NO KINTOKI. MINAMOTO NO YORITOMO. TAWARA NO TOTA.
LIKE THOSE LEGENDARY STRONGMEN AND YOKAI SLAYERS...
...HE BELONGS TO THAT RARE BREED OF HUMAN BORN ONLY ONCE EVERY FEW GENERATIONS.
FORGET THE RANDOM AYASHIMON RABBLE. HE HAS THE STRENGTH TO GO TOE-TO-TOE WITH THE EXECUTIVES OF A MAJOR SYNDICATE.
ONE OF THE DUMBEST THINGS ABOUT THIS UNDERWORLD IS ITS RELIANCE ON THE RITUAL DUEL...
...WHICH DISREGARDS CUNNING AND RESOURCES IN FAVOR OF BRUTE FORCE.
THAT MAKES MARUO THE PERFECT PIECE FOR MY PLANS.

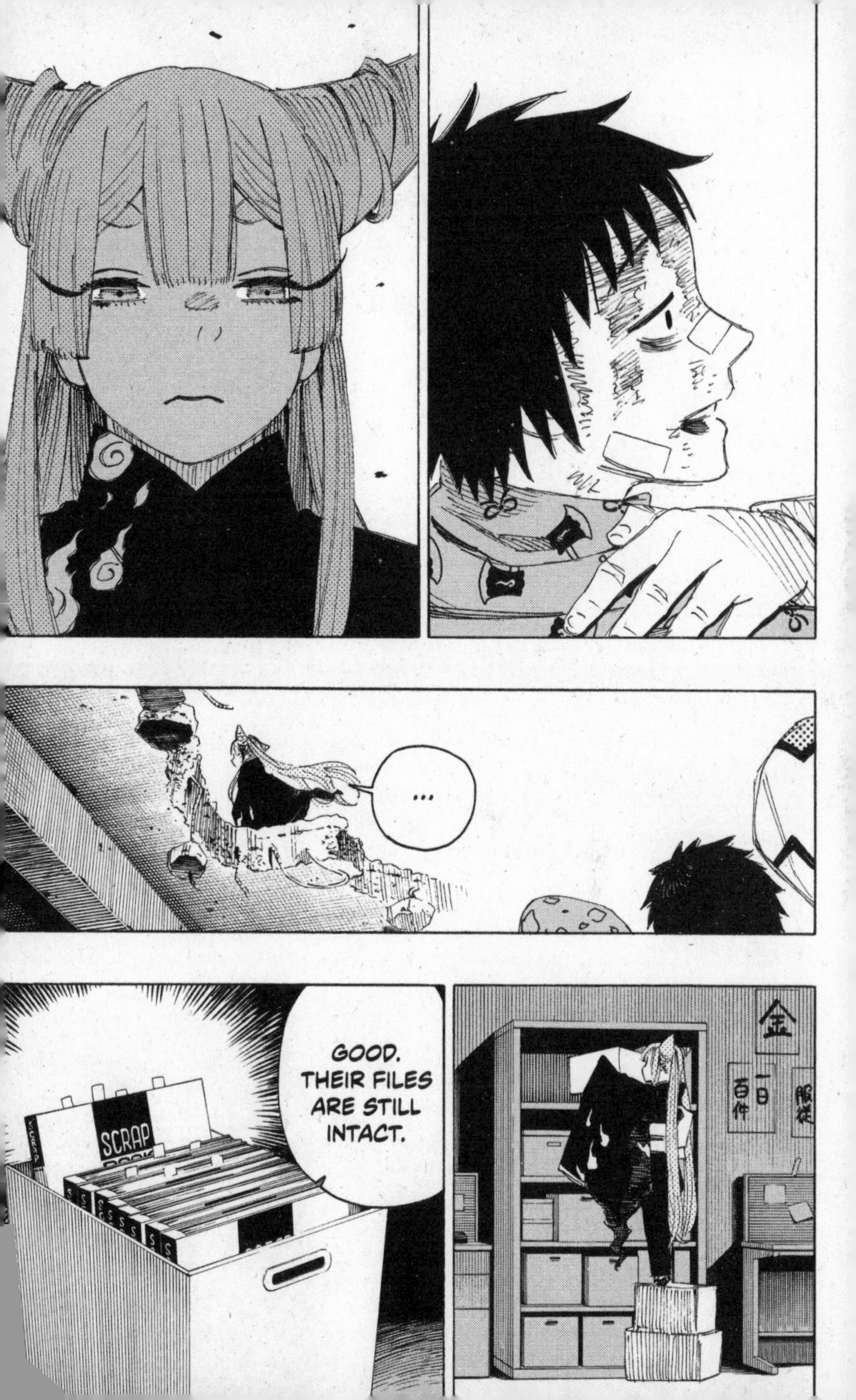
...
金
一日百件
服従
GOOD. THEIR FILES ARE STILL INTACT.
SCRAP

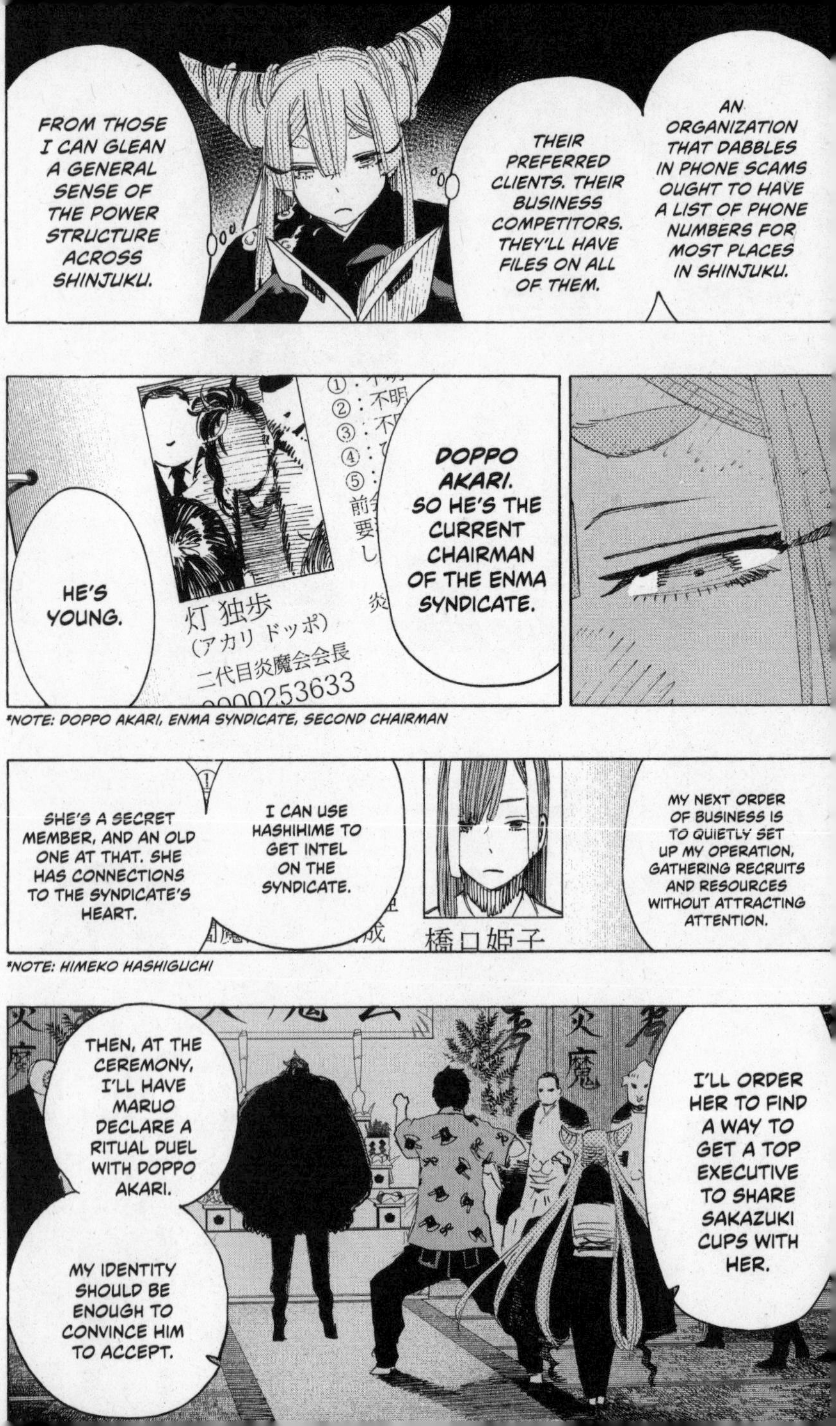
AN ORGANIZATION THAT DABBLES IN PHONE SCAMS OUGHT TO HAVE A LIST OF PHONE NUMBERS FOR MOST PLACES IN SHINJUKU.
THEIR PREFERRED CLIENTS. THEIR BUSINESS COMPETITORS. THEY'LL HAVE FILES ON ALL OF THEM.
FROM THOSE I CAN GLEAN A GENERAL SENSE OF THE POWER STRUCTURE ACROSS SHINJUKU.
DOPPO AKARI. SO HE'S THE CURRENT CHAIRMAN OF THE ENMA SYNDICATE.
HE'S YOUNG.
灯 独歩
(アカリ ドッポ)
二代目炎魔会会長
*NOTE: DOPPO AKARI, ENMA SYNDICATE, SECOND CHAIRMAN
MY NEXT ORDER OF BUSINESS IS TO QUIETLY SET UP MY OPERATION, GATHERING RECRUITS AND RESOURCES WITHOUT ATTRACTING ATTENTION.
I CAN USE HASHIHIME TO GET INTEL ON THE SYNDICATE.
SHE'S A SECRET MEMBER, AND AN OLD ONE AT THAT. SHE HAS CONNECTIONS TO THE SYNDICATE'S HEART.
橋口姫子
*NOTE: HIMEKO HASHIGUCHI
I'LL ORDER HER TO FIND A WAY TO GET A TOP EXECUTIVE TO SHARE SAKAZUKI CUPS WITH HER.
THEN, AT THE CEREMONY, I'LL HAVE MARUO DECLARE A RITUAL DUEL WITH DOPPO AKARI.
MY IDENTITY SHOULD BE ENOUGH TO CONVINCE HIM TO ACCEPT.

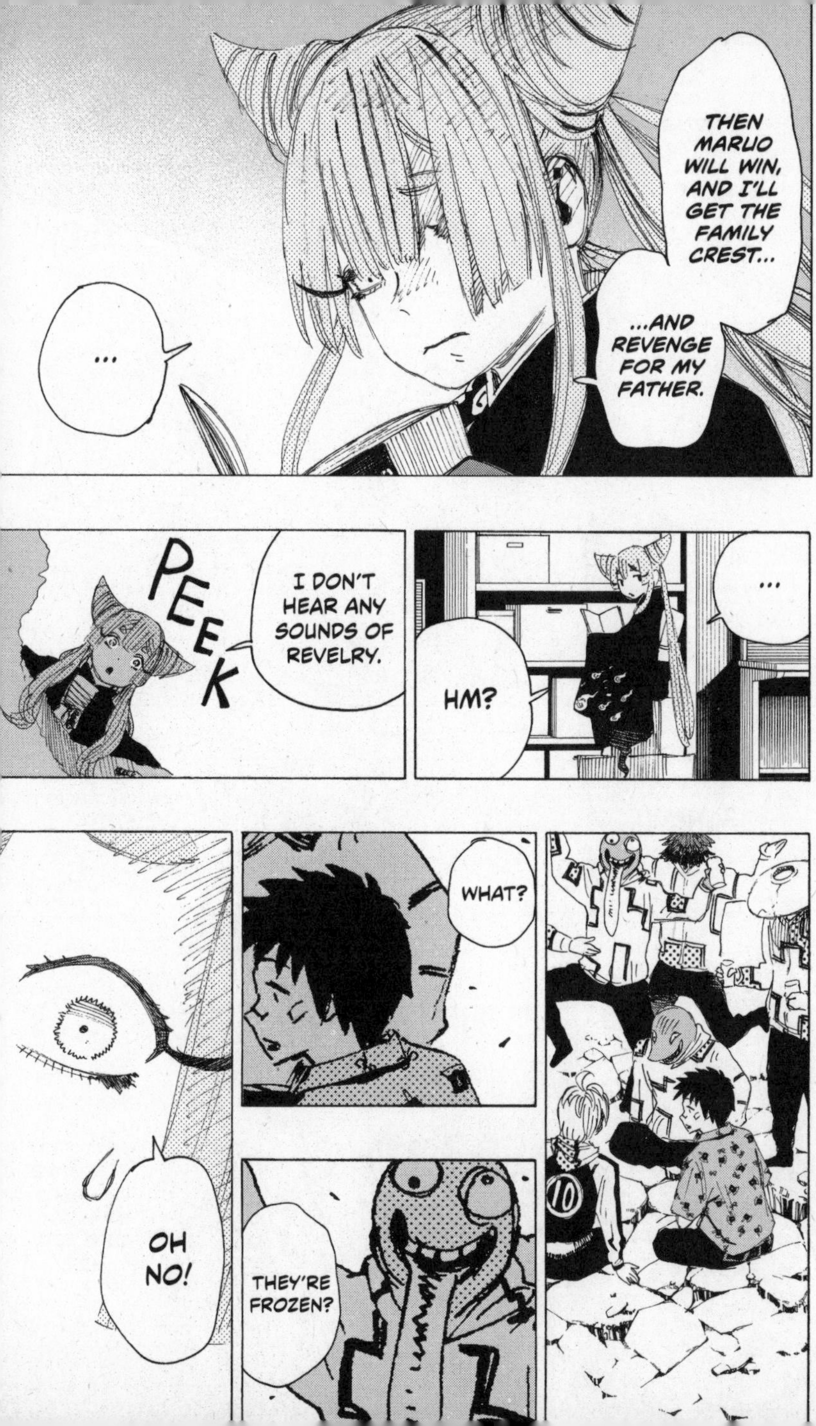
THEN MARUO WILL WIN, AND I'LL GET THE FAMILY CREST...
...AND REVENGE FOR MY FATHER.
...
...
HM?
I DON'T HEAR ANY SOUNDS OF REVELRY.
PEEK
WHAT?
THEY'RE FROZEN?
OH NO!

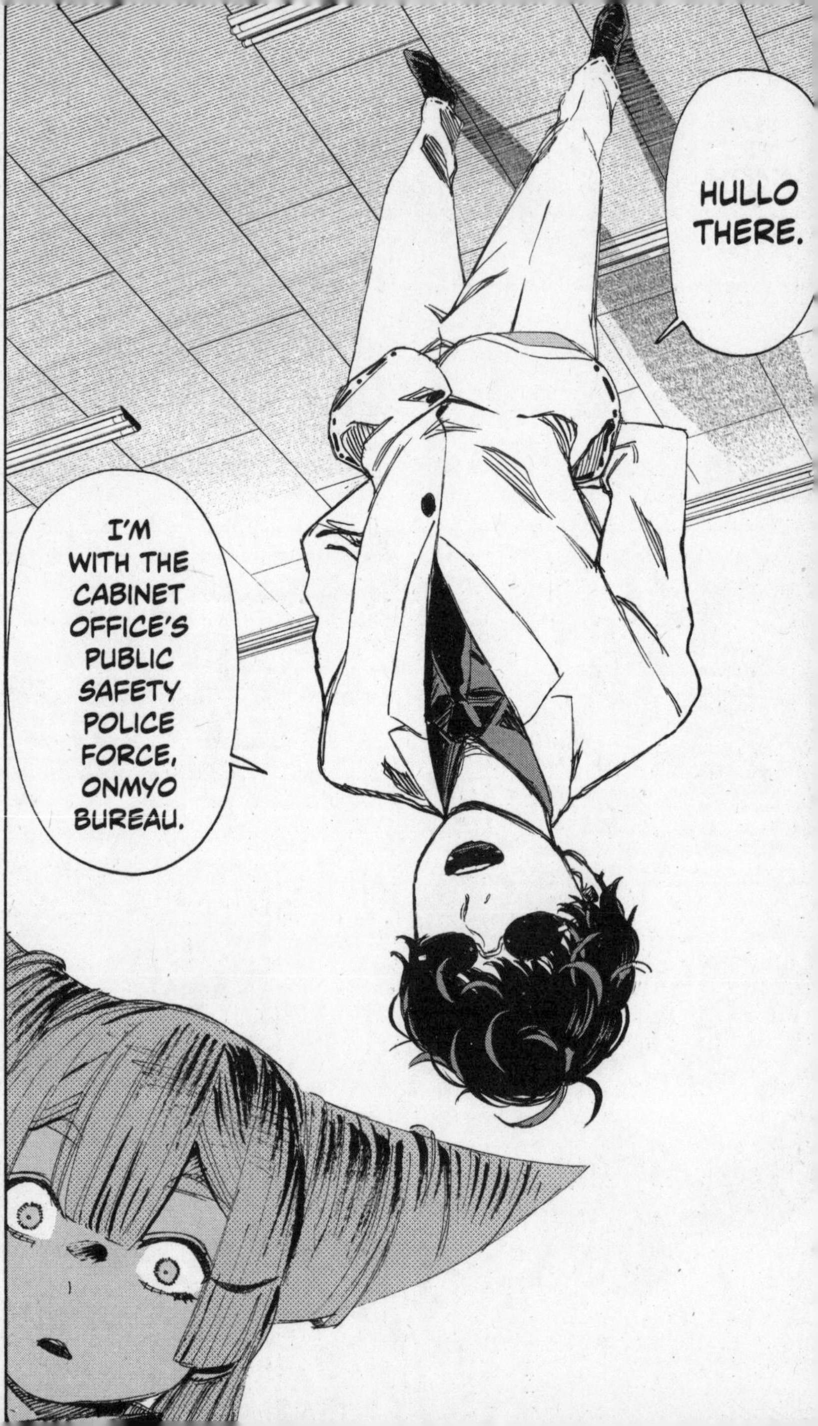
HULLO THERE.
I'M WITH THE CABINET OFFICE'S PUBLIC SAFETY POLICE FORCE, ONMYO BUREAU.

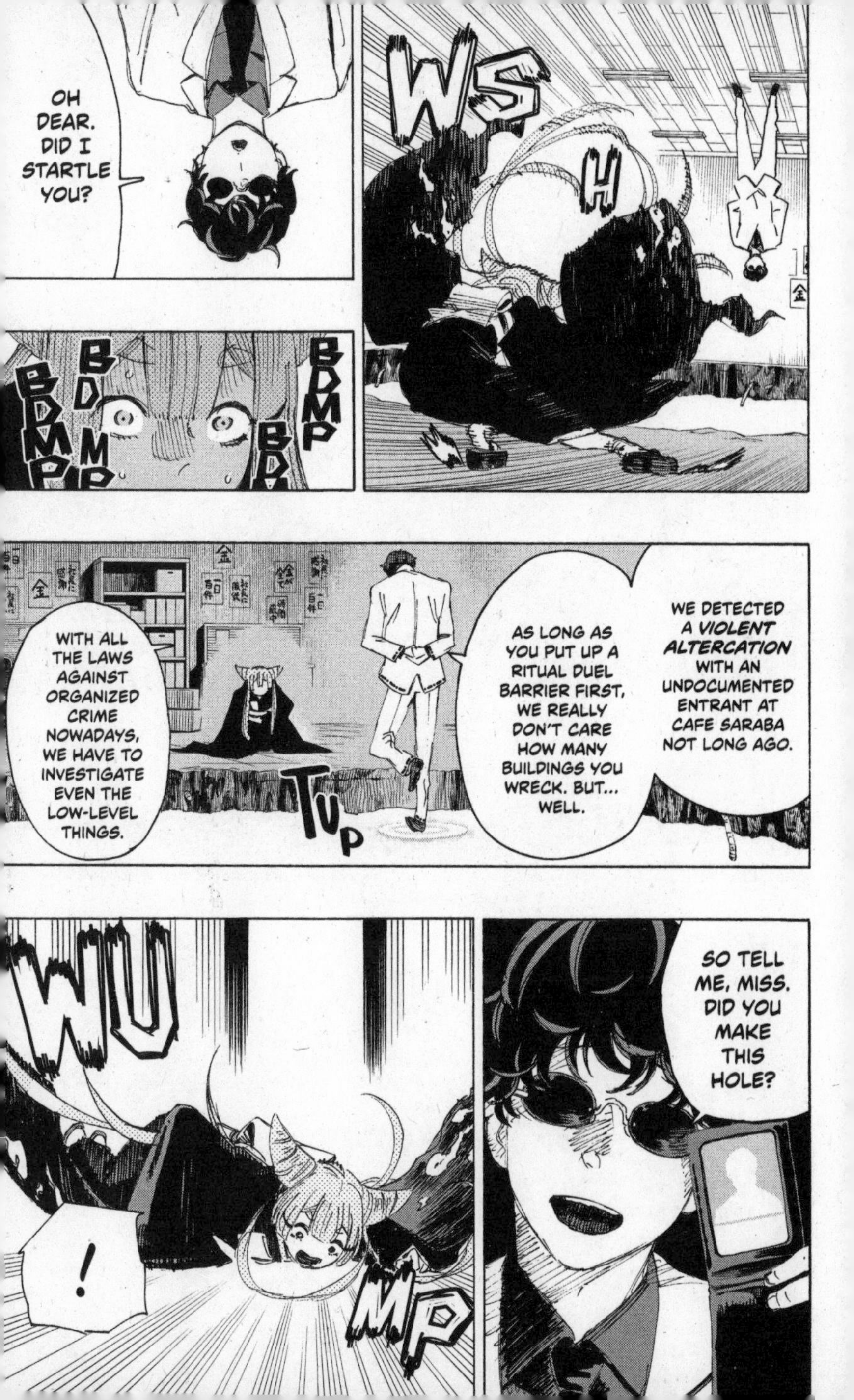
WSH
OH DEAR. DID I STARTLE YOU?
BDMP BDMP
BDMP BDMP
WE DETECTED A *VIOLENT ALTERCATION* WITH AN UNDOCUMENTED ENTRANT AT CAFE SARABA NOT LONG AGO.
AS LONG AS YOU PUT UP A RITUAL DUEL BARRIER FIRST, WE REALLY DON'T CARE HOW MANY BUILDINGS YOU WRECK. BUT... WELL.
TUP
WITH ALL THE LAWS AGAINST ORGANIZED CRIME NOWADAYS, WE HAVE TO INVESTIGATE EVEN THE LOW-LEVEL THINGS.
SO TELL ME, MISS. DID YOU MAKE THIS HOLE?
WUMP
!

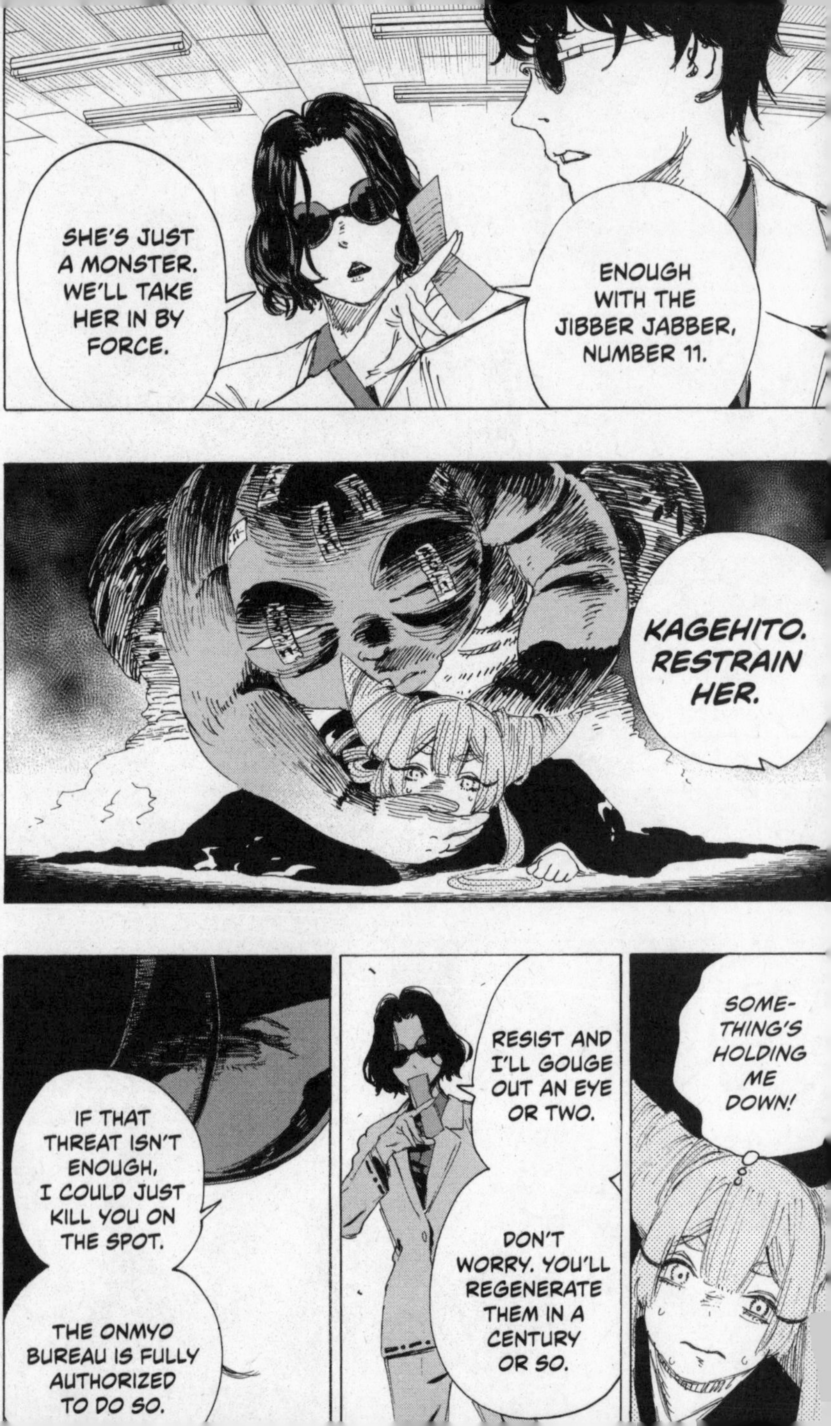
ENOUGH WITH THE JIBBER JABBER, NUMBER 11.
SHE'S JUST A MONSTER. WE'LL TAKE HER IN BY FORCE.
KAGEHITO. RESTRAIN HER.
SOME-THING'S HOLDING ME DOWN!
RESIST AND I'LL GOUGE OUT AN EYE OR TWO.
DON'T WORRY. YOU'LL REGENERATE THEM IN A CENTURY OR SO.
IF THAT THREAT ISN'T ENOUGH, I COULD JUST KILL YOU ON THE SPOT.
THE ONMYO BUREAU IS FULLY AUTHORIZED TO DO SO.

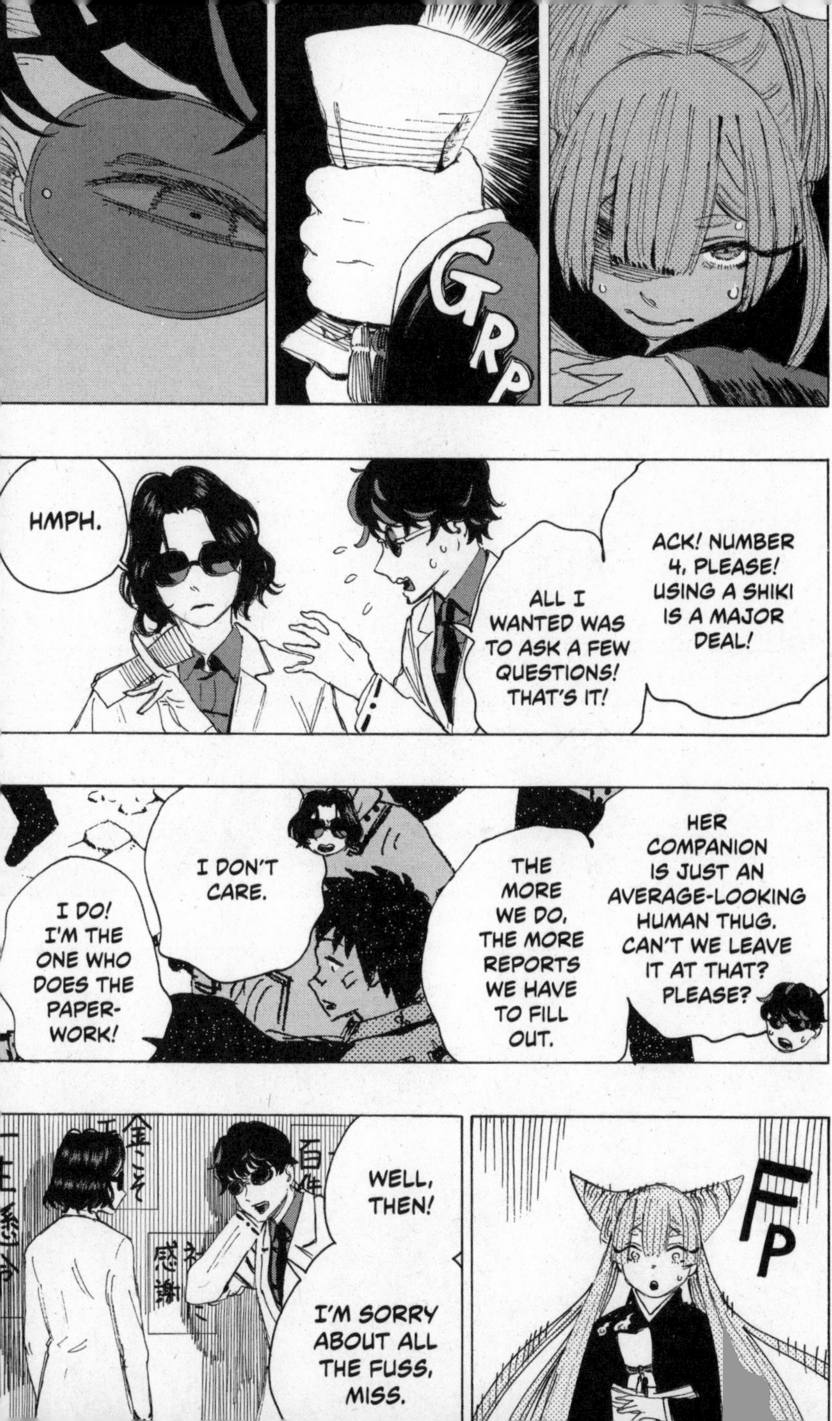
GRP
ACK! NUMBER 4, PLEASE! USING A SHIKI IS A MAJOR DEAL!
ALL I WANTED WAS TO ASK A FEW QUESTIONS! THAT'S IT!
HMPH.
HER COMPANION IS JUST AN AVERAGE-LOOKING HUMAN THUG. CAN'T WE LEAVE IT AT THAT? PLEASE?
THE MORE WE DO, THE MORE REPORTS WE HAVE TO FILL OUT.
I DON'T CARE.
I DO! I'M THE ONE WHO DOES THE PAPER-WORK!
FP
WELL, THEN!
I'M SORRY ABOUT ALL THE FUSS, MISS.

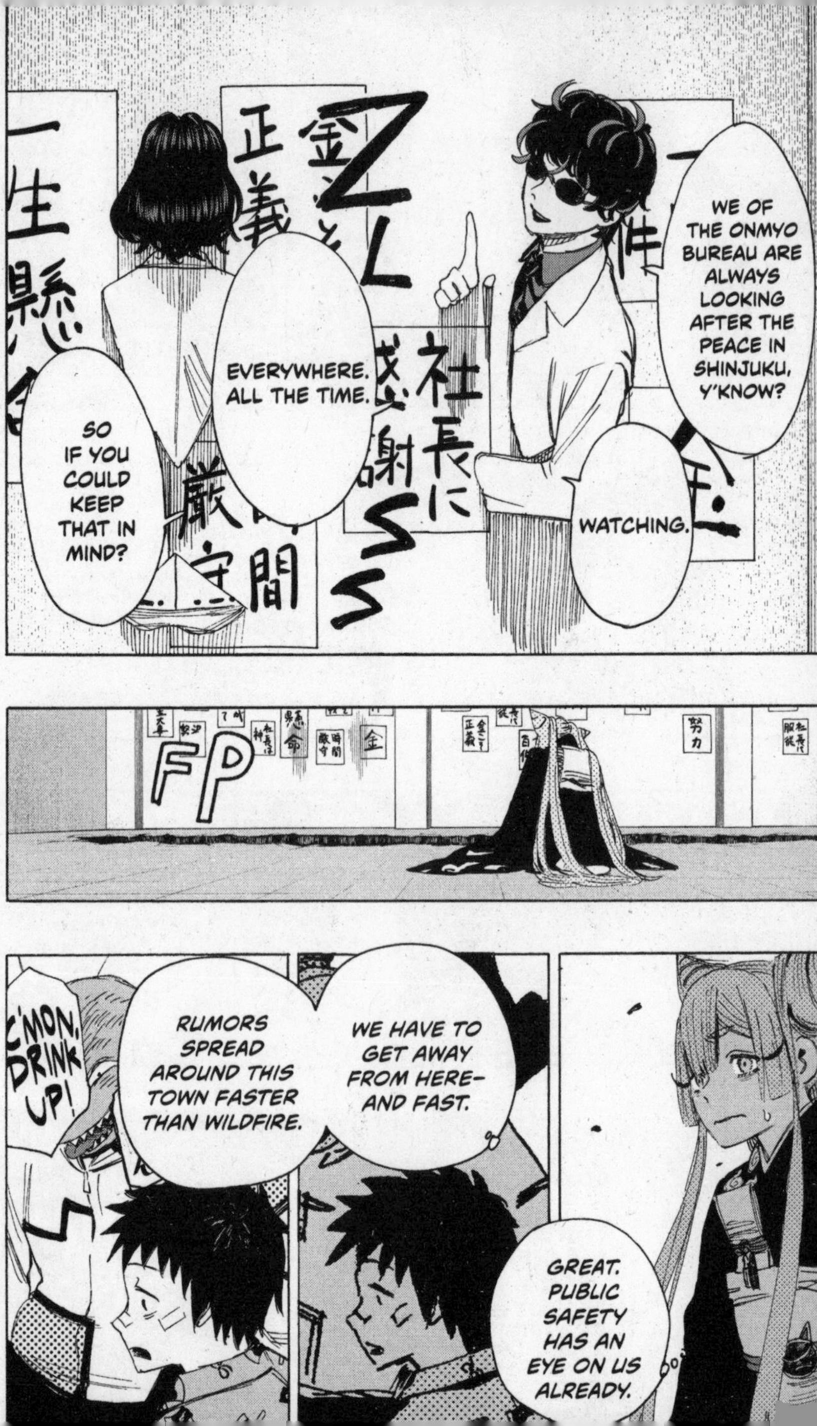
WE OF THE ONMYO BUREAU ARE ALWAYS LOOKING AFTER THE PEACE IN SHINJUKU, Y'KNOW?
WATCHING.
EVERYWHERE. ALL THE TIME.
SO IF YOU COULD KEEP THAT IN MIND?
ZL
SS
FP
GREAT. PUBLIC SAFETY HAS AN EYE ON US ALREADY.
WE HAVE TO GET AWAY FROM HERE-AND FAST.
RUMORS SPREAD AROUND THIS TOWN FASTER THAN WILDFIRE.
C'MON, DRINK UP!

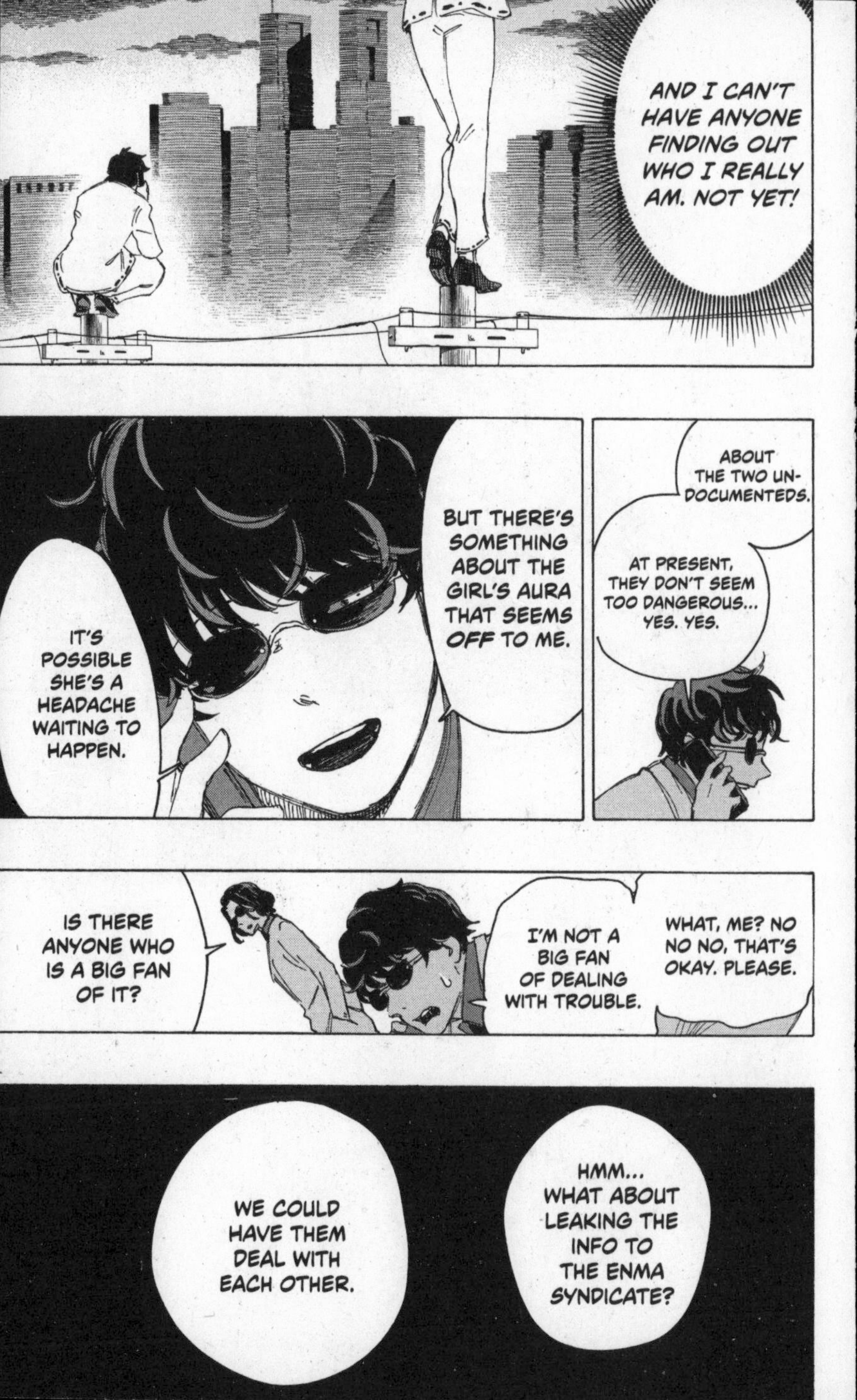
AND I CAN'T HAVE ANYONE FINDING OUT WHO I REALLY AM. NOT YET!
ABOUT THE TWO UN-DOCUMENTEDS.
AT PRESENT, THEY DON'T SEEM TOO DANGEROUS... YES. YES.
BUT THERE'S SOMETHING ABOUT THE GIRL'S AURA THAT SEEMS *OFF* TO ME.
IT'S POSSIBLE SHE'S A HEADACHE WAITING TO HAPPEN.
WHAT, ME? NO NO NO, THAT'S OKAY. PLEASE.
I'M NOT A BIG FAN OF DEALING WITH TROUBLE.
IS THERE ANYONE WHO IS A BIG FAN OF IT?
HMM... WHAT ABOUT LEAKING THE INFO TO THE ENMA SYNDICATE?
WE COULD HAVE THEM DEAL WITH EACH OTHER.

KABUKICHO MONSTER MANUAL

Yokai: Inokuma Nyudo

Just a basic thug, he has a hard time holding down a job. His *karakusa*-flame tattoos cover his entire body, and he has a shirt with the same pattern. He wears the same outfit year-around—most ayashimon can't be bothered with paying attention to the seasons...

Chapter 6

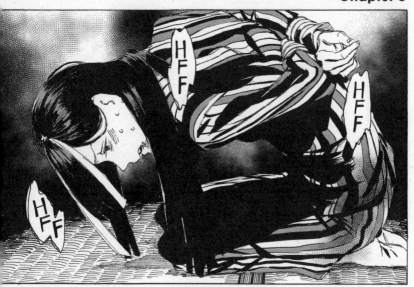

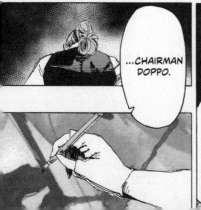

...CHAIRMAN DOPPO.

I BROUGHT HASHIHIME, AS YOU REQUESTED...

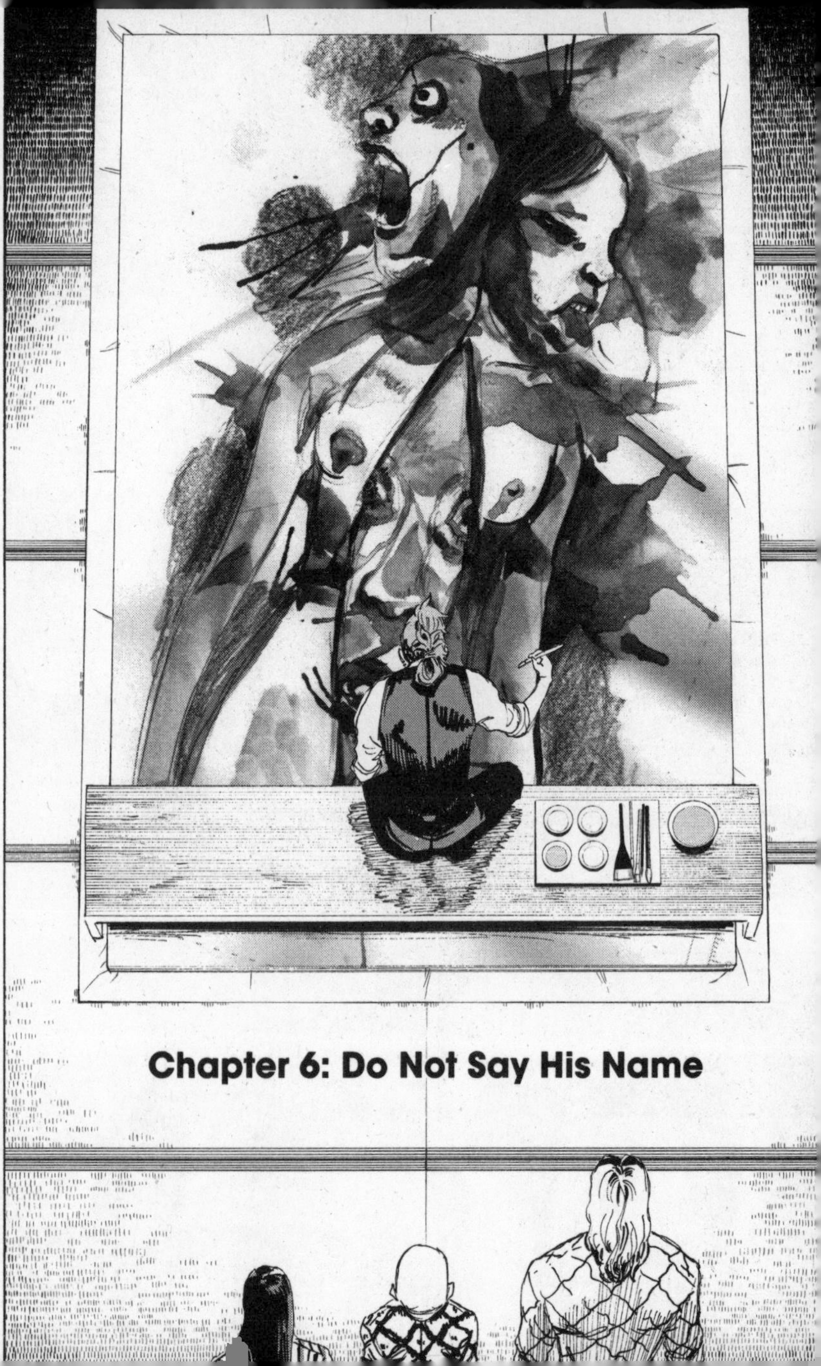
Chapter 6: Do Not Say His Name

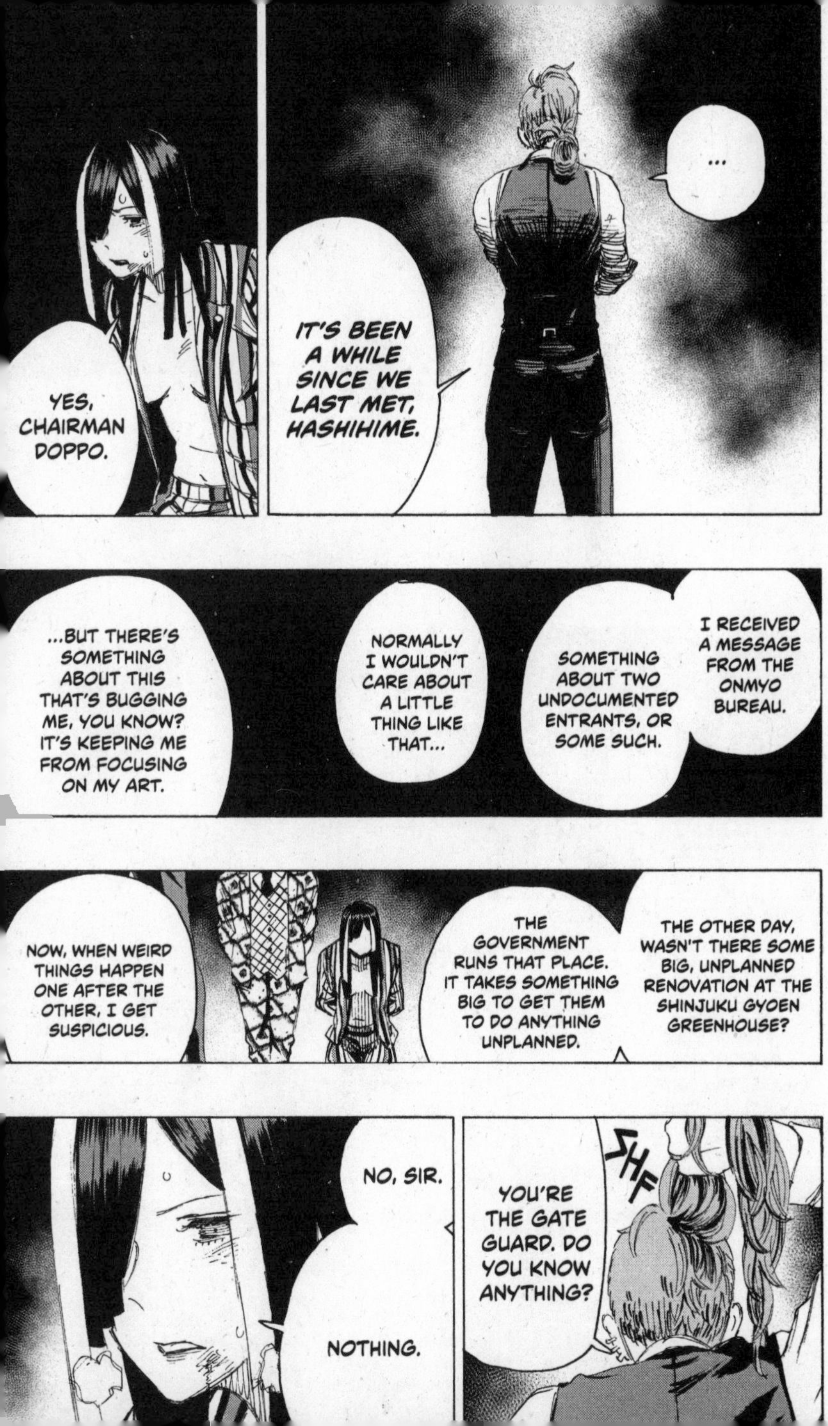
...
IT'S BEEN A WHILE SINCE WE LAST MET, HASHIHIME.
YES, CHAIRMAN DOPPO.
I RECEIVED A MESSAGE FROM THE ONMYO BUREAU.
SOMETHING ABOUT TWO UNDOCUMENTED ENTRANTS, OR SOME SUCH.
NORMALLY I WOULDN'T CARE ABOUT A LITTLE THING LIKE THAT...
...BUT THERE'S SOMETHING ABOUT THIS THAT'S BUGGING ME, YOU KNOW? IT'S KEEPING ME FROM FOCUSING ON MY ART.
THE OTHER DAY, WASN'T THERE SOME BIG, UNPLANNED RENOVATION AT THE SHINJUKU GYOEN GREENHOUSE?
THE GOVERNMENT RUNS THAT PLACE. IT TAKES SOMETHING BIG TO GET THEM TO DO ANYTHING UNPLANNED.
NOW, WHEN WEIRD THINGS HAPPEN ONE AFTER THE OTHER, I GET SUSPICIOUS.
SHF
YOU'RE THE GATE GUARD. DO YOU KNOW ANYTHING?
NO, SIR.
NOTHING.

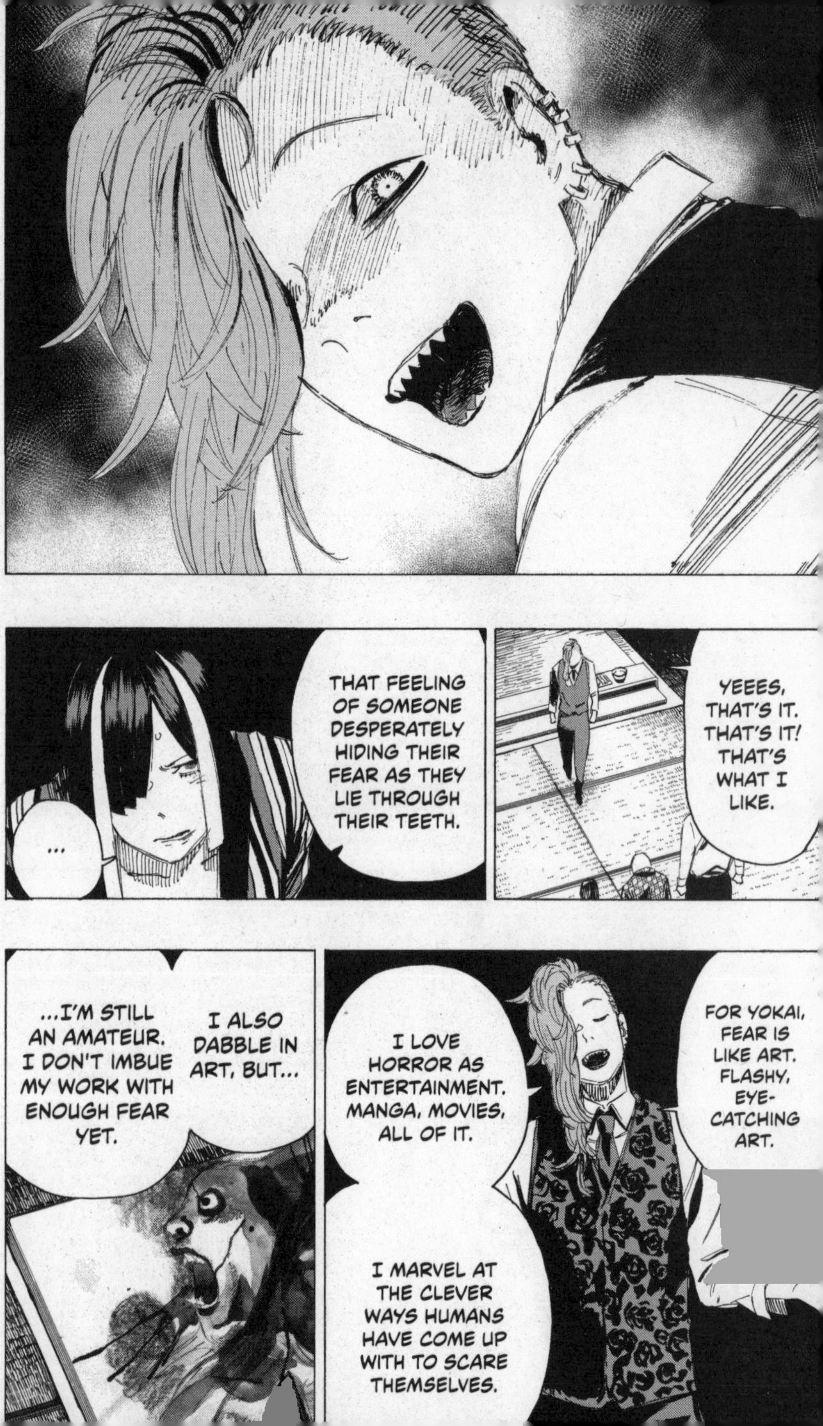
YEEES, THAT'S IT. THAT'S IT! THAT'S WHAT I LIKE.
THAT FEELING OF SOMEONE DESPERATELY HIDING THEIR FEAR AS THEY LIE THROUGH THEIR TEETH.
...
FOR YOKAI, FEAR IS LIKE ART. FLASHY, EYE-CATCHING ART.
I LOVE HORROR AS ENTERTAINMENT. MANGA, MOVIES, ALL OF IT.
I MARVEL AT THE CLEVER WAYS HUMANS HAVE COME UP WITH TO SCARE THEMSELVES.
I ALSO DABBLE IN ART, BUT...
...I'M STILL AN AMATEUR. I DON'T IMBUE MY WORK WITH ENOUGH FEAR YET.

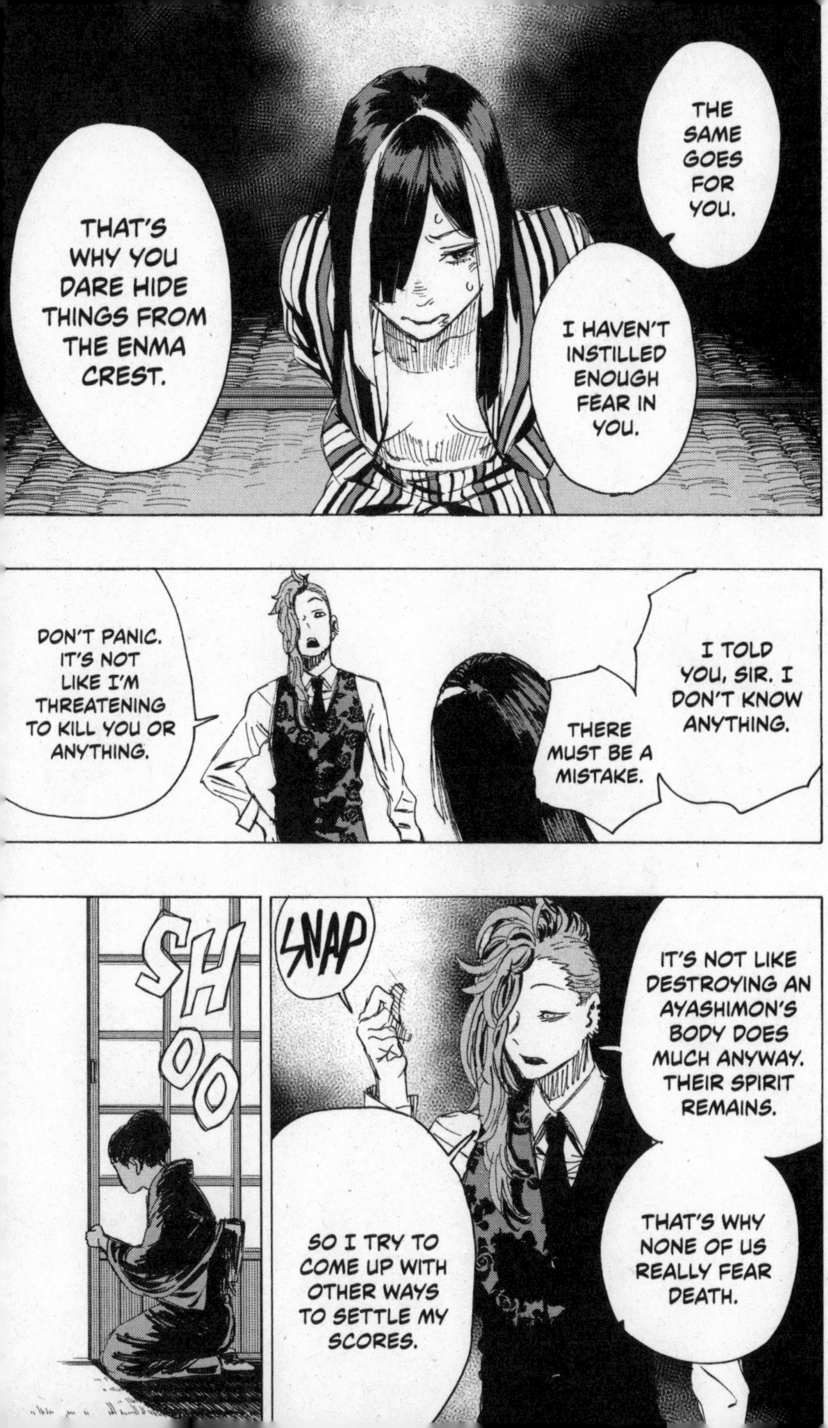
THE SAME GOES FOR YOU.
I HAVEN'T INSTILLED ENOUGH FEAR IN YOU.
THAT'S WHY YOU DARE HIDE THINGS FROM THE ENMA CREST.
I TOLD YOU, SIR. I DON'T KNOW ANYTHING.
THERE MUST BE A MISTAKE.
DON'T PANIC. IT'S NOT LIKE I'M THREATENING TO KILL YOU OR ANYTHING.
IT'S NOT LIKE DESTROYING AN AYASHIMON'S BODY DOES MUCH ANYWAY. THEIR SPIRIT REMAINS.
THAT'S WHY NONE OF US REALLY FEAR DEATH.
SNAP
SO I TRY TO COME UP WITH OTHER WAYS TO SETTLE MY SCORES.
SHOOO

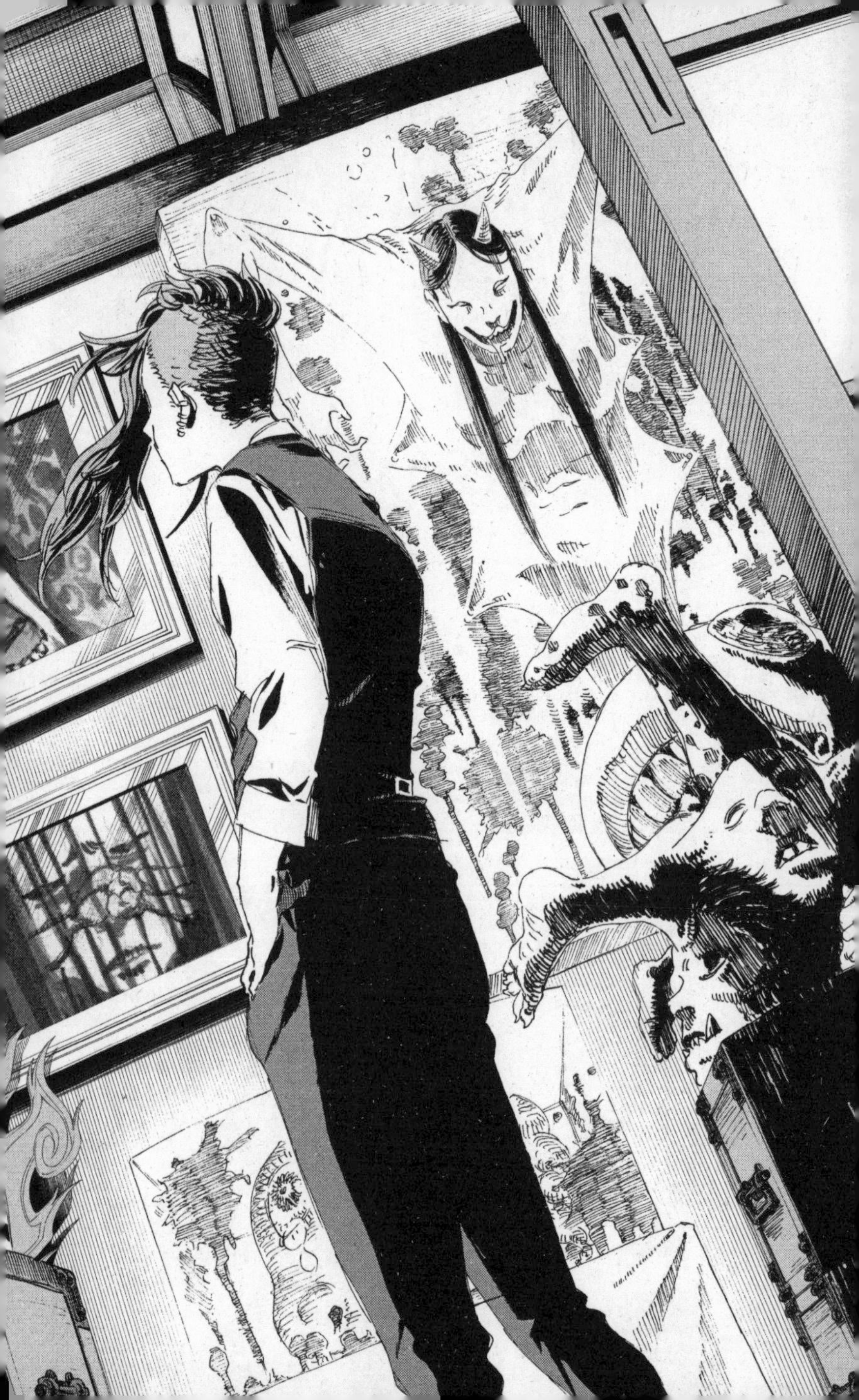

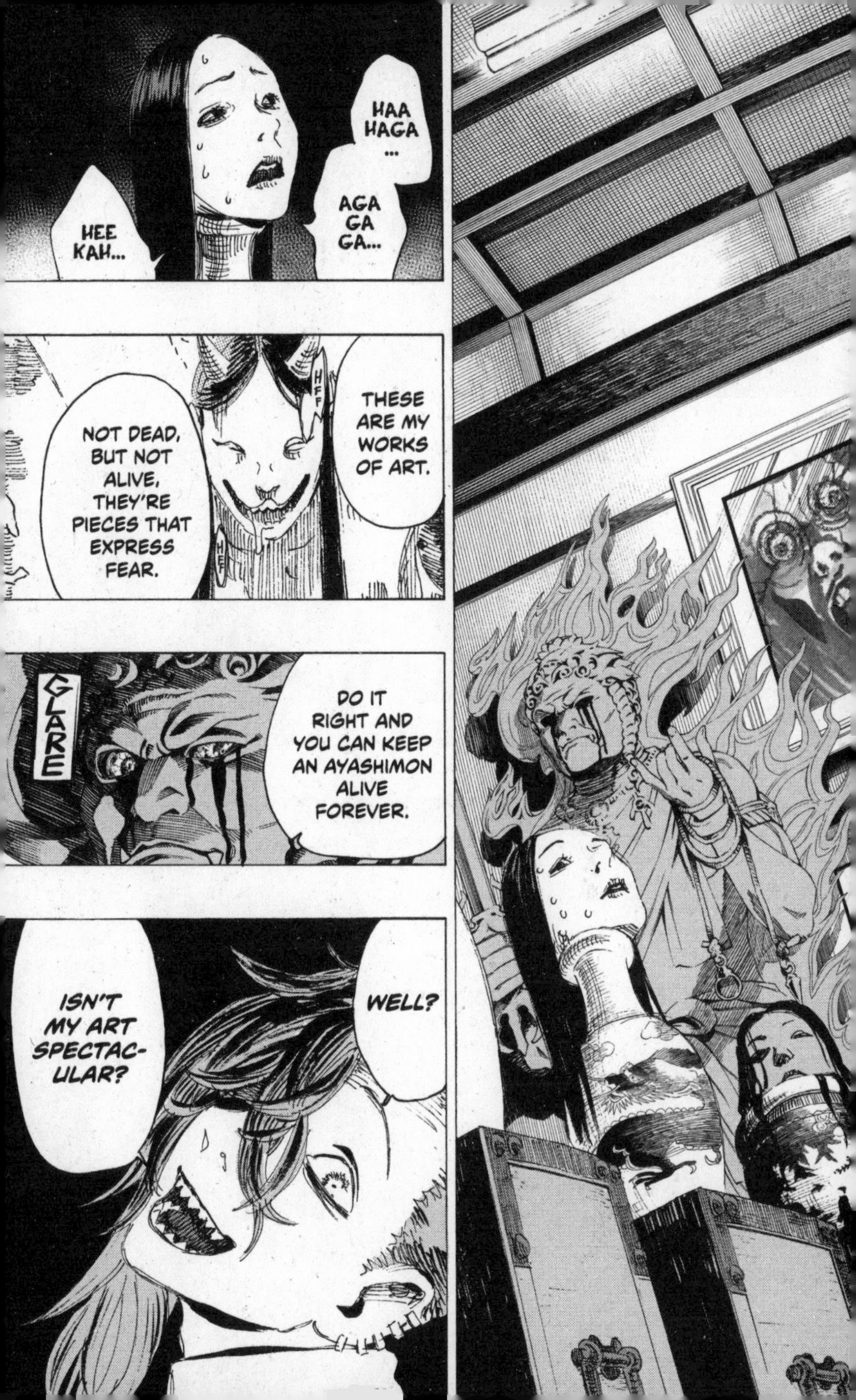
HAA HAGA ...
AGA GA GA...
HEE KAH...
THESE ARE MY WORKS OF ART.
HFF
NOT DEAD, BUT NOT ALIVE, THEY'RE PIECES THAT EXPRESS FEAR.
HFF
DO IT RIGHT AND YOU CAN KEEP AN AYASHIMON ALIVE FOREVER.
GLARE
WELL?
ISN'T MY ART SPECTACULAR?

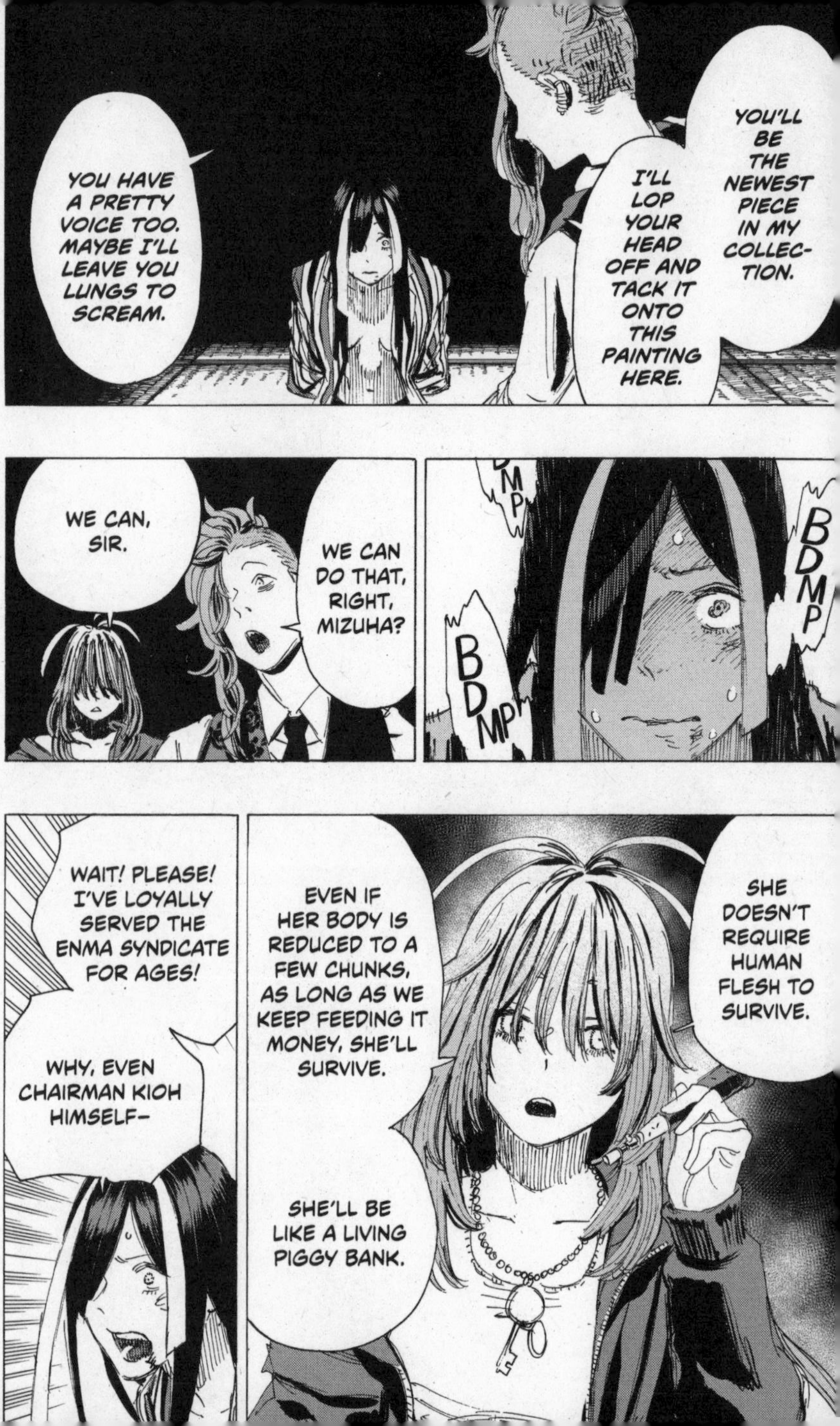
YOU'LL BE THE NEWEST PIECE IN MY COLLECTION.
I'LL LOP YOUR HEAD OFF AND TACK IT ONTO THIS PAINTING HERE.
YOU HAVE A PRETTY VOICE TOO. MAYBE I'LL LEAVE YOU LUNGS TO SCREAM.
BDMP
BDMP
WE CAN DO THAT, RIGHT, MIZUHA?
WE CAN, SIR.
SHE DOESN'T REQUIRE HUMAN FLESH TO SURVIVE.
EVEN IF HER BODY IS REDUCED TO A FEW CHUNKS, AS LONG AS WE KEEP FEEDING IT MONEY, SHE'LL SURVIVE.
SHE'LL BE LIKE A LIVING PIGGY BANK.
WAIT! PLEASE! I'VE LOYALLY SERVED THE ENMA SYNDICATE FOR AGES!
WHY, EVEN CHAIRMAN KIOH HIMSELF–

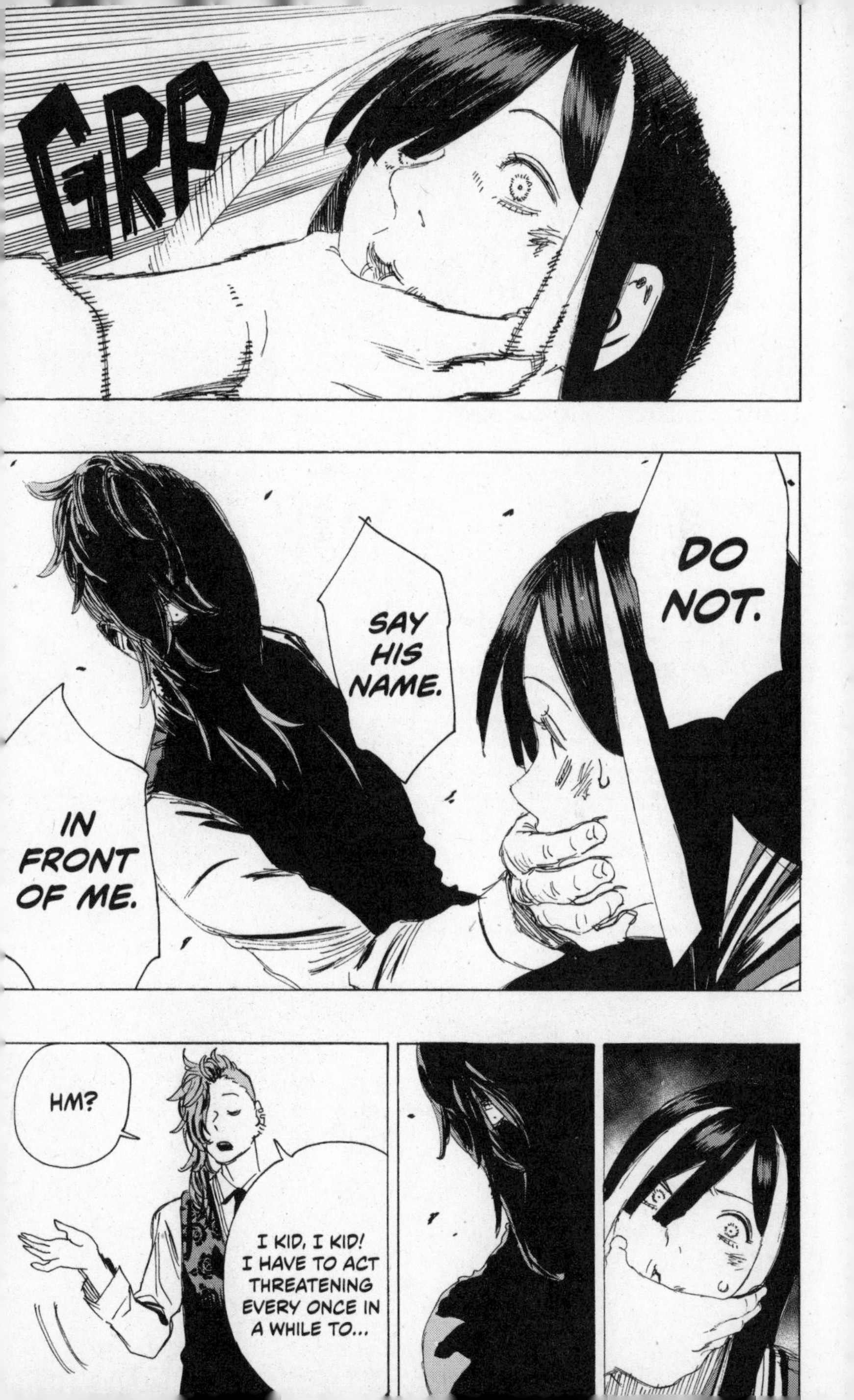
GRP
DO NOT.
SAY HIS NAME.
IN FRONT OF ME.
HM?
I KID, I KID! I HAVE TO ACT THREATENING EVERY ONCE IN A WHILE TO...

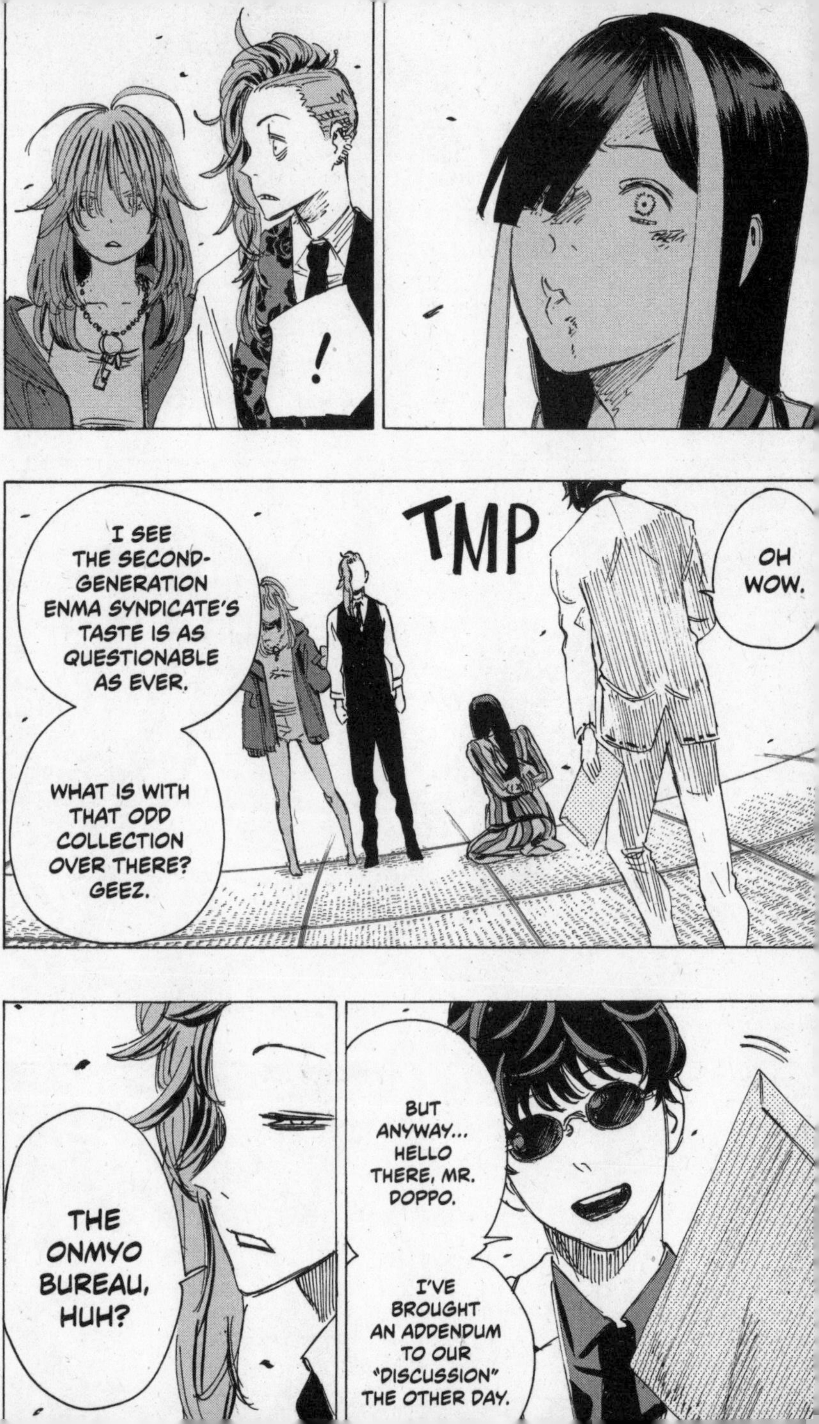
!
OH WOW.
TMP
I SEE THE SECOND-GENERATION ENMA SYNDICATE'S TASTE IS AS QUESTIONABLE AS EVER.
WHAT IS WITH THAT ODD COLLECTION OVER THERE? GEEZ.
BUT ANYWAY... HELLO THERE, MR. DOPPO.
I'VE BROUGHT AN ADDENDUM TO OUR "DISCUSSION" THE OTHER DAY.
THE ONMYO BUREAU, HUH?

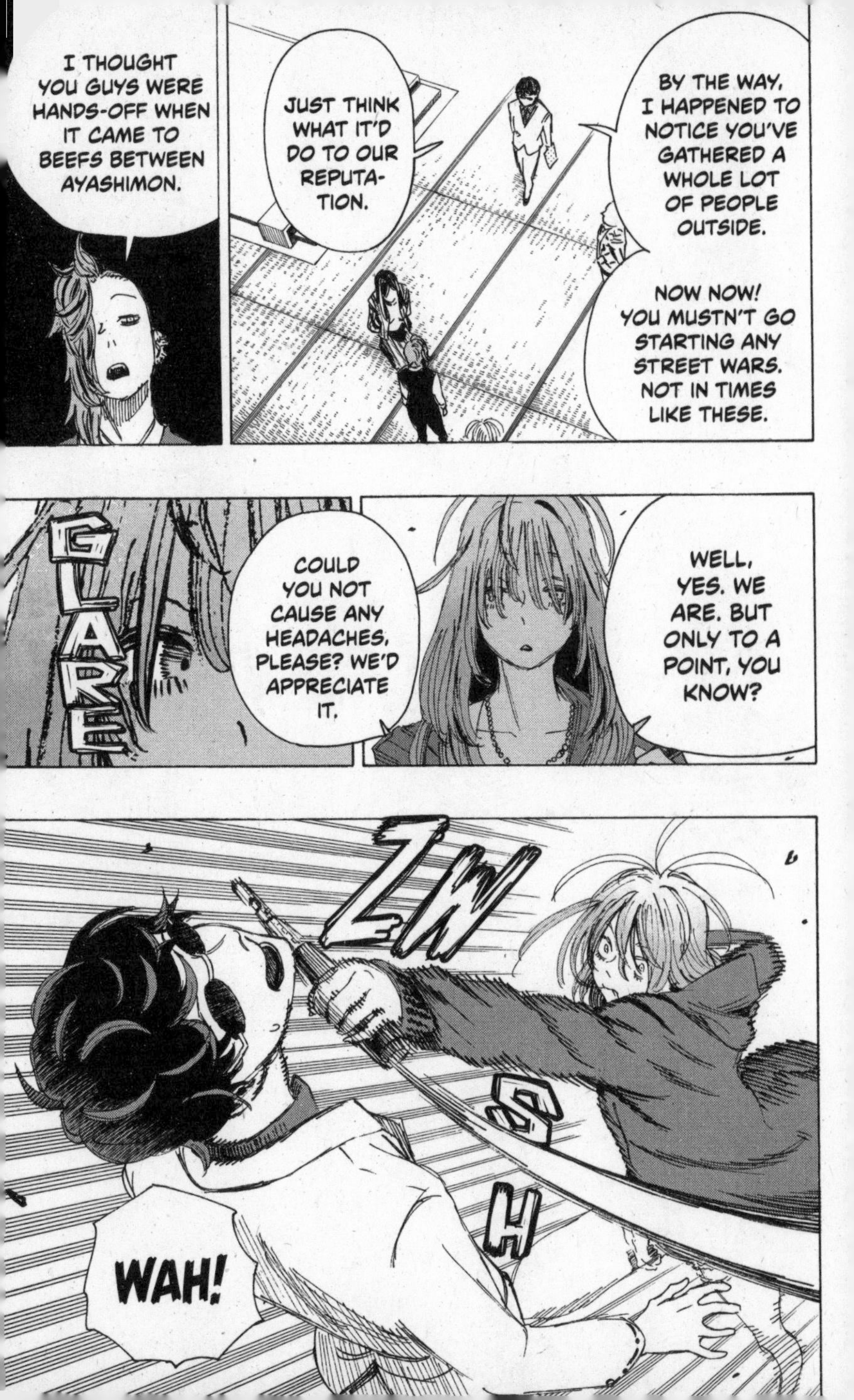
BY THE WAY, I HAPPENED TO NOTICE YOU'VE GATHERED A WHOLE LOT OF PEOPLE OUTSIDE.
NOW NOW! YOU MUSTN'T GO STARTING ANY STREET WARS. NOT IN TIMES LIKE THESE.
JUST THINK WHAT IT'D DO TO OUR REPUTATION.
I THOUGHT YOU GUYS WERE HANDS-OFF WHEN IT CAME TO BEEFS BETWEEN AYASHIMON.
WELL, YES. WE ARE. BUT ONLY TO A POINT, YOU KNOW?
COULD YOU NOT CAUSE ANY HEADACHES, PLEASE? WE'D APPRECIATE IT.
GLARE
ZWSH
WAH!

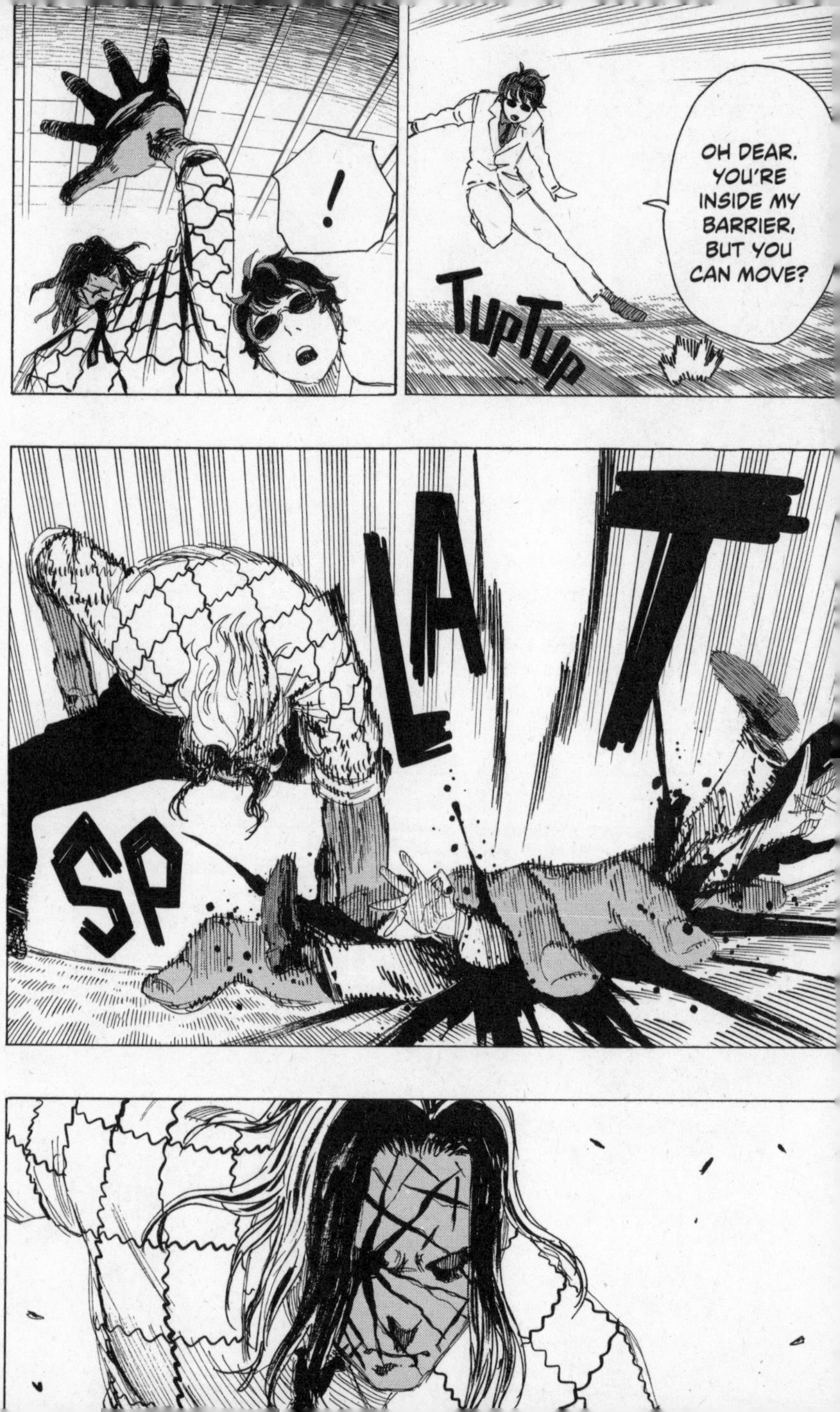
OH DEAR. YOU'RE INSIDE MY BARRIER, BUT YOU CAN MOVE?
TUPTUP
!
SPLAT

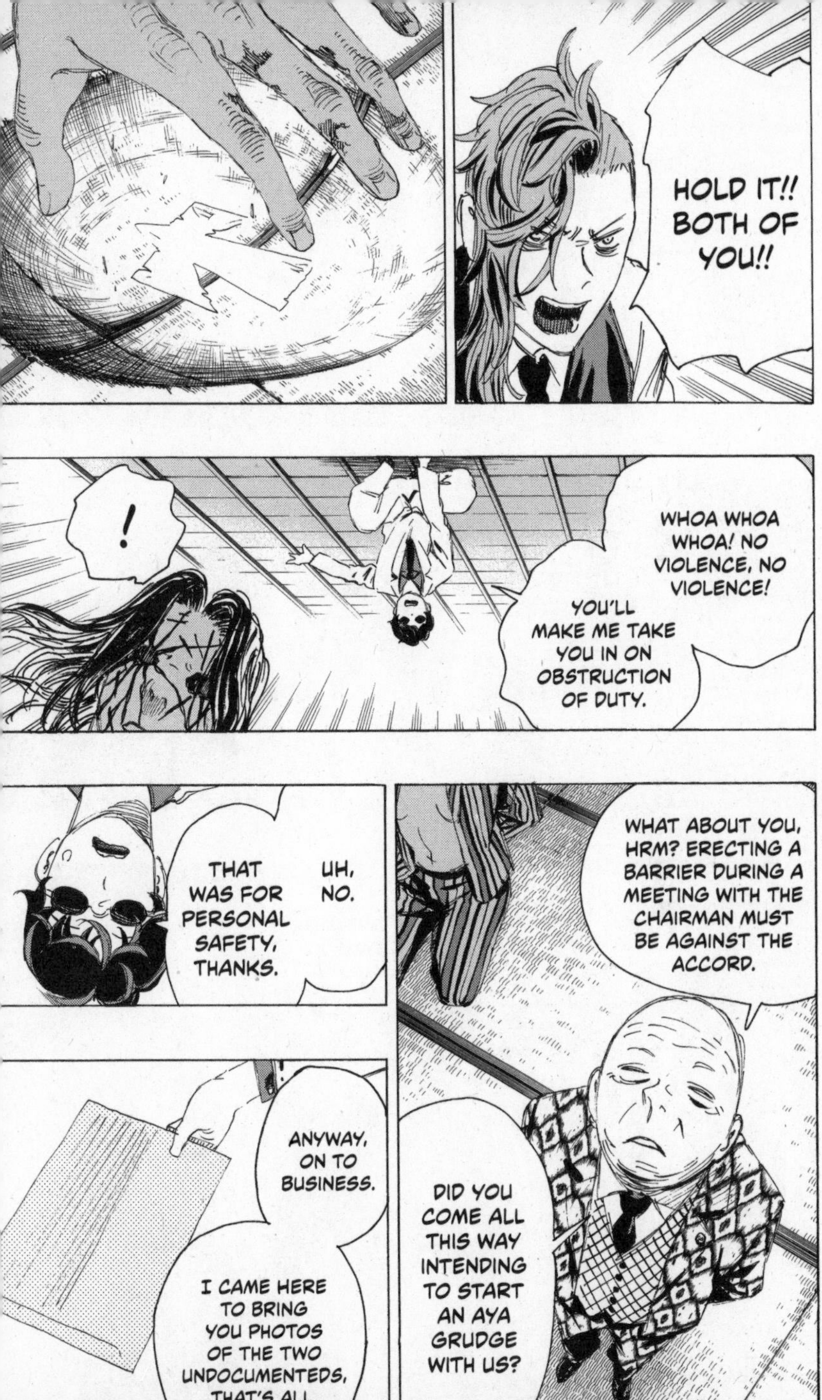
HOLD IT!! BOTH OF YOU!!
WHOA WHOA WHOA! NO VIOLENCE, NO VIOLENCE!
YOU'LL MAKE ME TAKE YOU IN ON OBSTRUCTION OF DUTY.
!
WHAT ABOUT YOU, HRM? ERECTING A BARRIER DURING A MEETING WITH THE CHAIRMAN MUST BE AGAINST THE ACCORD.
DID YOU COME ALL THIS WAY INTENDING TO START AN AYA GRUDGE WITH US?
UH, NO.
THAT WAS FOR PERSONAL SAFETY, THANKS.
ANYWAY, ON TO BUSINESS.
I CAME HERE TO BRING YOU PHOTOS OF THE TWO UNDOCUMENTEDS, THAT'S ALL.

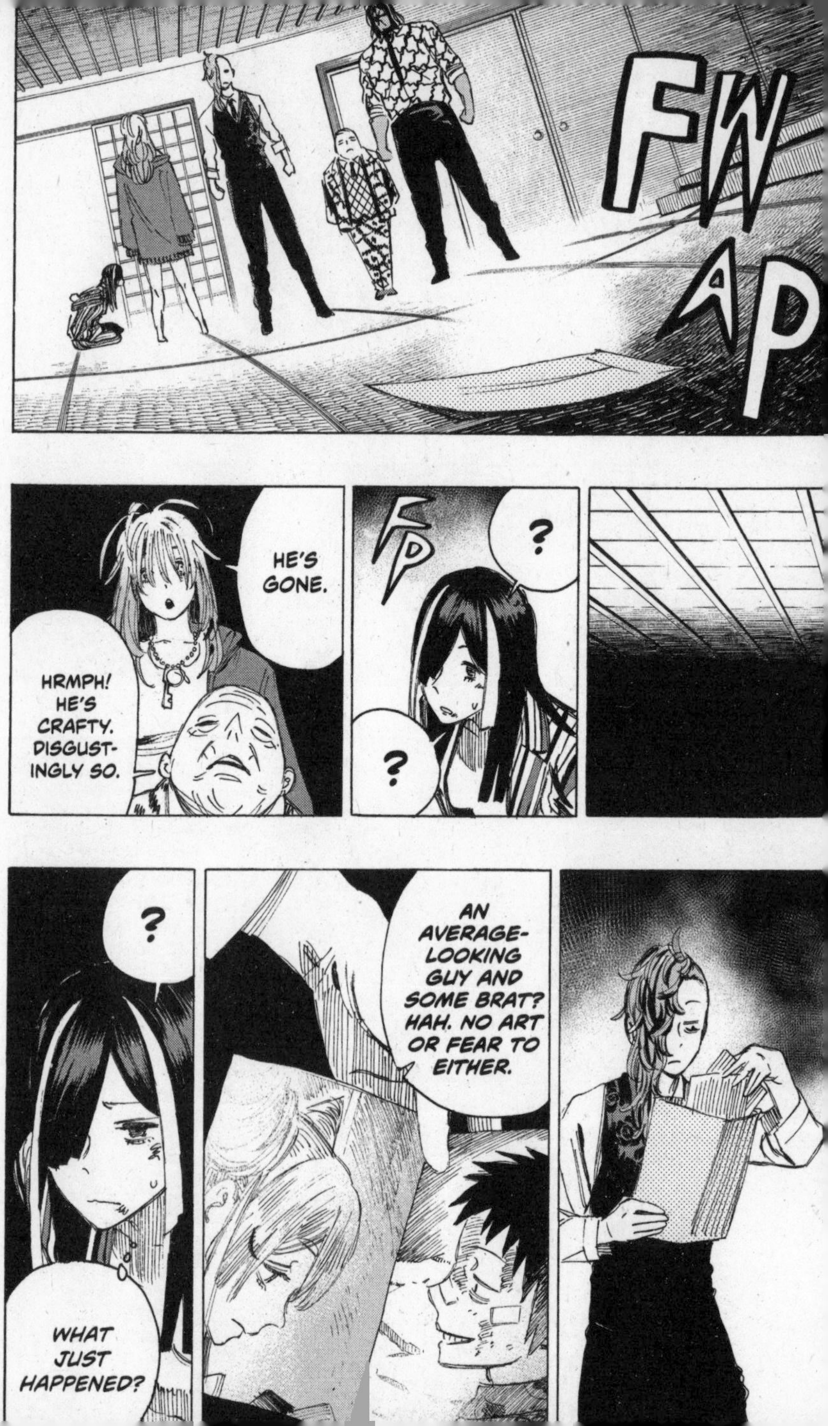
FWAP
FP
?
?
HE'S GONE.
HRMPH! HE'S CRAFTY. DISGUST-INGLY SO.
AN AVERAGE-LOOKING GUY AND SOME BRAT? HAH. NO ART OR FEAR TO EITHER.
?
WHAT JUST HAPPENED?

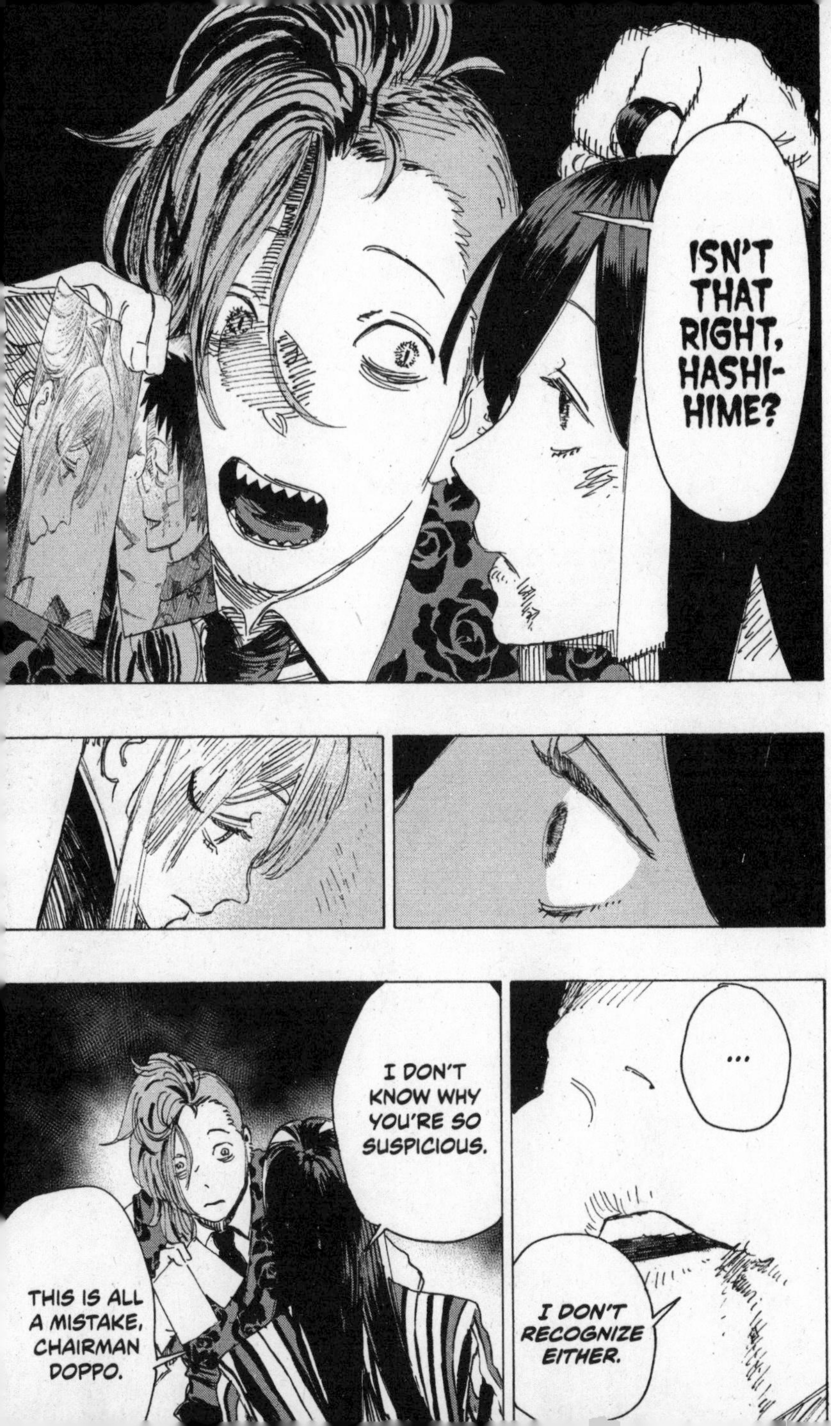
ISN'T THAT RIGHT, HASHI-HIME?
...
I DON'T RECOGNIZE EITHER.
I DON'T KNOW WHY YOU'RE SO SUSPICIOUS.
THIS IS ALL A MISTAKE, CHAIRMAN DOPPO.

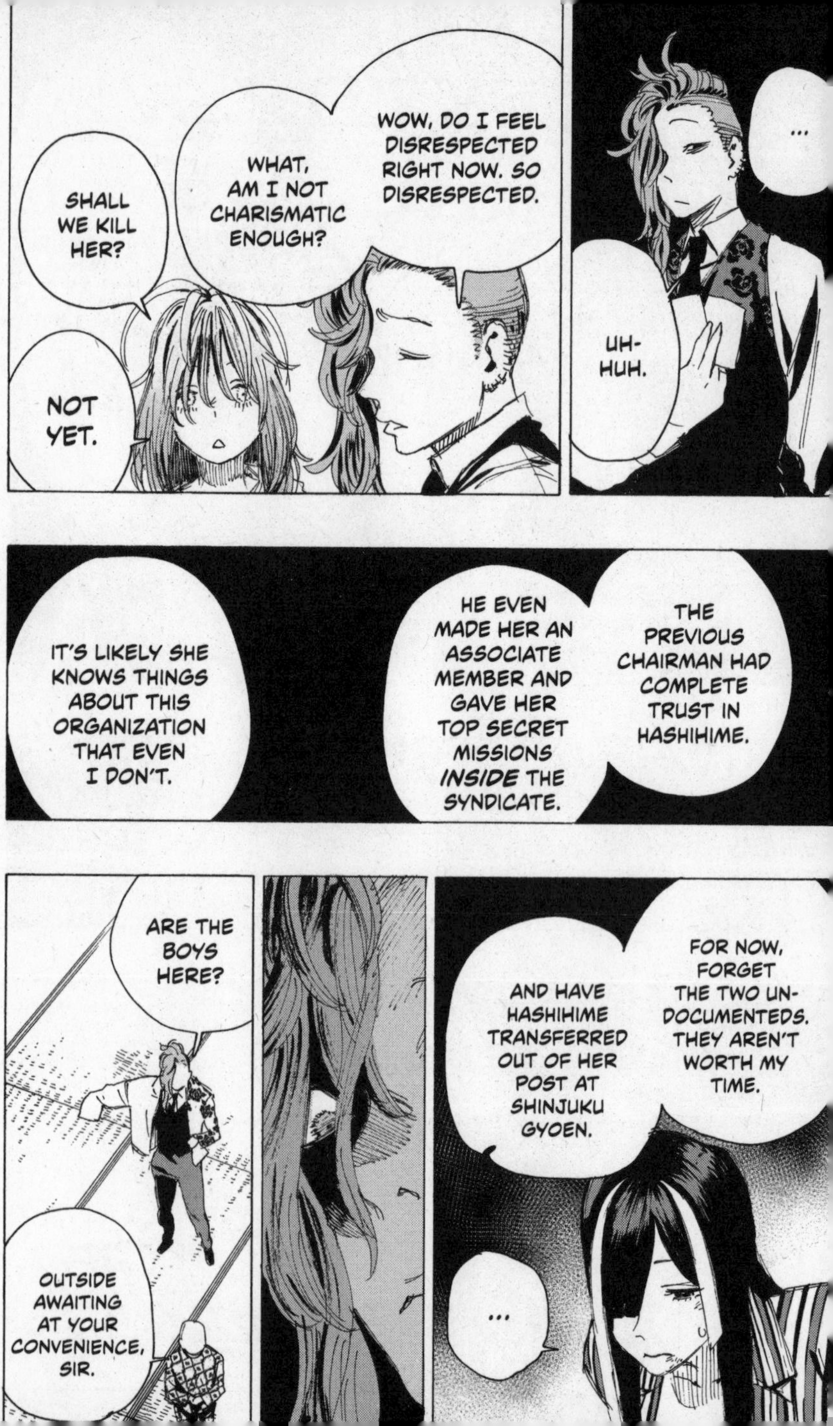
...
UH-HUH.
WOW, DO I FEEL DISRESPECTED RIGHT NOW. SO DISRESPECTED.
WHAT, AM I NOT CHARISMATIC ENOUGH?
SHALL WE KILL HER?
NOT YET.
THE PREVIOUS CHAIRMAN HAD COMPLETE TRUST IN HASHIHIME.
HE EVEN MADE HER AN ASSOCIATE MEMBER AND GAVE HER TOP SECRET MISSIONS *INSIDE* THE SYNDICATE.
IT'S LIKELY SHE KNOWS THINGS ABOUT THIS ORGANIZATION THAT EVEN I DON'T.
FOR NOW, FORGET THE TWO UN-DOCUMENTEDS. THEY AREN'T WORTH MY TIME.
AND HAVE HASHIHIME TRANSFERRED OUT OF HER POST AT SHINJUKU GYOEN.
...
ARE THE BOYS HERE?
OUTSIDE AWAITING AT YOUR CONVENIENCE, SIR.

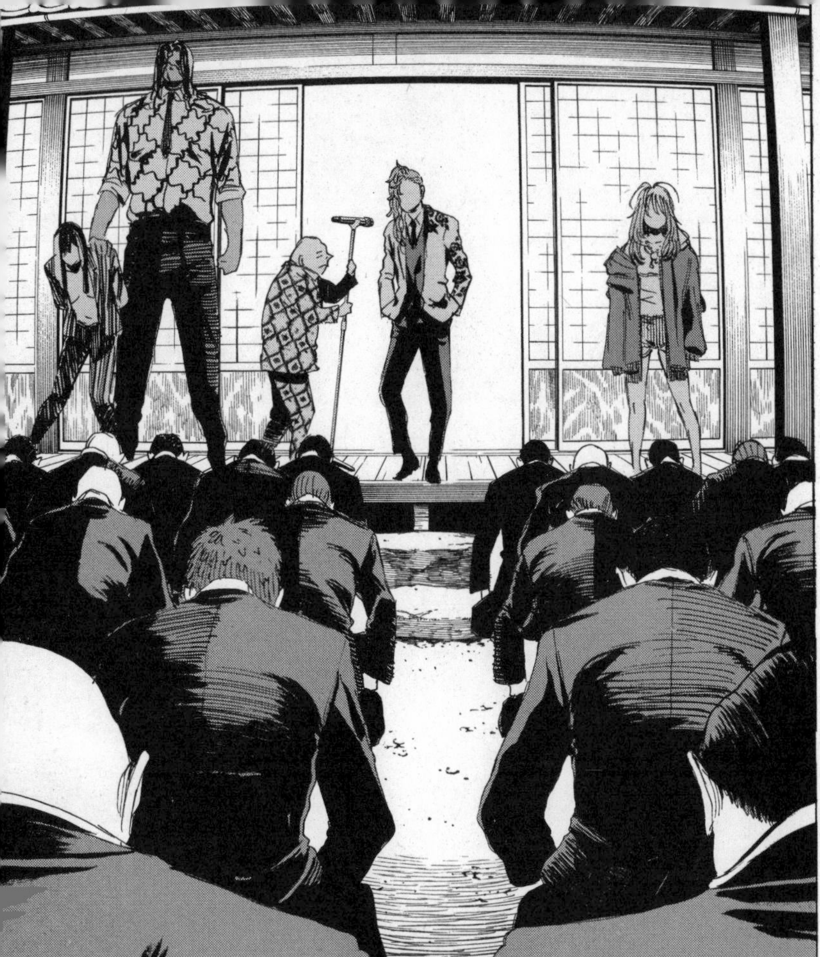

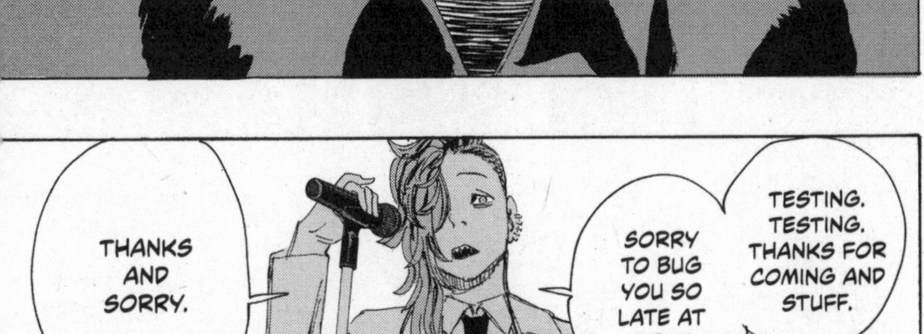
TESTING. TESTING. THANKS FOR COMING AND STUFF.
SORRY TO BUG YOU SO LATE AT NIGHT.
THANKS AND SORRY.

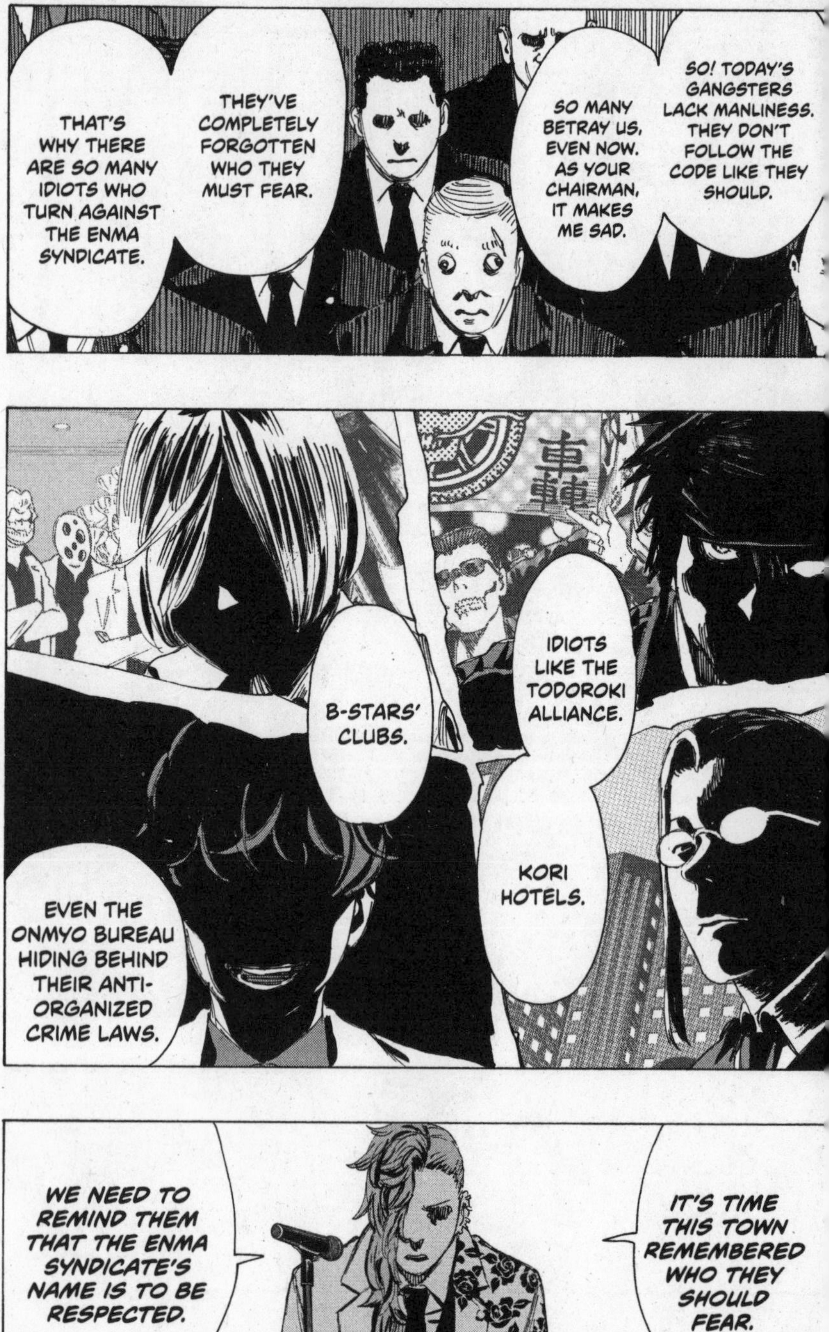
SO! TODAY'S GANGSTERS LACK MANLINESS. THEY DON'T FOLLOW THE CODE LIKE THEY SHOULD.
SO MANY BETRAY US, EVEN NOW. AS YOUR CHAIRMAN, IT MAKES ME SAD.
THEY'VE COMPLETELY FORGOTTEN WHO THEY MUST FEAR.
THAT'S WHY THERE ARE SO MANY IDIOTS WHO TURN AGAINST THE ENMA SYNDICATE.
車輌
IDIOTS LIKE THE TODOROKI ALLIANCE.
B-STARS' CLUBS.
KORI HOTELS.
EVEN THE ONMYO BUREAU HIDING BEHIND THEIR ANTI-ORGANIZED CRIME LAWS.
IT'S TIME THIS TOWN REMEMBERED WHO THEY SHOULD FEAR.
WE NEED TO REMIND THEM THAT THE ENMA SYNDICATE'S NAME IS TO BE RESPECTED.

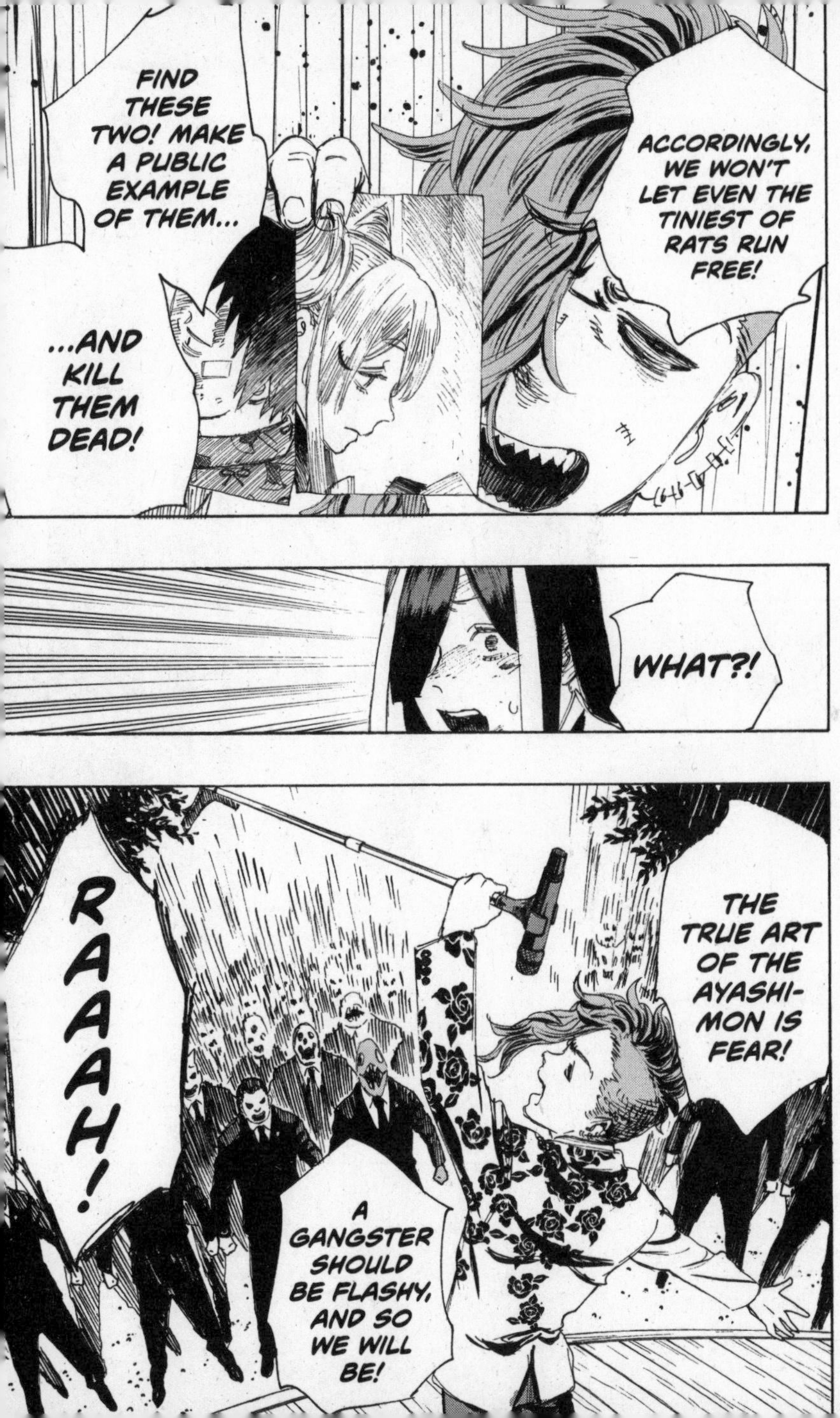
ACCORDINGLY, WE WON'T LET EVEN THE TINIEST OF RATS RUN FREE!
FIND THESE TWO! MAKE A PUBLIC EXAMPLE OF THEM...
...AND KILL THEM DEAD!
WHAT?!
THE TRUE ART OF THE AYASHI-MON IS FEAR!
RAAAAH!
A GANGSTER SHOULD BE FLASHY, AND SO WE WILL BE!

KABUKICHO MONSTER MANUAL

Yokai: Amamehagi

A hip-hop fan.

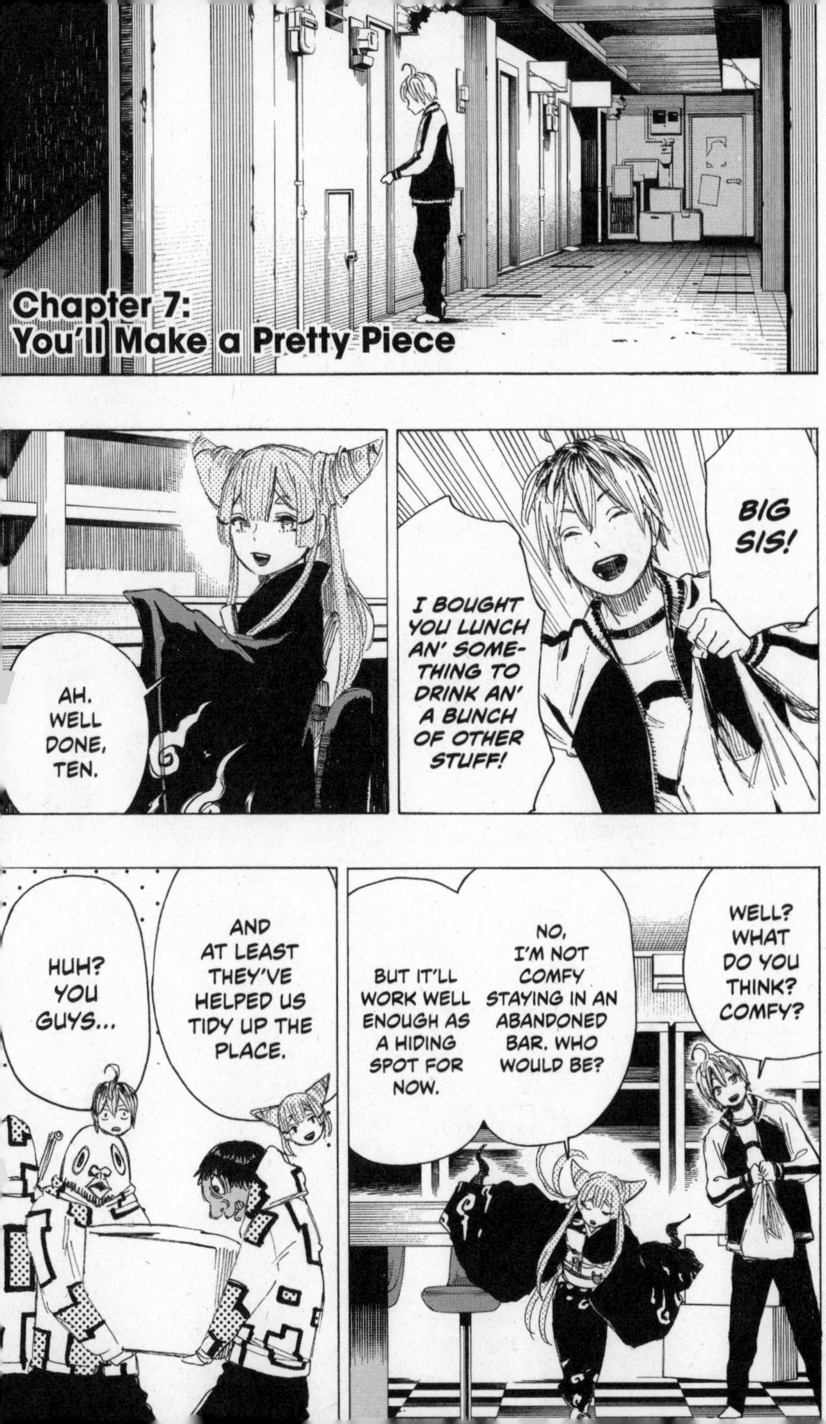
Chapter 7:
You'll Make a Pretty Piece
BIG SIS!
I BOUGHT YOU LUNCH AN' SOME-THING TO DRINK AN' A BUNCH OF OTHER STUFF!
AH. WELL DONE, TEN.
WELL? WHAT DO YOU THINK? COMFY?
NO, I'M NOT COMFY STAYING IN AN ABANDONED BAR. WHO WOULD BE?
BUT IT'LL WORK WELL ENOUGH AS A HIDING SPOT FOR NOW.
AND AT LEAST THEY'VE HELPED US TIDY UP THE PLACE.
HUH? YOU GUYS...

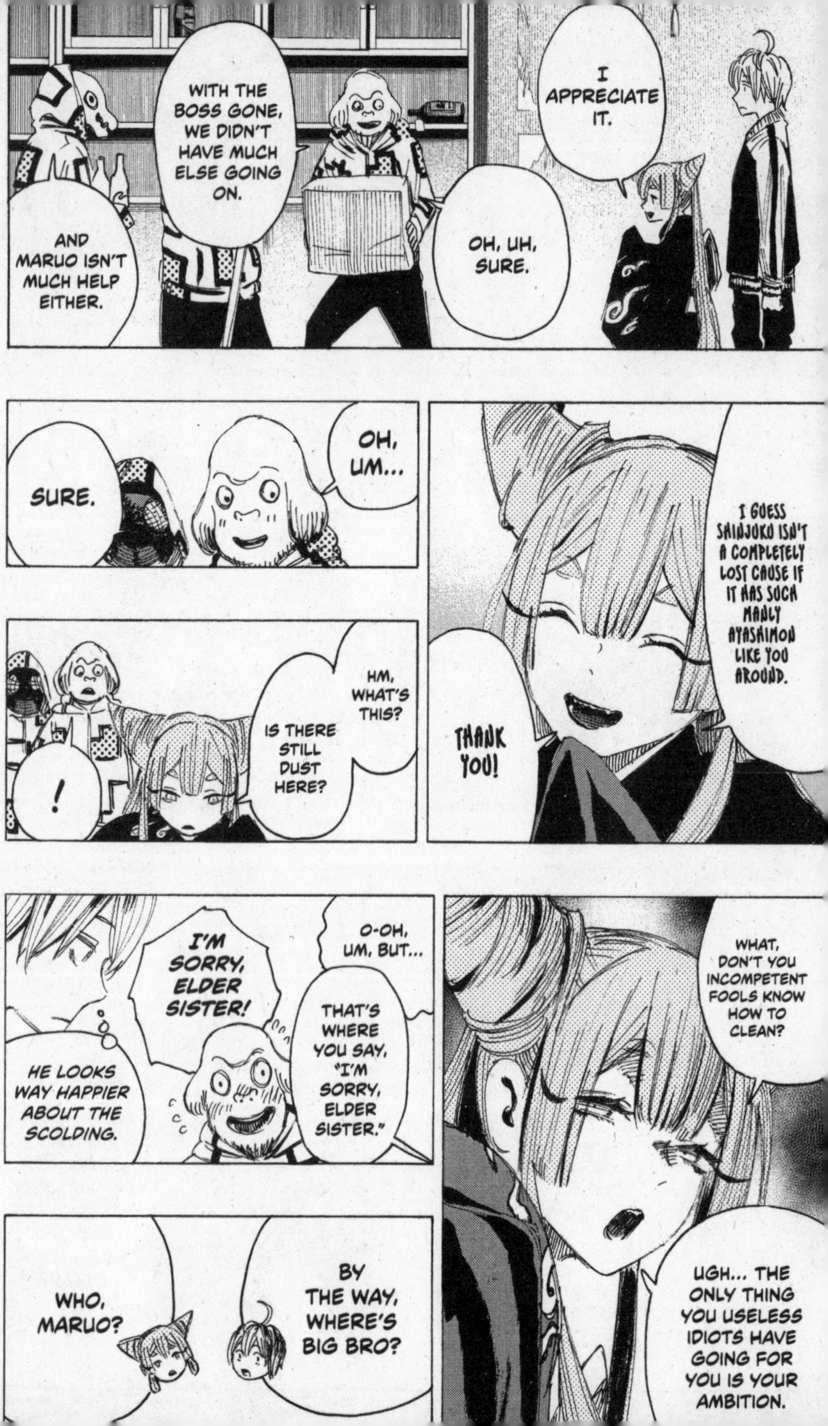
I APPRECIATE IT.
OH, UH, SURE.
WITH THE BOSS GONE, WE DIDN'T HAVE MUCH ELSE GOING ON.
AND MARUO ISN'T MUCH HELP EITHER.
I GUESS SHINJUKU ISN'T A COMPLETELY LOST CAUSE IF IT HAS SUCH MANLY AYASHIMON LIKE YOU AROUND.
THANK YOU!
OH, UM...
SURE.
HM, WHAT'S THIS?
IS THERE STILL DUST HERE?
!
WHAT, DON'T YOU INCOMPETENT FOOLS KNOW HOW TO CLEAN?
UGH... THE ONLY THING YOU USELESS IDIOTS HAVE GOING FOR YOU IS YOUR AMBITION.
O-OH, UM, BUT...
THAT'S WHERE YOU SAY, "I'M SORRY, ELDER SISTER."
I'M SORRY, ELDER SISTER!
HE LOOKS WAY HAPPIER ABOUT THE SCOLDING.
BY THE WAY, WHERE'S BIG BRO?
WHO, MARUO?

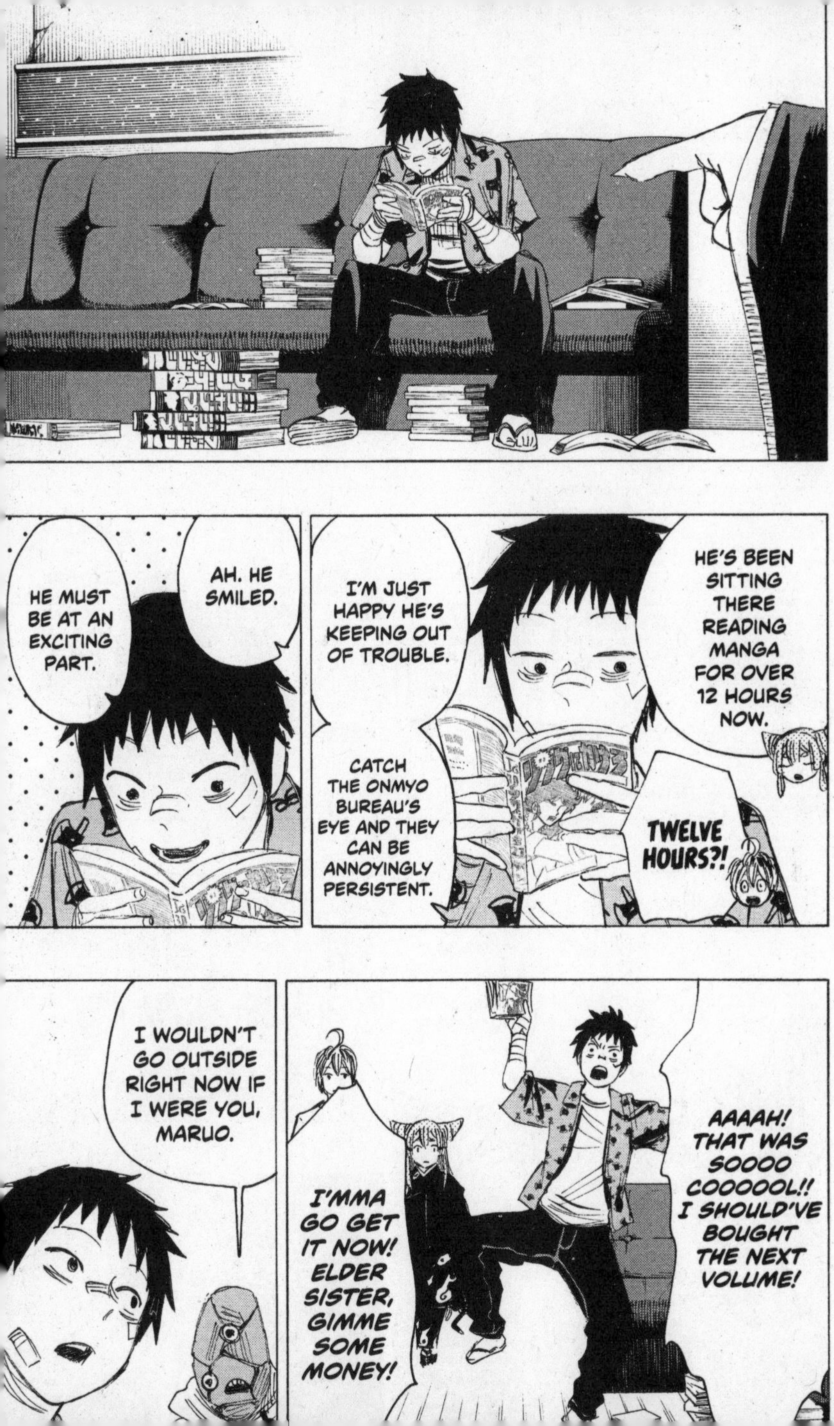
HE'S BEEN SITTING THERE READING MANGA FOR OVER 12 HOURS NOW.
TWELVE HOURS?!
I'M JUST HAPPY HE'S KEEPING OUT OF TROUBLE.
CATCH THE ONMYO BUREAU'S EYE AND THEY CAN BE ANNOYINGLY PERSISTENT.
AH. HE SMILED.
HE MUST BE AT AN EXCITING PART.
AAAAH! THAT WAS SOOOO COOOOOL!! I SHOULD'VE BOUGHT THE NEXT VOLUME!
I'MMA GO GET IT NOW! ELDER SISTER, GIMME SOME MONEY!
I WOULDN'T GO OUTSIDE RIGHT NOW IF I WERE YOU, MARUO.

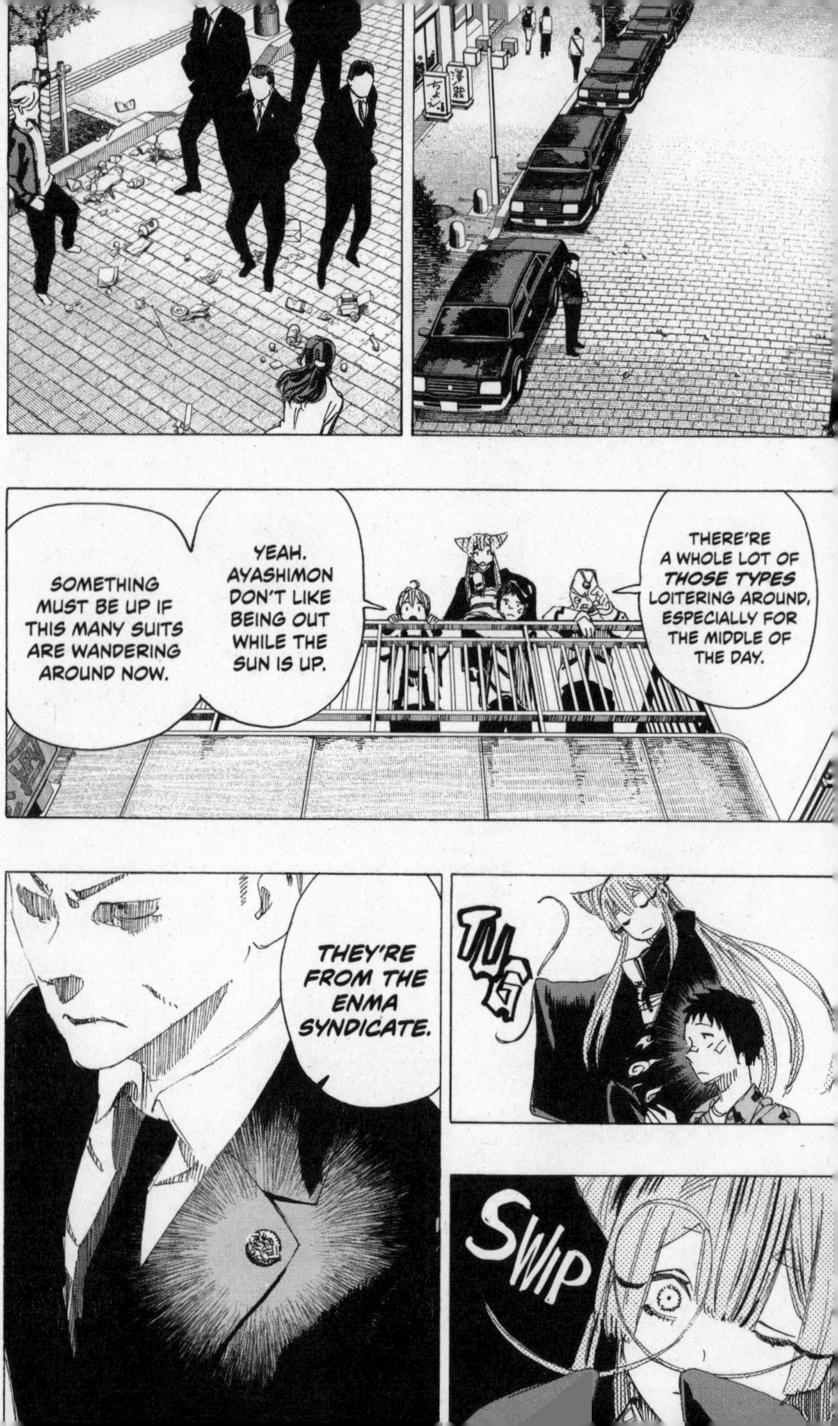
THERE'RE A WHOLE LOT OF THOSE TYPES LOITERING AROUND, ESPECIALLY FOR THE MIDDLE OF THE DAY.
YEAH. AYASHIMON DON'T LIKE BEING OUT WHILE THE SUN IS UP.
SOMETHING MUST BE UP IF THIS MANY SUITS ARE WANDERING AROUND NOW.
TUG
SWIP
THEY'RE FROM THE ENMA SYNDICATE.

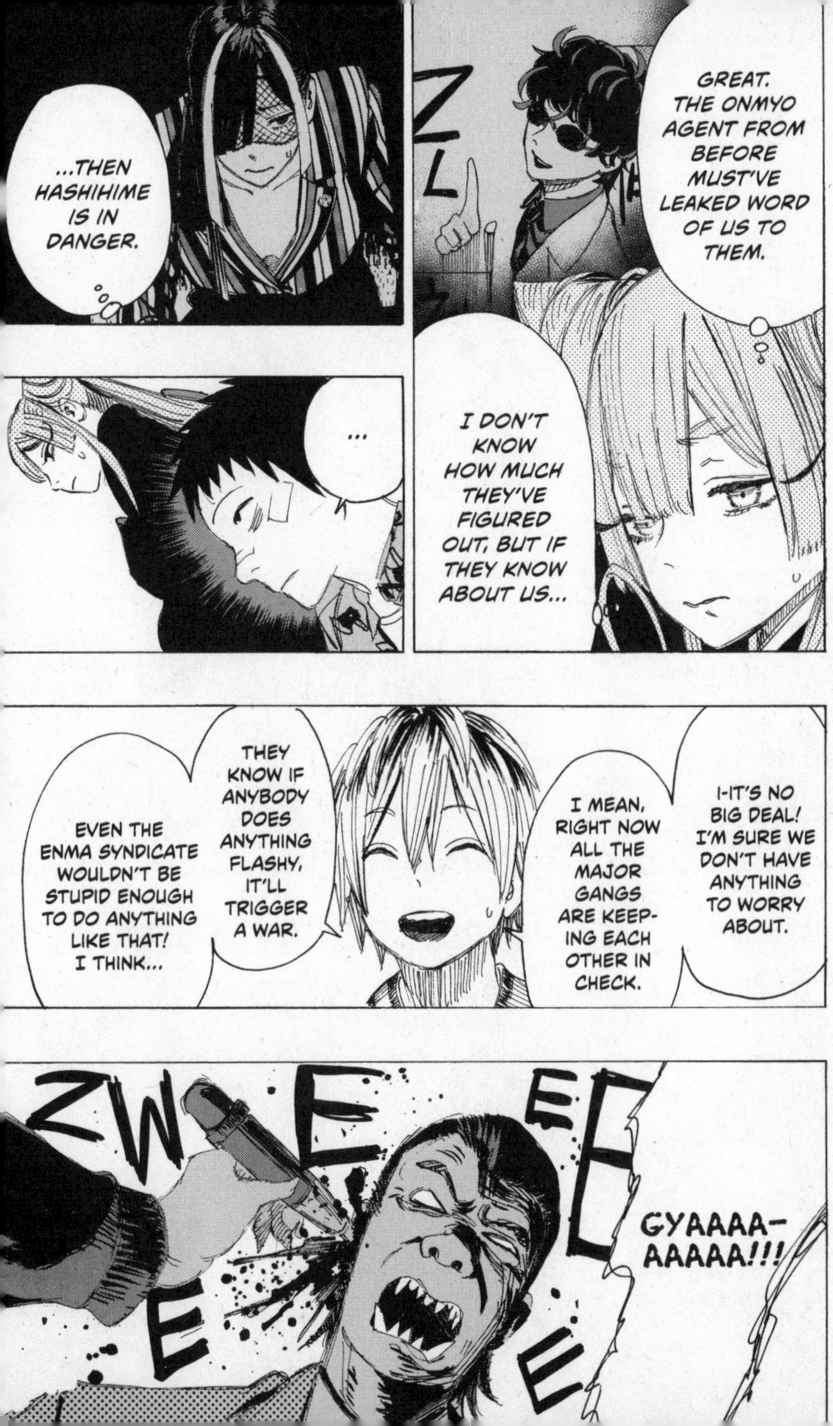
ZL
GREAT. THE ONMYO AGENT FROM BEFORE MUST'VE LEAKED WORD OF US TO THEM.
...THEN HASHIHIME IS IN DANGER.
I DON'T KNOW HOW MUCH THEY'VE FIGURED OUT, BUT IF THEY KNOW ABOUT US...
...
I-IT'S NO BIG DEAL! I'M SURE WE DON'T HAVE ANYTHING TO WORRY ABOUT.
I MEAN, RIGHT NOW ALL THE MAJOR GANGS ARE KEEP-ING EACH OTHER IN CHECK.
THEY KNOW IF ANYBODY DOES ANYTHING FLASHY, IT'LL TRIGGER A WAR.
EVEN THE ENMA SYNDICATE WOULDN'T BE STUPID ENOUGH TO DO ANYTHING LIKE THAT! I THINK...
ZWEEEEEEE
GYAAAA-AAAAA!!!

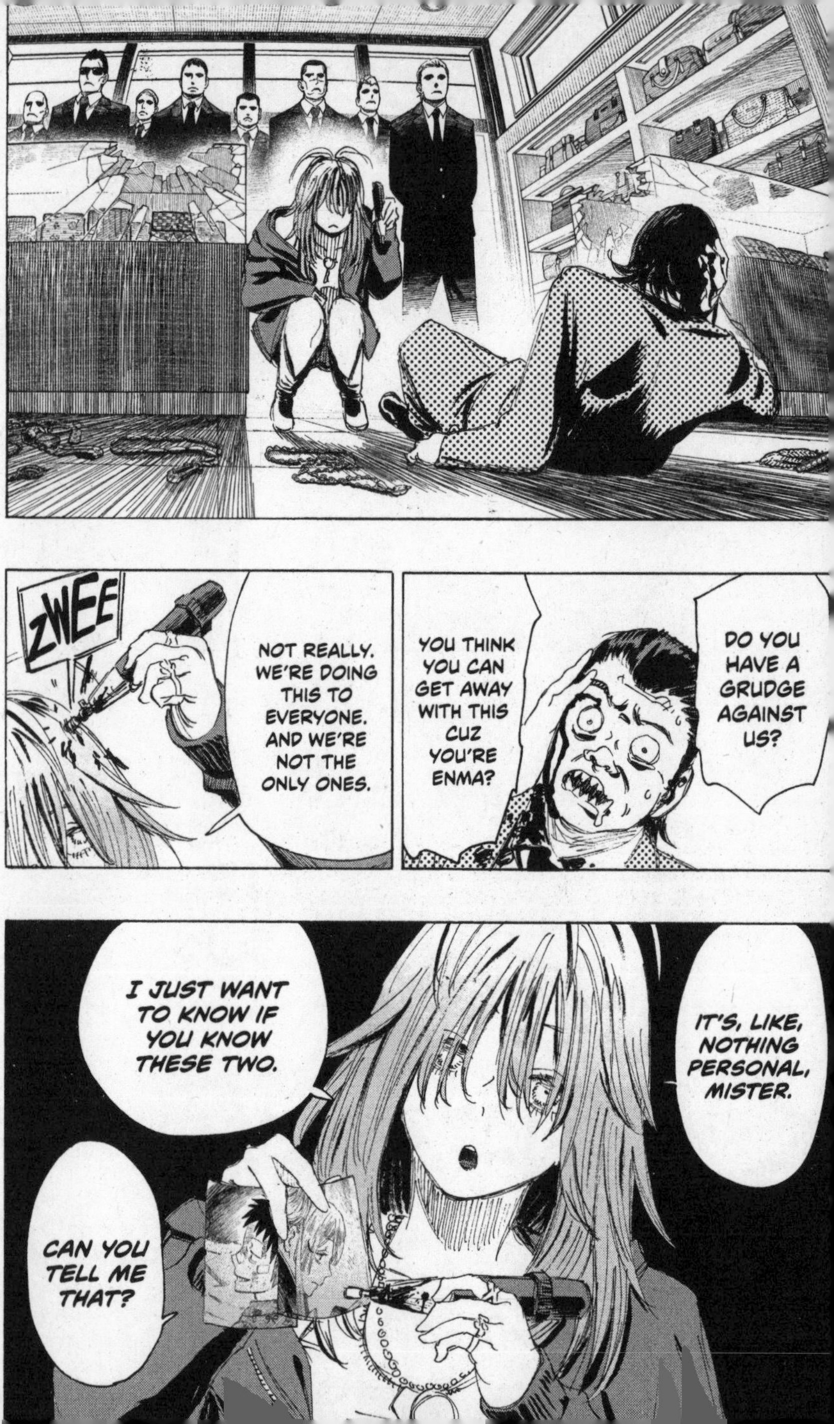
DO YOU HAVE A GRUDGE AGAINST US?
YOU THINK YOU CAN GET AWAY WITH THIS CUZ YOU'RE ENMA?
NOT REALLY. WE'RE DOING THIS TO EVERYONE. AND WE'RE NOT THE ONLY ONES.
ZWEE
IT'S, LIKE, NOTHING PERSONAL, MISTER.
I JUST WANT TO KNOW IF YOU KNOW THESE TWO.
CAN YOU TELL ME THAT?

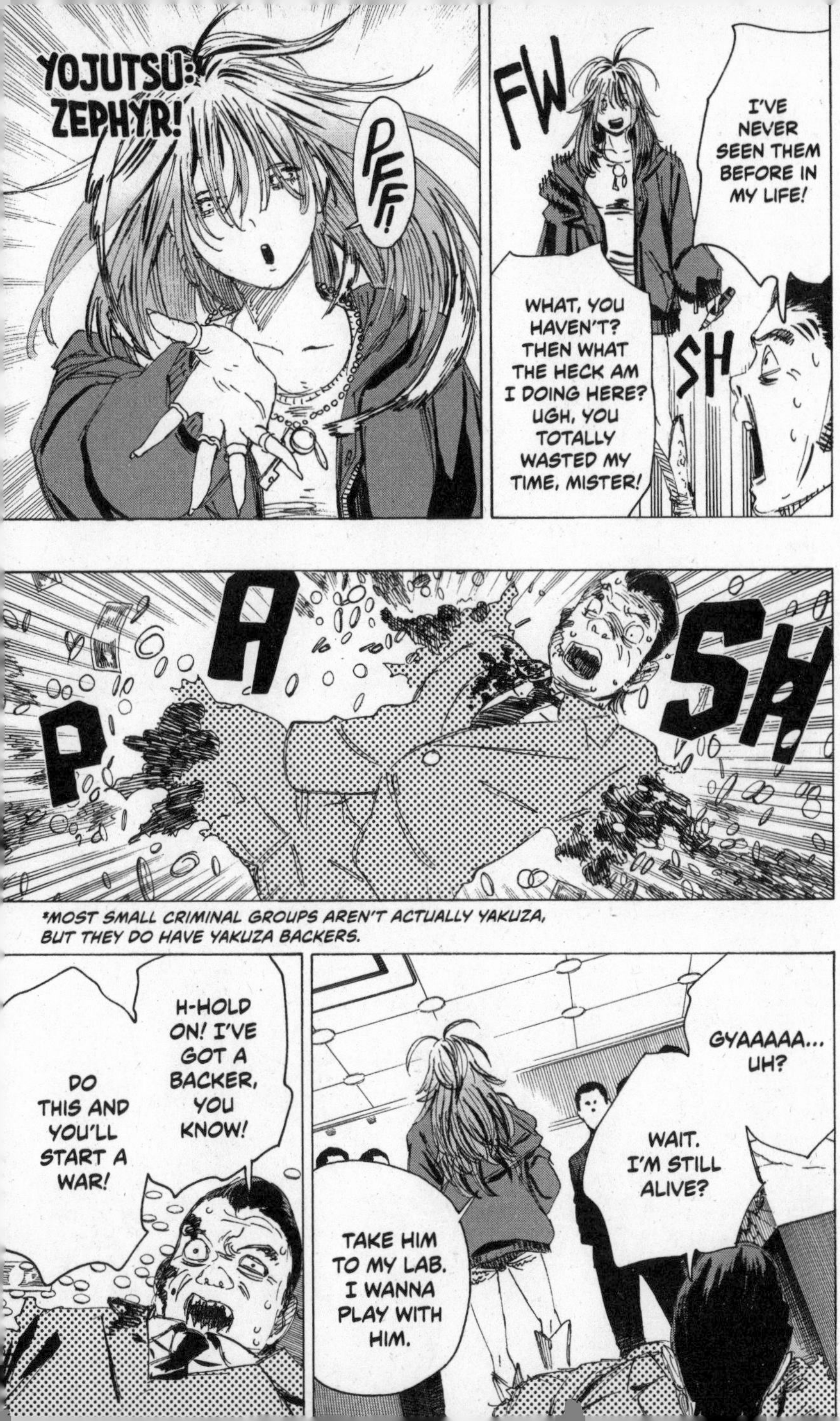
I'VE NEVER SEEN THEM BEFORE IN MY LIFE!
FW
WHAT, YOU HAVEN'T? THEN WHAT THE HECK AM I DOING HERE? UGH, YOU TOTALLY WASTED MY TIME, MISTER!
SH
YOJUTSU: ZEPHYR!
PFF!
PASH
GYAAAAA... UH?
WAIT. I'M STILL ALIVE?
TAKE HIM TO MY LAB. I WANNA PLAY WITH HIM.
H-HOLD ON! I'VE GOT A BACKER, YOU KNOW!
DO THIS AND YOU'LL START A WAR!

*MOST SMALL CRIMINAL GROUPS AREN'T ACTUALLY YAKUZA, BUT THEY DO HAVE YAKUZA BACKERS.

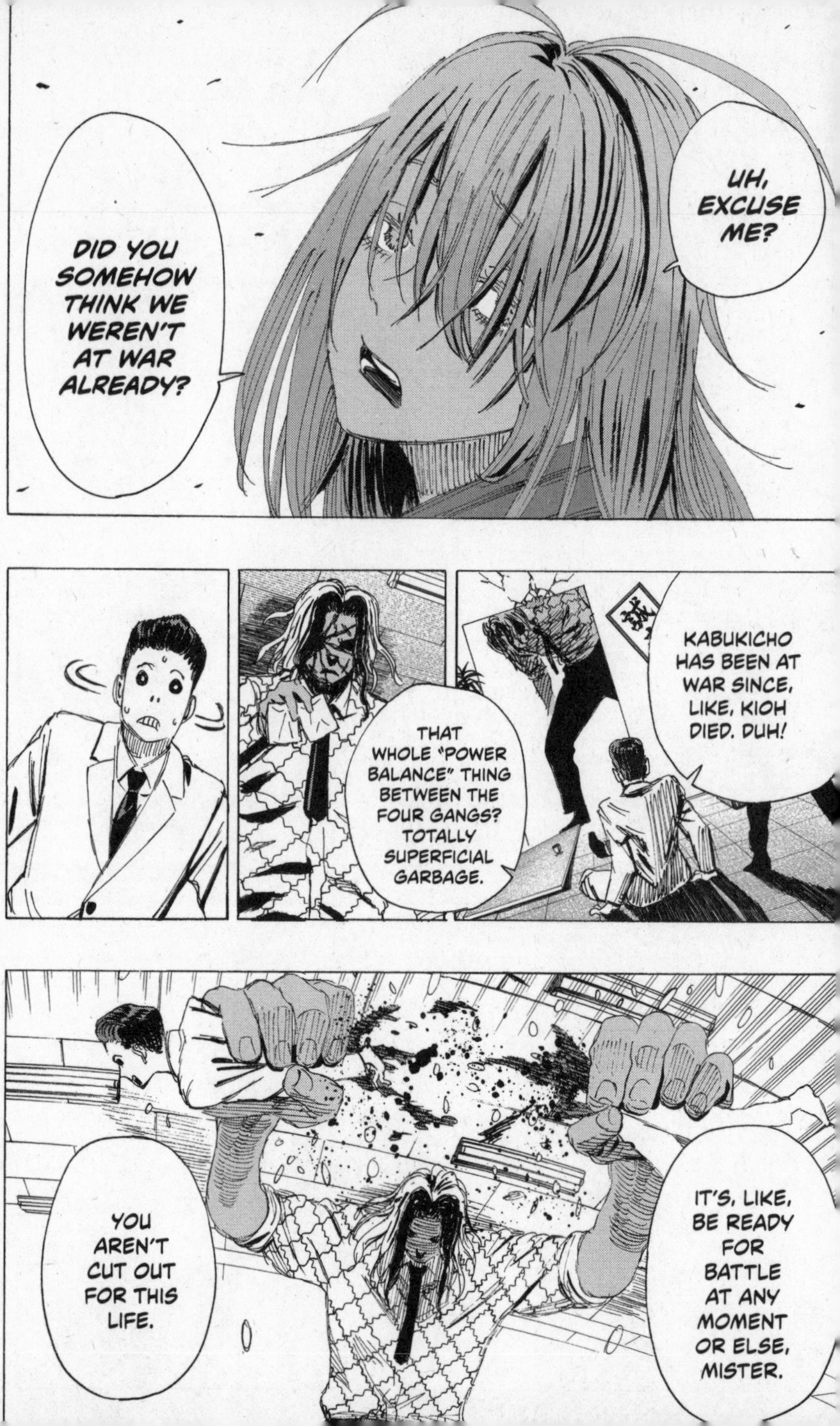
UH, EXCUSE ME?
DID YOU SOMEHOW THINK WE WEREN'T AT WAR ALREADY?
KABUKICHO HAS BEEN AT WAR SINCE, LIKE, KIOH DIED. DUH!
THAT WHOLE "POWER BALANCE" THING BETWEEN THE FOUR GANGS? TOTALLY SUPERFICIAL GARBAGE.
IT'S, LIKE, BE READY FOR BATTLE AT ANY MOMENT OR ELSE, MISTER.
YOU AREN'T CUT OUT FOR THIS LIFE.

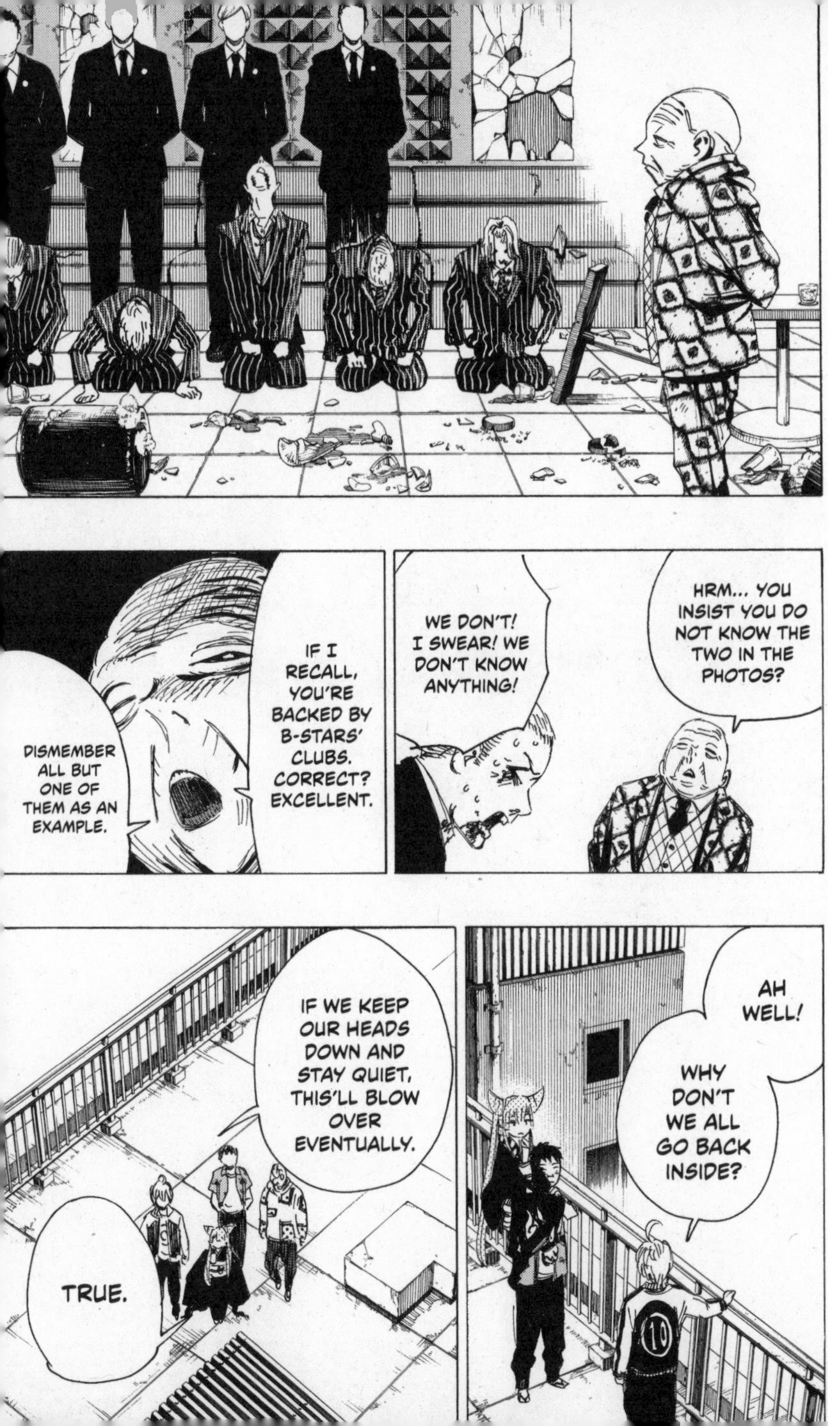
HRM... YOU INSIST YOU DO NOT KNOW THE TWO IN THE PHOTOS?
WE DON'T! I SWEAR! WE DON'T KNOW ANYTHING!
IF I RECALL, YOU'RE BACKED BY B-STARS' CLUBS. CORRECT? EXCELLENT.
DISMEMBER ALL BUT ONE OF THEM AS AN EXAMPLE.
AH WELL!
WHY DON'T WE ALL GO BACK INSIDE?
IF WE KEEP OUR HEADS DOWN AND STAY QUIET, THIS'LL BLOW OVER EVENTUALLY.
TRUE.

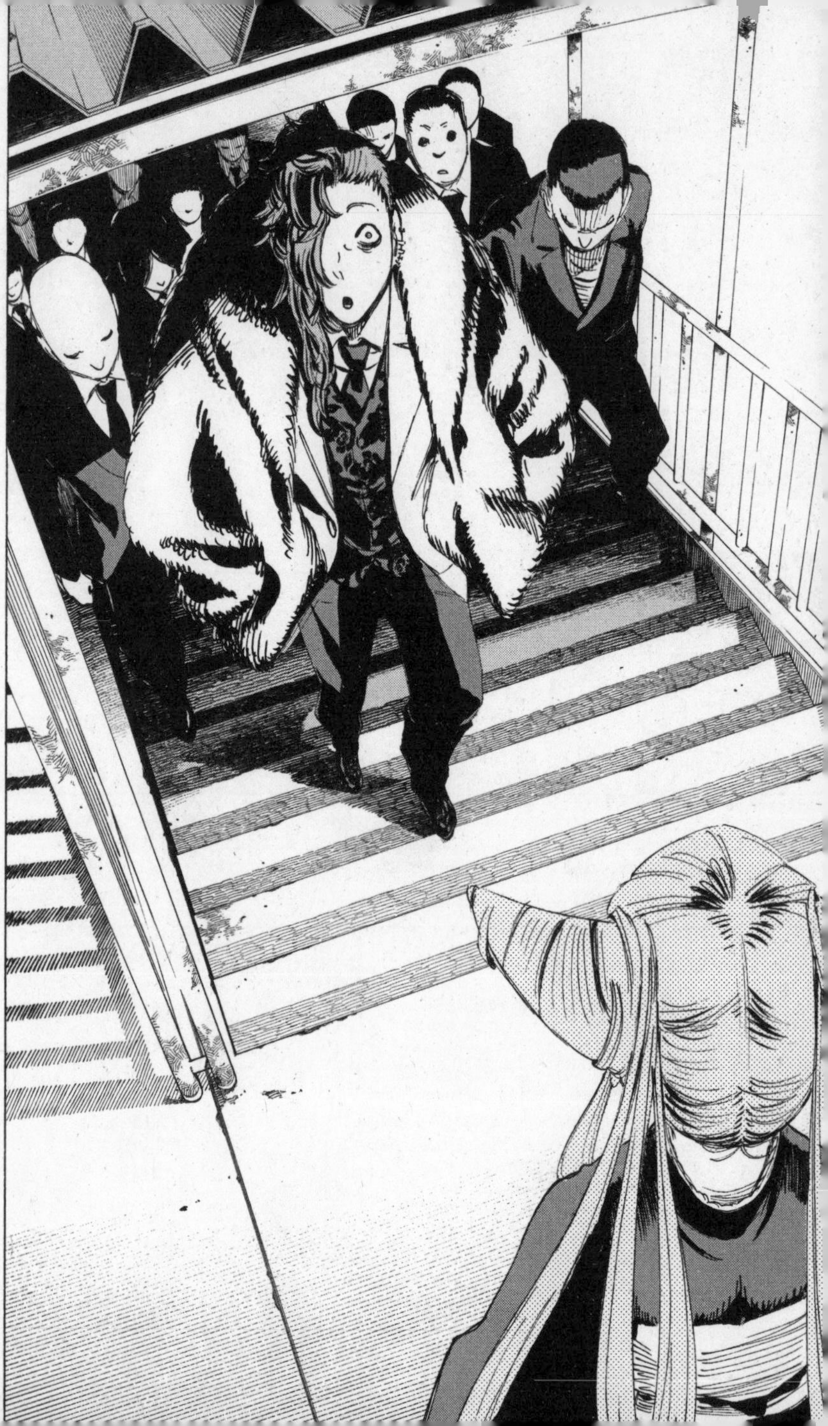

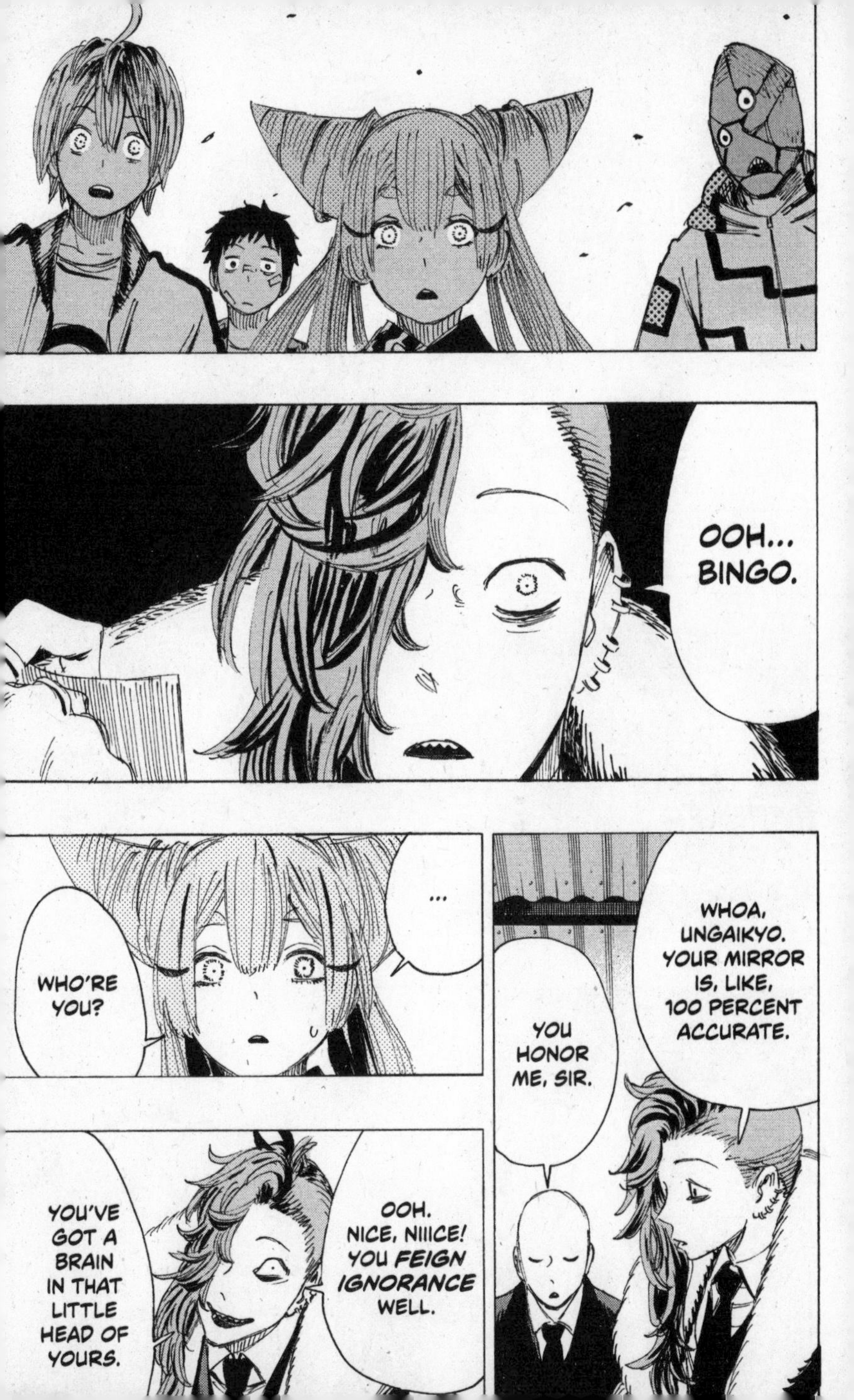
OOH... BINGO.
WHOA, UNGAIKYO. YOUR MIRROR IS, LIKE, 100 PERCENT ACCURATE.
YOU HONOR ME, SIR.
...
WHO'RE YOU?
OOH. NICE, NIIICE! YOU *FEIGN IGNORANCE* WELL.
YOU'VE GOT A BRAIN IN THAT LITTLE HEAD OF YOURS.

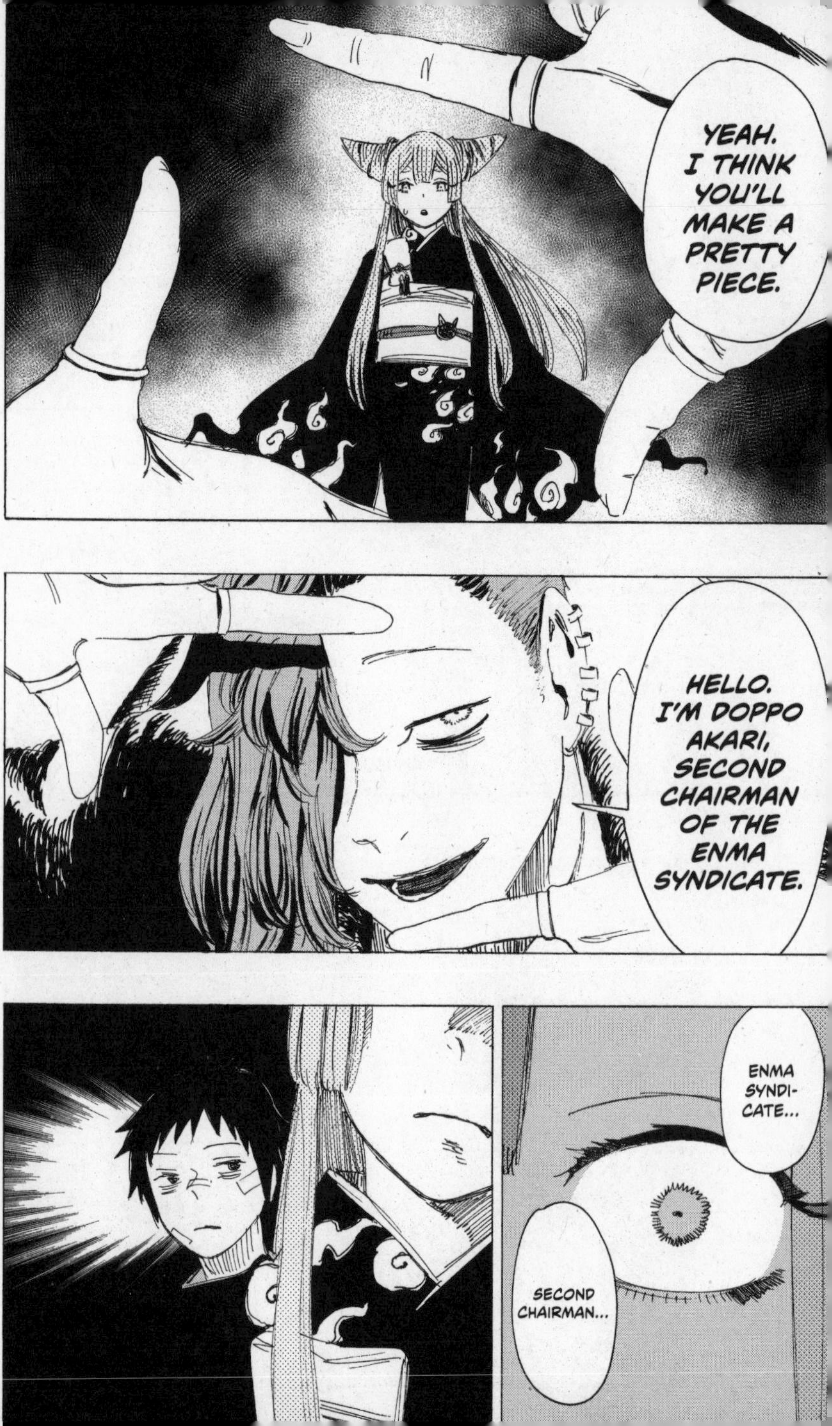
YEAH. I THINK YOU'LL MAKE A PRETTY PIECE.
HELLO. I'M DOPPO AKARI, SECOND CHAIRMAN OF THE ENMA SYNDICATE.
ENMA SYNDI-CATE...
SECOND CHAIRMAN...

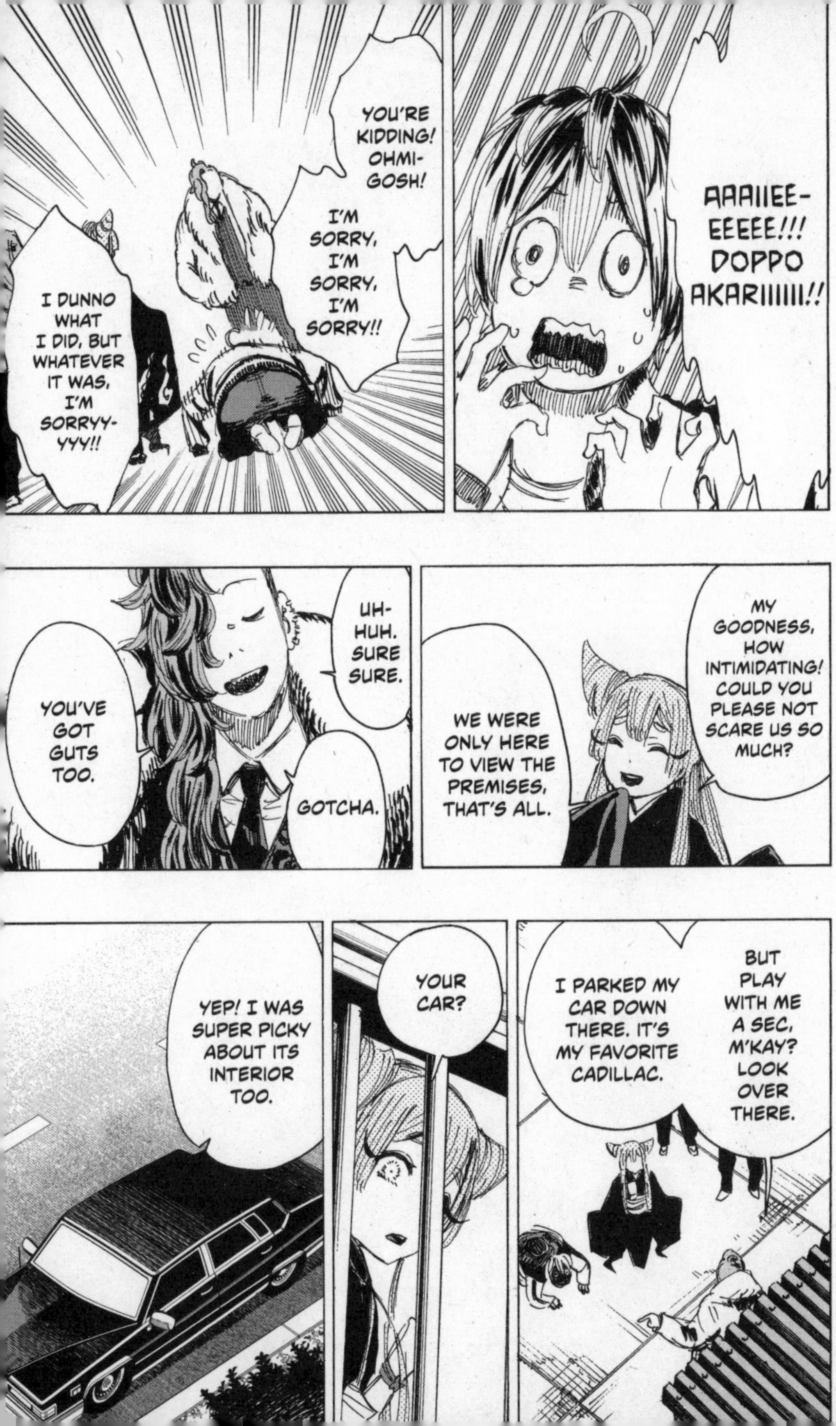
AAAIIEEE-EEEEE!!! DOPPO AKARIIIIIII!!
YOU'RE KIDDING! OHMI-GOSH!
I'M SORRY, I'M SORRY, I'M SORRY!!
I DUNNO WHAT I DID, BUT WHATEVER IT WAS, I'M SORRYY-YYY!!
MY GOODNESS, HOW INTIMIDATING! COULD YOU PLEASE NOT SCARE US SO MUCH?
WE WERE ONLY HERE TO VIEW THE PREMISES, THAT'S ALL.
UH-HUH. SURE SURE.
YOU'VE GOT GUTS TOO.
GOTCHA.
BUT PLAY WITH ME A SEC, M'KAY? LOOK OVER THERE.
I PARKED MY CAR DOWN THERE. IT'S MY FAVORITE CADILLAC.
YOUR CAR?
YEP! I WAS SUPER PICKY ABOUT ITS INTERIOR TOO.

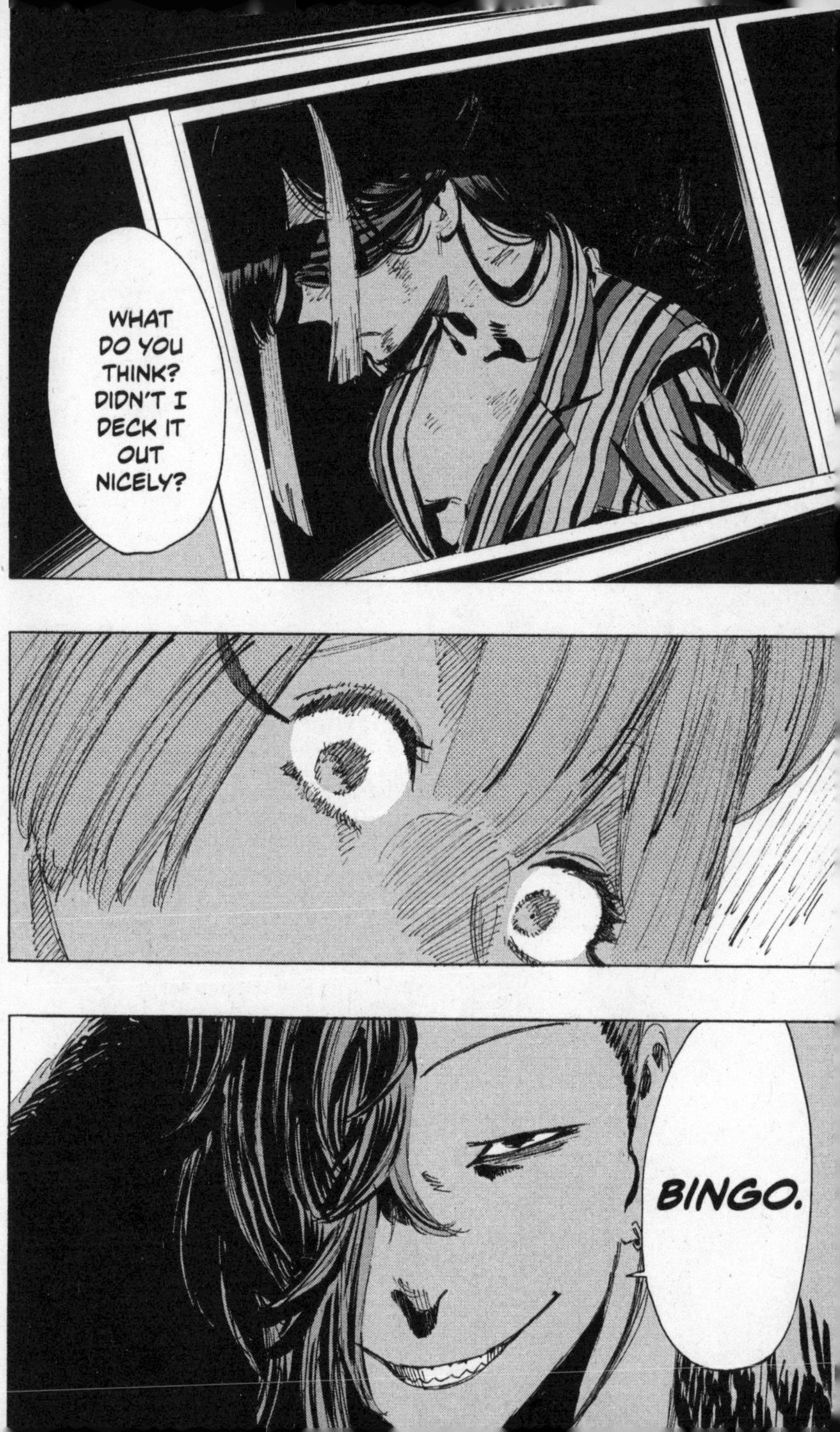
WHAT DO YOU THINK? DIDN'T I DECK IT OUT NICELY?
BINGO.

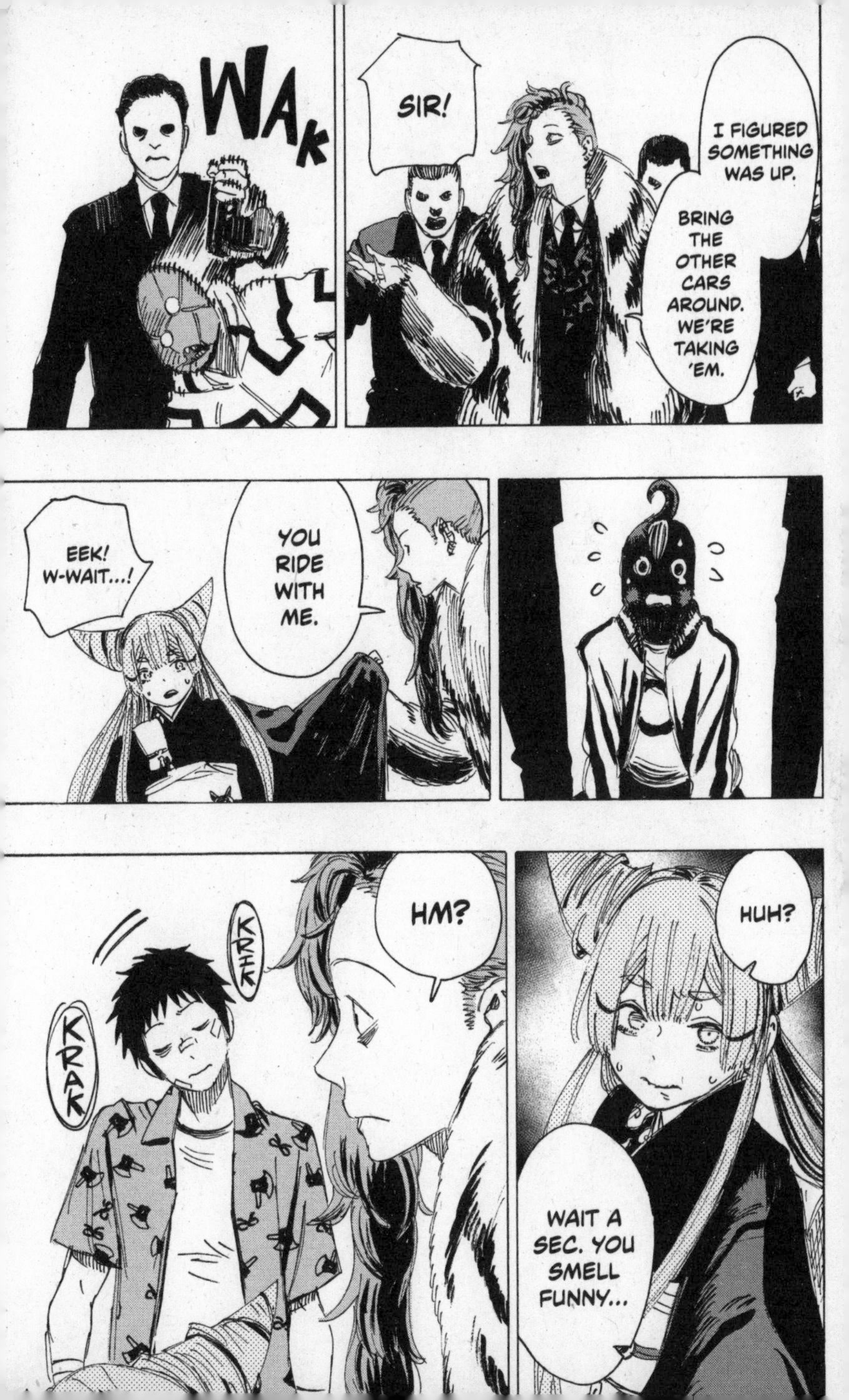
SIR!
I FIGURED SOMETHING WAS UP.
BRING THE OTHER CARS AROUND. WE'RE TAKING 'EM.
WAK
YOU RIDE WITH ME.
EEK! W-WAIT...!
HUH?
WAIT A SEC. YOU SMELL FUNNY...
HM?
KRIK
KRAK

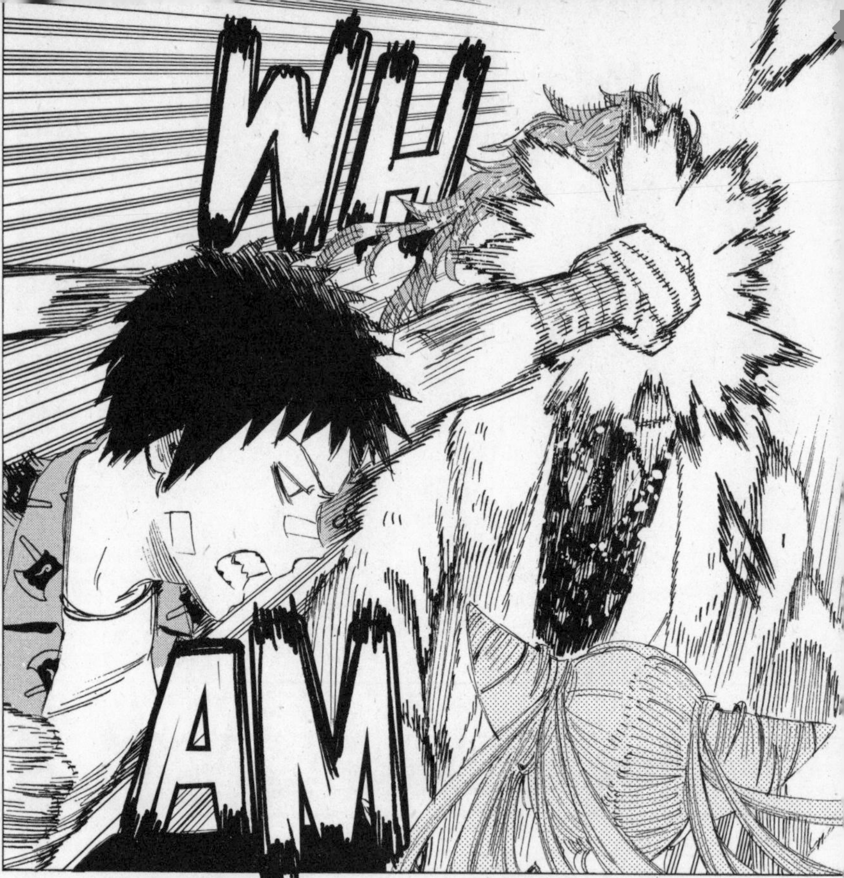
WHAM

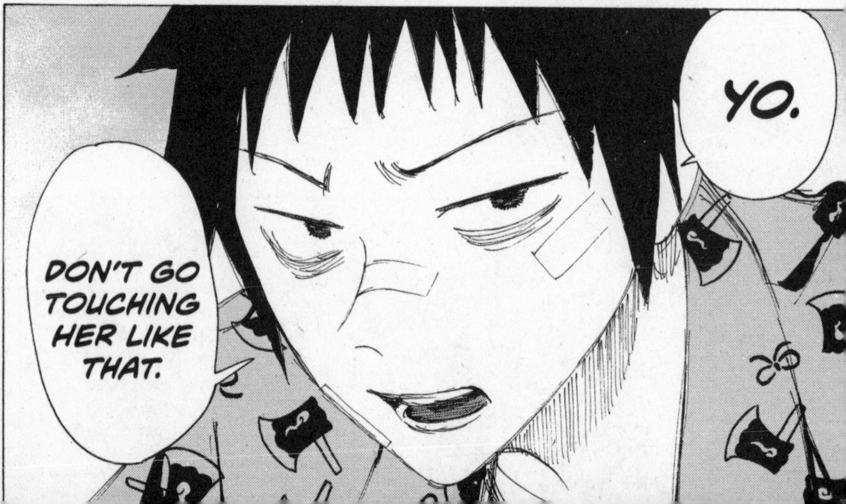
YO.
DON'T GO TOUCHING HER LIKE THAT.

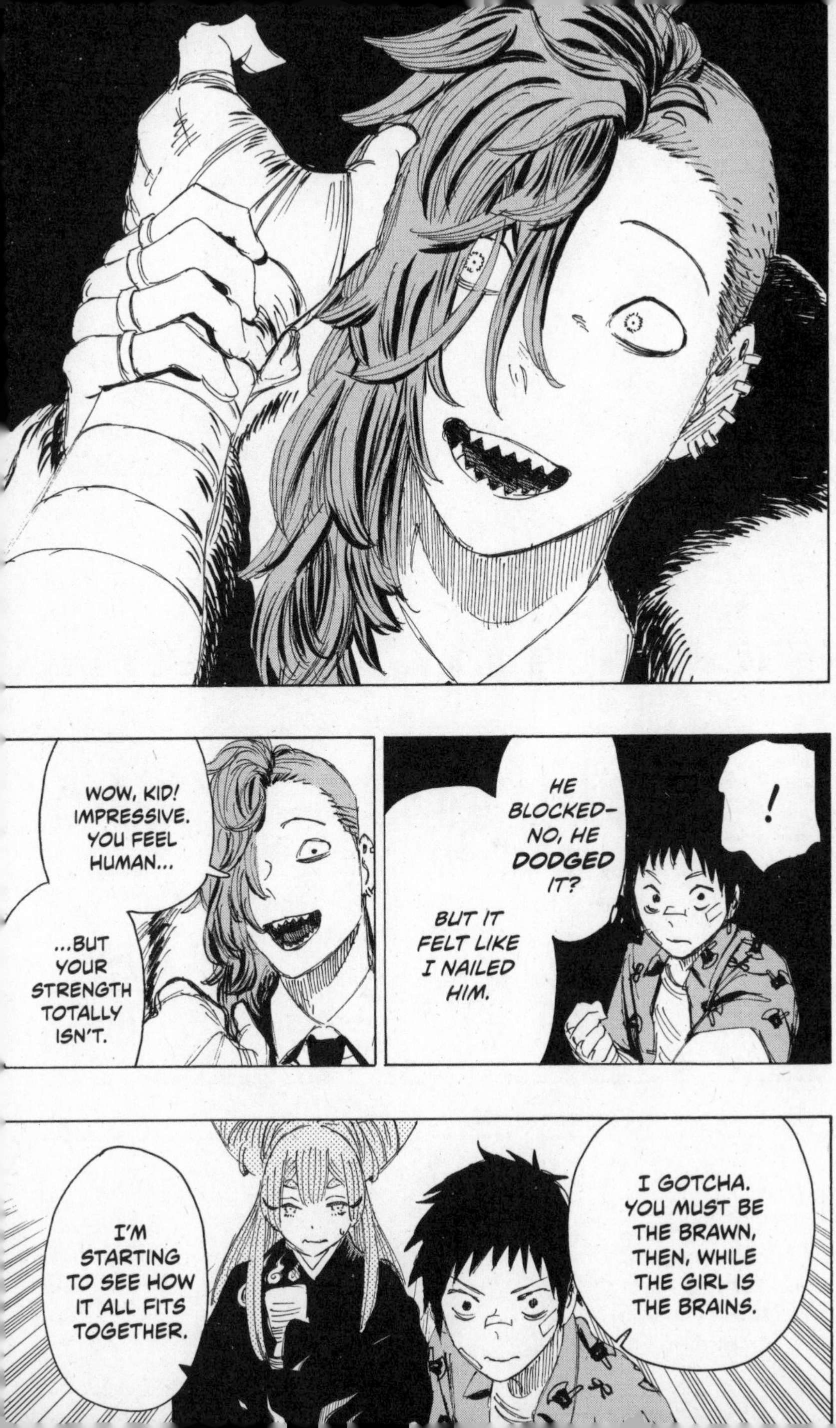
!
HE BLOCKED—NO, HE DODGED IT?
BUT IT FELT LIKE I NAILED HIM.
WOW, KID! IMPRESSIVE. YOU FEEL HUMAN...
...BUT YOUR STRENGTH TOTALLY ISN'T.
I GOTCHA. YOU MUST BE THE BRAWN, THEN, WHILE THE GIRL IS THE BRAINS.
I'M STARTING TO SEE HOW IT ALL FITS TOGETHER.

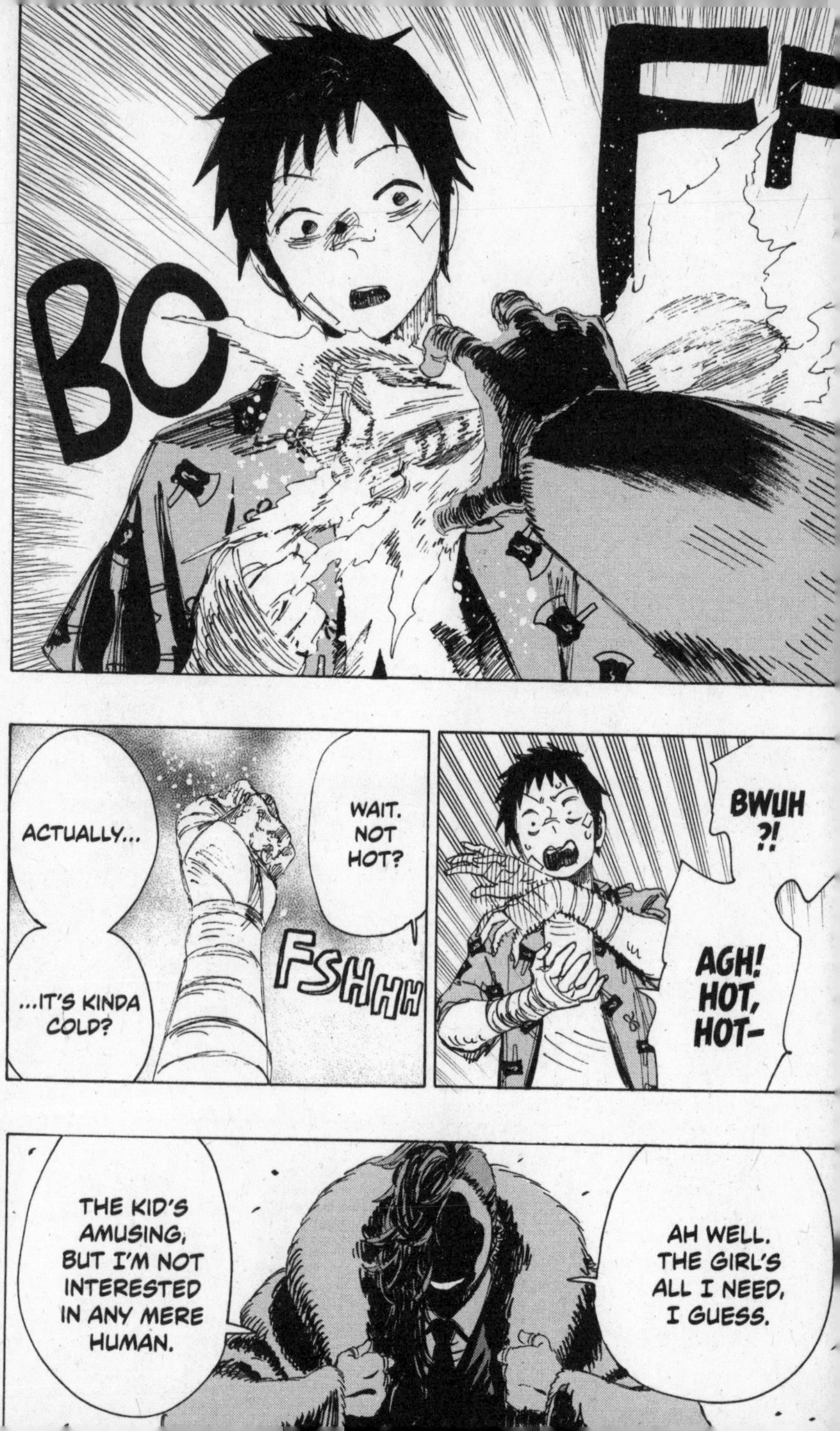
BOFF
BWUH ?!
AGH! HOT, HOT-
WAIT. NOT HOT?
FSHHH
ACTUALLY...
...IT'S KINDA COLD?
AH WELL. THE GIRL'S ALL I NEED, I GUESS.
THE KID'S AMUSING, BUT I'M NOT INTERESTED IN ANY MERE HUMAN.

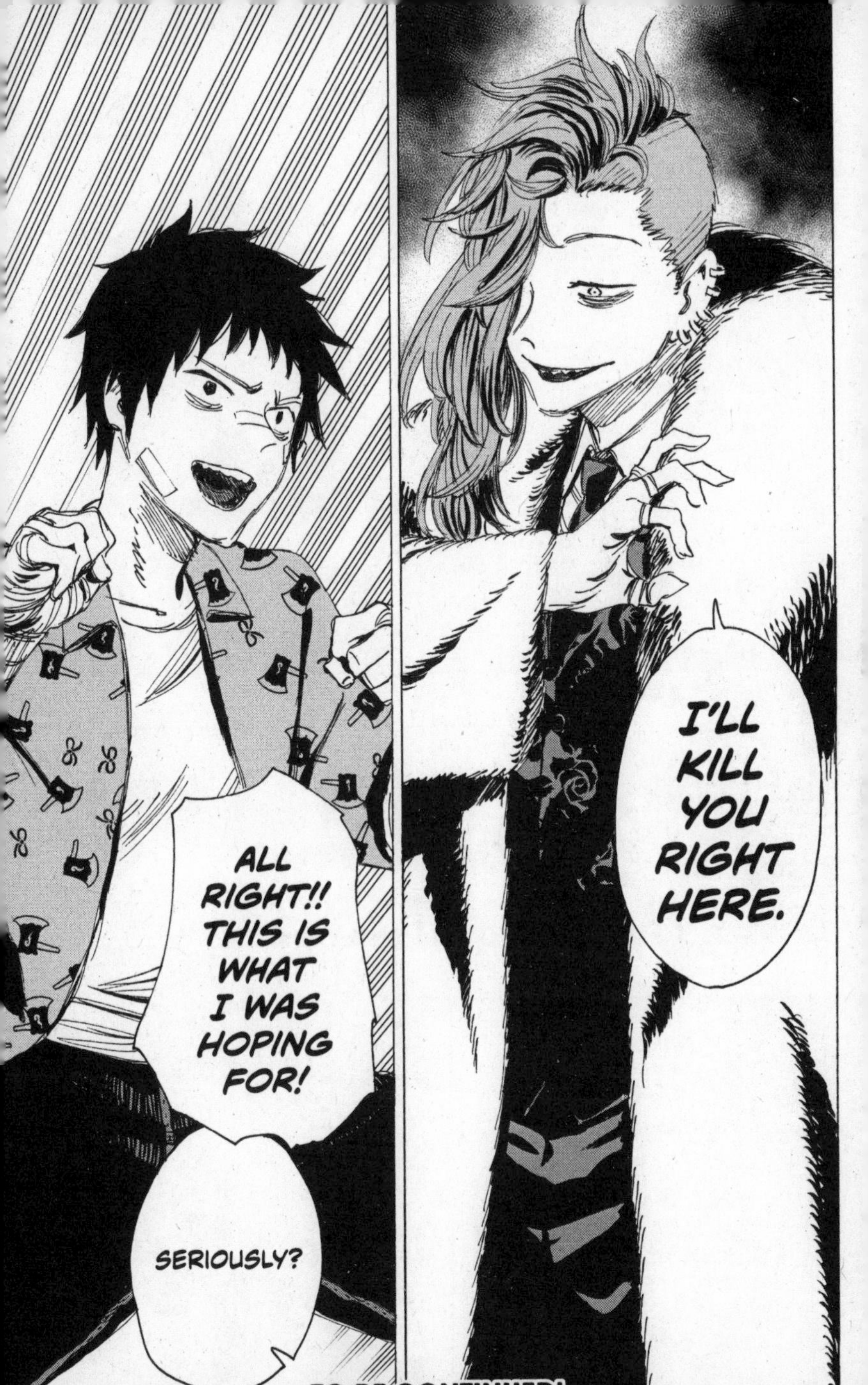
I'LL KILL YOU RIGHT HERE.
ALL RIGHT!! THIS IS WHAT I WAS HOPING FOR!
SERIOUSLY?

TO BE CONTINUED!

Bonus Story 1

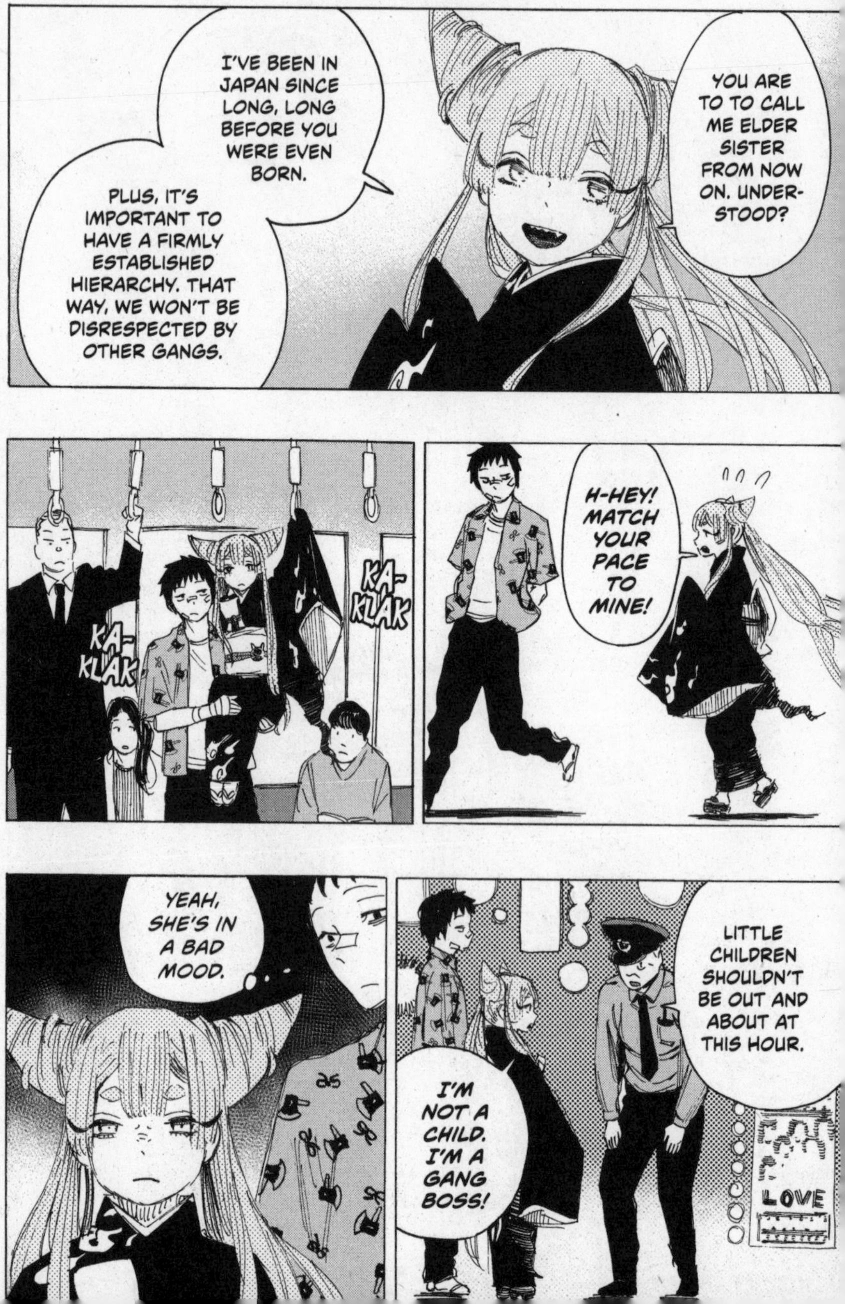
YOU ARE TO TO CALL ME ELDER SISTER FROM NOW ON. UNDER-STOOD?
I'VE BEEN IN JAPAN SINCE LONG, LONG BEFORE YOU WERE EVEN BORN.
PLUS, IT'S IMPORTANT TO HAVE A FIRMLY ESTABLISHED HIERARCHY. THAT WAY, WE WON'T BE DISRESPECTED BY OTHER GANGS.
H-HEY! MATCH YOUR PACE TO MINE!
KA-KLAK
KA-KLAK
LITTLE CHILDREN SHOULDN'T BE OUT AND ABOUT AT THIS HOUR.
I'M NOT A CHILD. I'M A GANG BOSS!
LOVE
YEAH, SHE'S IN A BAD MOOD.

Bonus Story 2

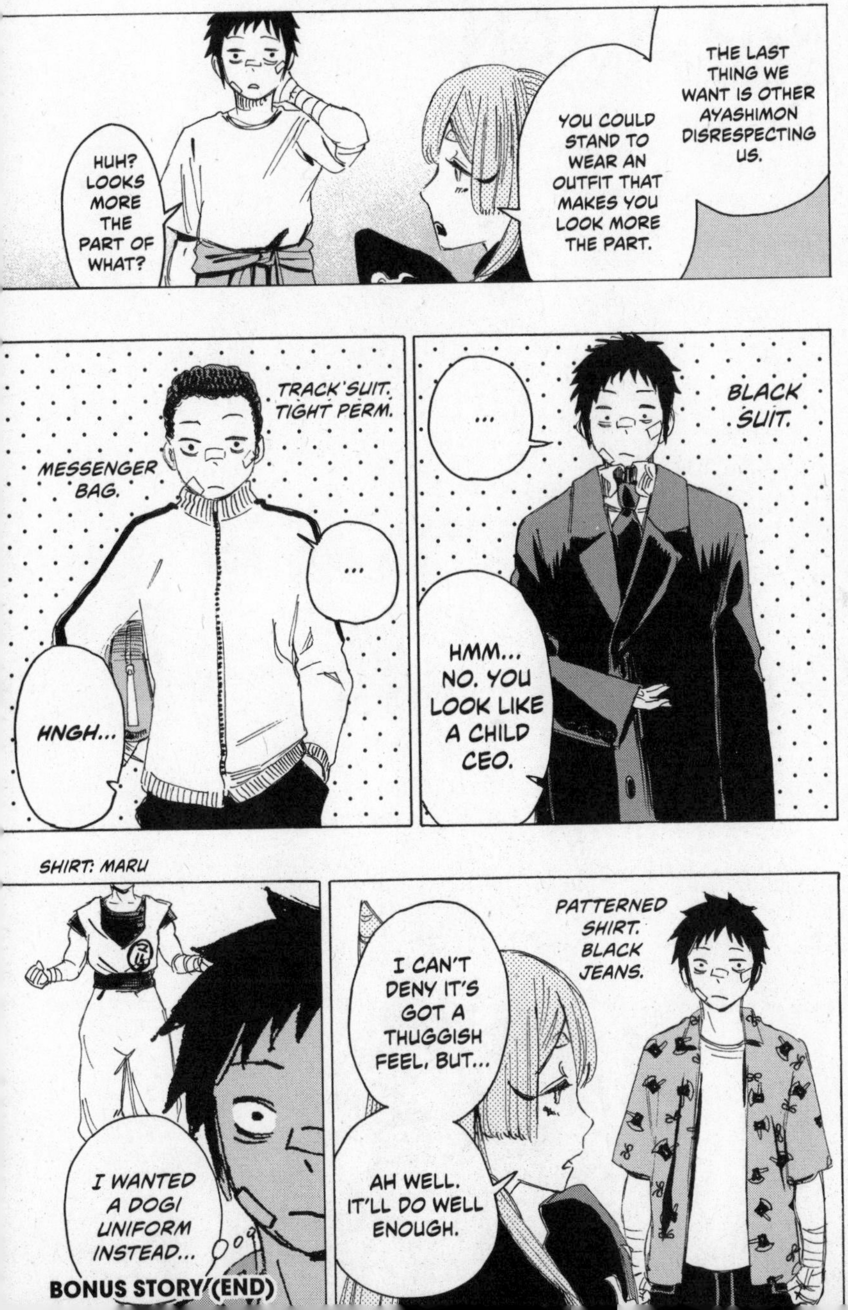

THE LAST THING WE WANT IS OTHER AYASHIMON DISRESPECTING US.
YOU COULD STAND TO WEAR AN OUTFIT THAT MAKES YOU LOOK MORE THE PART.
HUH? LOOKS MORE THE PART OF WHAT?
BLACK SUIT.
...
HMM... NO. YOU LOOK LIKE A CHILD CEO.
TRACK SUIT. TIGHT PERM.
MESSENGER BAG.
...
HNGH...
PATTERNED SHIRT. BLACK JEANS.
I CAN'T DENY IT'S GOT A THUGGISH FEEL, BUT...
AH WELL. IT'LL DO WELL ENOUGH.
SHIRT: MARU
I WANTED A DOGI UNIFORM INSTEAD...
BONUS STORY (END)

AYASHIMON

reads from right to left, starting in the upper-right corner. Japanese is read from right to left, meaning that action, sound effects, and word-balloon order are completely reversed from English order.

Check out the diagram shown here to get the hang of things, and then turn to the other side of the book to get started!

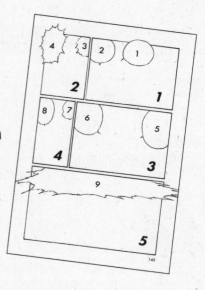